The Unwinding of the
Globalist Dream

EU, RUSSIA AND CHINA

The Unwinding of the Globalist Dream

EU, RUSSIA AND CHINA

Editors

Steven Rosefielde
University of North Carolina, Chapel Hill, USA

Masaaki Kuboniwa
Hitotsubashi University, Japan

Satoshi Mizobata
Kyoto University, Japan

Kumiko Haba
Aoyama Gakuin University, Japan

 **World Scientific**

NEW JERSEY · LONDON · SINGAPORE · BEIJING · SHANGHAI · HONG KONG · TAIPEI · CHENNAI · TOKYO

Published by

World Scientific Publishing Co. Pte. Ltd.

5 Toh Tuck Link, Singapore 596224

USA office: 27 Warren Street, Suite 401-402, Hackensack, NJ 07601

UK office: 57 Shelton Street, Covent Garden, London WC2H 9HE

Library of Congress Cataloging-in-Publication Data
Names: Rosefielde, Steven, editor.
Title: The unwinding of the globalist dream : EU, Russia and China / edited by
    Steven Rosefielde (University of North Carolina, Chapel Hill, USA), [and three others].
Description: New Jersey : World Scientific, [2017]
Identifiers: LCCN 2017015006 | ISBN 9789813222069 (hc : alk. paper)
Subjects: LCSH: European Union countries--Social conditions--21st century. |
    European Union countries--Economic conditions--21st century. | Russia (Federation)--
    Social conditions--21st century. | Russia (Federation)--Economic conditions--21st century. |
    China--Social conditions--21st century. | China--Economic conditions--21st century. |
    Globalization--Political aspects. | Globalization--Social aspects.
Classification: LCC HN373.5 .U579 2017 | DDC 306.0947--dc23
LC record available at https://lccn.loc.gov/2017015006

British Library Cataloguing-in-Publication Data
A catalogue record for this book is available from the British Library.

Desk Editors: Chandrima Maitra/Dong Lixi

Typeset by Stallion Press
Email: enquiries@stallionpress.com

Printed in Singapore

In memory of my beloved son, David Rosefielde

About the Authors

Torbjörn Becker is the Director of the Stockholm Institute of Transition Economics (SITE) at the Stockholm School of Economics in Sweden since 2006. He is also a board member of the Swedish Development Cooperation Agency (Sida) and several economics research institutes in Eastern Europe that together with SITE are part of the Forum for Research on Eastern Europe and Emerging Economies (FREE) Network. Prior to this he worked for 9 years at the International Monetary Fund (IMF) where his work focused on international macro, economic crises, and issues related to the international financial system. He holds a Ph.D. from the Stockholm School of Economics and has published in top academic journals. He has contributed to several books and authored policy reports focusing on Russia and Eastern Europe.

Olga Bobrova, Ph.D. in Management, is teaching students at Saint Petersburg State University of Economics, Russia. Bobrova currently works as an Associate Professor at the Department of Economics and Management of Enterprises and Industrial Complexes. In 2007, she presented her Ph.D. thesis titled *Forming a System of Socially Responsible Management of Enterprise*. She also has a wide experience working in NGO sector in Russia, since 2004. Her research interests include corporate social responsibility, entrepreneurship in Russia, stakeholder management, and Japanese management. Her recent works include *Business Essentials: Textbook and Practicum for Academic Bachelors* (published in Russian), *Stakeholder Management of Japanese Companies: The View from Russia* and *Implementation of Industrial Policy as One of the Factors of Modernization in Russia*.

Bruno Dallago, Ph.D., is a Professor of Economics at the Department of Economics and Management, University of Trento, Italy. He was Visiting Professor at various universities, including the University of California at Berkeley, USA, the University of North Carolina at Chapel Hill, Hitotsubashi University, Zhejian University, Kyoto University, the University of Pécs, Tshwane University of Technology. He is currently a member of the International Advisory Board of the Institute of Economics of the Hungarian Academy of Sciences and of the Corvinus University of Budapest. His research interests include the European Union, comparative economics, the transforming economies of Central and East Europe, SMEs and entrepreneurship, and local development. He is the author and editor of several scholarly books and journal articles, including *One Currency, Two Europe*, World Scientific Publishers, 2016; *Transformation and Crisis in Central and Eastern Europe: Challenges and Prospects* with Steven Rosefielde, Routledge, 2016; and *A Global Perspective on the European Economic Crisis* with Gert Guri and John McGowan, eds., Routledge, 2016.

Victor Gorshkov is an Associate Professor at the Department of International Liberal Arts, Faculty of International Liberal Arts, Kaichi International University (Japan). He received his M.A. in international economics and finance from Khabarovsk State Academy of Economics and Law (Russia) and Ph.D. in economics from Kyoto University (Japan). He is a charter member of the Japanese Association for Comparative Economic Studies. He has taught part-time at Kanagawa University (Japan) and conducted research as a Visiting Associate Professor at the Institute of Economic Research, Kyoto University. His research interests are in the fields of international economics, international economic relations, comparative economic systems, and international education.

Kumiko Haba is Professor of International Politics at Aoyama Gakuin University. She is also Director of Institute for Global International Relations, Jean Monnet Chair of the European Union, a Vice President of International Studies Association (ISA in USA), member of Science Council of Japan (SCJ). She has been Visiting Scholar at Harvard University (2011–2012), European University Institute, Florence (2007), Sorbonne University (2004), University of London, SSEES (1996–1997) and Hungarian Academy of Science (1995–1996, 2002). Her specialty is international relations and comparative politics between EU and Asian Regional Cooperation, and immigrants, minority questions and democracy.

She wrote 57 books (including as co-editors and co-writers and seven books as single author), and 160 articles on Central and Eastern Europe, the EU and Asian Regional Cooperation. Her recent publications include *Division and Integration in Europe — Nationalism and Border Question*, Chuokoronshinsya, 2016; *Challenge for Enlarged Europe — The EU as a Global Power*, Chuokoronshinsya, 2014; *Great Power Politics and Asian Regional Cooperation* at Harvard University, Aoyama Gakuin University, 2013. *Power Shift — World Crisis and Nationalism* will be published soon.

Iikka Korhonen has worked at the Bank of Finland since July 1995, when he joined the Institute for Economies in Transition (BOFIT). At the BOFIT he has followed, among other things, banking and financial systems of the Baltic states and Russia. His past duties include working as BOFIT's research supervisor, and since October 1, 2009, he has been the Head of BOFIT. His research interests include exchange rates and inflation in transition as well as emerging market countries. In addition, he has published widely, e.g. on the correlation of economic activity between different countries, as well as on the effects of oil prices on economic activities.

Anna Kovaleva is an Associate Professor at the Department of International Business, Saint Petersburg State University of Economics (Russia). She received her M.E. in Human Studies from the Herzen State Pedagogical University of Russia and M.A. in Sociology from the European University at St. Petersburg. She defended her Ph.D. thesis at the Saint Petersburg

State University of Economics. She is also an International Coordinator at the Centre for Research in the Economics of the Firm and Organizational Innovation in Saint Petersburg State University of Economics. She has conducted her research studies and participated in different summer schools, conferences, and internships in 10 countries. She realized a project "Comparative Study of Management System of Innovative Companies in Japan and Russia" as a JREX fellow at the Institute of Economic Research at the Kyoto University Kyoto, Japan in 2014–2015. Her research interests are in the fields of innovation ecosystem in cross-cultural perspective, innovation-driven companies, and international education.

Yoji Koyama, Ph.D., is Professor Emeritus at Niigata University (Japan). He studied International Relations and Area Studies and graduated from the University of Tokyo in 1967. Over time he gradually shifted his focus from International Relations to Economics. He was a Visiting Scholar in Belgrade from October 1978 to March 1980 under the Yugoslav government fellowship scheme. He authored several Japanese books including *A Study of Yugoslav Self-managed Socialism: Movement of the Regime of the 1974 Constitution* (in 1996) and three English books including *The EU's Eastward Enlargement: Central and Eastern Europe's Strategies for Development* (in 2015). He edited an English book *The Eurozone Enlargement: Prospect of New EU Member States for the Euro Adoption* (in 2016).

Masaaki Kuboniwa with a Ph.D. in economics from Hitotsubashi University is a Professor Emeritus at Hitotsubashi University, Tokyo, Japan. He has been a Professor at International Graduate School, New Zealand and a Visiting Professor at National Universities in New Zealand and Taiwan for 2015–2017. He has received an honorary doctorate from the Central Economics and Mathematics Institute of Russian Academy of Sciences in 2003, and a W.W. Leontief Medal in 2004. His books and articles in English have been published by noted publishers and journals including the Oxford University Press and *Journal of Comparative Economics*.

Yiyi Liu gained her Ph.D. from UNC Chapel Hill and majored in Microeconomics (Mechanism Design). She is working at the Department of Development and Reform in National Gui'an New Area. She is a trained game theorist and has devoted her efforts to studying Public–Private Partnerships in providing public services.

Wenting Ma is a Ph.D. student in Economics at the University of North Carolina, Chapel Hill. Her research fields are real estates and finance labour. Her latest working paper, Merger and Acquisition, Technological Change and Inequality (with Paige Ouimet and Elena Simintzi), has been presented at 2016 Tsinghua Finance Workshop, 2016 CSEF-EIEF-SITE Conference on Finance and Labor and NBER Productivity Seminar, and has been scheduled to present at 2017 WFA, 2017 SFS Finance Cavalcade Conference, 2017 Annual Meetings of the Society of Labor Economics and 2017 Financial Intermediation Research Society Conference.

Satoshi Mizobata is a Professor and Director at the University of Kyoto, Kyoto Institute of Economic Research. His research areas are comparative studies in economic systems, corporate governance and business organization and the Russian and East European economies, focusing on the enterprises and market structure. He is editor of *The Journal of Comparative Economic Studies* in Japan and member of the Executive Committee of European Association for Comparative Economic Studies. His recent works include *Melting Boundaries: Institutional Transformation in the Wider Europe* (co-edited with K. Yagi), Kyoto University Press, 2008; "Diverging and Harmonizing Corporate Governance in Russia", in John Pickles ed., *State and Society in Post-socialist Economies*, Palgrave Macmillan, 2008; *Two Asias: The Emerging Postcrisis Divide* (co-edited with S. Rosefielde and M. Kuboniwa), World Scientific, 2012; "Restructuring of the Higher Educational System in Japan" (with Masahiko Yoshii); "Restructuring of the Higher Educational System in Japan" (with Masahiko Yoshii), in J.C. Brada, W. Bienkowski and M. Kuboniwa eds., *International Perspectives on Financing Higher Education*, Palgrave Macmillan, 2015, and others.

Steven Rosefielde is a Professor of Economics at the University of North Carolina, Chapel Hill. He received his Ph.D. in Economics from

Harvard University, and is a member of the Russian Academy of Natural Sciences (RAEN). He has taught in Russia, China, Japan, and Thailand. Most recently, he published *Democracy and Its Elected Enemies: The West's Paralysis, Crisis and Decline*, Cambridge University Press, 2013; *Inclusive Economic Theory* (with Ralph W. Pfouts), World Scientific Publishers, 2014; *Global Economic Turmoil and the Public Good*, (with Quinn Mills), World Scientific Publishers, 2015; *Transformation and Crisis in Central and Eastern Europe: Challenges and Prospects* (with Bruno Dallago), Routledge, 2016; *Kremlin Strikes Back: Russia and the West after Crimea's Annexation*, Cambridge University Press, 2017; *The Trump Phenomenon and Future of US Foreign Policy* (with Quinn Mills), Singapore World Scientific Publishers, 2016; *Trump's Populist America*, World Scientific Publishers, 2017; *China's Market Communism: Challenges, Dilemmas, Solutions* (with Jonathan Leightner), Routledge, 2017.

Pi-Han Tsai is an Assistant Professor of Economics at Zhejiang University, China. She received her Ph.D. in Economics at the University of California, Irvine in 2014. She holds an M.P.I.A. degree in International Relations and Pacific Studies at the University of California, San Diego and B.A. degree while majoring in both Political Science and Economics at National Taiwan University. Her areas of specialization include public economics, political economy, and Chinese economy. She has published in academic journals such as *International Tax and Public Finance* and *Public Finance Review*.

Zhikai Wang is Professor of Economics and Ph.D. Supervisor, at Zhejiang University, Hangzhou, China. In 1993, he became a civil servant and started working for Jiangsu provincial government at the Development & Reform Commission, in Nanjing for the next 10 years. In 2002, he moved to the Zhejiang University. Wang now serves as the General Secretary of Centre for Research of Private Economy (CRPE), Zhejiang University. His publications include *Rebalancing China's Economy for Long-term Growth* (in Chinese), Fudan University Press, 2016; *Private Sector Development and Urbanization in China* (in English), Palgrave & Macmillan, 2015; *Research on Regional Development* *of China's Private Sector* (in Chinese), Zhejiang University Press, 2009; *The Private Sector and China's Market Development* (in English), Chandos Publishing, 2008; *The Chinese Seafood Industry: Structural Changes and Opportunities for Norwegians* (in English), edited with Knut Bjorn Lindkvist *et al.*, SNF Press, 2005; *Comparative Welfare Economy Analysis* (in Chinese), Zhejiang University Press (2004), etc.

Acknowledgments

The editors thank their institutions for their generous support. The University of North Carolina (Chapel Hill), Hitotsubashi University, Aoyama Gakuin University and the Kyoto Institute for Economic Research provided conference facilities and financial assistance critical to this volume's success.

Contents

Introduction

Steven Rosefielde

Globalism was the new millennial utopia, until Donald Trump's stunning electoral victory. Supporters believed that a harmonious, just, peaceful, and prosperous future was dawning that soon would be realized by building global economic, political, and social networks. They reasoned that nationalism limited the world's potential and spawned international conflict in much the same way that communists claimed private property was the root of evil. Eliminate nations, or render them obsolete by adopting a common ideal, and, as Francis Fukuyama surmised, the planet will arrive at the "end of history."

Globalization in the new millennial utopia serves as the engine of globalism. It is today's ineluctable materialist dialectic. The logic is appealing. Eliminate national barriers to trade and everyone will prosper. Construct international institutions to harness collective know-how and things will be even better. Create a superior blended common sociopolitical culture, and global well-being will soar beyond the stratosphere.

Globalists believed that globalization was unstoppable. Each advance provided rewards that would be lost if the process reversed, tutoring everyone that the only rational course was fast forward. The vision inspired several generations and became an article of faith until the global financial crisis of 2008, when the unimaginable happened. Globalism began unwinding economically, socially, politically, and internationally.

1

Recovery from the 2008 global financial crisis morphed into secular stagnation.[1] Rapid Third World economic development became a fading
memory. European Union (EU) dreams unraveled with Grexit and Brexit,
and Russia and China began vigorously challenging Western (American
and EU) dominance. Where it once seemed that the world was heading
toward a common Western-style economic, political, social, and cultural
order (a politically correct variant of the traditional "American Dream"),
this no longer seems plausible. Not only are Russia and China contesting
the West's concept of the global ideal, and expanding their own national
spheres of influence, Donald Trump has declared that he is hostile to the
concept. He advocates "America First," and seeks to disempower or
eradicate flagship globalist institutions like the United Nations and the
Trans-Pacific Partnership.

Globalists, however, need not despair. Trump will not be forever.
Perhaps, utopia will eventually reign across the globe, but it is still useful
to consider why the globalist dream in the EU, Russia, and China went
awry and to gauge the crosscurrents hidden beneath the headlines.
Unwinding of the Globalist Dream examines why the EU, Russia, and
China went astray after the 2008 global financial crisis. It scrutinizes the
West's triumphalist decline (America and the EU)[2]; highlighting the

---

[1] Robert Barro and Tao Jin, "Rare Events and Long-run Risks," *NBER Working Paper*
21871, January 2016, available at http://www.nber.org/papers/w21871: "On average,
during a recovery, an economy recoups about half the GDP lost during the downturn. The
recovery is typically quick, with an average duration around two years. For example, a
4% decline in per capita GDP during a contraction predicts subsequent recovery of 2%,
implying 1% per year higher growth than normal during the recovery. Hence, the growth
rate of U.S. per capita GDP from 2009 to 2011 should have been around 3% per year, rather
than the 1.5% that materialized."
[2] Krauthammer (1990, 2002/2003). "The new unilateralism argues explicitly and
unashamedly for maintaining unipolarity, for sustaining America's unrivaled dominance
for the foreseeable future. It could be a long future, assuming we successfully manage the
single greatest threat, namely, weapons of mass destruction in the hands of rogue states.
This in itself will require the aggressive and confident application of unipolar power rather
than falling back, as we did in the 1990s, on paralyzing multilateralism. The future of the
unipolar era hinges on whether America is governed by those who wish to retain, augment
and use unipolarity to advance not just American but global ends, or whether America is
governed by those who wish to give it up — either by allowing unipolarity to decay as they

complexities of Russia's and China's geopolitical ascent, secular economic stagnation, social discord, and EU unraveling. This volume has three parts. Part I addresses Western secular stagnation, social strife, and EU fragmentation, focused on the EU. Chapter 1 sets the scene with a summary account of the West's woes, followed by five chapters on the EU's unfolding economic, political, and social plights.

Part II illuminates Russia's resurgence and interplay with the Western-dominated globalist order. It focuses on developments after Russia's annexation of Crimea and on the possibilities of the Kremlin's expansion of its sphere of influence at the West's expense. Seven chapters are devoted to these themes.

Part III extends the story by examining China's growing economic and military potential against the backdrop of the West's reciprocal decline. Six chapters are devoted to these important topics.

A conclusion briefly summarizes the unwinding of the globalist dream and offers some insights into the impending brave new populist age that seems likely to replace paradise lost.[3]

---

retreat to Fortress America, or by passing on the burden by gradually transferring power to multilateral institutions as heirs to American hegemony. The challenge to unipolarity is not from the outside but from the inside. The choice is ours. To impiously paraphrase Benjamin Franklin: History has given you an empire, if you will keep it." Available at http://belfercenter.ksg.harvard.edu/files/krauthammer.pdf.

Cf. Andrew J. Bacevich, "American Triumphalism: A Postmortem," *Commonweal*, January 26, 2009, available at https://www.commonwealmagazine.org/american-triumphalism-0: "Triumphalist thinking derived from two widely held perceptions. The first was that the unraveling of the Soviet empire had brought history to a definitive turning point. According to this view, the *annus mirabilis* of 1989 truly was a year of wonders, sweeping aside the old order and opening the door to vast new possibilities. The second conviction was that it was up to the United States to determine what was to come next. Basic arithmetic told the story: there had previously been two superpowers; now only one remained. Henceforth, the decisions that mattered would be Washington's to make." The term "American triumphal" for the reasons made clear above is associated with Conservatives and neo-Conservatives, but its roots go back to Woodrow Wilson and Theodore Roosevelt before him.

[3] Danny Quah and Kishore Mahbubani, "The Geopolitics of Populism," *Project Syndicate*, December 9, 2016, available at https://www.project-syndicate.org/commentary/populism-driven-by-geopolitical-change-by-danny-quah-and-kishore-mahbubani-2016-12. Cf. Yuri Friedman, "What the World Might Look Like in 5 Years, According to US Intelligence," *Atlantic*, January 11, 2017, available at http://www.defenseone.com/ideas/2017/01/

References

Fukuyama, Francis (1992), *The End of History and the Last Man Standing*, New York: Simon and Schuster.

Krauthammer, Charles (1990), "The unipolar moment: America and the world," *Foreign Affairs*, July/August 2002, 70(1), 23–33.

Krauthammer, Charles (2002/2003), "The unipolar moment revisited," *The National Interest*, Winter, 5–17.

Mills, Quinn and Steven Rosefielde (2016), *The Trump Phenomenon and Future US Foreign Policy*, Singapore: World Scientific Publishers.

Rosefielde, Steven (2016), "Grexit and Brexit: Rational choice, compatibility, and coercive adaptation," *ActaOeconomica*, September, 66, 77–91.

Rosefielde, Steven and Quinn Mills (2017), *Trump's Populist America*, Singapore: World Scientific Publishers.

---

what-world-might-look-5-years-according-us-intelligence/134511/?oref=d-river: "Even America's own government analysts see the American Era drawing to a close. Every four years, a group of U.S. intelligence analysts tries to predict the future. And this year, in a report released just weeks before Donald Trump assumes the presidency, those analysts forecast a massive shift in international affairs over the next five years or so: 'For better and worse, the emerging global landscape is drawing to a close an era of American dominance following the Cold War,' the study argues. 'So, too, perhaps is the rules-based international order that emerged after World War II.' The National Intelligence Council (NIC), a unit within the Office of the Director of National Intelligence, is essentially marking the potential end not just of America's status as the world's sole superpower, but also of the current foundation for much of that power: an open international economy, U.S. military alliances in Asia and Europe, and liberal rules and institutions — rules like human-rights protections and institutions like the World Trade Organization — that shape how countries behave and resolve their conflicts." "Today, however, major powers are struggling to cooperate on issues of global consequence and acting aggressively in their respective parts of the world, the NIC observes. In the coming years, the council envisions the current international system fragmenting 'toward contested regional spheres of influence.'"

Part I
Western Secular Stagnation and Social Strife

Chapter 1
Overreach and Discord

Steven Rosefielde

The Industrial Revolution catapulted the West to the top of the heap, inspiring dreams of global dominion, despite a series of devastating world wars and a 73-year ideological death dance between Soviet communism and Western capitalism. Over the centuries, the West gradually forged a coherent idealist agenda ("American Dream") founded on the principles of reason, democracy, private property, free enterprise, liberty, humanitarianism, social justice, and the rule of law.

The dissolution of the Soviet Union on December 25, 1991, appeared to clear the way for the West to transform the world in its own likeness (Fukuyama 2006). The movement seemed to be succeeding with unstoppable momentum spearheaded by North Atlantic Treaty Organization's and the European Union's eastward march and soft power more broadly between 1991 and 2008, but supremacy did not endure. The one-two punch of the global financial crisis of 2008 and post-crisis economic stagnation sent the West reeling. The Washington consensus went the way of the dodo. A simmering social–economic–political and cultural crisis exacerbated by wealth inequality, Islamic immigration, and a deluge of refugees came to a boil. Russia's annexation of Crimea, China's provocative actions in the South China Sea, the emergence of the ISIS Middle East challenge, terrorism, the Syrian imbroglio, Iran's machinations, and nuclear proliferation further savaged the West's aura of inevitability. Suddenly, it became a stretch to imagine a unipolar reality where the idea of the West becomes the World's idea.

The new reality is multipolar, including America, Britain, the EU, Russia, China, and other great powers. While America can console itself as *primus inter pares* and the EU is affluent, there no longer seems any prospect for a second Western unipolar moment. The West appears increasingly militarily, economically, politically, and socially vulnerable. The old Western imperial dream of cloning the world in its own image is dead, and Russia, China, Iran, and the ISIS appear capable of expanding their spheres of influence and even augmenting their territories at the West's expense.

Western leaders, including Donald Trump, know that the correlation of forces has taken a nasty turn but cannot muster their resolve, while Russian and Chinese leaders rub their eyes in disbelief. There is time to right the ship. Trump is committed to trying in some important respects. He will restore American naval forces to the 1992 level and significantly increase military preparedness. He is committed to reinvigorating the economy by shifting to a government regulatory regime that incentivizes entrepreneurship, innovation, and growth and reduces anti-productive influences. His proposed adjustments are not panaceas and will not restore America's (the West's) unipolarity. America, however, should be able to hold its own in Trump's brave new world. It should be able to prosper and peacefully coexist with Russia and China, while containing them.

Reference

Fukuyama, Francis (2006), *End of History and the Last Man Standing*, New York: Free Press.

Chapter 2

Europhoria

Bruno Dallago

After years of euphoria for the common currency ("europhoria"), a deepening and broadening fault line is growing in the Eurozone between vulnerable and resilient countries.[1] The fault line became evident with the 2008 crisis, although its causes had been preexistent to it and predominantly internal to the Eurozone. Policies and common procedures are strengthening the financial situation of resilient countries, while the negative effect of austerity policies and the difficulty of vulnerable countries in reforming their economies are weakening their position. The latter are meeting increasing costs and weakening their performance, without the former being advantaged proportionally in a negative sum game. The Eurozone is consequently ailing and splitting, to the dissatisfaction and disadvantage of its inhabitants and economic agents.

---

[1] Vulnerable countries are those having an unbalanced macroeconomic or financial situation and whose economy is not competitive. They need policies to adjust their situation, but they miss policy sovereignty as members of a monetary union. External shocks may have particularly damaging consequences on these economies. The following countries are considered as vulnerable: Cyprus, Greece, Italy, Portugal, and Spain. Ireland is also considered in this group, since this country shared the basic features of vulnerable countries for years. Countries in balanced macroeconomic or financial situation do not have these problems. The following countries are considered as resilient: Austria, Belgium, Finland, France, Germany, Luxembourg, and the Netherlands. Other Eurozone countries are not considered because they are in between and share features of both groups.

While all countries apparently are greatly supporting their participation in the common currency and some of them are undergoing serious sacrifices imposed upon their population in order to comply with the common rules and requirements, the Eurozone seems to be unable to get out of a clearly undesirable and even dangerous situation. Anti-euro political parties and movements are slowly, but safely, becoming more popular and vociferous. The perspective of "Brexit," i.e., the exit of an important member country from the European Union (EU) — but not the Eurozone of which it was not part — dramatically strengthened such negative sentiments in the short run. However, the difficulties that the British polity and economy are meeting after the June 23, 2016, referendum and the opposition to Brexit by Scotland and Northern Ireland may well have a different outcome in the medium-to-long run.

The debate on the euro and related policies was replaced by procedures, threats, and orders that increasingly lack credibility. The lack of enthusiasm for a currency that a few years ago was seen as the crown jewel of European integration is increasingly evident. Countries that still a few years ago were longing to enter the euro, such as Central European countries, canceled this event from their agenda. In 2015, the first accession country, Iceland, unilaterally withdrew and canceled negotiations for EU membership. A Eurozone country, Greece, was close to exiting the euro in 2015, and a non-euro country, Great Britain, held a referendum which decided in favor of Brexit. Differences among member countries are growing, thereby making the common currency increasingly unsustainable and costly. The perspective of Brexit is apparently acting as a detonator that could lead to any outcome for the Eurozone: from its strengthening in a probably multispeed EU to the disruption of the Eurozone.

What are the causes of a potential economic, political, and social disaster? Why is the EU unable to find a solution, in spite of the bold and increasingly determined action of its Central Bank? Why is the European Commission so evidently powerless? And why are national governments, the real repositories of power in the EU together with the European Central Bank (ECB), so clearly unable to find a viable compromise, let alone a solution to mounting dangers? Why is the present situation so evidently dangerous for democracy and the constructive cooperation among European countries? Is this the beginning of the end or is it the end of an ineffective period from which a new Europe will emerge?

Theories of optimum currency areas (OCAs) are a good starting point for analyzing these problems and assessing the Eurozone perspectives. The chapter starts by considering why it is important that a monetary union is an OCA, in order to avoid the internal differences becoming structural factors that jeopardize the sustainability of the monetary union (Section 1). Section 2 reviews the benefits and the costs and disadvantages of an OCA. In Section 3, OCA criteria are considered and used to compare the Eurozone situation, with the United States taken as a benchmark. When a monetary union such as the Eurozone is not a perfect OCA, adjustment is more problematic and costly and requires policies and reforms. This is discussed in Section 4. However, as is considered in Section 5, the Eurozone is an incomplete and asymmetric monetary union, and this situation makes adjustment to asymmetric shocks problematic and leads to perverse consequences. As stressed in Section 6, the fundamental problem is the existence of incompatible and conflicting economic and fiscal philosophies within the Eurozone, in particular due to the dominance of the German ordoliberal approach in combination with austerity policies imposed by international organizations for years. Since this standard approach has failed to reestablish a viable situation, the Eurozone is in search of alternative policies, which Brexit makes dramatically urgent. Section 7 concludes in discussing some recent proposals.

Monetary Unions and OCAs

Any social undertaking including a monetary union has costs and benefits (Baldwin and Wyplosz 2012). A common currency area has one unique central bank and monetary policy, which cannot deal with the asymmetric effect of shocks in the different parts of the monetary union. Since asymmetric shocks cannot be avoided and the countries that form a monetary union have differences,[2] there must exist both market and policy devices for the monetary union to be viable. Market devices work without

---

[2]There are two fundamental types of differences that matter in a common currency area. These are economic, social, and institutional features of countries (such as different labor market institutions and structures, price elasticities of exports, energy intensity of the economy, industrial structures, and size of enterprises) and different financial structures (such as sources of investment financing, features of banks, financial and capital markets, role of the state, and size of the public debt).

requiring any explicit intervention by policymakers. However, they require proper institutional frameworks to be effective. OCA theories highlight the most important among them. One important device that was invoked for years as sufficient to guarantee the sustainability of the Eurozone is the so-called private insurance mechanism.[3]

National policy devices include fiscal policies (growth policies, internal devaluation[4]) and structural and institutional reforms that make the economic system more effective and efficient, with lower transaction costs. Various devices were discussed at European level, but hardly implemented. An important yet slowly implemented direct device is the creation of a European Banking Union, which includes a Single Supervisory Mechanism providing a framework for a more integrated banking market, and a Single Resolution Mechanism facilitating greater risk-sharing across borders. The Banking Union should also include, soon, a European Deposit Insurance Scheme, but this step is meeting serious resistance, particularly from Germany.

A country which is part of a monetary union cannot make use of depreciation of its nominal exchange rate to bring its cost level in line with its competitors. When incomes converge to the competitors' level, but productivity and prices do not, a monetary union leads to the appreciation of the real exchange rate for the vulnerable economies. This was evident until the crisis (Figure 2.1). Such appreciation has to be adjusted by improving performance or decreasing costs and incomes in vulnerable countries through structural (internal devaluation)[5] and institutional

---

[3] By private insurance mechanism, market solutions fixing the asymmetric effect of shocks within a monetary union is what is meant. When such mechanisms work, resources flow from countries with strong financial situations to countries in more vulnerable conditions through market processes.

[4] The concept of internal devaluation, to indicate a general direct decrease of costs with effects similar to those of the external devaluation, was first used during the economic crisis of Sweden during the 1990s and when Finland prepared to join the EU in 1995. With the 2008 crisis, the concept and related policies became a standard in Eurozone countries with the aim of restoring competitiveness and balancing national budgets (Piton and Bara 2012).

[5] The meaning and content of structural reforms is subject to some disagreement among scholars and policymakers. According to the European Commission (EC 2015a), structural reforms address impediments to the fundamental drivers of growth by unshackling labor, product, and service markets to foster job creation, investment, and productivity. There is

reforms[6] or by increasing them in resilient countries. The latter step is likely to be opposed, since this would decrease the international competitiveness of resilient countries. However, this adaptation has negative long-run consequences for the vulnerable countries and may lead to tensions, and even the disruption of the union. In the Eurozone, the recovery of competitiveness of vulnerable countries was implemented entirely through the decrease of unit labor costs, due to internal devaluation policies (Figure 2.1).

There are different ways for reducing costs and improving performance in a monetary union through: (1) decreasing public expenditure and cutting taxes; (2) structural reforms that decrease costs (e.g., by cutting wages, pensions, and welfare); and (3) fostering investments (e.g., to make infrastructure better and more efficient). Each of these solutions presents trade-offs and disadvantages. Decreasing public expenditure is

---

an international agreement, strongly supported by the EU and international organizations such as the International Monetary Fund (IMF), the World Bank, and the Organisation for Economic Co-operation and Development (OECD), that the revival of vulnerable countries needs structural reforms. These reforms aim at enhancing an economy's competitiveness, growth potential, and adjustment capacity. As a matter of fact, in vulnerable countries the policy accent is mostly, sometimes nearly exclusively, on labor and often on decreasing the remuneration and rights of employees and diminishing the welfare state. Generally, what the EU means by this term are the changes that lead to or are preconditions of internal devaluation. The perspective is mostly of macroeconomic nature and consists primarily of changes to the labor market or the pension system that decrease production costs, ease dismissals, and decrease public expenditures. There is no clear evidence that these changes improve the microeconomic efficiency and effectiveness of European economies, in particular in the case of vulnerable countries. Moreover, these changes contribute to decrease the size of the domestic market and worsen the economic, social, and political moods of most consumers.

[6] Institutional reforms are aimed at revitalizing the working of markets and making policies effective, thus acting particularly at microeconomic level. Prominent among institutional reform at EU level are a broader ECB mandate, the creation of a Eurozone banking federation, a stronger EU budget and fiscal union, and a common ministry of finance. At a national level, particularly in vulnerable countries, fundamental institutional reforms include a more effective and less costly public administration, increased competition, more efficient labor markets, more effective fiscal systems, and improvement in the quality of human resources. In the EU, many of these reforms were important components of the Lisbon strategy and play an important role in the ongoing Europe 2020 strategy.

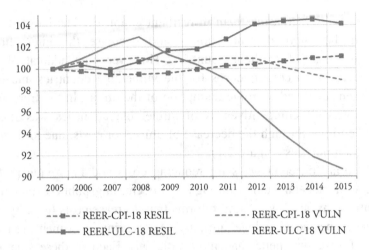

Figure 2.1   Real Effective Exchange Rate.

Note: Deflator: Unit labor costs in the total economy and consumer price indices (18 Trading Partners), 2005 = 100. A rise in the index means a loss of competitiveness. Data in this figure and the following figures refer to unweighted averages.

Source: Author's own figure based on data from Eurostat.

likely to decrease employment and weaken services and perhaps effectiveness in collecting tax revenues. Investments are a strategic and fundamental answer, but are costly in the present and give positive outcomes after some time, thus making their financing problematic in vulnerable countries.

The decrease of wages and the weakening of the rights of workers (e.g., decreasing welfare or pension rights) meet social opposition and are likely to increase income disparities. These effects may easily weaken aggregate demand and incentives to work. The consequence may be smaller internal market and lower investment, with long-term negative consequences (Figure 2.2).

Moreover, the depressive effect of wage cuts is usually fast and permanent, while prices are sticky. This redistributes income to the disadvantage of labor and depresses consumption and consequently investment. However, austerity policies may help to adjust current accounts of vulnerable countries, mainly through import cuts. The most noticeable effect is that adjustment falls entirely upon vulnerable countries and further

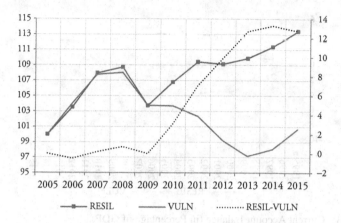

Figure 2.2   Cumulative Gain or Loss of Gross Domestic Product (GDP) in the Eurozone, 2005 = 100.

Note: Right scale for RESIL-VULN. The recovery for vulnerable countries in 2014 is entirely due to the strong growth of the Irish economy, which continued in 2015. In 2015, the economies of Spain and Cyprus had good performances.

Source: Author's own analysis of Eurostat data.

worsens their economic situation (Figure 2.3).[7] In the long run, price and wage reduction and investment decrease can push vulnerable countries to a low-level equilibrium and low-skill specialization and slow technical progress.

A sounder solution is institutional reform, i.e., reforms that reestablish the conditions for an efficient and effective economic system that supports the economy's competitiveness. Institutional reforms include fundamental solutions for decreasing transaction costs of economic activity, upgrading competition, linking wages to productivity and checking profits through competition, disrupting rents, and activating incentives. Examples are the reform of public administration, flexibility of markets, efficient welfare system, liberalization and effective regulation, entrepreneurship, and innovation.

---

[7] Much depends on the strength of the common currency compared to other currencies. If the former reflects the position of resilient member countries, vulnerable countries may find export difficult. The ECB effort to depreciate the euro since summer 2015 played an outstanding role in easing the situation of vulnerable countries, while also supporting resilient countries, which further increased their current account surplus.

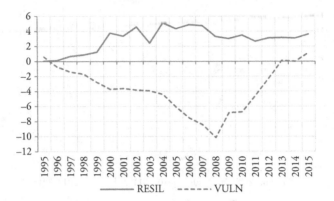

Figure 2.3   Current Account Balance (in Percentage of GDP).
Source: Author's own figure based on data from the Eurostat database.

Both structural and institutional reforms require time to be effective, involve serious costs, and may foster political and social opposition. A reasonable precondition for a well-working monetary union is, then, to include economies that are reasonably similar, so as to decrease costs and difficulties. An OCA is a group of countries that presents such economic and institutional features that make the use of one common currency more advantageous and efficient than having two or more currencies. OCA theories identify a set of features that are important to assess whether countries share the conditions for building a currency union that guarantees superior advantages. The classical benchmark of an OCA is the United States, but the approach is also used to assess whether the Eurozone presents the features that make the adoption of a common currency economically efficient and sustainable.

In a large and internally dissimilar monetary union such as the Eurozone, the unique currency and monetary policy have asymmetric effects that decentralized fiscal policies should fix (Buti and Sapir 1998). Asymmetric effects may be negligible if resources flow freely and rapidly within the union. The situation may be different when the instability of the external context goes beyond a certain threshold and economic agents perceive that the flow of resources is insufficient to balance the situation in the different parts of the union. This is exactly what happened during the crisis.

It has long been known that the Eurozone does not constitute a perfect OCA (Eichengreen 1991; Eichengreen *et al.* 1990; Feldstein 1991; Friedman 1997; Obstfeld 1997; Sala-i-Martin and Sachs 1991). However, the leaders of the monetary integration considered that consistent integration of markets, the activation of the private insurance mechanism, and reforms and strong political will and commitment would either create or complement the missing factors. *Ex post*, it is fair to say that this adaptation worked up to the crisis. In fact, the external effects of an expanding international economy and careful policy management created incentives to economic activity and avoided asymmetric shocks. However, tensions accumulated and the international crisis revealed such tensions and put the euro at risk. Unfortunately, the quality of an institutional setup, like a monetary system, corresponds to its value and resilience in a stressful situation. The institutional architecture of the EU in general, and the Eurozone in particular, proved to be questionable.

The Benefits and Drawbacks of an OCA

There are sizable benefits in going from a set of national currencies to a common currency (De Grauwe 2014; Marer 2016). Most of these benefits are of microeconomic nature in that they lead markets and economic actors to pursue efficiency. However, efficiency gains of a monetary union are diminished by the costs of the latter. These have mostly to do with macroeconomic management and institutional reforms.

Some gains and benefits are of general character, although the exact nature and size of others depend on the features of the economies that participate in the monetary union. In general, the benefits of a monetary union should be larger for small open economies and for their firms. The most important benefits are as follows:

1. The elimination of foreign exchange markets within the currency area reduces the costs of exchanging currencies and thus decreases transaction costs. These benefits go mainly to the advantage of enterprises, consumers, and tourists and are likely to attract more foreign investment to the common currency area. A fully integrated payment system is necessary within the common currency area to get the full

advantage of the reduction of transaction costs. The EU set up Single Euro Payments Area (SEPA) in 2012 for this purpose.[8] Thanks to lower transaction costs and integrated markets, it should be easier and more advantageous to conduct banking and insurance activities with a common currency.

2. Currency risk and exchange rate uncertainty disappear, and this should promote trade and investment, and consequently growth.

3. Greater transparency of prices should reduce price differentials among the member countries and should make prices converge to the cheapest level under the pressure of competition.

4. Monetary unions are credited for having positive impact on trade (Frankel and Rose 1998; Rose 2000).

5. A currency area — being larger, deeply integrated, financially disciplined, and sharing macroeconomic policies — should be more resilient and better able to absorb external shocks and thus guarantee greater macroeconomic stability and lower inflation.

6. The international role of a common currency creates seigniorage gains for the currency union.

7. Other benefits include economizing on foreign currency reserves and policy autonomy, thanks to its larger size and its monetary and financial stability. It should also lead to political and social benefits, including longer time horizon of economic actors, in that a monetary union endorses political stability and unity and common identity.

There are three main drawbacks of an OCA. They are as follows:

1. A country joining a monetary union loses monetary policy instruments, including control over the exchange rate, and has to afford an impossible trinity or trilemma (Baldwin and Wyplosz 2012; Obstfeld *et al.* 2004). Based on the condition of interest rate parity, a country in a monetary union can pursue at the same time only two among the following: a fixed exchange rate, free capital movement, or an

---

[8] SEPA is implemented by the European banks with the support of the ECB and the European Commission. It has the goal of making cashless payments across Europe fast, cheap, and safe.

independent monetary policy. In the Eurozone, only the ECB has an independent monetary policy, which includes the ability to set interest rates independently, with free capital movements. However, the ECB cannot fix exchange rates, and the euro is part of an international floating exchange rate system. Member countries guarantee free capital movement and give up exchange rates management, thus they cannot run an independent monetary policy.

2. Asymmetric shocks require that adjustment is left to flexible fiscal policies managed by national governments (Buti and Sapir 1998). However, member countries cannot have fiscal freedom, which would jeopardize the monetary sustainability of the area. Thus member countries lose flexibility in the use of fiscal policy instruments.

3. In being part of a monetary union, a government has to give up deficit spending and consequently a fundamental instrument of countercyclical policy (Goodhart 1998; Toporowski 2013; Wray 2000).

In the case of symmetric shocks, a monetary union is advantageous compared to monetary independence. The common central bank can effectively deal with these shocks and avoid policy competition among countries. Conversely, independent monetary policies can easily generate "beggar-my-neighbor" measures, such as competitive depreciation of national currencies. Unfortunately, it is a rare case of a monetary union that includes only countries or regions which are institutionally and structurally so similar that no asymmetric effects can be felt internally. The outcome depends on how the union's ability to manage these asymmetric effects is managed.

When shocks are asymmetric, a monetary union is the origin of costs compared to monetary independence. The common central bank cannot deal with these asymmetries, and fiscal policies should be left in the domain of national governments, as the EU did for years. For this mechanism to work effectively, countries should follow the same fiscal rules and behave in the same way, in particular, by keeping the same public and private budget constraints. In the long run, this is possible only if national economies are competitive or the private insurance mechanism assures intercountry flow of resources sufficient to smooth intercountry differences even in times of economic and financial distress. When these conditions do not hold, it will be necessary sooner or later to restrict the independent use of national financial policies. This is exactly what happened with the Maastricht criteria and the Stability and Growth Pact (SGP) and in particular with such clauses as the no-bailout clause of the Lisbon Treaty.

OCA Criteria and a Comparison with the United States

The classical analysis of an OCA stresses that member economies must be open, their production profile should be wide and production diversified, resources should be mobile, and prices and wages should be flexible. Under those conditions, the common currency assures its benefits without major costs or threats. Robert Mundell's seminal article (Mundell 1961) is usually credited to have introduced the concept of OCA. According to Mundell, in a world where asymmetric shocks are pervasive, a floating exchange rate regime can adjust economies to such shocks without causing unemployment, provided that prices and wages are flexible. Although financial capital can move fast in a monetary union, physical capital is transformed slowly, which prevents adjustment mechanisms from being sufficiently fast and effective. Consequently, it is particularly important that labor mobility is high and works as a shock absorber, spreading the effect of the shock over a much larger area (Mundell 1973).

Peter Kenen (1969) stressed the role of product diversification among countries as a necessary condition of an OCA. Countries with highly specialized production profile that form a currency union are liable to the asymmetric consequences of an external shock that concerns the goods or services in which they are specialized, without having the possibility to adapt to the shock through the variation of the exchange rate. Wide product differentiation in each member country of the monetary union and similarity of the production profile of the member countries is a guarantee that the effects of shocks concerning particular goods are not asymmetric to start with and are dispersed through a wide array of goods and services that each country produces.

According to Ronald McKinnon (1963), in open markets, goods are intensely traded and their price tends to be the same in each country by the force of international competition. As a consequence, if the nominal exchange rate varies, the internal price of the goods also changes, so that their external price is equal to the world price. Market openness also guarantees that business cycles in member countries are synchronized, thus supporting coordinated, non-competitive stabilization policies. In these conditions, the exchange rate loses much of its importance in support of the competitiveness of national goods and the adjustment of the economy to the effect of external shocks.

Since external shocks hit activities and countries randomly; it is in the interest of the countries that form a currency union to activate a sort of mutual insurance mechanism by transferring resources to the advantage of the members of the union in need. Intercountry fiscal transfers have the advantage of alleviating the recession in the country hit by the shock and mitigating the expansion in others. Such a solution can be implemented through market mechanisms or through the common fiscal capacity (a common budget) that acts as a mechanism of shock absorption and risk-sharing. It is generally important in a monetary union that policy preferences are homogeneous among member countries and mutual trust is strong. These sentiments help the union to foster mutual solidarity that can temper tensions and prolong the time horizon of all the involved actors.

In contemplating the Eurozone as an OCA, it is useful to consider how it fares compared with the typical benchmark, the United States (Dallago 2016a). Clearly the fundamental difference is that the United States comprehensively governs its economy, while the Eurozone does not. The litmus test of an OCA consists in assessing whether member countries activate risk-sharing through both market and fiscal means, in order to smooth intercountry differences to a level compatible with a sustainable common currency.

Various studies, referring to different periods of time, have found that labor market shocks lead to weaker migration in Europe than in the United States (Bentivogli and Pagano 1999; Bonin *et al.* 2008; Dallago 2016b; Decressin and Fatás 1995; Gáková and Dijkstra 2010), although recently inverse dynamics were observed (Molloy *et al.* 2011). Not only is labor mobility to another EU country or to another region of the same country much lower than in the United States, but there is also much higher spatial concentration of mobility of the working-age migrants in the EU than in the United States. Lower labor mobility than in the United States is a typical feature of the entire EU and is irrespective of the time of joining the EU, the level of development of the country or region, and the degree of openness of labor markets. Among the reasons that explain this dissimilarity, cultural and linguistic factors apart, are the differences in labor legislation between the EU and the United States, and there are still some obstacles to the free movement of labor in some parts of the EU. With the recent (2015) immigration crisis, such obstacles are growing further.

The role of labor mobility in reducing the differences in economic development between the states is important in the United States, thanks to a rather high share of the US working-age population moving every year to another state of residence. In the EU, however, this effect is much lower and labor mobility is not an important factor in reducing the disparities between EU member countries. Moreover, in the EU, there are important cross-country differences in labor mobility. In particular, there is a clear distinction between the new and the old member countries. In the latter, the share of the working-age population who changed their region of residence is nearly four times higher than in the Central and Eastern member countries.

The general situation of substantially lower labor mobility in the EU than in the United States changes somehow when interregional mobility within EU member states is considered. Although differences with the United States decrease in this case, these still remain important. Gáková and Dijkstra (2010) estimate that 85% of overall labor mobility in the EU was among regions of the same country. However, even in this case, mobility was very unequal through regions — also interregional mobility presents much higher dispersion in the EU than interstate mobility does in the United States. Thus, taking the US situation as a benchmark for OCA requirements, labor mobility is insufficient as an adjustment mechanism in the European monetary union featuring important interregional differences of performance.

However, the EU reacted more strongly to changes in labor market conditions than the United States during the more recent migration waves (Jauer *et al.* 2014). One important source of increased labor mobility within the EU was Eastern enlargements in 2004 and 2007 (Von Weizsäcker 2008), which increased disparities among countries and regions. Divergent situations among EU immigration countries changed the attractiveness of destinations to the advantage of Germany and other resilient countries and the disadvantage of vulnerable countries (Bertoli *et al.* 2013). These differences are larger in the EU, with unemployment at the regional level being more than two times higher in Europe than in the United States. Although there were positive developments, a host of problems and obstacles still hamper intra-EU labor mobility (BS 2014).

Important and growing differences also exist among EU-15. Yet so far, these differences did not push migration from vulnerable countries to resilient countries on a significant scale. Within the Eurozone, it was mainly labor migration from Central and Eastern European Countries (CEECs) that fed labor market adjustment through labor migration, in particular thanks to CEECs citizens who have taken on the nationality of a Eurozone country.

The second fundamental criterion for an OCA is openness of markets and integration. Openness of markets includes various aspects of an economy, such as foreign trade, foreign direct investments, external debt, and participation in global value chains. Openness of markets of Eurozone countries is high and, if infra-Eurozone exchanges are included, higher than the United States. According to the International Chamber of Commerce (ICC) Open Markets Index (ICC 2013), the Eurozone economy is more open than the US economy (based on the unweighted average of the scores of individual Eurozone member countries) (Dallago 2016a). Resilient Eurozone countries have a clear advantage over the United States: the former group of countries has above-average openness, while the United States is in the group of average openness and features and has a remarkable similarity to vulnerable countries. In the case of economic openness, then, the Eurozone is, on average, better off than the United States.

Much of the trade involving European countries is intra-industry trade, i.e., EU and Eurozone member countries trade mainly components of complex products. Their high product differentiation takes place within the same industries and in the production of components of similar goods or variants of the same product (e.g., cars). Moreover, as integration proceeds and leads to greater regional concentration of production, this concentration is inattentive to the countries' borders (De Grauwe 2014).

In fact, border regions attract a disproportionate share of the relocation of high technology and increasing-returns industries (Tsiapa 2013). Thus, productive activities localize where it is more convenient and involve more countries. Under these conditions, demand shocks are dispersed through countries.

Fiscal transfers are an important component of an OCA. However, this is one of the most problematic aspects of the Eurozone (Baldwin and Wyplosz 2012). In fact, the Eurozone lacks a fiscal pillar complementing the monetary pillar, since the common EU budget is negligible (around 1% of the EU GDP) and is used for structural convergence purposes. This compares to an average share of national public budget to GDP of 50% in EU member countries and 27% in the United States (to this, the states' public budgets should be added). Thus, the bulk of stabilization through transfers can only be managed by national governments in the Eurozone. However, national finances are constrained by restrictive common rules, and no effective common umbrella protects vulnerable countries.

The Eurozone is vulnerable to large country-level shocks since it lacks fiscal schemes for sharing income risk across member countries. These national shocks can become systemic for the area as a whole. According to an IMF Technical Background Notes (Bornhorst *et al.* 2013), cross-country risk-sharing in the Eurozone amounts to only half the sharing existing in other federal states and is similar to that in the EU. Moreover, risk-sharing also decreases sharply in severe downturns. All these features lead to an increased vulnerability of the Eurozone compared to any other arrangement existing in modern economies.

Business cycle coordination is another factor that decreases the possibility of asymmetric shocks in a monetary union. Saiki and Kim (2014) compare the Eurozone with East Asia. They find that business cycle correlation increased over time in both regions. However, synchronization progressed much faster in East Asia. Intra-industry trade, and in particular vertical intra-industry trade, unambiguously increased business cycle correlation. Both increased in East Asia, a finding consistent with the rapid increase in business cycle correlation in East Asia, but not in the Eurozone.

Konstantakopoulou and Tsionas (2011) find that synchronization is stronger among subgroups of Eurozone countries. In particular, there is a core of resilient countries (Germany, France, Belgium, the Netherlands, and Austria) showing the strongest synchronization. Other vulnerable countries (such as Greece and Portugal), but also Luxembourg and Finland, present no synchronization with the rest. However, Furceri and Karras (2008) find that there was an increase in synchronization after the establishment of the Economic and Monetary Union (EMU). Pentecôte *et al.* (2015) show that external demand is a particularly important determinant of business cycle synchronization in the case of the 11 founding members of the EMU over the 1995–2007 period.

Differences in synchronization are, in part, the outcome of national specialization and productive structure and the different situation of public finances. Such differences require uncoordinated fiscal policies. Since these policies are under common fiscal discipline, the national capacity for countercyclical action may be constrained, which generates uncoordinated business cycles.

It is clear that, under the OCA criteria, the Eurozone is disadvantaged compared to the United States, even if the distance is not unbridgeable. Yet this disadvantage could be bridged through political engagement and social support. After years of austerity policies that imposed serious strains on the citizens of most Eurozone countries, it is remarkable that political engagement continues and there is a majority of European citizens who continue to support the common currency, even in the countries which were most heavily hit by austerity policies. It seems fair to conclude that the commonality of destiny is rather sound in the Eurozone. Or, in any case, citizens generally do not want to lose the economic and political advantages of the common currency and afford the costs, disadvantages, and uncertainty that the return to a national currency would imply. This provides the common currency with an important support.

Perhaps the most convincing support for this conclusion is found in the evolution of the Greek crisis. In spite of the heavy sacrifices imposed on the citizens of that country by European authorities and other member states' governments, a majority of the population continues to support the participation in the monetary union. As to Brexit, it does not appear that it will change the general support to the common currency in the Eurozone member countries and could lead even to strengthening of the monetary unification, although probably not the willingness of other countries to join it.

Only one-third of the respondents living in the Eurozone considered negatively the euro for their own country in 2014, while 57% considered it as a good thing (Eurobarometer 2014a; see also Stokes 2015). The situation improved one year later, when negative feelings decreased to 30% of respondents, while support increased to 61% (Eurobarometer 2015a). However, there are significant differences among countries, and the support for the euro is definitely stronger in resilient countries. Although the majority of respondents thinking that the euro is good for their own country is larger than those having a negative opinion, this share was 50% in Cyprus and 49% in Italy in 2015. However, in both countries there was an improvement compared to 2014. Most Europeans are also convinced that the euro is good for the Union: 71% thought so at the end of 2015, compared to 19% of those having a negative opinion. The favorable trend, stronger than in the case of member countries, has been going on since 2012, in coincidence with the more active stance of the ECB. In this case, the positive opinion is much stronger than negative opinions in any country, even if intercountry differences are significant in this case.

The support is also strong for European policies and reforms: 78% of Europeans think that there is need for significant economic reforms in their own country, and more than seven out of ten Europeans (71%) support the perspective of having more coordination in Eurozone policies, including budgetary policies. Both data are on the rise compared to one year earlier, and intercountry differences are relatively mild: positive answers vary between 72% in Germany and 88% in Cyprus (Eurobarometer 2014a, 2015a).

However, citizens' trust is still shaky, although improving on average: the share of respondents having trust in the EU increased from 31% in Spring 2014 to 40% in 2015. In the same period, trust in the main European institutions — the European Parliament, the European Commission, and the ECB — increased significantly. These shares are higher than in the case of national parliaments and governments. Conversely, the percentage of people having a negative image of the EU decreased from 29 to 19% in the same period. Trust in the EU is stronger in resilient countries (more than 40%) than in vulnerable countries (nearly 29% of respondents). In the latter countries, those who have trust are only

Table 2.1   The Eurozone and the United States as OCAs.

OCA criterion	Eurozone	United States
Labor mobility (Mundell)	Low, but growing	Yes
Trade openness (McKinnon)	Yes	Yes
Product diversification (Kenen)	Yes	Yes
Fiscal transfers	Low, but growing	Yes
Homogeneity of preferences	Partial	Yes
Commonality of destiny	Partial (support to euro, trust)	Yes

one-third of those who do not have trust (69%). The Eurozone is split even in this case (Eurobarometer 2014a, 2015b, 2015c).

The intergovernmental trust is perhaps the most fundamental asset in an EMU that is increasingly becoming an intergovernmental integration (Piattoni 2016). It is not easy to assess the real state of this trust in the Eurozone. While Brexit undoubtedly distressed intergovernmental trust in the EU, it is not necessarily so in the Eurozone. The perception of the danger coming from Brexit is apparently pushing Eurozone countries to move prudently and in a concerted way.

The overall situation of the Eurozone as an OCA compared to the United States is summarized in Table 2.1.

Adjustment in a Non-OCA Monetary Union

A country outside a monetary union can adjust its economy, when hit unfavorably by an asymmetric shock, by depreciating the exchange rate. This is a rapid adjustment that decreases all prices and wages impersonally. The economy thus regains its competitiveness. Sovereign monetary and fiscal policies can be used to strengthen the adjustment. In a currency union, the unique monetary policy tends to enlarge the problems of the vulnerable part of the union. A symmetric shock, such as the appreciation of the common currency, is likely to create expansion in countries with rigid export demand and recession in member countries with elastic export demand. Since the common currency reputation depends typically upon the strongest countries in the Union, the common monetary policy is likely to reflect the needs of the economically, financially, and politically strongest partners. This is disadvantageous to vulnerable countries. However, vulnerable countries may take advantage of the strength of the former through capital import and expanded exports within the Union. This was the situation of the Eurozone until 2008. The outcomes in vulnerable countries depend on the use of the additional resources: growth and additional employment may follow, or financial and real bubbles may occur. These consequences may create political and social tensions within the monetary union that are not easy to manage, given the incomplete institutional and policy setting.

Integrated capital markets offer an alternative mechanism that can be compared to a private insurance system. With integrated capital markets, the mobility of capital allows for automatic insurance against shocks if capital flows where there is more need and higher returns, i.e., to deficit countries. However, there are three problems with this private mechanism. First, the insurance works at the cost of higher returns in the deficit country. This takes the form of a positive spread over benchmark return rates in balanced countries. Second, there is no guarantee that capital accrues to finance activities useful to bridge the financial gap and may create financial or real bubbles. Third, if capital markets perceive the deficit country as particularly risky, capital may abstain from flowing to the deficit country. Even worse, when risk is perceived as high, as when markets recognize that no common financial protection exists, domestic capital can leave the deficit country. Therefore, differential risk may hamper the working of integrated capital markets as insurance systems. This typically happens during a crisis.

These problems proved to be nearly intractable in the Eurozone during the crisis. The private insurance mechanism worked rather smoothly before the crisis but contributed to create bubbles. Capital of surplus countries, particularly Germany, financed deficits in Greece, Ireland, and Spain. However, when the crisis hit vulnerable countries, German capital left in spite of higher returns. Also, domestic capital of vulnerable countries expatriated to strong surplus countries, primarily because of the perceived excess risk.[9]

---

[9] Private capital flows to vulnerable countries, in particular to southern European countries (Greece, Italy, Ireland, Portugal, and Spain), increased significantly as a share of their GDP from 2002 to 2007–2009. The share of cumulative inflow of private capital was as high as 90% of the 2007 GDP in Portugal, 80% in Greece, and 70% in Spain. In Ireland and

Trans-European Automated Real-time Gross Settlement Express Transfer System (Target2) is an integrated and harmonized European payment system that provides for the automatic transfers among central banks to adjust balance of payments disequilibria.[10] A further development, close to full completion in summer 2017, is Target2-Securities. This system aims at setting up a single IT platform — built, owned, and operated by the Eurosystem — for moving securities and money between buyers and sellers. The system intends to integrate and harmonize the currently fragmented securities settlement infrastructure in Europe. It also aims at reducing the costs of cross-border securities settlement within the euro area and participating non-euro countries and at increasing competition and choice among providers of post-trading services. The ECB also operates the Correspondent Central Banking Model (CCBM), a framework set up in 1999 to enable banks in the Eurozone to submit all assets eligible for use as collateral for Eurosystem monetary policy operations or intraday credit in Target2. The new CCBM2, under development, should be based on one single platform, thus allowing more standardization.

Target2, which measures balance of payment settlements, allows for an estimate of the multilateral effects of sovereign debt. Target2 balances

---

Italy, it was slightly above 25% (Merler and Pisani-Ferry 2012b). This remarkable inflow was followed by a significant "sudden stop" (a common feature of balance-of-payments crises in emerging countries — see Calvo *et al.* 2004) between 2008 and 2011. Sudden stop episodes hit countries in three distinct periods, in function of country-specific risk factors (Schmidt and Zwick 2013): Greece in early 2008 and Ireland from October 2008, concomitant with the international financial crisis; Greece again in spring 2010, causing a contagion that hit Portugal and Ireland; Italy and Spain at the end of 2011 following the pressure in their sovereign bond market during the summer; and again Portugal (Merler and Pisani-Ferry 2012b; Pisani-Ferry and Merler 2012).

[10] As of February 2016, 25 central banks of the EU participate or are connected to Target2. These are the 20 euro area central banks (including the ECB) and 5 central banks from non-euro area countries (Bulgaria, Croatia, Denmark, Poland, and Romania) (https://www.ecb.europa.eu/paym/t2/html/index.en.html). According to the latest update on July 15, 2016, there were 1,007 banks directly participating in Target2 in 2014. To these, 837 indirect participants and 5,037 correspondents should be added. Around 56,000 banks worldwide can send and receive payments via the system. See https://www.ecb.europa.eu/paym/t2/html/index.en.html.

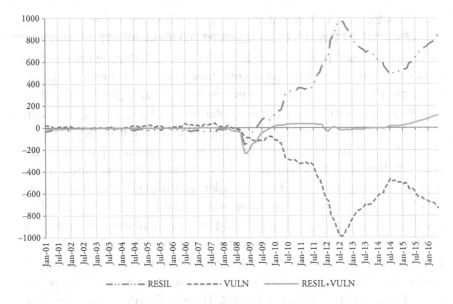

Figure 2.4   Target2 Balances, January 2001 to May 2016 (in billion €).

Source: Own elaborations on data from Steinkamp and Westermann (http://www.eurocrisismonitor.com/Data.htm).

measure the share of National Central Bank's (NCB) credit to private banks that is used for international transactions. In this way, according to some scholars, Target2 turns a domestic credit of an NCB which is part of the Eurosystem into a multilateral loan of the country with respect to the Eurosystem (Sinn 2014; Steinkamp and Westermann 2014). Surplus Eurosystem NCBs finance these losses. The striking difference of resilient and vulnerable countries during the crisis was evident and formed a mirror image (Figure 2.4).[11] The difference was striking particularly in summer 2012, when the negative position of Spain and Italy soared (respectively to nearly €435 billion and nearly €290 billion), with a mirror positive position of Germany of more than €750 billion.

One way of adjusting differences of macroeconomic conditions in a monetary union is to have different interest rates in different parts of the

---

[11] The positions of Austria, Belgium, and France were mildly negative throughout the period, while that of Italy was positive until mid-2011.

Union, perhaps following the Taylor rule.[12] Interest rates identified through the rule in both the Eurozone and the United States fit quite well in the past and corresponded well to the ECB interest rate policy. However, since the crisis, the Taylor rule identifies large differences in interest rates for the Eurozone-resilient and -vulnerable countries (Nechio 2011; Wynne and Koech 2012). Malkin and Nechio (2012) have found that divergences from Taylor-rule-based optimal interest rates are wider in the Eurozone than in the United States, which the authors attribute to lower labor mobility and lesser use of fiscal transfers. During the crisis, the gap between ECB and country-specific Taylor rates widened (Wynne and Koech 2012).

If the transfer of resources from other regions or countries is not possible, economic difficulties can be solved only by diminishing in some way costs, and hence prices, in the less-competitive country or region (internal devaluation). This can be done in different ways: through reforms that cut costs (e.g., by cutting taxation or rents or by implementing a more efficient and effective public administration), or decreasing the cost of production (e.g., through investments that make infrastructure more efficient or decrease the cost of energy), or increasing competition. These changes require far-reaching reforms. Alternatively, adjustment may take place through the decrease of wages, or by weakening the rights of workers (e.g., by decreasing welfare or pension rights). However, the latter is likely to increase income disparities and may easily weaken aggregate demand and incentives to work. The consequence may comprise lower domestic demand, including lower investment, with long-term negative consequences.

An institutionally incomplete currency area such as the Eurozone, one in which internal transfers are insufficient, risks to be left with internal devaluation as the only adjustment mechanism to an external shock. In this case, the adjustment takes a longer time and may have negative long-run consequences for production. Moreover, adjustment is typically costlier and more painful, because the downward adjustment of prices and wages must take place directly and nominally through explicit decisions and actions concerning individual prices and wages. However, prices and

---

[12] The Taylor rule is a "rule of thumb" that can be used for identifying optimal interest rates (Taylor 1993) as a function of inflation and unemployment gaps in different countries.

wages are typically sticky, firms and employees resist the unfavorable adjustment, and labor reallocation is slow.[13] This process may be cumbersome, since it requires the renegotiation of individual contracts, and may meet strong social opposition and creates uncertainty. Moreover, there is no guarantee that a decrease of wages translates into lower prices, since this depends on the conditions of competition in markets and the institutional setting of the economy. Perhaps more important, internal devaluation runs the risk of starting a race to the bottom, with negative social and long-term economic consequences. It shrinks the domestic market and causes substantial unemployment, unless increased exports and the inflow of investments smooth out the negative effect. Unemployment increases social expenditures from the state budget and decreases fiscal revenue. If GDP decreases, the real value of the debt inevitably increases. Through internal devaluation, vulnerable countries recovered competitiveness (Figure 2.1) at a lower GDP level (Figure 2.3).

Downward wage rigidity was strong before the crisis in many OECD countries, but has decreased since, due to labor market reforms and policy pressure in various countries. Holden and Wulfsberg (2008) find stronger downward nominal wage rigidity in southern European countries (Italy, Greece, Portugal, and Spain) and in northern European countries (Denmark, Finland, Norway, and Sweden). In these two groups of countries, employment protection legislation is stricter and/or unions are stronger. In resilient countries (Austria, Belgium, France, Germany, Luxembourg, and the Netherlands) and Anglo-Saxon countries (Canada, Ireland, New Zealand, the United Kingdom, and the United States), downward nominal wage rigidity is weaker. However, resilient countries typically have social institutions and programs for the protection and support of workers, which explain their greater labor market flexibility. With the crisis, downward rigidity of wages weakened further, particularly in vulnerable countries (Table 2.2).

---

[13] In the Eurozone, producer prices change slightly more often than consumer prices, probably because of lesser competition in the retail sector. The monthly frequency of price changes is respectively 15% and 21% (Dhyne *et al.* 2009). This frequency is lower than in the United States, where consumer prices change more often than producer prices, over 25% per month.

Table 2.2   Growth in Real Hourly Wages (Annual Average Growth Rates 2008–2013).

		2008–2013			2008–2013
VULN	Greece	-3.8	**RESIL**	Austria	0.9
	Ireland	-0.3		Belgium	0.4
	Italy	-0.3		Finland	1.0
	Portugal	-0.5		France	0.9
	Spain	-0.2		Germany	0.7
				Netherlands	0.1
	VULN, average	**-1.0**		**RESIL, average**	**0.7**

Source: Own elaboration on data from OECD (2014).

Eurozone: A Catch 22?

A currency union can proceed without a common government, provided that economies have similar levels of competitiveness and grow at approximately the same pace. In such a situation, each economy produces sufficient jobs and resources to be redistributed internally to welfare and public investment. Neither are absolute differences in productivity relevant, provided that they are compensated by cost and price differences and dissimilar specializations.

The situation becomes unbearable for those countries which see their relative productivity decrease while wages and other costs converge to resilient countries'. In this case, a monetary union leads to the appreciation of the real exchange rate for the vulnerable economies (Figure 2.1). If vulnerable countries are unable to upgrade their productivity through investment (which indeed fell significantly — Figure 2.5), such appreciation has to be adjusted by decreasing directly prices, incomes, and welfare in vulnerable countries or increasing them in resilient countries, a step that the latter is likely to oppose since this would decrease their international competitiveness (Figure 2.6).

However, this adaptation has negative long-run consequences for the vulnerable countries and may lead to further problems. In the short run, the depressive effect of wage cuts is usually faster and stronger than price decrease. This is due to both the employees' psychology impinging upon consumption expenditures and the control that enterprises and their

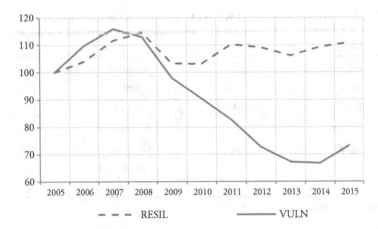

Figure 2.5   Gross Fixed Capital Formation, Chain-Linked Volumes, Index: 2005 = 100 (2005–2015).

Note: Eurostat **chain-linked level series** are obtained by successively applying price growth rates of the previous year to the current price figure of a specific reference year (2005).
Source: Author's own calculations based on Eurostat data.

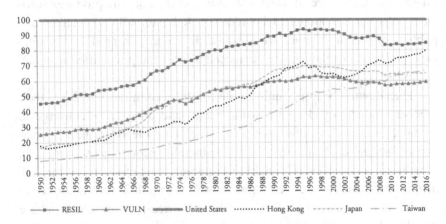

Figure 2.6   Productivity Gap: GDP per Hours Worked, 1950–2013 (Geary–Khamis Dollars, US = 100).

Source: Author's own figure based on "The Conference Board. 2016. The Conference Board Total Economy Database™, http://www.conference-board.org/data/economydatabase/".

associations have on prices. These effects create negative consequences for consumption and investment of vulnerable countries. In the long run, price and wage reduction can push the country to a low-skill specialization and slow down technical progress. Under these conditions, much depends on the strength of the common currency compared to other currencies. If the former reflects the position of resilient member countries, vulnerable countries may also find it difficult to export.

Under these conditions, the common currency deprives vulnerable countries of a fundamental instrument for adjustment: the depreciation of the exchange rate. It is therefore of utmost importance that the common currency and monetary policy are accompanied by compensating factors. A common budget and transfer of common resources to the advantage of regions in need is the strongest common solution, although it may be difficult to implement it in the absence of a common government. Other factors include fiscal equalization, independent national budgets and related policies, the intercountry transfer of resources by means of bilateral or multilateral government actions, through private insurance mechanisms or through automatic compensations among central banks (Target2).[14] Additional devices include a bank union and supervision. A common central bank that acts as a lender of last resort can ease asymmetries and tensions. Political will and social preferences supporting the common currency are also important components of success.

The Eurozone is implementing these devices at different levels and with different intensity. These devices are useful in supporting the cooperation among member countries, in avoiding heavy economic and social consequences and in gaining time for making the monetary union more effective and efficient. However, in themselves, these devices do not cure the causes of divergence, but only ameliorate its consequences. Two solutions are available: first, whenever the OCA solution is insufficient, it is necessary to reestablish the conditions for costs to be in line with (marginal) productivity through internal devaluation. Second, a more desirable

---

[14] There may be different ways to reach a balanced situation, going from a transfer union to fiscal equalization. A transfer union comprises different schemes, including — in its most complete form — permanent, direct, and horizontal transfers between Eurozone countries, a situation from which the EMU is still far away. Some see this outcome as desirable or inevitable (Hill 2014), others are afraid for the potential complicacies and conflicts it could bring (Heinen 2011). Fiscal equalization consists in the transfer of financial resources across countries or regions in order to balance out the consequences of disparities in incomes and revenue-raising capacity and provide all citizens with similar levels of public services at a similar tax burden (Blöchliger 2013; Blöchliger and Charbit 2008). The EU budget may be seen as a rather rudimentary and partial form of fiscal equalization.

solution is to activate the different features of an OCA, in particular labor mobility, price flexibility, and trade and product integration. This may require reforms and active policies, which may meet obstacles already in the short run and bring improvements in the long run. Establishing the preconditions of an OCA allows resources to flow freely from where they are abundant and unutilized to where they are most needed. The real alternative is to upgrade productivity through investments, technical progress, and institutional reforms, which can provide a real boost to the economy's development and competitiveness.

The issue of having a common government of the economy is certainly a central one in a monetary union. So far in the Eurozone, common rules and procedures replaced the common government. Unluckily, common rules and procedures cannot promote growth, employment, or investment and technical progress. They can only support the implementation of stabilization by constraining the behavior of member countries. This is important in a currency union but is insufficient to improve welfare and promote growth and employment and even less to adjust to external crises.

One problem is public debts. When countries in a currency area have similar growth rates but different debts, countries with higher debts may have to pay higher interest rates to finance their debt and devote an increasing share of their GDP to that purpose. This causes the growth of debt to GDP ratios (Figure 2.7).[15]

This is inevitable when markets stop believing in the existence of a common protective umbrella. This typically takes place when a general crisis tests the common willingness to support vulnerable countries. Since member countries are deprived of national monetary policies and have to run their debts in a currency they do not control, fiscal policies must be strictly disciplined and coordinated for the sake of stability of the common currency, to avoid countries with higher debts causing inflation and jeopardizing the value of the common currency to the disadvantage of low-debt countries. This is a disadvantage to vulnerable countries, which have a large share of their budget expenditures sunk to the payment of interests (Figure 2.8).

---

[15] In fact, even with balanced primary budgets, debt to GDP ratios grow if the real interest rate is higher than GDP growth rate.

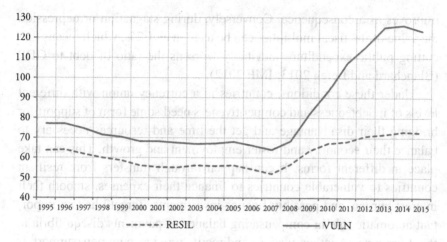

Figure 2.7 General Government Gross Debt (Percentage of GDP).
Source: Author's own figure based on data from Eurostat.

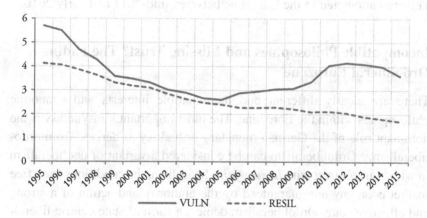

Figure 2.8 General Government Interest, Payable, Percentage of GDP.
Source: Author's own figure based on data from Eurostat.

Unfortunately, financial discipline meets the problem of the fiscal multiplier. Fiscal multipliers have much higher values in a stagnation or depression than they have in an expansion. According to the IMF calculations, the value of the fiscal multiplier in the expanding economies of the 1990s was around 0.5. This means that by decreasing public expenditure by 1%, the GDP only decreases by 0.5%. The ratio of debt to GDP improves as a consequence. Conversely, during stagnation or depression the value of the fiscal multiplier can be as high as 1.7%, which means that cutting public expenditure inevitably worsens the ratio of debt to GDP (Blanchard and Leigh 2013; IMF 2012).

Under these conditions, countries in a currency union with different levels of indebtedness and competitiveness need some form of support for bridging their disadvantage and get the time and resources necessary to balance their economy and foster employment and growth. This can take place in different forms. It can happen through transfers from resilient countries to vulnerable countries to finance their expenses, smooth their interest burden, and possibly finance investments. Target2 had an important automatic role in compensating balance of payments disequilibria in the Eurozone. Another way to indirectly provide common support is depreciating the common currency to a level that goes to the advantage of vulnerable countries, although it may be too low for resilient countries. This was attempted in the Eurozone between mid-2014 and early 2016.

Incompatible Philosophies and Missing Trust? The Fading Ordoliberal Eurozone

There are clearly different and incompatible interests and economic philosophies within the Eurozone. The most important idiosyncrasy is the dominant role of the German monetary orthodoxy as derived from ordo-liberalism.[16] Ordoliberalism can be considered a variant of neoliberalism in which, in contrast with *laissez-faire* liberalism, the conditions for a free market economy are guaranteed by the authority and action of a strong and effective state. Ordoliberalism depicts a form of state-centric liberalism, in which the strong state is the political form of free markets, and

---

[16] Ordoliberalism was developed at the Freiburg School by such economists as Walter Eucken and Franz Böhm, particularly in the 1930s and 1940s, and was the leading economic and social thought at the basis of the social market economy established in Germany after World War II. An important ordoliberal analysis of European monetary unification is Sinn (2014). Sinn maintains that the ECB has been too accommodating and that bailouts have created dangerous moral hazard. For ordoliberalism and related policies, their origin, content, and approach to the crisis, see Bonefeld (2011, 2012, 2013), Dullien and Guerot (2012), Ptak (2009), Sally (1996), Schnyder and Siems (2013), and Young (2014).

competition and enterprising are political tasks. Economic freedom is a fundamental tenet of ordoliberalism, but economic freedom is ordered freedom. Along with law and order, among the necessary conditions are also social policies. These aim at including and captivating workers and making them participate in the economy as repositories of property rights, both as private owners and through codetermination. This aim is addressed to avoid the radicalization of trade unions and workers' political movements (Bonefeld 2012, 2013; Schnyder and Siems 2013).

Equally important were German policy preferences, as influenced by the German historical experience with hyperinflation and its social and political consequences. When the project of the euro started to take form, Germans were prudent and lacked enthusiasm. They understandably feared the loss of control over a sound national currency. The German mark had a strong reputation as sound and well-managed currency and German monetary authorities had a strong reputation for prudence and soundness. The new currency looked ill-defined to them, since it was shared with countries that were not considered as good examples of monetary stability and soundness.

These German idiosyncrasies are the basis of the position that Germany consistently held and successfully imposed to European institutions during the crisis (Dullien and Guerot 2012; Young 2014). Unfortunately, this approach is at odds with much of the rest of the Eurozone, which has a different, albeit variegated, institutional and consequently policy stance. It is from this deep institutional and political difference that arises much of the conflict on policies within the Eurozone. While many countries need more relaxed stabilization policies, also attentive to growth, Germany sees the rule-based ordoliberal approach as a panacea for the Eurozone countries that have to regain competitiveness.[17]

---

[17] "Through its dominance of the euro system, Germany is exporting ordoliberal ideology to the rest of the single currency bloc. It is hard to think of a doctrine that is more ill-suited to a monetary union with such diverse legal traditions, political system and economic conditions than this one. And it is equally hard to see Germany ever giving up on this. As a result the economic costs of crisis resolution will be extremely large" (Münchau 2014). However, there may be an interesting, albeit prudent, change in the position of the German government going on, following the agreement over Greece in summer 2015. It is to be seen what the effect of Brexit will be.

Ordoliberal principles are at the basis of the construction of the ECB and its initial policy stance in support to austerity and price stability, the centerpiece of the Eurozone policies, at the expense of economic growth. They are at the core of European agreements which include such provisions as the no-bailout clause and no monetary financing. This construction held at least until the ECB, under the presidency of Mario Draghi, prudently and progressively changed position, under the fading transmission mechanism of monetary policy and the pressure of mounting problems. At the same time, the most rigid components of the ordoliberal approach, such as the fiscal compact,[18] became progressively ineffective. Acting as the only really common institution, the ECB endeavored to pursue monetary policies that could be effective for countries with non-ordoliberal institutional settings and economic situations. Although the German policy position slowly evolved, as a consequence of the failure of the policies it imposed on the Eurozone, the way toward sustainable and effective policies is still a long one.

Conclusion

Ordoliberalism is the German-centric Eurozone version of austerity that dominated economic philosophy and policymaking in Europe and the

---

[18] The Fiscal Stability Treaty, or simply fiscal compact (formally, the Treaty on Stability, Coordination and Governance in the EMU), is a stricter version of the SGP. The treaty was signed on March 2, 2012, and entered into force on January 1, 2013 for 16 countries; the remaining 9 countries joined by April 1, 2014. The Treaty builds on the budgetary rules outlined in the SGP. Signatories to the Treaty agreed to *implement a balanced budget rule* in their national legislation through permanent, binding provisions, preferably of a constitutional character. The Treaty includes a provision for (1) limiting deficits (annual structural government deficit *must not exceed 0.5 percent of GDP*; the deficit must be in line with the country-specific minimum benchmark figure for long-term sustainability; this figure is set by the preventive arm of the SGP); (2) automatic correction mechanism (countries must implement a correction mechanism, i.e., design measures to *reduce the budget deficit*; these measures are triggered automatically in the event of a significant deviation from the agreed benchmark figure for long-term sustainability); (3) reinforced coordination (Treaty signatories also agreed to inform each other, the Council of the EU, and the European Commission in advance when they plan to issue new debt; they also discuss all plans for major economic policy reforms); and (4) Euro Summit meetings (the signatories agreed to hold *Euro Summit meetings*, which bring together heads of state or government of the Eurozone, at least twice a year). The Eurogroup is responsible for the preparation and follow-up of these meetings.

international organizations, and in particular the IMF, until early 2010s. Policymaking and conditionalities that were imposed on countries needing support — Greece, Spain, Portugal, Cyprus, and Ireland — or in financial distress — Italy — owed to ordoliberalism as much as they were based on the unconvincing analyses of expansionary austerity (Blyth 2013). As mentioned above, they were also based on the gross mistakes of considering the value of the fiscal multiplier to be the same during the crisis as it was during the high expansion years. The institutional incompleteness of the Eurozone made these issues terribly costly and dangerous.

What is to be done? In consideration of the great benefits of the monetary union for all its member countries and the unpredictable costs of its disruption, the Eurozone can only proceed. The turmoil following Brexit strengthens this perception. Yet mutual trust is necessary to proceed. Mutual trust is the necessary basis for proceeding with common institutions and for implementing different policies in different countries. But mutual trust requires that all member countries share the same view of the monetary union and pursue the common good.

When looking at the effects of a monetary union, it is necessary to consider the institutional and structural features of the countries, knowing that these differences lead to asymmetric effects. Under these conditions, the classical solution is to have a common government of the economy that can transfer resources from the countries benefiting from the common monetary policy to the disadvantaged member countries. A further solution is to have a common central bank that acts as a lender of last resort. So far, neither solution exists within the Eurozone, even if the quantitative easing enacted since March 2015 led the ECB to be a *de facto* lender of last resort and the depreciation of the euro helped significantly vulnerable countries.

In a period of turmoil and internal and external threats, the European integration is at risk. This has prompted interesting and important developments in early 2016. The most promising are perhaps some moves toward a common government of the economy, however timid these are. Of particular interest is the recent article by the presidents of the French and German central banks (Villeroy de Galhau and Weidmann 2016). The importance of this piece is that one of the authors is the president of the German Central Bank, who is known for his extremely prudent and conservative attitude in the common monetary policy.

The article clearly outlines two scenarios: greater determination in accelerating the integration, or tougher fiscal and monetary discipline. The latter becomes inevitable if the former fails and takes directly to a rigorous implementation of the fiscal compact: "However, if governments and parliaments in the euro area were to shy away from the political dimension of a fully-fledged union, this would leave just one viable option — a decentralized approach based on individual responsibility and even stronger rules."

The force of the authors' insight is to remind all member countries about the "political dimension of a fully-fledged union" and to warn that "Europe's future cannot be built on renationalisation but on strengthening its foundations." "To successfully enhance the prosperity and stability of the euro area, three economic pillars have to be built."

The first pillar includes "resolute national structural reform pro-grammes." What is interesting is that the authors include under the term structural reforms many of what we termed as institutional reforms. This means that internal devaluation is not enough and may even be dangerous when not complemented by institutional reforms. Written by one of the main keepers of ordoliberal orthodoxy, this is a promising position.

Reforms are costly, and vulnerable countries are in a difficult situation to finance them. For this reason, "growth-enhancing measures at the European level" are also necessary. Here comes the second pillar, which consists of "an ambitious financing and investment union." This is impor-tant to mobilize the abundant amount of savings existing in the Union and that do not find an appropriate use in financing investments. The solution would start from implementing and streamlining in a stronger and effec-tive way already existing initiatives (such as the Capital Markets Union, the Juncker investment plan, and the completion of the banking union). This pillar may appear not particularly bold in light of the Eurozone prob-lems, but it is certainly noteworthy for the origin of the statement in core Eurozone central banks.

Finally, the third pillar is improved euro-area fiscal and economic governance: "More integration appears to be the most straightforward solution to restore confidence in the euro area, as it would foster common strategies for public finances and reforms, and thus growth." This conclusion comes for the evident failure of fiscal and economic governance in the Eurozone so far. Yet, it foresees what the most determined supporters of the European integration have requested in vain for years: "euro-area member states would clearly have to allow a comprehensive sharing of sovereignty and powers at the European level, which, in turn, would require greater democratic accountability." Clearly, to achieve this, a new integration framework should be designed and implemented for restoring "the balance between liability and control": "an efficient and less fragmented European administration, to build a common Treasury for the euro area in conjunction with an independent fiscal council; and a stronger political body for policy decisions, under parliamentary control."

This seems to be a reasonable agenda for proceeding to European integration. Clearly, the two central bankers admitted the limits of central banks and monetary policy and passed the burden to politicians. It is to be seen whether national governments are willing to give up such a fundamental component of their sovereignty and what the actual consequences of Brexit will be. So far, the main difficulties in finding a coordinated response to the crisis came from national governments that often gave the impression of being more concerned with pursuing unilaterally the supposed (short-run) interest of their national constituencies than being interested to do so within the frame of European integration. It seems that some national governments believe that there are no further gains from cooperation and that European integration is becoming a negative sum process.

The prevailing game in most countries in recent years has been to blame the EU for all the difficulties. The worst case is certainly that of Great Britain. After obtaining unilateral benefits from the European Commission, the British government went to a referendum on June 23, 2016 that ended with the narrow victory of the supporters of leaving the EU. This outcome opened a new and unexpected scenario for the EU, not necessarily negative. In the present situation, an external shock may even be beneficial.

While having an important, albeit reluctant, member country leaving the EU is certainly a negative event, both politically and economically, there are also positive perspectives. Great Britain was so far an important, perhaps insurmountable obstacle to a deeper integration, in particular in the case of capital markets, taxation, and the EU budget. In spite of all its political and trade drawbacks, Brexit may open new and promising perspectives for a more effective and less bureaucratic integration. Political will and determination by member countries to proceed in a coordinated and forward-looking way and based on mutual trust are critically important to do so. Inevitably, here lie serious dangers of failure. Although Great Britain is not part of the Eurozone, Brexit gives more importance and greater responsibility within the European integration to the group of countries which invested most of all in European integration by sharing the common currency. There are reasons to believe that after Brexit, the Eurozone will become the real essence of the EU, while the remaining countries may remain integrated in a looser way.

European integration used to move slowly and react to apparently insurmountable problems and threats. This time around, problems are even more irresolvable and threatening than ever. An approach bolder than the traditional one and perhaps more determined and faster in defining the long-run strategy and goals is necessary.

References

Afonso, António and Ana Sequeira (2010), "Revisiting business cycle synchronization in the European Union," School of Economics and Management, Technical University of Lisbon, *Working Papers*, WP 22/2010/DE/UECE. http://pascal.iseg.utl.pt/~depeco/wp/wp222010.pdf (accessed on June 28, 2017).

Aiginger, Karl and Wolfgang Leitner (2002), "Regional concentration in the United States and Europe: Who follows whom?," *Weltwirtschaftliches Archiv*, 138(4), 652–679. DOI: 10.1007/BF02707656.

Baldwin, Richard and Charles Wyplosz (2012), *The Economics of European Integration*, 4th ed., New York: McGraw Hill.

Beine, Michel, Pauline Bourgeon and Jean-Charles Bricongne (2013), "Aggregate fluctuations and international migration," *CESifo Working Paper* No. 4379, August.

Bentivogli, Chiara and Patrizio Pagano (1999), "Regional disparities and labour mobility: The Euro-11 versus the USA," *Labour*, 13, 737–760.

Bertoli, Simone, Herbert Brücker and Jesús Fernández-Huertas Moraga (2013), "The European Crisis and migration to Germany. Expectations and the diversion of migration flows," *IZA Discussion Paper* No. 7170 (accessed on June 28, 2017).

Blanchard, Olivier and Daniel Leigh (2013), "Growth forecast errors and fiscal multipliers," *IMF Working Paper*, *WP/13/1*, January.

Blöchliger, Hansjörg (2013), "Fiscal Equalisation — A Cross-Country Perspective," in: Hansjörg Blöchliger, *Fiscal Federalism 2014: Making Decentralisation Work*, Paris: OECD, pp. 99–116.

Blöchliger, Hansjörg and Claire Charbit (2008), "Fiscal Equalisation," *OECD Economic Studies* No. 44, 2008/1.

Blyth, Mark (2013), *Austerity: The History of a Dangerous Idea*, Oxford: Oxford University Press.

Bonefeld, Werner (2011), "Social market economy and big society: German neo-liberalism and the politics of austerity," Paper Presented at the meeting of the Northern IPE Network Meeting, Sheffield University, November 4.

Bonefeld, Werner (2012), "Freedom and the strong state: On German ordoliberalism," *New Political Economy*, 17(5), 633–656.

Bonefeld, Werner (2013), "German neoliberalism and the idea of a social market economy," *Journal of Social Sciences*, Pre-print, Phitsanulok, Thailand, 139–171, http://www.academia.edu/6758422/German_Neoliberalism_and_the_Idea_of_a_Social_Market_Economy_Free_Economy_and_the_Strong_State (accessed on June 28, 2017).

Bonin, Holger, Werner Eichhorst, Christer Florman, Mette Okkels Hansen, Lena Skiöld, Jan Stuhler, Konstantinos Tatsiramos, Henrik Thomasen and Klaus F. Zimmermann (2008), "Geographic mobility in the European Union: Optimising its economic and social benefits," *IZA Research Report* No. 19, July.

Bornhorst, Fabian, Esther Perez-Ruiz, John C. Bluedorn, Davide Furceri, Florence Jaumotte, Franziska Ohnsorge, Tigran Poghosyan, and Aleksandra Zdzienicka (2013), *Toward a Fiscal Union for the Euro Area: Technical Background Notes*, Washington D.C.: International Monetary Fund, September.

Boschma, Ron and Gianluca Capone (2014), "Relatedness and diversification in the EU-27 and ENP countries," *Papers in Evolutionary Economic Geography* # 14.07, Utrecht University, Urban & Regional Research Centre Utrecht.

Bräuninger, Dieter and Christine Majowski (2011), "Labour mobility in the euro area," Deutsche Bank Research, *Reports on European Integration EU Monitor 85*.

Brülhart, Marius and Rolf Traeger (2003), "An account of geographic concentration patterns in Europe," *HWWA Discussion Paper* No. 226.

BS (2014), *Harnessing European Labour Mobility. Scenario Analysis and Policy Recommendations*, Gütersloh: Bertelsmann Stiftung.

Buti, Marco and André Sapir (eds.) (1998), *Economic Policy in EMU: A Study by the European Commission Services*, Oxford: Clarendon Press.

Calvo, Guillermo A., Alejandro Izquierdo and Luis-Fernando Mejía (2004), "On the empirics of sudden stops: The relevance of balance-sheet effects," *Working Paper* 10520, *NBER Working Paper Series*, http://www.nber.org/papers/w10520.pdf.

Caroleo, Floro Ernesto and Francesco Pastore (2010), "Structural change and labour reallocation across regions: A review of the literature," in: Caroleo, F.E. and F. Pastore (eds.), *The Labour Market Impact of EU Enlargement, A New Regional Geography of Europe?* Heidelberg: Physica/Springer, pp. 17–47.

Caudal, Nicolas, Nathalie Georges, Vincent Grossmann-Wirth, Jean Guillaume, Thomas Lellouch and Arthur Sode (2013), "A budget for the euro area," *Trésor-Economics* No. 120, October, http://www.tresor.economie.gouv.fr/file/392340 (accessed on June 28, 2017).

Dallago, Bruno (2016a), *One Currency, Two Europe: Towards a Dual Eurozone*, Singapore: World Scientific Publishing Co.

Dallago, Bruno (2016b), "The monetary union and migration," in: Dallago, B., G. Guri and J. McGowan (eds.), *A Global Perspective on the European Economic Crisis*, Abingdon, Oxfordshire: Routledge, pp. 143–161 (accessed on 28 June 2017).

Dao, Mai, Davide Furceri and Prakash Loungani (2014), "Regional labour market adjustments in the US and Europe," *IMF Working Paper* No. 14/26, February.

Decressin, Jörg and Antonio Fatás (1995), "Regional labor market dynamics in Europe," *European Economic Review*, 39, 1627–1655.

De Grauwe (2014), *Economics of Monetary Union*, 10th ed., Oxford: Oxford University Press.

De Grauwe, Paul and Ji (2012), "Self-fulfilling crises in the Eurozone: An empirical test," *CEPS Working Document* No. 366, June.

Dhyne, Emmanuel, Jerzy Konieczny, Fabio Rumler and Patrick Sevestre (2009), "Price Rigidity in the euro area: An assessment," Final Report, *European Economy*, Economic Papers No. 380, May.

Dullien Sebastian and Ulrike Guerot (2012), "The long shadow of ordoliberalism: Germany's approach to the euro crisis," European Council on Foreign Relations, *Policy Brief*, ECFR/49, February.

EC (1990), "One market, one money: An evaluation of the potential benefits and costs of forming an economic and monetary union," European Commission, *European Economy*, Economic Papers No. 44, October.

EC (2015a), "'Structural reforms', economic and financial affairs, Brussels: European Commission," available at http://ec.europa.eu/economy_finance/structural_reforms/index_en.htm (accessed on July 30, 2015).

Eichengreen, B. (1991), "Is Europe an optimum currency area?," No. w3579, National Bureau of Economic Research.

Eichengreen, Barry, Maurice Obstfeld and Luigi Spaventa (1990), "One money for Europe? Lessons from the US currency union," *Economic Policy*, 5(10), 117–187.

Elsner, Benjamin and Klaus F. Zimmermann (2013), "10 years after: EU enlargement, closed borders, and migration to Germany," *IZA Discussion Paper* No. 7130, January.

Eurobarometer (2014a), *The Euro Area. Report*, Flash Eurobarometer 405, European Commission, October.

Eurobarometer (2014b), *Public Opinion in the European Union. First Results*, Standard Eurobarometer 82, European Commission, December.

Eurobarometer (2014c), *Tables of Results. Public Opinion in the European Union*, Standard Eurobarometer 82, European Commission, November.

Eurobarometer (2014d), *Europeans in 2014. Report*, Special Eurobarometer 415, European Commission, July.

Eurobarometer (2015a), *The Euro Area. Report*, Flash Eurobarometer 429, European Commission, October.

Eurobarometer (2015b), *Public Opinion in the European Union. First Results*, Standard Eurobarometer 83 Spring, European Commission, July.

Eurobarometer (2015c), *Public Opinion in the European Union. Report*, Standard Eurobarometer 83 Spring, European Commission, July.

Ezcurra, Roberto, Pedro Pascual and Manuel Rapún (2006), "Regional specialization in the European Union," *Regional Studies*, 40(6) (August), 601–616.

Feldstein, Martin (1991), "Does one market require one money? Policy implications of trade and currency zones," 1991 Annual Conference of the Federal Reserve Bank of Kansas City, USA, pp. 77–84, https://pdfs.semanticscholar. org/09ca/f05a80ea954dab1b2309a22087700e0f499c.pdf (accessed on June 28, 2017).

Frankel, Jeffrey A. and Andrew K. Rose (1998), "The endogeneity of the optimum currency area criteria," *Economic Journal*, 108(449), 1009–1025.

Friedman, Milton (1997), "The euro: Monetary unity to political disunity?" *Project Syndicate*, August 28, https://www.project-syndicate.org/commentary/ the-euro--monetary-unity-to-political-disunity (accessed on June 28, 2017).

Furceri, Davide and Georgios Karras (2008), "Business-cycle synchronization in the EMU," *Applied Economics*, 40(12), 1491–1501.

Gáková, Zuzana and Lewis Dijkstra (2008), "Labour mobility between the regions of the EU-27 and a comparison with the USA," EPC, *European Union Regional Policy* No. 02/2008, p. 7, http://ec.europa.eu/regional_policy/ sources/docgener/focus/2008_02_labour.pdf (accessed on June 28, 2017).

Gáková, Zuzana and Lewis Dijkstra (2010), "Labour mobility between the regions of the EU-27 and a comparison with the USA," *Princeton Working*

Paper No. 100976, p. 13, http://epc2010.princeton.edu/papers/100976 (accessed on June 28, 2017).

Glăvan, Bogdan (2004), "The failure of OCA analysis," *Austrian Economics*, 7(2) (Summer), 29–46.

Goodhart, Charles A.E. (1988), "The two concepts of money: Implications for the analysis of optimal currency areas," *European Journal of Political Economy*, 14, 407–432.

Hallet, Martin (2000), "Regional specialisation and concentration in the EU," European Commissions, *Economic Papers* No. 141, March.

Hayek, F.A. (1990), *Denationalisation of Money — The Argument Refined. An Analysis of the Theory and Practice of Concurrent Currencies*, 3rd ed., London: The Institute of Economic Affairs.

Heinen, Nicolaus (2011), "A European Transfer Union. How large, how powerful, how expensive?," *EU Monitor 81*, Frankfurt am Main: Deutsche Bank Research, 2 August.

Heinz, Frigyes Ferdinand and Melanie Ward-Warmedinger (2006), "Cross-border labour mobility within an enlarged EU," *Occasional Paper Series* No. 52, ECB.

Hill, Steven (2014), "Ready or not, Transfer Union here we come," *Social Europe*, February 21, available at http://www.socialeurope.eu/2012/02/ready-or-not-transfer-union-here-we-come/.

Holden, Steinar and Fredrik Wulfsberg (2008), "Downward nominal wage rigidity in the OECD," *The B.E. Journal of Macroeconomics*, 8(1) (Article 15), 48.

Huber, Peter (2007), "Regional labour market developments in transition: A survey of the empirical literature," *European Journal of Comparative Economics*, 4, 263–298.

Huber, Peter (2009), *Regional Diversity and Local Development in the New Member States*, in: Bruno Dallago and Paul Blokker (eds.), Houndmills, Basingstoke: Palgrave Macmillan, pp. 122–165.

ICC (2013), *Open Markets Index*, Paris: ICC Research Foundation, International Chamber of Commerce, April.

IMF (2012), *World Economic Outlook — Coping with High Debt and Sluggish Growth*, Washington D.C.: International Monetary Fund.

Jansen, W. Jos and Ad C.J. Stokman (2014), "International business cycle co-movement: The role of FDI," *Applied Economics*, 46(4), 383–393, DOI: 10.1080/00036846.2013.844327.

Jauer, Julia, Thomas Liebig, John P. Martin and Patrick Puhani (2014), "Migration as an adjustment mechanism in the crisis? A comparison of Europe and the United States," *OECD Social, Employment and Migration Working Papers* No. 155, January, Paris: OECD.

Kenen, Peter, (1969), "The theory of optimum currency areas: An eclectic view," in: Mundell, Robert and Alexander K. Swoboda (eds.), *Monetary Problems of the International Economy*, Chicago: University of Chicago Press, pp. 59–77.

Konstantakopoulou, Ioanna and Efthymios Tsionas (2011), "The business cycle in Eurozone economies (1960 to 2009)," *Applied Financial Economics*, 21(20), 1495–1513, DOI: 10.1080/09603107.2011.579060.

Kouparitsas, Michael A. (2001), "Is the United States an optimum currency area? An empirical analysis of regional business cycles," Federal Reserve Bank of Chicago, *WP 2001-22*, https://ideas.repec.org/p/fip/fedhwp/wp-01-22.html (accessed on June 28, 2017).

Krugman, Paul (1991), *Geography and Trade*, Cambridge, MA: The MIT Press.

Malkin, Israel and Fernanda Nechio (2012), "U.S. and euro-area monetary policy by regions," *FRSBSF Economic Letter*, 2012-6, February 27, available at http://www.frbsf.org/economic-research/publications/economic-letter/2012/february/us-europe-monetary-policy/.

Marer, Paul (2016), "The euro and east Europe: Six insiders, six outsiders. Why so?," in: Dallago, B., G. Guri and J. McGowan (eds.), *A Global Perspective on the European Economic Crisis*, Abingdon, Oxfordshire: Routledge, pp. 187–206.

McKinnon, Ronald (1963), "Optimum currency areas," *American Economic Review*, 53, September, 717–724.

Meade, James E. (1957), "The balance of payments problems of a free trade area," *The Economic Journal*, 67(267) (September), 379–396.

Merler, Silvia (2013), "The liquidity quandary: On the risk connected to normalisation of the Eurozone liquidity condition," *Bruegel*, available at http://www.bruegel.org/nc/blog/detail/article/1177-the-liquidity-quandary/.

Merler, Silvia and Jean Pisani-Ferry (2012a), "Sudden stops in the euro area," *Bruegel Policy Contribution* No. 2012/06, March.

Merler, Silvia and Jean Pisani-Ferry (2012b), "Sudden stops in the euro area," *Review of Economics and Institutions*, 3(3) (Article 5), pp. 1–23, http://www.rei.unipg.it/rei/article/view/97 (accessed on June 28, 2017).

Molloy, Raven, Christopher L. Smith and Abigail K. Wozniak (2011), "Internal migration in the United States," *NBER Working Paper Series* No. 17307, 1–47, http://www.nber.org/papers/w17307 (accessed on June 28, 2017).

Mundell, Robert (1961), "A theory of optimum currency areas," *American Economic Review*, 51(4), 657–665.

Mundell, Robert (1969), "A plan for a European currency," Paper Prepared for discussion at the American Management Association Conference on Future of the International Monetary System, New York, December 10–12, available at http://www.knopers.net/webspace/marketupdate/A_Plan_For_a_European_ Currency.pdf.

Mundell, Robert (1973), "Uncommon arguments for common currencies," in: Johnson, H.G. and A.K. Swoboda (eds.), *The Economics of Common Currencies*, Abingdon: Routledge, pp. 114–132.

Münchau, Wolfgang (2014), "The wacky Economics of Germany's parallel Universe," *Financial Times online*, November 16, available at http://www.ft.com/intl/cms/s/0/e257ed96-6b2c-11e4-be68-00144feabdc0.html.

Nechio, Fernanda (2011), "Monetary policy when one size does not fit all," *FRBSF Economic Letter* 2011-18, June 13, available at http://www.frbsf.org/publications/economics/letter/2011/el2011-18.html.

North, Douglass C. (1990), *Institutions, Institutional Change and Economic Performance*, Cambridge: Cambridge University Press.

Obstfeld, Maurice (1997), "Discussants: Alberto Alesina and Richard N. Cooper, 'Europe's gamble'," *Brookings Papers on Economic Activity* (2), 241–317.

Obstfeld, Maurice, Jay C. Shambaugh, and Alan M. Taylor (2004), "The trilemma in history: Tradeoffs among exchange rates, monetary policies, and capital mobility," *NBER Working Paper Series* 10396, available at http://www.nber.org/papers/w10396.

OECD (2014), *OECD Employment Outlook 2014*, OECD Publishing, http://dx.doi.org/10.1787/empl_outlook-2014-en.

O'Rourke, Kevin H. and Alan M. Taylor (2013), "Cross of euros," *Journal of Economic Perspectives*, 27(3), 167–192.

Pasimeni, Paolo (2014), "An optimum currency area," *The European Journal of Comparative Economics*, 11(2), 173–204.

Pentecôte, Jean-Sébastien, Jean-Christophe Poutineau and Fabien Rondeau (2015), "Trade integration and business cycle synchronization in the EMU: The negative effect of new trade flows," *Open Economies Review*, 26(1), 61–79.

Piattoni, Simona (2016), "The European crisis: Testing the trust foundations of an economic and monetary union," in: Dallago, B., G. Guri and J. McGowan (eds.), *A Global Perspective on the European Economic Crisis*, Abingdon, Oxfordshire: Routledge, pp. 79–95.

Pisani-Ferry, Jean and Silvia Merler (2012), "Sudden stops in the Eurozone," *VOX CEPR's Policy Portal*, April 2, available at http://www.voxeu.org/article/public-capital-flows-replacing-private-flows-eurozone-what-it-means-policy.

Piton, Sophie and Yves-Emmanuel Bara (2012), "Internal devaluation: Nothing but sweat and tears?," *le blog du CEPII*, August 7, available at http://www.cepii.fr/blog/bi/post.asp?IDcommunique=121.

Ptak, Ralf (2009), "Neoliberalism in Germany: Revisiting the ordoliberal foundations of the social market economy," in: Mirowski, P. and D. Plehwe (eds.), *The Road from Mont Pèlerin: The Making of the Neoliberal Thought Collective*, Cambridge, MA: Harvard University Press, 124–125.

Reinstaller, Andreas, Werner Hölzl, Johannes Kutsam, Christian Schmid (2012), "The development of productive structures of EU member states and their international competitiveness," European Commission, DG Enterprise and Industry, Vienna: WIFO (Austrian Institute of Economic Research), November.

Rose, A.K. (2000), "One money, one market: The effect of common currencies on trade," *Economic Policy*, 15, 7–46.

Saiki, Ayako and Sunghyun Henry Kim (2014), "Business cycle synchronization and vertical trade integration: A case study of the Eurozone and East Asia," *Working Paper* No. 407, Amsterdam: De Nederlandsche Bank NV, January.

Sala-i-Martin, Xavier and Jeffrey Sachs (1991), "Fiscal federalism and optimum currency areas: Evidence for Europe from the United States," *NBER Working Papers Series* No. 3855, NBER.

Sally, Razeen (1996), "Ordoliberalism and the social market: Classical political economy from Germany," *New Political Economy*, 1(2), 233–257.

Schmidt, Torsten and Lina Zwick (2013), "Uncertainty and episodes of extreme capital flows in the euro area," *Ruhr Economic Papers* No. 461, October, available at http://en.rwi-essen.de/media/content/pages/publikationen/ruhr-economic-papers/REP_13_461.pdf.

Schnyder, Gerhard and Mathias Siems (2013), "The ordoliberal variety of neoliberalism," in: Konzelmann Suzanne J. and Marc Fovargue-Davies (eds.), *Banking Systems in the Crisis: The Faces of Liberal Capitalism*, Abingdon, Oxfordshire: Routledge, pp. 250–268, available at http://papers.ssrn.com/sol3/papers.cfm?abstract_id=2142529.

Scitovsky, Tibor (1958), *Economic Theory and Western European Integration*, Abingdon: Routledge.

Sinn, Hans-Werner (2000), "Germanys economic unification. An assessment after ten years," *NBER Working Paper* No. 7586, pp. 1–26, http://www.nber.org/papers/w7586.pdf (accessed on June 28, 2017).

Sinn, Hans-Werner (2014), *The Euro Trap. On Bursting Bubbles, Budgets, and Beliefs*, Oxford: Oxford University Press.

Smets, Frank and Raf Wouters (2005), "Comparing shocks and frictions in US and euro area business cycles: A Bayesian DSGE approach," *Journal of Applied Econometrics*, 20, 161–183.

Steinkamp, Sven and Frank Westermann (2014), "The role of creditor seniority in Europe's sovereign debt crisis," *Economic Policy*, 29(79), 495–552.

Stokes, Bruce (2015), *Faith in European Project Reviving. But Most Say Rise of Eurosceptic Parties Is a Good Thing,* Washington, D.C.: Pew Research Center, June 2, available at http://www.pewglobal.org/files/2015/06/Pew-Research-Center-European-Union-Report-FINAL-June-2-20151.pdf.

Taylor, John B. (1993), *Macroeconomic Policy in a World Economy: From Econometric Design to Practical Operation,* New York: W.W. Norton.

Toporowski, Jan (2013), "International credit, financial integration, and the euro," *Cambridge Journal of Economics,* 37(3) (May), 571–584.

Tsiapa, Maria (2013), "New aspects on the industrial concentration patterns of the European Union," *Discussion Paper Series,* 19(2): 35–62, Department of Planning and Regional Development University of Thessaly.

Varela, Gonzalo J. (2013), "Export diversification in twelve European and Central Asian countries and the role of the commodity boom," *Policy Research Working Paper* No. 6472, June, Washington D.C.: The World Bank.

Villeroy de Galhau, François and Jens Weidmann (2016), "Europa braucht mehr Investitionen," *Süddeutsche Zeitung* (English version: "Europe at the crossroads"), February 8, available at https://www.bundesbank.de/Redaktion/EN/Standardartikel/Press/Contributions/2016_02_08_weidmann_galhau.html?startpageId=Startseite-EN&startpageAreaId=Teaserbereich&startpageLinkName=2016_02_08_weidmann_galhau+361962.

Von Weizsäcker, J. (2008), "Divisions of labour: Rethinking Europe's migration policy," *Bruegel Blueprint Series* No. 6, Brussels.

Wray, L. Randall (2000), "The neo-Chartalist approach to money," *CFEPS Working Paper* No. 10, Center for Full Employment and Price Stability, July.

Wynne, Mark A. and Janet Koech (2012), "One-Size-Fits-All Monetary Policy: Europe and the U.S.," *Economic Letter,* 7(9), Federal Reserve Bank of Dallas, September, pp. 1–4, https://webcache.googleusercontent.com/search?q=cache:X3CgqbTCqAEJ; https://www.dallasfed.org/assets/documents/research/eclett/2012/el1209.pdf+&cd=1&hl=it&ct=clnk&gl=it (accessed on June 28, 2017).

Young, Brigitte (2014), "German ordoliberalism as agenda setter for the euro crisis: Myth trumps reality," *Journal of Contemporary European Studies,* 22(3), 276–287.

Zimmermann, Klaus F. (2009), "Labor mobility and the integration of European labor markets," *Discussion Papers* 862, Berlin: DIW, March.

Chapter 3

European Union after Brexit

Steven Rosefielde

The European Union (EU) during the last decade has shown itself to be less robust than globalists imagined. Globalists believed that supranationality was weatherproof, that it would always outperform national alternatives, and that it would survive adversity. Economic stagnation and Brexit falsified these expectations. This chapter investigates one aspect of the EU's transnationalist plight — incompatible goals and the difficulty of mutual accommodation, especially during hard times. Globalists contend that the harmony of shared dreams assures that dreams will come true and that there is no need for some nations to impose their will on others. EU experience has belied the supposition. Close investigation reveals that supranational government is less robust than advocates claim, precisely because conflicting national interests make it difficult for members to subscribe to a common dream. This causes some to try to impose their will on others, and dissenters to head for the exits. Latent incompatibility does not doom globalization, but it does expose the vulnerability of globalism's premises and the schemes propensity to malfunction. Indeed, it is possible that transnationality instead of being a hallmark of EU superiority is an albatross.[1]

---

[1]An albatross is a metaphor for burden that feels like a curse. The allusion is to Samuel Taylor Coleridge's poem "The Rime of the Ancient Mariner" (1798).

The EU today is prone to disunion because its members no longer share a common view of mutually acceptable transnational government and policy, powerful members insist on bending recalcitrant members to their will (coercive adaptation), and participants hold contradictory attitudes toward solidarity on a variety of issues. The precise impact of the internecine struggle and its ultimate resolution on global relations is difficult to discern with precision, but the broad geopolitical and economic prognosis appear to be negative.

Transnational Clubs

The EU can be likened to a transnational club composed of sovereign nations outsourcing some governing powers to club officials. The division of powers between self-regulating members and club officials creates a two-level control regime intended to harmonize personal (local) and board members (transnational interests). The approach works adequately when club officials and members see eye to eye, but requires mutual accommodation otherwise.

There is no ideal transnational club. Bounded rationality and ethical pluralism permit multiple satisfying arrangements, but no universal best (Simon 1957, 1990, 1991; Tisdell 1996; Rubinstein 1998; Gigerenzer and Selten 2002; Kahneman 2003; Rosefielde and Pfouts 2014). Nonetheless, general competitive individual utility-seeking with learning and permissible taste change provides an instructive benchmark. It requires members to negotiate and renegotiate rules as circumstances dictate so that participants continuously maximize their utility and well-being, including rules of entry, expulsion, withdrawal, and reentry. The watchword is free choice. Members decide for themselves whether to accept or reject the group consensus. When acquiescence is tolerable, they stay. If it is not, they leave.[2]

Formation and evolution of the euro club

Nation states before World War II never voluntarily surrendered control over their fiscal, monetary, financial, legal, defense, education, social,

---

[2] This is how the South defined the United States prior to the Civil War.

and foreign policies as part of a package to achieve common goals, even though they participated in international institutions like the League of Nations. The horrors of World War II, combined with Cold War politics and the welfare state tide, however, propelled Europe along a novel supranational trajectory with some unintended consequences. On September 19, 1946, Winston Churchill gave a speech in Zurich not only advocating Franco-German rapprochement but also a kind of United States of Europe called a European "Third Way." Churchill can be considered the EU's founder. He also advocated a "Council of Europe" formed thereafter with the assistance of French Foreign Minister Robert Schuman, mandated to create supranational communities on the path to a fully democratic, integrated Union.[3] The Schuman Declaration May 9, 1950, reaffirmed the concept in conjunction with the formation of the European Coal and Steel Community (ESCS). It proclaimed the European Community (EC) as the world's first supranational institution, marking the "birth of modern Europe" and initiating an epoch where intra-European wars were impossible.[4]

Schuman's utopian vision, which can be traced back to France's first socialist Claude Henri de Rouvroy, comte de Saint-Simon (1760–1825) (On the Reorganization of European Industry, 1814), was the prelude to a succession of developments culminating in today's EU including the European Economic Community, known as the Common Market (1958), the EC (1967) (together with the European Commission and the European Council of Ministers); the European Council (1974), the European Monetary System (1979), the European Parliament (1979), the Schengen Agreement (1985), which opened intraunion borders; the Single Market Act (1986), the Maastricht Treaty (1993) founding the EU,[5] and the European Monetary Union (2002), which inaugurated the euro.

---

[3] The term "supranational community" was coined by Jean Monnet, head of France's General Planning Commission.

[4] In 2012, the EU received the Nobel Peace Prize for having "contributed to the advancement of peace and reconciliation, democracy, and human rights in Europe."

[5] The EU's seven principal decision-making bodies are the European Council, the Council of the European Union, the European Parliament, the European Commission, the Court of Justice of the European Union, the European Central Bank (ECB), and the European Court of Auditors.

On December 1, 2009, the Lisbon Treaty entered into force and reformed many aspects of the EU. In particular, it changed the legal structure of the EU, merging the EU's three-pillar system into a single legal entity,[6] created a permanent President of the European Council, and strengthened the High Representative of the Union for Foreign Affairs and Security Policy.[7]

Membership in Churchill's and Schuman's club was open to any European nation willing to participate in a supranational community on the path to discovering whether the group could devise a satisfactory fully democratic federal entity. Belgium, France, Germany, Italy, Luxembourg, and the Netherlands accepted the agenda in 1958 and seem content with their decision, with the possible exceptions of the Netherlands and France which are under pressure for Nexit and Frexit.[8] They were pleased both with the Common Market and subsequent efforts to expand the political, social, juridical, police, foreign, and defense policy aspects of the Union. They all want to continue the search for an amicable united European

---

[6]The term "three pillars" refers to (1) economic, social and environmental policies performed by the EC, the ECSC (until its expiry in 2002), and the European Atomic Energy Community; (2) foreign policy and military under the jurisdiction of the Common Foreign and Security Policy (CFSP); and (3) judicial and police matters undertaken Police and Judicial Co-operation in Criminal Matters.

[7]The military of the EU comprises the various cooperative structures that have been established between the armed forces of the member states, both intergovernmentally and within the institutional framework of the union; the Common Security and Defence Policy (CSDP) branch of the CFSP.

The policy area of defense is principally the domain of nation states. The main military alliance in Europe remains the intergovernmental North Atlantic Treaty Organization (NATO), which presently includes 22 EU member states together with 4 non-EU European countries, Albania, Iceland, Turkey, and Norway, as well as the United States and Canada. The development of the CSDP with regard to the existing role of NATO is a contentious issue. The military form of European integration has however intensified in the beginning of the 21st century, bringing about the deployment of numerous CSDP operations and the establishment of EU battle groups. The latter have, however, never been engaged in operations, and other recent examples of military integration, such as the European corps, gendarmerie force, and air transport command, are intergovernmental and outside the institutional framework of the union.

[8]A poll by the Pew Research Center in June 2016, before the British referendum, found the Dutch to have a 46% negative view of the EU, less than the 51% of their population found to have a positive view toward it. The Pew Research Center poll found that 61% of the French population held an unfavorable view of the EU, second only to Greece's 71%, with the United Kingdom on 48%.

federative state with supranational characteristics, and perhaps without them (superstate).[9]

Great Britain, Ireland, and Denmark joined the founding six members in 1973. The British and Danish publics were Eurosceptics from the outset. Their leaders were attracted to the economic benefits of tariff elimination in a common market, but were more ambivalent about deeper economic and political integration including subsequent monetary union, and proposals for supranational regulation fiscal, political, social, juridical, police, foreign affairs, and defense matters.[10] Britain and Denmark refused to join the Eurozone.

Greece and Spain became EU members in the 1980s, both aware of efforts to construct a European monetary union, open borders (Schengen agreement), and create a "single market." They and the 15 other countries that signed on after the Soviet Union's demise primarily sought economic benefits, but also agreed to explore the federative possibilities urged by the founding six under the slogan "more Europe." The details of federation with supranational characteristics remain as elusive today as they were at the outset of the project. What will be the characteristics of an all-union transnationalized culture, and who will rule at the end of the day? Will there be a hegemon, or will democracy prevail?

---

[9] Margret Thatcher warned against an EU superstate in 1988 (Palmer 1988).

[10] The governing bodies of the EU's supranational governance tier are the European Parliament, Council of the European Union, European Commission, the European Council, European Central Bank, Court of Justice of the European Union, and European Court of Auditors. Supranational bodies have exclusive competence over: (1) the "customs union," (2) competition policy, (3) Eurozone monetary power, (4) a common fisheries policy, (5) a common commercial policy, (6) conclusion of certain international agreements. They also have the right to shared competence in (7) the internal market, (8) social policy for aspects defined in the treaty, (9) agriculture and fisheries, excluding the conservation of marine biological resources, (10) environment, (11) consumer protection, (12) transport, (13) trans-European networks, (14) energy, (15) the area of freedom, security, and justice, (16) common safety concerns in public health aspects defined in the treaty, (17) research, development, technology, and space, (18) development, cooperation, and humanitarian aid, (19) coordination of economic and social policies, (20) common security and defense policies. Additionally, supranational bodies enjoy supporting competence in (21) protection and improvement of human health, (22) industry, (23) culture, (24) tourism, (25) education, youth sport, and vocational training, (26) civil protection (disaster prevention), and (27) administration.

Fiscal union

Proponents of "more Europe" understandably are loath to offer specifics about the distribution of real authority, but nonetheless have pressed this agenda under the banner of fiscal union. The slogan "more Europe" for the moment means perfecting the single market, establishing a lender of last recourse for the Eurozone, and complementing monetary union with a unified transnational fiscal system that will supplant aspects of national taxing authority and strengthen supranational public policymaking. Most macroeconomic theorists believe that a federation will empower sound macroeconomic management and restore prosperity (De Grauwe 2010; Rosefielde and Razin 2012a, 2012b; Sargent 2012; Rosefielde 2015; Razin and Rosefielde 2016). It promises a generally competitive, optimally macromanaged economically integrated system with "inclusive" sensibilities (Tirole 2015; Dallago 2018).

Euroscepticism

Eurosceptics do not deny the virtues of economic efficiency, stability, integrated macroeconomic management, coordinated supranational public policy, and social humanism. They acknowledge the microeconomic benefits of widened markets, free trade, and finance, but contend that Eurocrats cannot deliver what they promise and have hidden agendas (Mundell 1961, 1963; Fleming 1962; McKinnon 1963). They believe that full costs will exceed the gains. Specifically, they assert that Brussels and Berlin abuse their decision-making powers in their own interest and seek to undemocratically expand their control not only over the EU economy but also comprehensively over all dimensions of members' political, social, cultural, foreign, and defense activities (Bolton 2016). They recognize that Brussels and Berlin portray themselves as skillful benevolent technocrats, but contend that "more Europe" insiders act primarily on their own behalf at others' expense.[11]

---

[11] According to Gretschmann (2016), "Both in economic and political terms, the EU is on life support. Its former attractiveness as an economic powerhouse, a political 'soft power' and a much appreciated social model seems to be waning in the face of the Eurozone troubles and the political and military challenges at its borders."

Eurosceptics also maintain that members like Britain which had hoped to cherry pick, taking the good and avoiding the bad by insisting on strong national autonomy within a transnationalizing framework, are discovering that this is a losing game. The "more Europe" camp is gradually imposing its will on the EU, forcing dissenters to accept the new normal, or leave. There are no longer any prospects for "less Europe" to accommodate club members who prefer a weaker form of association. Transnationalism and supranationalism in the eyes of Eurosceptics have become hollow concepts.

They see the European transnational economic union as a failing project, compounded by democratic disempowerment (Dallago 2016a; Dallago *et al.* 2016). The Greeks are particularly adamant on this point. The British by contrast place emphasis the other way round. They do not want to be ruled by Brussels and Berlin and are less concerned about economics. A large segment of population is disgruntled by EU economic rules and regulations, but the pain is less acute than in Greece. The issue of democratic disempowerment voiced by Greece and Britain has been widely documented in the political science literature where the problem is characterized as a "democratic deficit" (Piattoni 2016). The term taken seriously by many political scientists has gained little traction among economists but deserves attention when trying to comprehend Grexit and Brexit. British voters came to believe that the EU bureaucracy is opaque, and British interests are overwhelmed by those of other EU members, especially Germany. A non-partisan analysis concluded that approximately 60% of all legislation enacted by Britain's Parliament was dictated, in whole or in part, by decisions already reached by Brussels bureaucrats or EU diplomats (Bolton 2016; Dallago 2016a).

Empty promises

Eurosceptics might grin and bear lost national political and economic autonomy if the EU and Eurozone were uniformly prosperous.[12] However,

---

[12]According to Greer and Jarman (2016), "[T]he whole apparatus of fiscal governance and conditional lending… is entrenched in law, treaties, and member state constitutions, and in theory subjects member states to a broad, deep, and automatic mechanism that shapes their fiscal and therefore public policies."

there is no convincing economic evidence that all club members have benefited (Rosefielde 2016). This seems counterintuitive because theory stresses the benefits of liberalization, free labor and capital mobility, outsourcing, technology transfer, and globalization (Razin and Rosefielde forthcoming). Many prominent economists at the time of Brexit insisted that it was irrational for Britain to withdraw from the club (e.g., Giles 2016). However, there is more to economics than optimally competitive utility-seeking. Bounded rationality and power often generate and entrench undeserving winners and losers. Moreover, the economic costs of exiting are easily overstated by ignoring alternative opportunities. Much can be accomplished in all these regards without the single market, as the experiences of China, Vietnam, India, and Israel attest (Razin and Rosefielde forthcoming). Moreover, the economic benefits of club membership have steadily diminished. EU growth rates have been declining asymptotically toward zero since the United Kingdom and Denmark joined the EC in 1973 (Eurosclerosis), with the exception of the short-lived growth spurt during 2000–2008 accompanying the euro's adoption (Maddison 2003). The EU has been afflicted by secular stagnation since 2008, and double-digit member unemployment is widespread. Real wages have fallen precipitously, income and wealth inequality have burgeoned, and the EU has underperformed the United States (Piketty 2014). All these negatives can be blamed on other forces, or it always can be argued that the EU saved members from even worse fates, but it is also easily understood why Eurosceptics deem these claims excuses. Klaus Gretschmann reminds us that the EU regulators extended their reach without cogent justification.[13] Overregulation is wasteful by definition and often impedes growth by warping and disincentivizing innovation, technological progress, entrepreneurship, and investment. Overregulation devitalizes national economies; hegemonic supranational overregulation compounds the problem by adding a second level of obstruction and waste.

---

[13] According to Gretschmann (2016), "The EU has turned into a legislative machine trying to interpret her fields of competence ever more widely. Ceaselessly, the Commission is working on weaving an ever closer web of harmonized European laws and regulations — the result thereof, the *'acquis communautaire'*, is presently estimated to comprise some 100,000 printed pages."

Grexit

Greece provides an object lesson on complexities swept under the rug by assuming that competition and solidarity heal all wounds under prevailing Lisbon Treaty arrangements. Athens was both an early beneficiary and victim of the Maastricht Treaty. It joined the Eurozone in 2001 (a subclub of the EU) and immediately enjoyed an investment bonanza as EU and foreign funds flooded Greece, Italy, Ireland, Portugal, and Spain in response to an implied Eurozone creditworthiness guarantee (Rosefielde and Razin 2012a). Hard asset prices, especially land and property values, skyrocketed. Per capital gross domestic product (GDP) rose 25%, narrowing the gap with the EU average during 2001–2008. Unemployment, especially among the youth, declined significantly. The Greek government capitalized on the strong euro and the implied creditworthiness guarantee to amass a huge national debt, much of it owed to foreigners. A large portion of these capital inflows funded an expansion of public service sector jobs, increased salaries, and benefits. Athens and German investors were both delighted until the bubble burst.

The global financial crisis of 2008 reversed the process. Suddenly, Greece was no longer creditworthy and Germany demanded that Athens adopt "austere" fiscal measures to assure debt repayment to German banks and private investors. Greek leaders appealed for debt relief and were accommodated four times (2010, 2012, 2015, and 2016), but to little avail. By 2012, Greeks' per capita share of real GDP was the same as in 2001 and had fallen to 74% of the EU average. Employment gains vanished and youth unemployment rose above 50% (Figure 3.1), despite a sharp austerity-impelled internal devaluation (Tartar 2015).

The hardship inflicted by this roller-coaster ride prompted a democratic revolt. On July 5, 2015, 62% of Greeks voted to reject an EU, ECB, and International Monetary Fund (IMF)-backed debt relief package, effectively opting for Grexit. If the Greek people had their druthers, their leaders would have canceled Greece's club membership. Prime Minister Alexis Tsipras, however, decided instead that discretion was the better part of valor. He chose to sign a deal worth €86 billion over three years laden with conditions, such as tax hikes and pension reforms, considered by critics to be so tough that social media buzzed with talk of a *coup d'etat.*

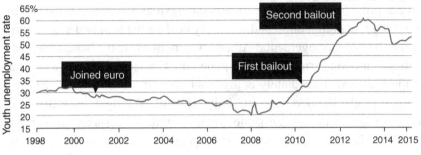

Source: Eurostat.

Note: Youth unemployment refers to people under 25 years of age.

Figure 3.1   Labor Gains Quickly Erased

Tsipras's capitulation in the face of a popular mandate can be variously interpreted.[14] Some construe it to mean that the Prime Minister grasped the indispensability of Eurozone membership regardless of the intermediate term costs. Some portrayed it as a "sellout" that sacrificed the public good for the benefit of powerful insiders, while others attributed his action to the risk of devastating punitive actions by the ECB. The latter interpretation is the most interesting from the standpoint of appraising the EU's future. It points to the possibility that the EU's merit depends not only on rational free choice but also on the risks of hegemonic economic and political coercion.

Supranational capital flight

Greece may have been brought to its knees by capital flight of a novel sort that took most observers by surprise. Greeks began withdrawing

---

[14] Polls taken before July 15 showed a plurality of Greeks favored remaining in the EU. Although, Greek voters knew that a vote against the EU, ECB, and IMF-backed debt relief package could be construed as a vote for Grexit if creditors stuck to their guns, earlier poll data gave Tsipras the wiggle room he needed to capitulate on the debt and Grexit. This was the course that he chose.

unsustainable amounts of euro deposits from private banks because they correctly feared that the ECB might cut off currency supplies in an attempt to jawbone Tsipras into accepting structural reform. Capital flight traditionally has been associated with hot money fleeing currencies ripe for devaluation. The Greek case was different. Euro devaluation was not an issue. Depositors fled Greek banks because they wanted to retain access to the euro, not because they feared euro devaluation. They recognized that the ECB might curtail euro access and that Greek banks might collapse if a run-for-the-liquid-euro could not be accommodated because banks assets were illiquid.[15]

The phenomenon can be labeled supranational capital flight because it is a logical consequence of the EU governance scheme which allows national banks to operate with a currency that national authorities do not control. Rational actors foreseeing a looming confrontation between supranational and national authorities will always find it costless to take their money and run, holding euros in cash, redepositing them in Helsinki, or purchasing other currencies.

---

[15] The literature on borrowing (incentive compatible) constraints is based on Holmstrom and Tirole (1997). One basic mechanism outlined in recent currency crisis models is where unhedged foreign currency liabilities play the key role in causing and transmitting crises. One of the first models to capture this joint problem was presented in Krugman (1999), and Schneider and Tornell (2004). In this approach, firms suffer from a currency mismatch between their assets and liabilities: their assets are denominated in domestic goods, and their liabilities are denominated in foreign goods. Then, real exchange rate depreciation increases the value of liabilities relative to assets, leading to deterioration in firms' balance sheets. Chang and Velasco (2001) show the vicious circle between bank runs and speculative attacks on the currency. On the one hand, the expected collapse of the currency worsens banks' prospects, as they have foreign liabilities and domestic assets, and thus generates bank runs. On the other hand, the collapse of the banks leads to capital outflows that deplete the reserves of the government, encouraging speculative attacks against the currency. Accounting for the circular relationship between currency crises and banking crises complicates policy analysis. For example, a lender-of-last-resort policy or other expansionary policy during a banking crisis might backfire as it depletes the reserves available to the government, making a currency crisis more likely, which in turn might further hurt the banking sector that is exposed to a currency mismatch. See De Grauwe and Ji (2013) for the lender-of-last-resort role and Razin (2015) for a survey.

This vulnerability and the difficulty of quickly readopting the drachma was invisible as long as cooperation and consensus were mandatory.[16] Shutting the ECB spigot (Trans-European Automated Real-time Gross Settlement Express Transfer System [Target2]) was unimaginable.[17]

---

[16] As Bulow and Rogoff (2015) write:

> "It is true that a major early motivation for the EU to lend to Greece was to subsidize its banks, but it is not true that Greece's creditors were taking money out of the country, at least until the Greeks chose to postpone or stop meeting the terms of its second bailout deal in the second half of 2014. Europe continued to provide cash inflows to Greece until that time, on top of the banking system support it still provides, and arguably does not really expect to be a net receiver of very much if any money over the next few years (at the very least). The bailout deals negotiated with Greece were meant to provide it with the cash needed to ease the transition from running primary deficits in its heavy borrowing years and to help keep its banks running and its private creditors at bay. The problems that Greece faces are due to a loss of confidence in the state, not only by foreign private investors but also by Greece's own citizens. Indeed, the latter have withdrawn over a hundred billion euros from the banking system since the onset of the crisis in early 2010. While Europe has replaced much of this money through Target2 loans (now primarily 'Emergency Liquidity Assistance') the Greek banks have also been weakened by the 33.5% of their private loans that are non-performing, reducing their capacity to take on new risky loans. It is partly for this reason, as well as because of the losses Greek banks suffered in 2012 on their holdings of Greek Government Bonds, that a significant part of the new money that Greece received over the past five years had to be used to recapitalise Greek banks.
>
> Whereas the EU has actually been a net provider of funds to Greece since the beginning of the crisis, this is not to say that its motivation has been entirely charitable. Greece has been able to combine the threat of default (which would create an unknown and potentially massive risk for the EU), a promised commitment to economic reforms that would put it on the road to self-sufficiency, and its 'too small to fail' status to gain extraordinary financial support. Over time, the risks of 'Grexit' — Greece leaving the euro — while still unknown, appear to have lessened for most observers. At the same time, the Greeks have recently elected a party seemingly intent on rolling back some of the country's hard-won economic reforms, negotiations have become harder. Nevertheless, it seems unlikely that in any deal Greece would be asked to pay back as much cash as it receives in net subsidies from the EU, at least for a long time to come."

[17] Target2 is the real-time gross settlement (RTGS) system for the Eurozone and is available to non-Eurozone countries. There is no upper or lower limit on the value of payments. Target2 is a RTGS system with payment transactions being settled one by one on a

Now that the genie is out of the bottle, however, it can be assumed that coercive methods, including Eurozone supranational capital flight, could be invoked whenever debt to GDP ratios expand and the danger of confrontation within EU governance structures looms.

Brexit

Britain's decision to cancel its membership in club EU is only obliquely connected with Grexit. Voters were aware of Greece's plight, but Britain was not a Eurozone member. Supranational capital flight therefore was irrelevant. Nor was Britain overindebted by the standards of other EU members.[18] The postfinancial crisis growth and employment were the best in the EU. Some argued that Britain's macroperformance would have been more vibrant if it were not entangled with the EU; however, the principal grievance motivating referendum voters was forced public goods substitution, including control over migrants and refugees. Eurosceptics felt that Eurocrats restricted local public policy choice, generated strong downward wage pressure, exacerbated involuntary unemployment, intensified unwelcome foreign labor migration (Dallago and McGowan 2016), increased terrorist risk, and drew them too deeply into Germany's political orbit (Mills and Rosefielde 2016). They argued, moreover, that Eurocrats were unelected and unresponsive to the British people's will.[19]

---

continuous basis in central bank money with immediate finality. This means that the ECB had an instrument in place to prevent Greek Euro capital flight if it had chosen to do so. Instead, it permitted Greece and others to receive long-term low-interest credit in lieu of instantaneous settlement. This technically is what gave the ECB the power to jawbone the Greek government over its bank capital flight. The ECB could have approached the problem earlier on a prudential basis, but for reasons unknown to the author, it did not.

[18] *CIA World Factbook*, available at https://www.cia.gov/library/publications/the-world-factbook/geos/uk.html. United Kingdom's debt to GDP ratio in 2015 was 90.6%. Portugal's debt to GDP ratio in the same year was 129%. The figure includes intragovernmental debt which is substantially lower than the American counterpart figure.

[19] These issues were not bolts from the blue. They appear to the author to have come to a head because of mounting concerns about terrorism, refugees, and immigration; the resentment of local authorities to Brussels's encroachment; the political determination of Brexit advocates; and mounting antagonism between EU winners in London and loser everywhere else in England.

It can be counterargued that British voters were ill-informed about these issues in varying degrees, but truth is peripheral to the larger question of EU survivability. Advocates of "more Europe" displayed an inability to defuse grievances essential for the survival of the Greater Europe project.

One country, two systems

Brussels and Berlin are unlikely to significantly accommodate demands for "less Europe" anytime soon. Their convictions are deeply held. Nonetheless, the time seems at hand for an intra-EU discussion of a third way. The Chinese concept of "one country, two systems" employed by Beijing to accommodate Hong Kong may provide a fruitful institutional compromise. Advocates of strong supranationality including a superstate with token transnational characteristics can be likened to Beijing — club members desiring "less Europe" to Hong Kong. Both systems can share a mutually agreeable core set of supranational arrangements, adjusted to reflect local needs. EU's strong supranationalists in this framework would be free to negotiate more comprehensive common rules and a unified monetary-fiscal transnational accord among themselves, while weak supranationalists either abided by the common core or narrowed it to taste, and members of both EU groups were permitted to switch sides. Europhoric and Eurosceptic countries under this scheme could modify the terms of membership to suit their changing needs without having to ponder exiting the club.

Other considerations

The one country, two systems formula also provides a suggestive framework for dealing with non-economic issues. The scope of the EU concerns broadened in 1967 to include political, social, defense, and foreign policies when the club became the EC. The interests of the six founding members were sufficiently congruent to make this possible, and the same principles were applied as membership grew, facilitated by the demise of the Soviet Union and the breakup of its empire. The diversity of interest among club members proved manageable during the halcyon days, but the façade of unanimity is wearing thin today as a consequence of mounting global terror threats, refugee crises, ethnic and religious pressures, and Putin's annexation of Crimea. The Visegrad four, for example, do not want to compromise their national identities, a concern easily accommodated in a less doctrinaire "united Europe."

Prospects

The powers that be in Brussels and Berlin are doctrinaire. This is the rub. "More Europe" advocates, despite claims of shared community values and chatter about compromise, want solidarity on their terms. They do not want members to have the freedom to disagree, and waywardness will be punished. Brussels is steeled to increase, not retract its regulatory reach (undemocratic directives). Berlin is intent on consolidating monetary and fiscal control over the entire EU space, and the inner circles of both establishments will resolutely strive to impose their cultural vision, including the management of immigrants and refugees.

Brussels and Berlin plan to win through tenacity. Their strategy for tomorrow is prefigured in their past actions. Brussels will relentlessly expand its regulatory reach behind a façade of inspiring slogans[20] and claim that it is tweaking shared mandates. Berlin will strengthen its control over the Eurozone and pressure members for fiscal accommodation. Both will badger those who resist their cultural policies. Although, the approach requires patience, they expect to win by wearing down and engulfing dissident members. They anticipate social and political turmoil, but are prepared to muddle through and bear the cost.

If their dreams come true, Europe will achieve "pax Berlin," an outwardly tranquil German-dominated superstate with ambiguous implications for Asia. If Brussels and Berlin's tenacity envenoms the Union, there will be substantial turbulence, and if they accept rational free choice, the outcome will be Pareto superior.

---

[20] According to Jones (2016), "'Europe' is about making sure every country (nation, people) has the opportunity to succeed and no country (nation, people) is left behind."

The world may gain or lose materially from the EU's travails, but observers of globalism will have an opportunity to learn constructive lessons come what may.

Conclusion

The EU today is prone to conflict and disunion because its members in response to changing global realities no longer share a common view of mutually acceptable transnational government and policy; powerful members insist on bending recalcitrant members to their will (coercive adaptation), and participants hold contradictory attitudes toward solidarity on a variety of economic, political, social, and cultural issues. Brussels and Berlin are likely to redouble their efforts for "more Europe" rather than meaningfully accommodate the disaffected and may well muscle their way forward (Dallago 2016b, 2016d). However, a more flexible plan B analogous to China's "one country, two systems" scheme that accommodates special needs within a broader union may well prove more effective. Any virtuous solution requires members to negotiate and renegotiate rules as circumstances dictate, so that participants continuously maximize their utility and well-being, including rules of entry, expulsion, withdrawal, and reentry. The watchword is democratic free choice for all antiauthoritarian clubs, and by extension the construction of a larger and harmonious World Order.

References

Bolton, J. (2016), "Brexit victory is a true populist revolt," *American Enterprise Institute,* June 24, available at http://www.aei.org/publication/brexit-victory-is-a-true-populist.

Bulow, J. and K. Rogoff (2015), "The modern Greek tragedy," *CEPR Vox,* June 10.

Chang, R. and A. Velasco (2001), "A model of financial crises in emerging markets," *Quarterly Journal of Economics,* 116(2), 489–517.

CIA World Factbook, https://www.cia.gov/library/publications/the-world-factbook/geos/uk.html.

Dallago, B. (2016a), "Europhoria and its aftermath," in: Rosefielde, S. (ed.), *Western Economic Stagnation and Social Turmoil: Lessons for Asia.* Singapore: World Scientific Publishers.

Dallago, B. (2016b), "The crisis, the monetary union, and migration," in: Dallago, B. and J. McGowan (eds.), *Crises in Europe in the Transatlantic Context: Economic and Political Appraisals*, London: Routledge, pp. 1–18.

Dallago, B. (2016d), "The progressive rift of the Eurozone: Risks and remedies," *Singapore Economic Review*, 2018.

Dallago, B., G. Guri and J. McGowan (eds.) (2016), *A Global Perspective on the European Economic Crisis*, London: Routledge.

De Grauwe, P. (2010), "The Greek crisis and the future of the Eurozone. The structural problem in the Eurozone is created by the fact that the monetary union is not embedded in a political union," *Eurointelligence*, February 11.

De Grauwe, P. and Y. Ji (2013), "Self fulfilling crises in the Eurozone: An empirical test," *Journal of International Money and Finance*, 34(April), 15–36.

Fleming, M. (1962), "Domestic financial policies under fixed and flexible exchange rates," *IMF Staff Papers* 9(November), 369–379.

Gigerenzer, G. and R. Selten (2002), *Bounded Rationality*, Cambridge: MIT Press.

Giles, C. (2016), "Brexit in seven charts — the economic impact," *Financial Times*, June 27.

Greer, S. and H. Jarman (2016), "Reinforcing Europe's failed fiscal regulatory state," in: Dallago, B., G. Guri and J. McGowan (eds.), *A Global Perspective on the European Economic Crisis*, Chapter 8, London: Routledge.

Gretschmann, K. (2016), "The EU in stormy seas: Beginning of the end or end of the beginning," in: Dallago, B., G. Guri and J. McGowan (eds.), *A Global Perspective on the European Economic Crisis*, Chapter 3, 33–47, London: Routledge.

Holmstrom, B. and J. Tirole (1997), "Financial intermediation, loanable funds, and the real sector," *Quarterly Journal of Economics*, 112(3), 663–691.

Jones, Erik (2016), "A compelling vision for Europe," *Politics and Strategy*, September 15, available at http://www.iiss.org/en/politics%20and%20strategy/blogsections/2016-d1f9/september-a44b/a-compelling-vision-for-europe-df6b?_cldee=c3RldmVuVuckBlbWFpbC51bmMuZWR1&recipientid=contact-46ecb47ad8b9e3119fa3005056be6986-9891cf2baabd4addb83f3e72d2919889&urlid=8.

Kahneman, D. (2003), "Maps of bounded rationality: Psychology for behavioral economics," *The American Economic Review*, 93(5), 1449–1475.

Krugman, P. (1999), "Balance sheets, the transfer problem, and financial crises," *International Tax and Public Finance*, 6, 459–472.

Maddison, A. (2003), "The world economy: Historical statistics," OECD, available at http://www.ggdc.net/maddison/Historical_Statistics/horizontal-file_03-2009xls. Statistics on World Population, GDP and Per Capita GDP 1-2006AD. (last update: March 2009, horizontal file; copyright Angus Maddison).

McKinnon, R. (1963), "Optimum currency areas," *American Economic Review*, 53(4), 717–725.

Mills, Q. and S. Rosefielde (2016), *The Trump Phenomenon and Future US Foreign Policy.* Singapore: World Scientific Publishers.

Mundell, R. (1961), "A theory of optimum currency areas," *American Economic Review*, 51(4), 657–664.

Mundell, R. (1963), "Capital mobility and stabilization policy under fixed and flexible exchange rates," *Canadian Journal of Economic and Political Science*, 29(4), 475–485.

Palmer, J. (1988), "Thatcher sets face against united Europe. Margaret Thatcher's speech to the college of Europe: 'The Bruges Speech,'" *The Guardian*, September 21.

Piattoni, S. (2016), "Institutional innovations and EU legitimacy after the crisis," in: Dallago, B. and J. McGowan (eds.), *Crises in Europe in the Transatlantic Context: Economic and Political Appraisals*, London: Routledge, pp. 119–136.

Piketty, T. (2014), *Capital in the Twenty-First Century*, Cambridge MA: Harvard University Press.

Razin, A. (2015), *Understanding Global Crises: An Emerging Paradigm*, Cambridge: MIT Press.

Razin, A. and S. Rosefielde (2016), "The European project after Greece's near default," *Israel Economics Journal*.

Razin, A. and S. Rosefielde (2017), "Israel and global developments 1990–2015: Riding with the global flows and weathering the storms," in: Ben-Bassat, A., R. Grunau and A. Zussman (eds.), *Israel Economy in the 21st Century.* Cambridge: MIT Press.

Rosefielde, S. (2015), "Secular crisis: The Mundell–Fleming trilemma and EU de-legitimation," in: Dallago, B. and J. McGowan (eds.), *Crises in Europe in the Transatlantic Context: Economic and Political Appraisals*, London: Routledge, pp. 71–83.

Rosefielde, S. (2016), "The European project: Moving forward with dry eyes," in: Dallago, B., G. Guri and J. McGowan (eds.), *A Global Perspective on the European Economic Crisis*, London: Routledge, 21–32.

Rosefielde S. and A. Razin (2012a), "A tale of a politically-failing single-currency area," *Israel Economic Review*, 10(1), 125–138.

Rosefielde, S. and A. Razin (2012b), "What really ails the Eurozone? Faulty supranational architecture," *Contemporary Economics*, 6(4), 10–18.

Rosefielde, S. and R.W. Pfouts (2014), *Inclusive Economic Theory*, Singapore: World Scientific Publishers.

Rubinstein, A. (1998), *Modeling Bounded Rationality*, Cambridge: MIT Press.

Sargent, T. (2012), "Nobel lecture: United States then, Europe now," *Journal of Political Economy*, 120(1), 1–40.

Schneider, M. and A. Tornell (2004), "Balance sheet effects, bailout guarantees and financial crises," *Review of Economic Studies*, 71(3), 883–913.

Simon, H.A. (1957), *Models of Man: Social and Rational — Mathematical Essays on Rational Human Behavior in a Social Setting*, New York: John Wiley and Sons.

Simon, H.A. (1990), "A mechanism for social selection and successful altruism," *Science*, 250(4988), 1665–1668.

Simon, H. (1991), "Bounded rationality and organizational learning," *Organization Science*, 2(1), 125–134.

Tartar, A. (2015), "Here's what membership in the euro did for Greece," *Bloomberg*, July 17.

Tirole, J. (2015), "Country solidarity in sovereign crises," *American Economic Review*, 105(8), 2333–2363.

Tisdell, C. (1996), *Bounded Rationality and Economic Evolution: A Contribution to Decision Making, Economics, and Management*, Cheltenham, UK: Brookfield.

Chapter 4

Balkans

Yoji Koyama

Introduction

The Western Balkans is a region consisting of Albania and successor countries of the former Yugoslavia except Slovenia and Croatia. Although Croatia was excluded from the grouping of the Western Balkans when it was admitted to the European Union (EU) in July 2013, it is discussed for comparison in this chapter. As there were ethnic conflicts in former Yugoslav Republics in the 1990s, this region has been unstable. Reflecting such unstable situations in the region, the amount of foreign direct investment (FDI) inflow has been far less than Central Europe and the Baltic States. Frankly speaking, in the 1990s the EU had no options to deal with problems in the Western Balkans. The Kosovo problem became increasingly serious, leading to the Kosovo war in 1999. Finally, only at that time, urged by the United States, the EU launched an active policy for the Western Balkans. In 1999, the Stability Pact for South Eastern Europe was concluded by EU member states, the United States, neighboring countries in Europe, and international organizations. When the Kosovo War ended in mid-1999, the Stabilization and Association Process (SAP) started. Stabilization and Association Agreement corresponds to the European Agreement for Countries in Central and Eastern Europe (CEE). Instead of strengthening its cooperation *vis-à-vis* individual candidate countries,

73

SAP adopts a "regional approach" in which the EU encourages regional cooperation among neighboring countries and their development with the Western Balkans as a regional unit.

In the 21st century, in a series of its documents the EU gave the Western Balkan countries a message that if these countries make continuous efforts toward reforms, eventually they would be able to join the EU. For example, the European Council in Brussels in March 2003 states, "The future of the Western Balkans is within the EU" (European Commission 2003a). Also, the European Commission states that the unification of Europe will not be completed until these countries join the EU (European Commission 2003b). At present Macedonia,[1] Serbia, Montenegro, and Albania[2] are EU candidates. Among them, Montenegro and Serbia began accession negotiations with European Commission in June 2013 and in January 2014, respectively. Bosnia and Kosovo[3] are potential candidates.

Currently, in addition to "enlargement fatigue," the EU faces some serious issues like a refugee problem and Brexit. It seems that the EU cannot afford to accept any new member state. However, the Western Balkans is as it were "a backyard" for the EU, and if the region is left in a state of being poor, it would remain a hotbed of organized crime and a route for drug smuggling and human trafficking, threatening the stability of the EU itself. Therefore, for mainly political reasons, the EU will be obliged to deal with the Western Balkans' European integration. After the United Kingdom's EU referendum turned out Brexit, Federica Mogherini, the High Representative of the Union for Foreign Policy and Security Affairs, was reported to have said "we are determined to implement the enlargement procedure as before" (*Asahi Shimbun*, July 6, 2016).

This chapter considers challenges facing the Western Balkans after the global financial crisis. To begin with, an overview of the Western Balkans is given and the necessity for switchover of their economic development model is discussed. Then, taking Serbia's case as an example, the current situation is examined more concretely and the necessity for industrial policy is stressed. Finally the chapter reaches some conclusion.

---

[1] For Macedonia, more in detail, see Chapter 7 of Koyama (2015).
[2] For Albania, more in detail, see Chapter 8 of Koyama (2015).
[3] For Kosovo, more in detail, see Chapter 3 of Koyama (2015).

Overview of the Western Balkans

All countries in the Western Balkans are small. Aside from Croatia, which is an upper middle-income country, they are all poor. Their economies heavily depend on foreign funds including remittances from expatriates. The unemployment in these countries is extremely high, recording double-digit unemployment rates (see Table 4.1). Reflecting the history, the region lacks cohesion.

World population is rapidly increasing, whereas in Southeastern Europe population is decreasing (see Table 4.2). During the period 1989–2007, due to fierce ethnic conflicts the case of Bosnia was striking as the population was decreasing at an annual rate of 1.25. In spite of the absence of ethnic conflicts, in Albania the population was decreasing at an annual rate of 0.75%. In the rest of the Western Balkans, the population decrease has been also substantial due to emigration related to wars in this region and subsequent economic difficulties.

As of 2015, Bosnia's and Serbia's GDPs still have not recovered to the 1989 level. In addition to the transformational depression, Bosnia and Serbia suffered damages from ethnic conflicts in the first half of the 1990s. Reflecting such tragic incidents, economic activities of these two countries declined considerably. Serbia suffered severe damage from the

Table 4.1 Basic Indicators of the West Balkan Countries.

	Area (1,000 km^2)	Population (1,000) 2015	GDP/capita (EUR) 2015	Unemployment rate (%) 2015	Remittance from abroad (% of GDP) 2006*	National currencies
Croatia	57	4,220	10,400	16.6	2.9	Kuna
Macedonia	26	2,080	4,400	27.0	4.3	Denar
Montenegro	14	625	5,800	18.0	13.6**	Euro
Serbia	88	7,040	4,700	17.0		Dinar
Bosnia	51	3,820	3,700	27.7	17.6	Convertible Mark (KM)
Albania	29	2,889	3,600	17.0	14.9	Lek
Kosovo	11	1,830	3,200	34.0	14.3***	Euro

Note: *World Bank (2010), p. 59; **data for Serbia and Montenegro; ***as of 2007, IMF (2013), Country Report. GDP — gross domestic product.
Source: *Forecast Report*, Spring 2016, wiiw.

Table 4.2   Population Dynamics in Southeastern Europe 1985–2005 (1,000 People).

	Population	Emigration (outflow)	Immigration (inflow)	Difference	Percentage of outflow
	[1]	[2]	[3]	[2–3]	[2:1]
Southeastern Europe					
(A) Western Balkans	25,775	5,727	818	4,909	22.6
Albania	3,563	860	83	777	24.1
Bosnia and Herzegovina	4,430	1,472	41	1,431	33.2
Croatia	4,442	726	661	65	16.3
Macedonia	2,045	371	121	250	18.1
Serbia and Montenegro	10,829	2,298	512	1,786	21.2
(B) EU member states					
Bulgaria	7,450	937	104	833	12.6
Romania	22,330	1,244	133	1,111	5.6
Slovenia	2,011	134	167	−33	6.7

Source: Jovancevic (2009, p. 19).

Kosovo war in 1999, causing another decline in the economic activities (see Figure 4.1). Serbia's GDP in 2015 is still only 76.6, which is below the level of Bosnia (79.0).

From the second half of the 1990s to the early 2000, foreign banks — mostly Greek, Italian, and Austrian — advanced to this region where local banks were in financial difficulties. The presence of foreign banks in the region is remarkable. As of early 2010, the share of banks controlled by foreign capital in total assets ranged from 75.3% in Serbia to 95.0% in Bosnia (see Table 4.3). As interest rates for euro-denominated loans have been cheaper than those for national currency-denominated loans, euro-denominated loans have become widespread in the region and at the same time deposits in euro have also increased. Therefore, it is said that their economies have become euro-ized. These banks gave loans actively to households and enterprises, contributing to the economic development.

We are concerned about very low export-to-import ratio in foreign trade of the Western Balkan countries. It means low export ability and

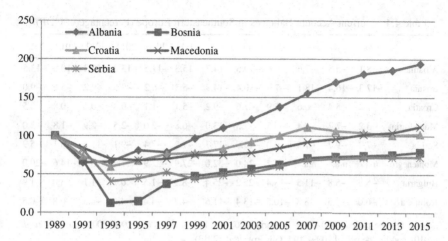

Figure 4.1   Changes in Real GDP Growth in the Western Balkans.

Note: Montenegro is omitted in this figure because together with Serbia it consisted of a country (Federal Republic of Yugoslavia in 1992–2003 and Serbia and Montenegro in 2003–2006) until 2006.

Source: Extrapolated by the author based on data in *Transition Report*, various issues.

Table 4.3   Banking Sector in the Western Balkans.

| | (% of GDP) | | | The share of | |
	Domestic credit to private sector	Domestic credit to households	Banking sector's asset	foreign-owned banks in total asset (%)	Loan-to-deposit ratio (%)
Albania	35.3	13.2	91	93.6	65.1
Bosnia and Herzegovina	53.5	27.2	87.2	95	118.3
Croatia	67.4	37.1	122	90	129.1
Macedonia	43.9	15.5	77.8	93.1	98.4
Montenegro	87.2	31.5	113.8	84.5	122.6
Serbia	39.7	13.9	67.9	75.3	130.6

Source: Country Report, February 8, 2010, UniCredit Group, p. 4.

low international competitiveness. The worst case is Montenegro, where exports of goods have been only one-fourth of the imports of goods. These countries have had chronic trade and current account deficits (Table 4.4). A huge current account deficit in Montenegro has been

Table 4.4   Current Account Balances in Southeastern Europe (Percentage of GDP).

	2003	2004	2005	2006	2007	2008	2009	2010	2011	2012	2013	2014
Albania	−8.1	−5.5	−7.6	−6.6	−10.6	−14.7	−15.3	−11.5	−13.0	−10.2	−10.6	−13.5
Bosnia	−17.3	−16.4	−18.1	−7.9	−10.4	−14.9	−6.3	−6.2	−9.6	−9.2	−5.9	−9.0
Croatia	−7.2	−5.4	−6.6	−6.9	−7.6	−9.2	−5.1	−1.1	−0.8	−0.1	0.8	0.5
Macedonia	−3.2	−7.7	−1.4	−0.5	−7.3	−13.0	−6.8	−2.0	−2.5	−2.9	−1.8	−2.0
Serbia	−7.2	−9.7	−7.5	−10.0	−15.6	−17.7	−7.2	−7.4	−9.1	−11.5	−6.1	−5.9
Montenegro	n.a.	n.a.	n.a.	−24.7	−24.0	−32.0	−27.9	−22.9	−17.7	−18.7	−14.6	−20.0
Bulgaria	−5.5	−5.8	−11.3	−18.4	−25.2	−25.4	−8.9	−1.5	0.1	−1.1	3.0	1.9
Romania	−6.0	−7.5	−8.8	−10.5	−13.4	−11.6	−4.2	−4.4	−4.6	−4.5	−0.8	−0.5

Source: For the period 2000–2005, Kathuria (2008), p. 13; for the period 2006–2008, Gligorov *et al.* (2010); and for the period 2009–2011, Gligorov *et al.* (2013).

covered by a huge amount of FDI inflow, but it would fall into difficulties once FDI inflow sharply decreased. As for Croatia, after negative economic growth for six consecutive years since 2009, it turned to positive economic growth only in 2015. During the period of the negative economic growth, its current account deficit continued to decrease and the current account balance turned positive in recent years. However, as long as its industrial structure remains unchanged, it is likely that the country will fall into a critical situation (a second Greece)[4] — Koyama (2016) not to mention other Western Balkan countries.

The Western Balkans except Albania and Kosovo were hit hard by the 2008 global financial crisis. The reasons for Albania and Kosovo being the exception are as follows: after a long-lasting policy of national isolation, Albania turned to an open-door policy in the early 1990. As it is not very long since then, the country, albeit a small country, has smaller dependency on foreign trade. Even though foreign-owned banks advanced to this country in the 1990s and it came to have linkage with the world of international finance, it has been relatively insulated from the international finance. As for Kosovo, it was part of the Republic of Serbia in the former

---

[4]For the Croatian economy, see Chapter 5 of Koyama (2015) and Chapter 8 of Koyama (2016).

Yugoslavia for a long time. It is not very long since its independence, and therefore it has smaller dependency of foreign trade.

Small countries usually have high dependency of foreign trade, but in the case of the Western Balkan countries their dependency on foreign trade has been low. In order to promote economic development, it is necessary for them to enhance foreign trade, and they have enough room to increase foreign trade. Reflecting the history of the Balkans with repeated conflicts, the amount of regional foreign trade has so far been smaller. Each country tended to skip neighboring countries and have close economic relation directly with EU member states. In 2000, the government of Western Balkan countries concluded bilateral free-trade agreements (FTAs) with one another, but it proved ineffective in increasing the regional trade. In 2006, governments of Western Balkan countries agreed to use CEFTA, the framework for free trade which Central European countries used until their EU accession, and established CEFTA-2006. The new framework was intended to remove all tariff and non-tariff barriers to foreign trade and realize foreign trade liberalization of both agricultural and non-agricultural goods, services, and investment by the end of 2010 (Kikerkova 2014). This has contributed to modest increase in the regional foreign trade, but it has not brought remarkable results as expected.

To sum up, the Western Balkan countries face the following challenges: since mid-1999 this region has been gradually stabilizing, and seemingly their economies have been developing. FDI went mainly to services and only a smaller portion of FDI went to manufacturing industry, especially production of tradable. Consequently, the international competitiveness of their economies has not enhanced. Their economic growth was led by consumption, heavily financed by the foreign borrowings, which foreign-owned banks actively facilitated. As a result, their trade balances and current account balances have recorded chronic deficits. These external deficits have been covered by FDI inflow. Therefore, their economies have become very vulnerable to changes in external environment. When the global financial crisis broke out in 2008, their economies faced sharp output decline and severe disruption in financing flows. Hence, these countries have the necessity for conversion of the economic development model.

Challenges Facing Serbia

Privatization and FDI

From the period of self-managed socialism, the Serbian economy has inherited a tendency of strong dependence on imports. It is quite important for the economy to overcome this tendency and increase exports. Therefore, the country is required to improve its international competitiveness. In order to attain rapid economic development, this country keenly needs FDI inflows.

Until 2001, FDI inflows were negligible. In spite of an early start of the transition to a market economy in 1990, it was not successful due to very difficult situation in the 1990s. Only after the collapse of the Milosevic regime in October 2000 did Serbia embark on transition to a market economy and European integration with 10 years' lag. In parallel with full-fledged privatization, the amount of FDI inflows increased since 2002. In Serbia, there were three waves of privatization: The first wave was the privatization implemented from 1990 to 1994, which gave priority to insiders (employees and managers in enterprises). It proved utterly unsuccessful due to ethnic conflicts deriving from a breakup of the Federation and United Nations (UN) sanctions as well as hyperinflation. The second wave was the privatization starting in 1996. The law on privatization enacted in 1996 schemed at spontaneous privatization and gave priority to insiders. In fact, however, there was substantially no progress until the collapse of Milosevic regime, and only after the collapse of the regime in October 2000 through February 2001 was the privatization hurriedly implemented. As the sale of the state-owned enterprises' share brought very limited amount of proceeds to the government, the law on privatization was soon abolished. The third wave was the implementation of a new law on privatization in 2001 (enacted in May 2001). The law required all state-owned enterprises to be privatized, and changed its method from an insider model to the sale in a commercial way. This method has eradicated any factors of self-management from the way of privatization. The privatization was to be implemented in the following ways: the first one was tender privatization. All of about 150 large enterprises were to be sold to strategic investors through tender privatization which the Agency of Privatization would implement. The second one was auction privatization. The number of small and medium-sized enterprises (SMEs) exceeded 7,000, and all of them were to be privatized through auction.

Vujacic *et al.* (2011) clarified that there were many problems also in the third wave of privatization. For example, the privatization did not bring as big amount of proceeds to the government as expected. Especially in the process of auction, there were many cases in which the number of bidders was extremely small, and consequently enterprises were sold at prices close to their reserved prices. There were many successful bidders who did not keep the condition of the requirement of business continuity. There were cases in which successful bidders, who should have paid by installments, used the enterprises as collateral for borrowing money and returned the enterprises to the Agency of Privatization without paying the second installment. There were also cases where purchases of enterprises were used for money laundering, i.e., transformation of illegal wealth — money obtained through drug trafficking — into legal wealth.

As the third wave of privatization proceeded, the amount of FDI inflow increased, but the structure of FDI inflows by sector was not satisfactory. Although total FDI inflow from 2004 to 2011 amounted to US$22.589 billion, manufacturing, the most expected one, accounted for only 20.0% (the second place). The first place was occupied by financial intermediary (28.1%), and the third place was occupied by wholesale and retail trade and repair (16.3%), followed by real estate and leasing (14.1%), and transport, storage, and communication (13.1%).

The Government of Serbia, especially the Serbia Investment and Export Promotion Agency (2011), endeavored to improve the investment climate in order to attract FDI inflows as much as possible. This Agency stresses that the corporate tax of 10% in Serbia, along with Bulgaria, is the lowest in Southeastern Europe. It is competition toward the bottom. As can be seen from cases in other transition countries, however, it seems that a low corporate income tax and low labor costs do not have decisive effects in the attraction of FDI. It seems that crucially important factors in the investment climate are macroeconomic stability, political stability, and the prospect for the EU accession.

Deindustrialization in progress and necessity for reindustrialization

Looking at changes in the contribution to gross value added by activities from 1999 to 2006, the share of agriculture, forestry, and fishery in the total gross value added decreased considerably from 17.3% to 9.2% during the period. Still, it is said that 44% of the total population live in rural areas. The share of industry decreased from 21.2% to 19.9%. Instead, trade and hotel, etc., transportation and telecommunication, and construction increased their contribution. During the period between 2001 and 2008, the GDP grew at annual average rate of 6%. It was a seemingly steady growth, but the growth rate of the industry was modest. Serbia attained the economic development led by domestic consumption, which was supported by banks' loans. According to an IMF report (IMF 2009), as of September 2008, loans to non-bank private sector as a percentage of GDP was a little over 70%, and nearly half of them, i.e., about 35%, were cross-border loans. Most of them went to non-tradable sectors, especially telecommunication, financial credits, and real estate.

About 55% of total exports go to the EU-27 countries. Its main sectors are agricultural products, accounting for about 20% of total export (mostly, grain, sugar, fruits and vegetables, confectionary products, and beverages). Others include steel and metal products (20%), machinery and transport equipment (17%), and chemicals. In parallel with an expansion of the domestic demand, imports increased faster than exports, expanding the external disequilibrium. Export of goods has always remained about half of import of goods. Although there has been some fluctuations depending on years, the rate of export of services and import of services have been almost the same. Looking at export and import including goods and services, the export-to-import ratio fluctuated between 55% and 63%. The trade deficit as a percentage of GDP has been very large, being between 20% and 25% until 2008. After the global financial crisis, the trade deficit has somewhat decreased as export has increased faster than import. Similarly, current account deficit, which recorded a GDP of 17.7% in 2008, has substantially decreased to 7.2% of GDP in 2009 due to the global financial crisis (see Table 4.5). In my

Table 4.5 Macroeconomic Indicators 2005–2014.

	2005	2006	2007	2008	2009	2010	2011	2012	2013	2014
GDP growth rate	5.6	3.6	5.4	3.8	−3.5	1.0	1.9	−1.7	2.6	−1.8
GDP/capita (EUR at ex. rate)	2,700	3,100	3,900	4,400	3,900	4,000	4,500	4,200	4,800	4,700
GDP/capita (EUR at purchasing power parity (PPP))	7,200	7,700	8,200	9,000	8,400	8,700	9,100	9,000	10,100	10,200
Gross fixed capital formation	5.0	15.2	12.0	8.0	−22.1	−5.5	4.6	13.2	−12	−3.6
Gross industrial production	0.8	4.2	4.1	1.4	−12.6	2.5	2.5	−2.2	5.3	−6.5
Unemployment rate, Labor Force Survey (LFS)	20.8	20.9	18.1	13.6	16.1	19.2	23.0	23.9	22.1	19.4
Average wages, annual change	6.4	11.4	19.5	3.9	0.2	0.7	0.1	1.0	−1.9	−1.7
Consumer prices	16.2	11.7	7.0	13.5	8.6	6.8	11.0	7.8	7.8	2.9
Central bank policy rate	8.5	14.0	10.0	17.8	9.5	11.5	9.8	11.3	9.5	8.0
General gov. budget balance	0.9	−1.6	−2.0	−2.6	−4.5	−4.6	−4.8	−6.8	−5.5	−6.6
Public debt(% of GDP)	50.5	37.7	30.9	29.2	34.7	44.5	45.4	56.2	59.6	70.4
Gross external debt (% of GDP)	66.2	60.9	60.2	64.6	77.7	84.9	72.2	80.9	75.1	77.3

Source: wiiw, *Current Analyses and Forecasts*, various issues.

opinion, however, reductions in trade deficit and current account deficit have been temporary phenomena, and there remains a challenge to improve the international competitiveness. According to the World Bank report of 2011, neighboring European and Central Asian economies have export shares of GDP in the range of 60–80%. In spite of being a small country, Serbia's export is too small. The report points out that there is substantial room for improvement as a share of GDP, currently at about 25%, could be to two to three times larger.

Due to the 2008 global financial crisis, the GDP in 2009 contracted by 3.5%, and it picked up somewhat in 2010 and 2011, but recorded negative growth again in 2012 and 2014, affected by the EU economy's stagnation. In January 2009, representatives of private financial institutions, headquartered in the EU, and public financial institutions met in

Vienna in order to prevent the financial crisis in CEE from expanding to the magnitude that East Asia experienced in 1997 ("Vienna Initiative"). It was targeted specifically at Latvia, Hungary, Romania, Serbia, and Bosnia. It is widely publicized that major banks from Western Europe, which had given loans to these countries, agreed not to withdraw a large quantity of capital and succeeded in achieving the expected results. As Serbia's decline in GDP in 2009 was 3.5%, smaller than that of many postsocialist countries, there might be some effect for Serbia, but it seems that there were no substantial effects. We have to pay attention to the content of the agreement that committed Western European banks to keeping their funds in their East European banks *if these governments committed to austerity to stabilize local banks' balance sheets* (Blyth 2013, p. 221) and to the fact that already only several months after the Lehman shock, austerity was imposed on these countries as a precondition for the financial support.

In 2013, Serbia's GDP has recovered only 72.4% of the 1989 level (see Figure 4.1), but the situation in the industry is even worse, with it recovering only 40.8. According to Savic and Kovacevic (2014), in 1990, the last year of "normal" development in the country, in industry 44% of GDP was generated and about 1.1 million workers were employed. Total exports in that year amounted to almost US$6 billion, of which 90% were industrial products. A quarter century later, only 275,000 workers (the same as in 1955) work in the Serbian industry, the level of industrial production is below a half of the level recorded in 1990, and only 17% of GDP was generated in the industry (Savic and Kovacevic 2014).

Thus a phenomenon of "de-industrialization" has occurred, say Savic and Kovacevic (2014). There is an argument that it is natural for industry in postsocialist countries to decrease its share of GDP since excessive industrialization was pursued at the sacrifice of the service sector during the socialist period[5] (de Melo *et al.* 1997), but in the author's opinion, this does not apply so much to successor countries of former Yugoslavia because during the period of self-managed socialism a mechanism of a

---

[5] Cerovic (2014b) makes a comparison of a proper share of industry in GDP which de Melo *et al.* (1997) have predicted and the real changes in 2007 for Albania, Bulgaria, Croatia, Macedonia, Romania, and Slovenia for which all necessary data are available.

kind of market economy worked to a certain extent there. Rather, as mentioned before, Serbia experienced ethnic conflicts deriving from the breakup of the federation in the first half of the 1990s and the Kosovo war in 1999 as well as UN sanctions during both periods, and consequently the Serbian industry has become weakened. In this connection, Savic and Kovacevic (2014) make a comparison as follows: during the period between 1990 and 2013, Serbia increased its export by 2.6 times, while the Czech Republic increased its export by 26.6 times (p. 85). In advanced industrial countries, growth and further expansion of the service sector followed development of industry, whereas in Serbia the service sector expanded as a result of the decay of its industry. Indeed a large number of SMEs in the service sectors such as restaurants, cafes, retail shop, boutiques, etc. have already been established, and they mitigated unemployment to a certain extent. However, Cerovic (2014b, p. 49) argues that it could be realistic if SMEs are established in cooperative relationship with larger firms that can become their main partners and customers and can involve them in their programs, but also organize them and help them in technology, know-how, management, etc.

In addition to a loss of the former Yugoslav common market, ethnic conflicts in 1992–1995, and Kosovo war in 1999, as well as UN sanctions, as causes of "deindustrialization," Savic and Kovacevic (2014) stress "an extremely bad development model" applied by governments after the change in October 2000 (fall of the Milosevic regime, democratization, and Serbia's return to the international community), specifically as follows: (1) direction of inflow of foreign capital; as mentioned above, FDI went mostly to services, real estate, etc. — consumption-led economic development; (2) wrong privatization model; the privatization has been implemented by the governments based on neoliberalism. They were so naïve to believe that "a majority of deeply stumbling industrial enterprises would be bought by rich foreigners who would rebuild them from the ruins into contemporary and efficient companies within a short time" (Savic and Kovacevic 2014, p. 70); (3) hasty liberalization of the Serbian market; a problem is that liberalization occurred in the second phase of transition when completely exhausted and devastated Serbian industry did not have any chances in competition with very efficient multinational companies (*ibid.*, p. 72); (4) a complete lack of a vision of long-term

Table 4.6   Balance of Payments 2006–2014.

	2006	2007	2008	2009	2010	2011	2012	2013	2014
Exports of goods + services*	6,948	8,686	10,157	8,478	10,070	11,145	11,469	13,937	14,451
Imports of goods + services*	11,970	15,578	17,877	13,578	14,838	16,487	17,655	17,783	18,096
Trade balance*	−5,022	−6,892	−7,720	−5,100	−4,768	−5,342	−6,186	−3,846	−3,645
Trade balance (% of GDP)	−21.4	−23.3	−22.5	−17.3	−17.0	−16.0	−19.5	−11.6	−10.9
Current account (% of GDP)	−10.0	−15.6	−17.7	−7.2	−7.4	−10.9	−11.6	−6.1	−6.0
FDI inflow (% of GDP)	14.4	8.5	5.9	4.8	3.6	10.6	3.2	4.7	4.5

Note: *EUR (in million).
Source: wiiw, *Current Analyses and Forecasts*, various issues.

development of Serbia; in this regard, they positively evaluate a role played by Japanese Ministry of International Trade and Industry.

"De-industrialization" has brought chronically large trade deficits and current account deficits and consequently a huge and increasing amount of external and public debts (see Table 4.6). Public debt emerged as a result of necessity for financing budget deficit, and only a part of funds was used for the construction of infrastructure. Foreign credits that domestic companies obtained were used not for investment but for financing current production with the exception of a few cases. Foreign credits should be used for investment to upgrade the economic structure and construct the industry's export ability (exports first of all in the EU market).

Looking at indicators of external solvency, the external debt reached 277% of the export revenue in 2009 (Table 4.7). Then the proportion declined gradually while the external debt as a percentage of GDP continued to increase and reached 86.6% in 2012. Looking at indicators of external liquidity, since 2006 the repayment of debt/GDP continuously exceeded 10% of GDP, being a heavy burden on the national economy. In 2009, the worst year, nearly half of the export revenue had to be allotted to the repayment of external debt. Current account deficit reached 21.8% of GDP, which was an extraordinary record figure. This miserable situation necessitates reindustrialization. Savic and Kovacevic (2014) stress the importance of the state's active approach, i.e., the industrial policy.

Table 4.7 Indicators of External Solvency and Liquidity of Serbia During the Period 2005–2014 (%)

	2005	2006	2007	2008	2009	2010	2011	2012	2013	2014*
Indicators of external solvency										
External debt/ GDP	60.7	61.3	61.1	64.2	76.9	84.1	76.6	86.6	80.6	79.9
External debt/ export of commodities and services	234.9	205.7	214.2	219.1	277.0	246.9	216.4	223.0	184.7	172.8
Indicators of external liquidity										
Repayment of debt/GDP	5.2	10.8	10.7	11.0	13.5	12.7	13.3	14.0	14.0	12.4
Repayment of debt/export of commodities and services	19.8	36.2	37.5	37.5	48.8	37.4	37.6	36.1	32.2	25.8
Current account as a percentage of GDP	−8.8	−10.1	−18.7	−21.8	−6.1	−7.4	−10.5	−12.3	−6.5	−4.7

Note: *Estimate.
Source: Savic and Kovacevic (2014, p. 83).

Importance of industrial policy

Until recently, industrial policy has been disregarded in Serbia. In recent years, Serbian economists such as Savic and Kovacevic (2014) and Cerovic (2014a, 2014b) came to emphasize its importance. A Japanese specialist of developmental economics Ken'ichi Ohno (2013) enumerates areas of the standard menus for the reinforcement of industrial ability: (1) framework on legislation and policymaking; (2) training of capable persons for industry (education and training); (3) reinforcement of enterprises (management and technology); (4) funding; (5) invitation of FDI; (6) marketing and intercompanies cooperation; and (7) innovation. In addition, maintenance and upgrading of infrastructure, transportation and physical distribution, appropriate measures for social and environment issues, and comprehensive regional development are enumerated. None of the enumerated policies is in breach of international rules such as the World Trade Organization (WTO), FTA, and Economic Partnership Agreement. It is preferential treatment for domestic products and domestic producers compared with imported products and foreign enterprises that the WTO prohibits.

In 2010 the labor participation rate, i.e., the share of people actually working and people seeking jobs in the productive age (15–64 years), was 58.9%. The employment rate, i.e., the share of people actually working in the productive age, was only 47.1%, and 11.7% of them were unemployed. In comparison with other countries, in 2004, the employment rate was 64.7% in EU-15, 68.6% in Japan, and 77.4% in Switzerland (Eurostat 2009, p. 270). If the labor participation rate and the employment rate in Serbia are increased to the same level as in EU-15, more rapid economic development could be expected. For that purpose, however, more investment is also required.

In order to increase inward FDI, it is necessary for the country to improve the investment climate. For that purpose, there are many challenges to be tackled, for example, the establishment of rule of law, the suppression of corruption and organized crimes, the promotion of regional cooperation, and so forth. Among others, it is of urgent necessity to improve the educational system. It is indispensable also for reindustrialization.

As many authors (Esch and Kabus 2014) indicate, there has been a big gap between what the educational system can offer students and what businesses request. A lack of skill in the labor market has also been pointed out. It seems that problems are concentrated in the secondary education. "Despite the oversupply of schools and teachers for the number of secondary school-aged youth, many students are not able to pursue the curricula of their choice. For instance, there is an abundance of spots available to take courses in textiles, wood processing, agriculture and other vocational trades, while the courses in health care, economics, law and general secondary education are oversubscribed. Serbia's system forces students to select narrow educational tracks at a young age; this has resulted in more than 76% of secondary school students attending vocational education (the second highest percentage in Europe)". As for university graduates, there has been a big gap between supply and demand in terms of skills and knowledge, and brain drain has become a serious problem (Djuricin and Vuksanovic 2010, p. 113). In this way, Serbia's educational system is now pressed to implement reforms in order to get rid of mismatch of supply and demand in the labor market and train capable people necessary for a knowledge-based economy.

Cerovic (2014b) sharply criticizes austerity measures,[6] which together with the IMF the European Commission recommended countries with budget deficits as a "universal recipe." Usually, expenditures for education, research, medical care, safety net, and culture have been targeted. Reduction of administrative employees is also problematic. He warns that reduction of these kinds of expenditures will inevitably lead to a substantial decrease of countries' economic activities and contribute to negative

---

[6] It is Blyth (2013) that sharply criticizes this point. The essentials of his argument are as follows: Politicians today, in both Europe and the United States, have succeeded in casting government spending as reckless wastefulness that has made the economy worse. In contrast, they have advanced a policy of draconian budget cuts — austerity — to solve the financial crisis. We are told that we have all lived beyond our means and now need to tighten our belts. This view conveniently forgets where all that debt came from. Not from an orgy of government spending, but as the direct result of bailing out, recapitalizing, and adding liquidity to the broken banking system. Through these actions, private debt was rechristened as government debt, while those responsible for generating it walked away scot-free, placing the blame on the state, and the burden on the taxpayer (Blyth, 2013, book cover). From a critical standpoint, a young Italian economist Paternesi Meloni (2015) explains the mistakes in austerity as follows: The European Commission recommended deficit countries to implement structural reforms on the grounds that current account differentials were almost exclusively referred to their weak competitiveness. He explains the logic underlying austerity measures which have been imposed on peripheral countries: First, in order to restore government debt sustainability — the reducing of the debt-to-GDP ratio, mitigating market losses of trust, and lowering of risk premiums (expansionary austerity); second, in order to restore external competitiveness through internal devaluation — real wage reduction and structural reforms (competitive austerity). This is the neoliberal view placing an emphasis on the supply side. As a matter of fact, an improvement in current account occurred not through these channels, but through a channel of a decrease in aggregate demand, leading to a decrease in total output and a decrease in consumption and a decrease in imports. In this way, this policy has brought debt deflation. Paternesi Meloni disproves the austerity–competitiveness linkage, and based on Keynesian economics, argues the necessity for putting an emphasis on the demand side.

growth rates. He also poses a question on reduction of subsidies for private investors when countries aim at a necessary structural change toward production of tradable and exporting goods in economies that are lacking local capital.

Inward FDI is very important. Contrary to short-term capital, FDI, staying in a host country for a longer time, contributes to the country's economic development and is therefore useful. However, multinational enterprises are fickle. FDI is never immobile as shown by the case of the Smederevo Steel Company. Since 2001, Serbia has pursued the economic development mainly depending on foreign capitals. For that purpose, the country has sold many enterprises to foreign companies. In contrast to Central European countries, however, FDI has not flowed into manufacturing so much as expected. Even if foreign capitals arrived in this country, multinational enterprises are fickle. For example, The US Steel Company acquired the Smederevo Steel Company in Serbia in 2003. In January 2012, when the Eurozone experienced a double-dip depression and demand for steel decreased due to the auto industry slump, the US Steel Company sold this steel factory to the Government of Serbia for only US$1 and withdrew from the country, concentrating steel production on Slovakia where automobile production has been in good shape. The government bought back the plant to avert the loss of 5,500 jobs (*EEM*, April 2012). This relocation was the logical behavior for a multinational enterprise, but unbearable for both employees and the government in Serbia.[7] Is it enough for the government to exclusively rely on FDI? It would be necessary for the government to have its own industrial policy. We are concerned about the fact that foreign banks account for almost all assets in the banking sector. Foreign banks always attach importance to efficiency. It is natural and quite important, but it is not enough for development of SMEs. In the light of experiences of East Asia, from mid- and long-term perspective, the government should have government-affiliated financial institutions that take care of SMEs while giving priority to creation of job opportunities. Hence, there is a necessity to increase the savings rate and investment rate.

---

[7] Finally in June 2016, a Chinese company Hesteel agreed with the Serbian government to acquire Smederevo Steel Company (*JICA Balkan News*, No. 11/2016, Summer Issue).

It is quite important for the country to promote the development of domestic companies. If the country succeeds in this regard, it would be able to restrain the tendency of people's outflow to the EU core member states. However, if domestic companies do not develop sufficiently, such a tendency would continue and unemployed people and low-wage workers would be absorbed by richer EU member states.

Free mobility of labor has been encouraged in the EU. In the author's opinion, it would be more desirable for labor to move two ways between country A and country B, but in practice it is not likely that emigration and immigration will be balanced. However, it would be problematic that people go one-sidedly and massively within a short period to richer countries from poorer countries. The ability of richer countries to accept immigrants is limited.[8] If depopulation continues in a poor country, it would lose people who could shoulder the future economic development in the country, and concomitantly local communities would collapse and traditional cultures would decay. It would be a great loss to a country that especially young and educated people who should shoulder the future development of the country leave their mother country massively. It is more important to create job opportunities for these people in poorer countries. Besides

---

[8] Current massive inflow of asylum seekers or illegal immigrants to Europe should be taken as an exceptional occurrence. The first thing to do is to get rid of the source of an enormous level of asylum seekers, which exceeded 1 million in 2015. In this regard, a Japanese economist residing in Hungary, Tsuneo Morita (2016) offers a valuable remark. He says that the fundamental cause of the occurrence of such massive asylum seekers is the Iraq war launched by the United States in 2003 and the US bombardment escalated from Iraq to Syria in 2014. It is stowaway business organizations in Turkey that have been guiding these people in refugee camps to illegal immigration into Europe. In addition, we have to take into account activities of international non-profit organizations which actively support "refugees" and "immigrants" by providing information on destinations and routes. There is a guidebook for asylum seekers. It is said that the guidebook has been produced and distributed by a charity group Open Society Foundation, which George Soros, a refugee from Hungary, now an American citizen and a world-famous investor, has established. He intends to transform Europe into a multiethnic society like the United States and activate the stagnating European society. Free mobility of capital and activation of the European society is favorable to him. It is interesting that Morita says. "Noteworthy is that anarchic words and actions of irresponsible European leftists and Soros' market fundamentalist idea of the abolishment of borders coincide." In my opinion, New EU member states cannot afford to accept a large number of "asylum seekers."

Structural Funds and Cohesion Fund in the EU, it is necessary to establish a mechanism at the EU level for inducing private funds in richer EU member states to the Western Balkan countries.

Conclusion

First, the Western Balkan countries including Serbia promoted the transition to a market economy, faithfully keeping neoliberal prescriptions recommended by the European Commission and international financial institutions. As a result, international competitiveness in these countries' manufacturing has stagnated or deteriorated, especially in the production of tradable goods. Since mid-1999, when the Western Balkans began to stabilize, their economies were seemingly developing, but the development was in fact led by consumption heavily relying on foreign capital. Therefore, their economies became vulnerable to changes in the external environment. The 2008 global financial crisis and the subsequent Eurozone crisis revealed their economic weakness. The high unemployment, especially among the young generation, is a matter of concern. It is of urgent necessity to make a switchover of their economic development model.

Second, governments should play important roles in the economies, especially when a switchover of their economic development model is made. Industrial policy should be attached more importance in the Western Balkan countries.

Third, inward FDI is very important for less-developed countries because it supplements capital-deficient economies, provides them with advanced technology, and enables them to have international linkage in production and sales. As the case of Smederevo Steel Factory shows, however, FDI is not always immobile. From a mid- and long-term perspective, the Western Balkan countries are required to make efforts in increasing their domestic savings. In addition, it is necessary for them to establish public financial institutions that will contribute to the promotion of SMEs.

Fourth, although there is the principle of free mobility of labor, the EU's development model, which has continuously been absorbing labor forces from poorer countries into its core member states, is problematic.

It is necessary for the EU to device a mechanism in which young and educated people in the Western Balkans need not emigrate to EU core member states excessively. For this purpose, it is necessary to establish a mechanism at the EU level for inducing private funds in richer EU member states to the Western Balkan countries.

Fifth, austerity, which the European Commission and the EU core member states, Germany in particular, and international financial institutions have been imposing on southern Europe and on candidates, is one of major factors causing the EU's secular stagnation. Compliance of fiscal discipline is of course important, but there should be a room for flexible policymaking to a certain extent in these countries.

References

Blyth, Mark (2013), *Austerity: The History of a Dangerous Idea*, New York: Oxford University Press.

Cerovic, Bozidar (ed.) (2014), *The Role of the State in the New Growth Model of the Serbian Economy*, Centrar za izdavcku delatnost: Univerzitet u Beogradu, Ekonomski fakultet.

Cerovic, Bizidar (2014a), "Western Balkans and Serbia: What are Way-outs from the Crisis?," in: Cerovic, B. (ed.), *The Role of the State in the New Growth Model of the Serbian Economy*, Centrar za izdavcku delatnost: Univerzitet u Beogradu, Ekonomski fakultet, pp. 3–13.

Cerovic, Bozidar (2014b), "Western Balkans: Late in Transition, Struck by the Crisis, Slow in Recovery — Which Road to Take?," in: Esch, V. and J. Kabus (eds.), pp. 46–52.

de Melo, M., A. Gelb, and S. Tenev (1997), "Circumstance and Choice: The Role of Initial Conditions and Policies in Transition Economies," *Policy Research Working Paper* No. 1866, The World Bank, Policy Research Department.

Djuricin, Dragan and Iva Vuksanovic (2010), "Population Risk and Sustainable Development in Combined Economic Crisis: The Case of Serbia," in: Domazet, T. (ed.), *Facing the Future of South East Europe*, Zagreb: Croatian Institute of Finance and Accounting, pp. 103–130.

Esch, Valeska and Juliana Kabus (eds.) (2014), *"EU Enlargement: Between Conditionality, Progress, and Enlargement Fatigue?,"* Germany: The Aspen Institute.

European Commission (2003a), Brussels European Council 20 and 21 March 2003: Presidency Conclusions, https://www.consilium.europa.eu/uedocs/

cms_data/docs/pressdata/en/ec/75136.pdf#search=%27Brussels+European+ Council+2003+March%27 (accessed on February 26, 2010).

European Commission (2003b), Communication from the Commission to the Council and the European Parliament: The Western Balkans and European Integration.

Eurostat (2009), *Europe in Figures Eurostat Yearbook 2009*, Luxembourg: Office of Official Publications of the European Communities.

Gligorov, Vladimir *et al.* (2010), *Crisis Is Over, but Problems Loom Ahead, Current Analyses and Forecasts 5*, Vienna: wiiw.

Gligorov, Vladimir, *et al.* (2013), *Animal Spirits still Dimmed: Slow Recovery Expected, Current Analyses and Forecasts 12*, Vienna: wiiw.

IMF (2009), Republic of Serbia: Request for Stand-By Arrangement — Staff Report; Press Release on the Executive Board Discussion; and Statement by the Executive Director for the Republic of Serbia.

IMF (2013), *Republic of Kosovo: Staff Report for the 2013 Article IV Consultation*, IMF Country Report No. 222.

Jovancevic, Radmila (2009), "The Impact of World Economic Crisis on the Sustainable Growth of the South-Eastern European Countries: Does Regional Cooperation Matter?," in Faculty of Economics — Skopje 2009, *Regional Trade Agreements and Regional Cooperation Challenges and Opportunities: Proceedings from the Third International Conference*, Skopje.

Kathuria, Sanjay (ed.) (2008), *Western Balkan Integration and the EU: An Agenda for Trade and Growth*, Washington, DC: World Bank.

Kikerkova, Irena (2014), "Administrative Barriers to Trade within CEFTA-2006," in: Esch, V. and J. Kabus (eds.), *EU Enlargement: Between Conditionality, Progress and Enlargement Fatigue?*, Berlin: The Aspen Institute.

Koyama, Yoji (2015), *The EU's Eastward Enlargement: Central and Eastern Europe's Strategies for Development*, Singapore: World Scientific.

Koyama, Yoji (ed.) (2016), *The Eurozone Enlargement: Prospect of New EU Member States for Euro Adoption*, NY: Nova Science.

Morita, Tsuneo (2016), *Consideration of the Problem of 'Refugees' Inflow in Europe, Russian Eurasian Economy & Society* No. 1002, Tokyo: Institute of Eurasian Studies.

Ohno, Ken'ichi (2013), *Designing Industrial Policies: Learning from Asia's Best Practices*, Tokyo: Yuhikaku (in Japanese).

Paternesi Meloni, Walter (2015), "Austerity and competitiveness: A misleading linkage," Paper presented at the 1st World Congress of Comparative Economic Studies, held at Rome Tre University on June 25–27, 2015.

Savic, Ljubodrag and Radovan Kovacevic (2014), "Izvozno orijentisana reindus-
trializacija kao prctpostavka dinamicnog razvoja Srbije," in: Cerovic, B. (ed.),
The Role of the State in the New Growth Model of the Serbian Economy,
Centrar za izdavcku delatnost: Univerzitet u Beogradu, Ekonomski fakultet,
pp. 67–87.

Serbia Investment and Export Promotion Agency (SIEPA) (2011), "Investment
guide to Serbia," available at http://siepa.gov.rs/files/pdf2010/ENG_
Brochure_FAQ_2010.pdf (accessed on August 23, 2014).

Vujacic, Ivan and Jelica Petrovic Vujacic (2011), "Privatization in Serbia —
Results and Institutional Failures," *Economic Annals*, LVI(191), 89–105.

World Bank (2010), "Enhancing regional trade: Integration in Southeast Europe,"
World Bank Working Paper No. 185.

Periodicals

Asahi Shimbun (a nationwide Japanese newspaper).

CEE Quarterly, UniCredit Group.

Emerging European Monitor (EEM): South Eastern Europe, London: Business
Monitor International.

JICA Balkan News, Beograd: Japan International Cooperation Agency.

Chapter 5

Immigrants, Xenophobia, and Terrorism

Kumiko Haba

Introduction

Immigration and asylum are increasing across the globe. There were 23 million immigrants in 2013, and 65 million were granted asylum in 2015.[1] The Syrian civil war, post-Afghan and Iraq conflagrations, and Arab Spring instabilities spurred 1 million refugees to flee to the European Union (EU) in 2015.

Most sailed across the Mediterranean. Capsized boats drowned several thousand voyagers. Several hundred thousand people, many with babies, children, and the elderly, trod the land route through the Balkan Peninsula. This journey was perilous because Hungary and other nations along the path shut their borders. Many Eastern and Central European countries like Hungary and Slovakia disregarded the EU's mandate of granting refugees transit rights. They closed their borders at the end of April in 2016.

---

[1] UNHCR Statistical Yearbook, http://www.unhcr.org/figures-at-a-glance.html and http://www.unhcr.org/globaltrends2016/. Hayashi, Reiko (2014), "Contemporary perspective of International Demographic Immigration," *Journal of Population Problems*, 70(3), 192–206, available at http://www.ipss.go.jp/syoushika/bunken/data/pdf/19981802.pdf. Asylum seekers reached 65 million at the end of 2015, UNHCR, *Tokyo News Paper*, June 20, 2016.

This chapter investigates:

(1) Why 1 million refugees fled to Europe?
(2) Why there was a xenophobic reaction?
(3) Whether today's immigrants can be assimilated to mitigate antago-
     nisms and deter EU defection? (Haba 2014, Haba 2016)

Immigrants–Refugees are Flooding into Europe: Statistics and Rationales

When, who, and how many are entering Europe?

The data reveal that immigrants arrived in Europe in three waves during the past 30 years, mostly from outside the region (see Figures 5.1 and 5.2). Non-European immigration usually exceeded intra-European flows, including movements from Eastern to Western Europe.

(1) The first wave was concentrated in Germany. It peaked in late 1990s to 2000s and ebbed after EU enlargement during 2004–2007. In the peak period, immigration from outside the EU was about 600,000. Internal immigration was 200,000–300,000. External migrants came mainly from Ukraine, Russia, and Belarus, peaking at about 1 million.

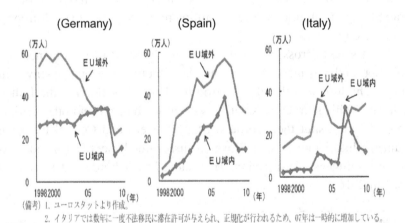

Figure 5.1   Transition of Immigrants and Refugees: Germany, Spain and Italy from 1998–2010.

Notes: Upper line indicates outside of the EU and lower line indicates inside of the EU.
Source: Eurostat, Japan Cabinet Office, Trend of the World Economy II, 2012.

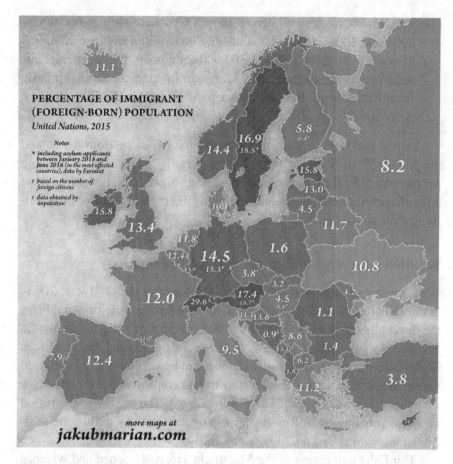

Figure 5.2   Immigrants Entering Europe Through Mediterranean Route and Balkan Route.

Notes: Immigrants came to Europe because (1) opening of the borders after the end of the Cold War, (2) wage disparity especially after the EU enlargement during 2005–2007, (3) Arab Spring after 2010–. (1) and (2) are the right arrows from Russia, CIS and Eastern Europe, and (3) is the lower arrow from Arab and Middle East countries, especially Syria, Afghanistan and Iraq.

Source: UN, 2015, https://jakubmarian.com/wp-content/uploads/2015/07/immigrants-europe.jpg.

(2)   The second immigrant wave hit Spain. The peak was from 2004 to 2007. Non-Europeans exceeded arrivals from EU enlargement states. They totaled about 450,000–600,000 people from African and Middle East countries (Shingo 2014). European arrivals were mostly Romanians and Bulgarians. They numbered 200,000–400,000, bringing the total to about 1 million.

(3)   The third wave washed across Italy. There were twin peaks, 2003–2004 and 2009–2010, with a steadily increasing flow thereafter, and a cumulative total of 200,000–300,000 newcomers. European migrants were mostly Romanians; non-European immigrants came primarily from Afghanistan, Iraq, and other parts of the Middle East after the Arab Spring.

During the 1990s, most immigrants to the EU came from Africa and the Middle East. Some of these migrants were "brain drainers," young people with high skills and education seeking higher pay; thereafter, most African and Arab arrivals were unskilled workers, refugees from instability in their native lands.

Relation between Immigrants and Xenophobia

What motivated immigrants to settle in Europe after the Cold War, 2003–2008, and after 2010? Reasons varied, but two factors were primary. First, the dismemberment of the Soviet satellite system facilitated emigration in Russia's former sphere of influence. Second, globalization (economic liberalization, competitiveness, and enhanced labor mobility) incentivized German, Spanish, Italian, French, and British employers to hire low-wage migrants. This was the pull (Armstrong 2011). The push was depressed economic conditions in Russia and its former satellites during the post-Soviet transition (Berend 2009; Kurti 2001).

Third, the ratification of the Maastricht Treaty deepened and widened EU integration after 1991. It also created a European identity that people in former socialist countries found attractive. Fourth, the broad process of EU democratization, liberalization, and marketization appealed to post-Soviet Russians and East Europeans. Many wanted to be part of the "one Europe" concept. They moved westward and did not return. At first they were welcome. Europhoria swept the region, but then Europeans began having second thoughts as local workers were displaced by migrants accepting lower wages. The EU as a whole benefited, but segments of the population were hard hit. They became resentful and prone to xenophobia (fear and hence dislike of strangers) (Bordeau 2009; Harrison 2005). The problem was not severe for the first generation of immigrants but has gradually intensified with subsequent new waves. Even though they have acquired European citizenship, many natives do not accept immigrants as worthy fellow citizens.

They frequently are victims of discrimination, and second- and third-wave immigrants are mostly poor and frustrated. The global financial crisis of 2008 and ensuing economic stagnation has exacerbated antagonisms.

Why Democratization Has Spread across the World and What Happened?

Democratization is an important aspect of the xenophobia story because it affects the political management possibilities of conflict among majorities and minorities, insiders and outsiders. Democracies however differ widely and with correspondingly diverse behavioral potentials. It is important therefore for us to sort out the complexities to fully appreciate the present xenophobic danger across Europe, both in long-established and new-arisen democratic states (Richard *et al.* 2006).

Anthony Lake, President William Jefferson Clinton's national security advisor described the role of democracy in American foreign policy as follows: "The expansion of democracy became the new strategy of the United States after the Cold War as an alternative to the containment policy against the Soviet Union during the Cold War."

Expanding democracy in this way became the cornerstone of America's post-Cold War policy of "Democratic Peace" (Russett 1994) But what is "democracy?" The literal definition is clear, but its substance is elusive and its practice diverse.

The origin of the word is Greek: *demos* (people) and *kratos* (rule, govern). It means rule in accordance with the people's collective will. This may merely require consent of the governed, or strict obedience to popular public preferences.

Democratic rule is not necessarily best. In Winston Churchill's words, "Democracy is the worst form of government, except for all the others."

Michel Mann plumbed the nuances in *The Dark Side of Democracy* and found that democracy works well in homogeneous societies, but sometimes malfunctions in heterogeneous ones, and may even cause massacres and genocide (Mann 2005).

He investigated and analyzed the genocide that occurred in democratizing Yugoslavia during the period 1991–1999, including the Kosovo bombing, and showed how the Serbians borrowed Nazi holocaust policies of inclusion and exclusion. Democracy, he discovered, sometimes is warped by xenophobia in Western countries, and the danger needs to be resolutely addressed. We need to be clear about who we are and who they are, and the moral obligations of majorities and minorities to each other.

Democratization Defeated Autocracy, but What is Next?

Democratization was a powerful weapon in the struggle against autocracy. The process began in Eastern Europe and Soviet Union in the 1980s as an element of communist reform.

All Eastern European "communist" regimes and the Soviet state were swept away by the democratic tide (Nakazawa 1999 writes another story), and replaced by parliamentary systems without recourse to violence. All disintegrated internally. Communists in East Europe hoped that socialism with a human face might be an antidote to democracy, but the effort failed. East Europeans chose democracy, and socialism with a human face has not been revived as a political force in the post-communist era.

Democratization in Eastern Europe and the Soviet Union was spear-headed by intellectuals but was quickly embraced by the people. The future appeared sky blue.

But storm clouds have appeared on the horizon. Conflicts have arisen among ethnic groups. Resentment against immigrants and refugees has added fuel to the fire. It appears that Michael Mann's concerns about the dangers of ethnic hostility and xenophobia against outsiders may be prescient.

Latent conflicts in heterogeneous democracies can be inflamed when powerful majorities self-righteously defend their privileges and minorities are exploited without hope of redress. Minorities under these circum-stances demand accommodation. Majorities refuse and respond with hatred and repression, triggering vicious cycles. The confrontation quickly becomes seemingly intractable, spawning xenophobic-driven violence against oppressed minorities and outsiders, and terrorist counterviolence by victims against society. Democracy fails under these circumstances because majorities feel entitled to oppress, and minorities cannot success-fully use the ballot to redress their grievances (Sakai 2008).

The problem can be solved by assimilation and adoption of construc-tive common values. This has been the American approach to managing its racial, ethnic, and religious diversity, but it requires time, patience, and mutual consideration that are in short supply when xenophobia sweeps nations (Mann 2005).

The issues until recently have been muted in Central Europe unlike the Balkans because Poland, Hungary, Slovakia, and Czechia are comparatively homogenous democracies, but the tranquility is jeopardized by the influx of Third World Muslim refugees from the Middle East, Afghanistan, and Pakistan. The same phenomenon is sweeping across Western Europe.

Why is Xenophobia on the Rise in Western Europe?

Xenophobia is on the rise in Western Europe for the following four reasons:

(1) Immigration has contributed to wage inequality inside Europe.
(2) Middle-class living stands are deteriorating.
(3) Migration is associated with perceptions of criminal behavior and terrorism. It has been claimed that more than 50% of all crimes are perpetrated by foreign immigrants.
(4) Many native Europeans infer that wage inequality and crime will escalate unless new immigration is reduced.

Xenophobia thus is rising because migrant flows are increasing, unemployment is worsening, and native Europeans are concerned about their personal safety European and National Identity, and terrorism. At that time conflicts happen under the increasing diversity (Mann 2005; Stone 2002).

Evolving Trends in European Nationalism

Western European countries are homogenous in Michel Mann's classification scheme. "Natives" form the majority and can be influenced by appeals to "nationalism" that implicitly segregate insiders from minority outsiders. Although, Mann argues that heterogeneous democracies are more violence prone, their homogenous twins also are at risk whenever xenophobia rears its ugly head. Nationalism is not intrinsically intolerant, but can be hijacked by xenophobia.

Post-Cold War European nationalism has manifested itself in three primary forms: liberal, radical, and xenophobic. The first (liberal nationalism) is exemplified by Central and Eastern Europe 1989–2004. Central and Eastern European nationalists during this era democratized their political governance, abandoned communist central planning, and defended their newly won independence by joining the EU and North Atlantic Treaty Organization (NATO). Ethnic hostilities within the region were subsidiary.

The second form (radical nationalism) applies to the Balkan countries (former Yugoslavia) and the successor states of the former Soviet Union. Many of these nations are ethnically divided with opposing groups struggling for political dominance. Balkan nationalism too often has meant civil wars, the suppression of the weak by the strong, and extreme violence spanning the gamut from rape to massacre and genocide during 1991–1999. Conflicts continue to smolder in Bosnia-Herzegovina and Kosovo.

The third type (xenophobic nationalism) is a pan-European nativist response to the influx of European migrants from the former Soviet bloc nations and non-Europeans from other parts of the globe. It began in France, the United Kingdom, and the Netherlands and then spread to Switzerland and Scandinavia during 2000–2016.

Liberal nationalism — Positive model

Central and Eastern Europe liberal nationalism (Auer 2004) began in 1989 as a wave of democratization, marketization, and liberalization. The governments of these post-communist states introduced representative democracy and free elections and began the process of acceding to the EU and NATO. The process worked well despite high unemployment, low wages, and the high cost of consumer goods imports from Western Europe (Dallago and Rosefielde 2016). Hungary, Poland, and Czech joined NATO in the late 1990s, and most of Eastern Europe with the exceptions of Romania, Bulgaria, and former Yugoslavia became EU members in 2004 (Berend 2009; Schubert 2011).

Admission to the EU came with strict conditionality. Central and Eastern European states were barred from participating in the Schengen Accord until they complied with the Common Agrarian Policy, the provisions of the *acquicommunautaire*, and Copenhagen criteria. This arduous task took a decade to accomplish.

Radical nationalism — Negative model

The Balkan nations and former Soviet Republics also tried to democratize in rudimentary fashion, marketize, and liberalize but remained fundamentally authoritarian. They focused on suppressing ethnic separatist opposition instead of harmonious and progressive nation-building (Ramet 1999; Prusin 2010 indicates historically Borderlands area were easily under the conflict especially nation building era).

Xenophobic nationalism — Prejudicial model

The core countries of the EU were well-established market-oriented democracies that had put their ethnic discords behind them. Xenophobic residues of the prewar past existed, but were fading. The recent influx of European immigrants from the former Soviet bloc and non-Europeans from Africa and the Middle East is reviving xenophobic animosities.

Conflict Over Open Borders

The Schengen Agreement permits immigrants to travel wherever they please in the EU. This has created frictions both in transit and recipient countries. Processing issues often force transit countries like Austria and Italy to host unwanted migrants, creating needless resentments. J. Hider's Austrian Liberal Party and Berlusconi's Forza Italia together with East German neo-Nazi groups vocally oppose open borders for immigrants. Unemployment and low wages attributed to immigrants has led trade unions in Austria, Germany, and Italy to advocate closed borders.

Restrictions and Expulsion

Anti-immigrant sentiment in France, Sweden, and Switzerland has led to the emergence of political parties advocating the restriction of immigrant rights and in some instances expulsion (Bordeau 2009; Nothwehr 2008 shows Catholic society sometimes induces racism and xenophobia). Jean-Marie Le Pen fared well at the polls running on this platform during the 2002 presidential election. President Nicolas Paul Stéphane Sarközy de Nagy-Bocsa (2007–2012) banned *burqas* in 2010–2011 and sought repatriation of the Roma. The Swedish Democratic Party stirred up animosity against immigrants by criticizing what was claimed to be their receipt of exorbitant welfare benefits. The slogan "Let's stop naturalization" became a rallying cry in Switzerland.

Exclusion from society: Insider and outsider

These xenophobic attitudes are creating societies of insiders and outsider of the sort prevalent during the Nazi era when only Germans living inside Deutschland including ethnic German minorities were considered insiders; those living abroad were deemed outsiders, unless they proved their loyalty. The distinction was not entirely genetic. Some non-Jewish naturalized non-Germans were treated as insiders. Those who failed to apply for naturalization remained outsiders. Loyal naturalized civil servants were treated as insiders; those whose loyalty was suspect were considered outsiders. Non-Germans who were viewed as potential loyal citizens were viewed as potential insiders; the rest as "rabble." The impact of these distinctions was to treat everyone who was not an actual or potential citizen as "rabble." (Kvistad 1999; Kvistad 1987). There are signs that these pernicious attitudes are returning and contributing to Islamist violence in France and elsewhere in Europe.

Home-Grown Terrorism in France, Europe

Islamic terrorist violence perpetrated by marginalized immigrants flared twice in Paris during 2015. In January, eleven editors and illustrators of Charlie Hebdo publisher, weekly cartoon journal that sometimes mocked Islam, were killed, and a synchronized terrorist attack was carried out in six locations during that year. A total of 128 people died and 300 were wounded. The IS claimed responsibility, but the masterminds were second- and third-generation home-grown Islamic immigrants. This home-grown terrorism is partly attributable to rising xenophobia, shifts in political power, and perhaps democratic failure. A large segment of second- and third-generation migrants have not been fully assimilated and suffer the tribulations of xenophobia discrimination, exclusion, and poverty. They remain outsiders with inadequate democratic recourse, making many resentful and susceptible to IS influence. Some are disaffected by Western intervention and carnage in the Middle East (particularly Libya, Syria) and see home-grown violence as their only recourse. Constructive policies aimed at mitigating their alienation and expediting full intercultural dialogue with protected diversity are needed to remedy these grievances.

Conclusion

The root of contemporary European xenophobia is a conflict between aggrieved insider members of Europe's middle class and poor immigrants. Both sides must be placated. Granting migrants citizenship is insufficient. Inclusion, welfare, and other antipoverty measures also would not be enough if middle-class incomes continue declining due to low-wage Asian competition (Lijphart and Crepaz 2007). This did not matter much in the United States where labor shortages existed in some sectors, but the situation there too is beginning to change. Donald Trump has called for the construction of a fence along the Mexican border to stem the flow of illegal immigration.

There are no simple solutions to today's clash of civilizations, especially in democratic systems. However, some principles deserve consideration.

1. Support diversity, open borders, and embrace heterogeneity.
2. Reduce income, wealth, and social inequalities.
3. Bolster inclusivity and competition.
4. Stop bombing Syria; collaborate with Turkey on asylum issues; increase competitiveness *vis-à-vis* Asia; cooperate with Asia, Middle East, and Africa; promote democracy in Asia; support Asia Infrastructure and Investment Bank and Silk Road (One Belt One Road) investment; and devise win–win policies for pluralistic societies everywhere.

The Unwinding of the Globalist Dream: EU, Russia and China

References

Armstrong, David, Valeria Bello *et al.* (eds.) (2011), *Civil Society and International Governance, The Role of Non-State Actors in Global and Regional Regulatory Frameworks,* Routledge Garnet Series: Europe in the World.

Auer, Stefan (2004), *Liberal Nationalism in Central Europe,* Routledge Curzon Contemporary Russia and Eastern Europe Series: Routledge.

Berend, Ivan T. (2009), *From the Soviet Bloc to the European Union: The Economic and Social Transformation of Central and Eastern Europe since 1973,* New York: Cambridge University Press.

Bordeau, Jamie (2009), *Xenophobia: The Violence of Fear and Hate,* New York: Rosen Publishing.

Crepaz, Markus M.L. (2007), Forward by Arend Lijphart, *Trust Beyond Borders: Immigration, the Welfare State, And Identity in Modern Societies* (Contemporary Political and Social Issues), Ann Arbor: University of Michigan Press.

Dallago, Bruno, and Steven Rosefielde (2016), *Transformation and Crisis in Central and Eastern Europe,* London: Routledge.

Haba, Kumiko (2014), *Challenge of Enlarged Europe: The European Union as a Global Power,* 2nd ed., Tokyo: Chuokoron Publisher Paperback.

Haba, Kumiko (2016), *Division and Integration in Europe: Nationalism and borders of Enlarged EU — Inclusion or Exclusion,* Tokyo: Chuokoron Publisher.

Harrison, Faye V. (ed.) (2005), *Resisting Racism and Xenophobia, Global Perspectives on Race, Gender, and Human Rights,* Oxford: Altamira, Toronto.

Hayashi, Reiko (2014), "Contemporary perspective of international demographic immigration," *Journal of Population Problems,* 70–3, 192–206.

Kato, Shingo (2014), "Continuity and change or Spanish media strategy on irregular immigration in Africa," NII-Electronic Library Service, Sofia University.

Kurti, Laszlo (2001), *The Remote Borderland, Transylvania in the Hungarian Imagination,* New York: State University of New York Press.

Kvistad, G. (1987), "Between state and society: Green political ideology in the mid-1980s," *West European Politics* 10.

Kvistad, G. (1999), *The Rise and Demise of German Statism.*

Lijphart, Arend, Markus M. L. Crepaz (2007), *Trust Beyond Borders: Immigration, the Welfare State, And Identity in Modern Societies* (Contemporary Political and Social Issues), Ann Arbor: Michigan University Press.

Mann, Michael (2005), *The Dark Side of Democracy — Explaining Ethnic Cleansing*, New York: Cambridge University Press.

Nakazawa, Takayuki (1999), *The Conspiracy of Belavezha Wood*, Ushio Publisher.

Nothwehr, Dawn M. (2008), *That they May be One, Catholic Social Teaching on Racism, Tribalism, and Xenophobia*, New York: Orbis Books.

Prusin, Alexander V. (2010), *The Lands Between, Conflict in the East European Borderlands, 1870–1992*, Oxford: Oxford University Press.

Ramet, Sabrina (1999), *The Radical Right in Central and Eastern Europe since 1989* (Post-Communist Cultural Studies), Pennsylvania: PSU Press.

Richard, Gunther, P. Nikiforos Diamandouros and Dimitri A. Sotifopoulos (eds.) (2006), *Democracy and the State in the New Southern Europe*, Oxford: Oxford University Press.

Russett, Bruce (1994), *Grasping the Democratic Peace: Principles for a Post-Cold War World*, Princeton: Princeton University Press.

Sakai, Keiko (2008), "Interrelation among conflicts, election and identity," *International Politics* No. 174, in: Saideman Stephen, M. and R. William Ayres (eds.), *For Kin or Country, Xenophobia, Nationalism, and War*, New York: Columbia University Press.

Schubert, Frank N. (2011), *Hungarian Borderlands, from the Habsburg Empire to the Axis Alliance, the Warsaw Pact and the European Union*, London: Bloomsbury.

Stone, John and Rutledge Dennis (eds.) (2002), *Race and Ethnicity, Comparative and Theoretical Approaches*, London: Blackwell Publishing.

Part II
Russia

Chapter 6
Great Power Resurgence

Steven Rosefielde

Russia and the West are entangled in an on-again, off-again cold war triggered by Crimea's annexation on March 18, 2014. The likelihood that the conflict will mimic Cold War I depends on what Nikolai Ogarkov, Marshal of the Soviet Union called the "correlation of forces" (balance of power) (Ogarkov 1982, 1985; Metz and Kievit 1995).

It is widely agreed that the correlation of forces favors the West. America's and the European Union's (EU) economies and North Atlantic Treaty Organization's (NATO) armed forces are more powerful than the Kremlin's. It would seem that Putin was foolish to annex Crimea and should withdraw and mend fences with Washington and Brussels. This would spare Russia the pain of further economic sanctions and the danger of forcible eviction from Crimea, Donetsk, and Luhansk. The West would be forgiving and gladly partner again with the Kremlin for their mutual benefit.

Although Putin recognizes that the West is economically and militarily stronger than Russia, and appreciates partnership's blessings, he is not swayed because he distrusts Washington (Rosefielde 2017). He believes that America is Russia's frenemy, that it wants Kremlin "regime change" (color revolution), and geopolitical domination achieved through EU and NATO eastward expansion and Moscow's submission to Western international law.

Putin is not intimidated by the superior size of the West's economy, military, and population because he is convinced that the West is vulnerable despite its advantages. He believes that Russia's economy is strong enough to endure Western economic sanctions and that NATO cannot muster sufficient resolve to forcibly expel Russia from Crimea, Donetsk, and Luhansk. He may even surmise that the West is willing to accommodate further territorial expansion in Novorossiya, that he can push back successfully against fresh EU and NATO incursions into Russia's sphere of influence, and even recapture some geopolitical influence lost in 1991 because Moscow can muster superior armed force in critical theaters of military operation (*teatr voennykh deistvii* [(TVD)]) without impoverishing the nation.

Could Putin be right? Should it be assumed that he is whistling past the graveyard and will soon relent, or is it possible that Russia can build sufficient military power to achieve some or all of the Kremlin's objectives without ruining the economy? Can Russia succeed today, where the Soviet Union failed?

The evidence suggests that Putin may be right, if the West insists on fighting with two hands tied behind its back by building down NATO and relying on soft power to discipline Moscow.[1]

---

[1] Zakheim (2016):

"Those challenges can be broken down into three areas: modernizing and growing our military capability to deter revisionist powers like China and Russia; rebuilding and restoring the readiness of our forces to sustain operations in a low-end terrorism fight as well as high-end warfare; and resourcing a strategy to truly defeat ISIS. In other words, we lack a military capable of deterring adversaries and assuring allies in three key regions of the world. Despite a public record chock full of testimony from military leaders pleading for relief and warning of dire consequences if unaddressed, the administration response to all three challenges has been anemic. It ranges from outright denial, in the case of the readiness crisis, to inadequate, in the case of military modernization."

Russia's Arms Buildup

The credibility of Russia's ability to militarily push back against NATO and EU eastward expansion, as well as counterattacking in Novorossiya and the Baltic states is supported by an authoritative inventory of Russia's military industrial accomplishments (budgetary expenditures and weapons procurement) recently compiled by Julian Cooper for FOI (Swedish Defense Research Agency) and serves as a baseline (Cooper 2016; Kogan 2016; Barabanov 2014; Renz 2014).[2] Cooper's appendix contains a complete line item inventory of Russia's weapons acquisitions between 2010 and 2015 for those desiring full documentation.

Armaments program for Russia for the years 2011–2020

Putin's goal of restoring Russia's great power — reflected in Crimea's annexation — depends critically on the past success of the Military Industrial Complex's (VPK) military industrial research and development (R&D) 2002–2010 initiative achieved under The Reform and Development of the Defense Industrial Complex Program 2002–2006 signed by Prime Minister Mikhail Kasyanov in October 2001 (Shlykov 2002; Izyumov *et al.* 2001a, 2001b) and the State Armaments Program for Russia for the years 2011–2020 signed by President Dmitri Medvedev at the end of 2010. Cooper summarizes the program and its accomplishment through 2015 as follows:

> This was a highly ambitious document setting out plans for the procurement of weapons and other military equipment, plus research and development for the creation of new systems, to a total value of over 20 trillion roubles, or US$680 billion at the exchange rate of the day. The aim of the programme was to increase the share of modern armaments held by the armed forces from 15 percent in 2010 to 30 percent in 2015 and 70 percent in 2020. The programme has been

[2]Cooper (2016): "This report provides an overview of the implementation of the Russian state armament programme to 2020 as the end of its first five year approaches. It is an empirical study designed to present data that is not readily accessible to analysts." Also see Barabanov (2014).

implemented through the budget-funded annual state defence order supplemented by state guaranteed credits. By 2014 the military output of the defence industry was growing at an annual rate of over 20 percent, compared with 6 percent three years earlier. The volume of new weapons procured steadily increased, the rate of renewal being particularly strong in the strategic missile forces and the air force, but not as impressive in the navy and ground forces. In 2014 the work of the defence industry began to be affected by the Ukraine crisis, with a breakdown of military-related deliveries from Ukraine and the imposition of sanctions by NATO and European Union member countries. The performance of the economy began to deteriorate, putting pressure on state finances. It was decided to postpone for three years the approval of the successor state armament programme, 2016–2025. Nevertheless, the implementation of the programme to date has secured a meaningful modernisation of the hardware of the Russian armed forces for the first time since the final years of the [Union of Soviet Socialist Republics] USSR.

Insofar as Cooper is correct (Rosefielde 2016; Ellman 2015; Gressel 2015),[3] despite the adverse consequences of the global financial crisis of 2008, Russia has not only succeeded in augmenting the size of its arsenal but has also significantly modernized its armed forces.[4] Eugene

---

[3] But cf. Gressel (2015): "The West has underestimated the significance of Russia's military reforms. Western — especially US — analysts have exclusively focused on the third phase of reform: the phasing in of new equipment. Numerous Russian and Western articles have stated that the Russian armed forces were still using legacy equipment from the Soviet Union and that its replacement was occurring more slowly than planned by the Kremlin. [ix]However, this is a misunderstanding of the nature of the reforms. The initial stages were not designed to create a new army in terms of equipment, but to ensure that existing equipment was ready to use, and to make the organization that uses it more effective and professional. Indeed, to successfully intervene in Russia's neighborhood, Moscow does not necessarily need the latest cutting-edge defense technology. Rather, such interventions would have to be precisely targeted and quickly executed to pre-empt a proper Western reaction."

[4] Bender (2016). Lieutenant General H.R. McMaster told the Senate Armed Services committee last week that "in Ukraine, the combination of unmanned aerial systems and offensive cyber and advanced electronic warfare capabilities depict a high degree of technological sophistication."

Kogan concurs.[5] The quantitative improvement may be partly attributable to restarting existing weapon production lines with negligible systemic implications (economic recovery), but modernization is another story.

---

[5] Kogan (2016):

> It can be said that the Russian military has indeed learnt their lessons from the Russia-Georgia war of August 2008. The manner that the military operated in Crimea, and most recently, in Syria demonstrated that military operations combined three most important components: surprise, mobility and swiftness (SMS). Whether or not the same lethal combination would be successfully replicated elsewhere remains to be seen. On the other hand, to state unequivocally that the Russian military is not capable of competing in conventional warfare beyond the post-Soviet space or in confrontation with NATO would be short-sighted and inaccurate. Such an assumption is no longer far-fetched but rather realistic even though experts in the field may disagree with the author. The Western perception of the current Russian military is undergoing a sea of change. It is evident that the agility and the rapidness of the military to perform before other actors intervene took the West at large by surprise. As a result, there is more and more talk about Russian military operations against the Baltic States even though they are NATO members and NATO famous dictum: an attack on one is an attack on all, appears to no longer be deterring Russia. In other words, the West at large can no longer take for granted that the Russian military will not seize the opportunity to intervene if they see fit. After all, President Vladimir Putin showed repeatedly his flair for being an opportunist and not being shy of military adventurism. Although the 2008–2012 military reform degraded Russia's combat capabilities in its western regions, Moscow's shift towards operations in limited conflicts [author's italics] riveted more attention to mobile and special operations forces. As a result, not only did the Airborne Forces avoid manpower cuts but they also kept their divisions and amplified their strength. Special Operations Forces (SOFs), too, began their buildup and increased combat readiness. The modernisation of Army Aviation units began swiftly and was accompanied by the procurement of a large number of new helicopters and a substantial number of new combat aircraft. As Barabanov continues, the procurement of a large number of new but not modernised helicopters accentuated mobility. In addition to mobility, large investments in human resources and combat training paid off generously in 2014 with a better army and more skillful personnel, especially among officers. Another positive factor is a large number of officers with real combat experience acquired in the Chechen wars, counter-terrorism operations in the North Caucasus and various local conflicts in the post-Soviet states. Additionally, numerous exercises have been held at all levels, including regular strategic manoeuvres, new education and combat training methods introduced

It demonstrates that Russia's post-communist economy, like its Soviet predecessor, is capable of manufacturing large quantities of technologically improved weapons systems.

---

and more professional soldiers recruited. New arms and hardware supplies since 2007 have considerably improved the army's material status and equipage, primarily in the Air Force and Army Aviation units. A major breakthrough was also made in logistics. After the Georgian campaign, the Russian army has been enhancing its strategic manoeuvre capabilities for years and practicing deployment over great distances which proved highly instrumental during the Ukrainian crisis. However, the Ukrainian crisis showed once again that the Russian army's weak spot was the dominating number of conscripts, the reduced length of military service (one year) and the lack of a sufficient number of contract servicemen. Although Russia had declared the goal of creating a permanent readiness army, many military units and formations were not used in full in 2014 due to both the shortage of personnel in the majority of units and the cyclic nature of conscript training. As a result, "permanent readiness" formations could send no more than two-thirds of their personnel to the operational area, leaving behind untrained soldiers drafted in the fall. Another serious issue is the reserve. No optimal reserve model has so far been worked out for the "new look." Additionally, there are still no clear-cut mechanisms for deploying additional units and formations and replacing lost personnel during wartime. Despite the abovementioned shortcomings, the efficiency with which Russian forces have assumed control over Crimea is hard to reconcile with the image of an inadequate military close to collapse. Despite claims to the contrary, Russia is much closer to having the military it needs that has often been suggested. In other words, the Western perception of the not sufficiently prepared Russian military was deeply mistaken. The 2008–2012 military reform prepared the military for the year 2013. The Kremlin began to set up a pool of rapid deployment forces in 2013 in order to be able to intervene in its neighbourhood. These well-equipped, well-trained, modern forces consist of Airborne Forces (four divisions, five brigades), Marines (four brigades, eight separate regiments), GRU Intelligence Forces (GRU Spetsnaz) brigades and three or four elite Ground Forces units as well as air and naval support. The MoD planned that, in the coming years, all of these units would be made up of professionals. On this basis, the Airborne Forces already count up to 20 battalions. There is every reason to believe that the 30,000 to 40,000 troops transferred to the south-eastern border of Ukraine in February 2014 were the backbone of these rapid deployment forces that realistically may have 100,000 and more troops ready for rapid deployment. The GRU Spetsnaz forces, in particular, have both expanded — with two new brigades: the 100th and the 25th — and developed. Most of the 15,000 to 17,000 Spetsnaz are essentially very well-trained light infantry and intervention forces. However, a growing awareness of the need for truly "tier one" special forces able to operate in small

Sources of quantitative growth and modernization

Quantitative weapons growth and modernization depend on engineering prowess and economic efficiency. Engineers design weapons and the factories needed to produce them. Russian military specifications, like

---

teams and complex political environment led to the decision to create the Special Operations Command (or KSO in Russian) in 2010. Becoming operational in 2013, the KSO first saw action in the seizure of Crimea in 2014. Numbering about 500 operators with integral airlift and close air support assets, the KSO represents a genuine enhancement of Russian capabilities and one designed for precisely the kind of military political operations described for the first time in the 2014 doctrine. On the other hand, attempts to increase the proportion of the Armed Forces staffed on a professional, volunteer basis continue to lag behind plans. As of December 2014 the total such kontraktniki in the military numbered 295,000: a solid increase from 2013's 186,000 but still well short of the 499,000 meant to be in the ranks by 2017. As of December 2015 the total of such kontraktniki in the military numbered 352,000 while their number should reach 384,000 in 2016. It can be assumed that the number of professional soldiers is likely to increase until 2017. Thus, the term lagging behind will become obsolete.

General Yuri Borisov, Deputy Minister of Defence for Procurement (hereafter cited as General Borisov), said in late January 2015 that: "The segment of modern equipment in the Aerospace Defence Forces (or VKO in Russian), the Navy and the Strategic Missile Forces (or RVSN in Russian) is at the rate of more than 40%." Currently, only 28% of the Russian Air Force inventory consists of modern equipment while the figure stands at 26% for the Ground Forces and the rest of the Russian military. RIA Novosti reported in early October 2015 by citing General Borisov that: "Modern hardware now makes up 45.8% of the Aerospace Forces (or VKS in Russian)." Finally, in early February 2016 General Sergei Shoigu, Minister of Defence, said that: "Forty seven percent of the country's arms and equipment inventory is now considered 'modern.'" The most modern area is its nuclear deterrent which between the three elements of its nuclear triad are reported to be 55% modernised. The Aerospace Forces are at 52% with the Navy sitting at 39% and the Ground Forces at 35% at the close of 2015. The further increase in modern equipment requires substantial funds that, despite the current economic crisis, President Vladimir Putin and his administration are ready to shoulder. Therefore, the pronounced target for the Armed Forces to have 70% of modern equipment by 2020 is no longer a far-fetched scenario but a fact that the West at large need to acknowledge, carefully monitor and think through as to what it can do about it. The author's assertion may be dismissed out of hand by the expert community but facts presented above reinforce the author's assertion. Furthermore, the section below, entitled Defence Spending, reinforces the author's view that the reshaping of the Russian military and equipping it with modern weapons is on the right track.

their counterparts in the West, are determined by military professionals, not private consumer preferences. The volumes of weapons produced, given prevailing technologies, depend formally on each good's production function, factor supplies, and allocative efficiency (Rosefielde and Pfouts 2013).[6] Output can be increased by building additional factories, employing more variable capital and labor, allocating factors to better use, and improving technology (Solow 1956, 1957; Swan 1956), even if factor and product prices in multiproduct firms are not generally competitive (Rosefielde 2007a). Just as in the West, optimization (maximal efficiency) cannot be fully achieved if prices are distorted by anticompetitive influences. This means that the Kremlin can increase weapons production from the achieved level to the extent that Putin desires within conventional "bounded rationality constraints" (Birman 1978; Selten 2002; Simon 1982, 1991) and in accordance with his willingness to divert resources from the civilian sector to military production. Even more can be achieved by improving production technologies and "second worst" allocative efficiency (Rosefielde 2015; Lipsey and Lancaster 1956; Meade 1955).[7] The claim that Russia's economy cannot support the creation and maintenance of formidable armed forces is fundamentally misguided on engineering and microeconomic grounds, an assertion confirmed by the Soviet experience. The same argument holds for improved weapons design, the development of new weapon systems, and the modernization of productive capacities. The Kremlin can and historically has continuously enhanced the technological proficiency of its weapons and modernized its armament production facilities and interindustrial material supplies networks. There are two highly classified programs (*federalnye tselevye progammy* [FTsP]) in place today, approved by President Dmitrii Medvedev on December 31, 2010, facilitating the implementation of the Russian State Armament Program, 2011–2020

---

[6] Mathematical and geometric proofs are provided in this volume.

[7] The term "second worst" emphasizes the magnitude of observable deviations from optimality. It is a word play on the more familiar term "second best." There is a tendency to downplay the consequences of Western anticompetitiveness in the neoclassical economic theory literature by describing suboptimal outcomes as "second best." Second worst cautions scholars the Western economic performance typically is substantially inferior to the ideal. The term was first coined by James Meade.

(gosudarstvennaia programma vooruzhenii) by funding the modernization of the industrial base of the defense sector (FTsP development of the
defense–industrial complex, 2011–2020) and interindustrial supply
(FTsP development, restoration, and organization of the production of
strategic scarce and import substituting materials and small-scale chemistry for armaments, military, and special technology in 2009–2011 and
period to 2015).[8]

VPK policy, institutional, and incentive reforms

The performance and potentials of Russia's military industrial system and
economy took a quantum leap after the 2008 global financial crisis. These
changes were planned as early as 2002, but materialized a few years later
than originally envisioned in the Reform and Development of the Defense
Industrial Complex Program 2002–2006. Military spending in Kasyanov's
document focused on designing and developing fifth-generation weapons
rather than augmenting inventories of standard equipment. Military R&D
temporarily took pride of place over procurement until new technologies
came on stream and manufacturing facilities were installed for the mass
production of advanced armaments. During this period and a few years
beyond, it seemed as if the directors of the VPK and enterprise managers
were content to throw money down a R&D black hole (Rosefielde 2007c).
There was no credible evidence of success, while reports indicated that
key officials managed to live comfortably by diverting funds to personal
use while feigning bold R&D ventures. The Russian defense budgetary
and weapons procurement data compiled by Cooper (2016), confirmed by
multiple sources, reveal that the VPK has moved beyond the R&D phase
of its military restoration project to rapid rearmament (Rosefielde 2016).
He contends that a meaningful modernization of the hardware of the
Russian armed forces occurred between 2010 and 2015 for the first time

---

[8] Cooper (2016): "It is a highly classified document in twelve sections. Ten are devoted to
particular services of the MOD — ground forces, navy, air force, etc. — one to all other
forces and one (the tenth) to R&D relating to the development of armaments — fundamental,
exploratory and Applied." "Total funding is usually given as 20.7 trillion roubles."

since the final years of the USSR, driven by the rapid procurement of new advanced weapons (Cooper 2016).

This means that not only has Putin adhered to the policy laid out in in the Reform and Development of the Defense Industrial Complex Program 2002–2006, albeit with a delay but also that the companion institutional and incentive reforms required for success were implemented, especially during the FTsP development of the defense–industrial complex 2011–2020 program. The surge in Russian weapons cannot be explained by revving up idled production lines for fourth-generation equipment. It reflects modernization of weapon characteristics, updating old production lines, building new modern production facilities, and switching from managerial regimes, rewarding executives for mass production rather than military R&D.

The literature on these subjects provides a clear, if incomplete, picture of what has transpired. First, after Yeltsin's experiment with privatization, the VPK and closely associated "strategic enterprises" like Transneft, Gazprom, Rosneftegaz, and Alrosa were renationalized in 2004. Initially, state ownership included some private shareholding participation, but now 100% state proprietorship is more frequently the norm (Sprenger 2008). However, unlike Soviet arrangements, state ownership does not bar VPK enterprises or public–private partnerships from competing among each other (Liu and Rosefielde 2016). Military industrial firms (including holding companies) are permitted to operate on a for-profit basis. They compete for state orders and export sales (contracts) and can outsource. Shareholders and/or managers are variously incentivized to profit-seek and incompletely profit-maximize rather than comply with Ministry of Defense (MOD) commands and/or rent-seek. They have fewer degrees of freedom than private Western defense corporations, like Boeing, but are self-motivated to efficiently produce in accordance with Herbert Simon's bounded rationality framework and William Baumol's satisficing concept (Baumol 1959). This bolstered VPK initiative when the MOD stopped prioritizing military R&D. Weapon producers could pretend to increase output, continue rent-seeking, and live passively off state funds. This may well have been the most likely outcome, but judging from Cooper's evidence Putin beat the odds by imposing firm discipline and containing rent-seeking, buttressed with competitive reforms and sufficient material incentives. No one denies that kleptocratic rent-seeking persists, and the latent threat it poses to Russia's military industrial revival. The system could relapse into indolence when Putin retires, but it now needs to be recognized that sustainable Russian military modernization is also a distinct possibility.

Escalation dominance

The Kremlin's drive to restore Russia's great power status has much in common with Soviet precedent, but it differs on several important scores. The genstab (Soviet General Staff) strove to achieve full spectrum strategic and tactical battlefield dominance. It maintained the World's largest tank armies for blitzkrieg attack against NATO and was prepared to use tactical nuclear and biological weapons in its order of battle. The USSR maintained vast strategic nuclear forces (including reloads) for disarming first strikes and second-strike retaliation. It constructed antiballistic missile defenses to reinforce strategic nuclear deterrence and sought to achieve escalation domination at all combat intensities across the globe and planned for prolonged warfighting engagements.

Russia's 2010 military doctrine retains these essentials Military doctrine of the Russian Federation (2010), Polina and Bettina (2015) but scales down the defense mission concentrating forces on its Western periphery, foregoing a Pacific blue-water navy and prolonged warfighting reserves. The goal is an economically cost-effective military capable of quick victories in key theaters of military operation (TVD) through the rapid deployment of superior battlefield forces, buttressed by strategic nuclear deterrence (Howe 2016; Adamsky 2016; Schneider 2016).[9] Instead of doing everything poorly, the new doctrine strives to do the essentials well (Giles 2016).

---

[9]The Kremlin's arms buildup has multiple purposes including the achievement of battlefield escalation dominance with conventional and nuclear ordnance up to the strategic nuclear threshold (a global reconnaissance/strike capability to wage intercontinental conventional war against the United States/allies and other adversaries in support of Russian national interests).

This means in practice that NATO cannot tactically deter Russia in the Baltics or Ukraine. The Kremlin has operational weapons fitted with tactical nuclear ordnance ready for employment on Europe's battlefields. Western leaders might be chastened by the methodical and rapid manner in which Moscow has transformed the military correlation of forces on Russia's western periphery, but are unfazed. They insist that tactical escalation dominance and rapid war winning capabilities are moot because mutually assured destruction (MAD) means that the tactical escalation dominance and quick victories cannot be exploited.[10] Moscow cannot employ its tactical escalation dominance because it fears America's strategic nuclear retaliation, and quick victories on periphery would lead to prolonged war with the West that Russia could not win. This reasoning is hardly failsafe, but Washington and Berlin are prepared to rely on it until something far more catastrophic than Crimea's annexation alters their outlook.

No one is suggesting that Russia's military can easily defeat the West in World War III or that the Kremlin's arms buildup will soon empower it to invade and conquer the NATO heartland, but many legitimately fret that Moscow can fight and win territory against two candidates for NATO membership — Ukraine and Georgia — and perhaps non-NATO Finland and the NATO Baltic states.[11] Needless to say, the military component of the correlation of forces is only one of many factors shaping Putin's actions; nonetheless, it merits close attention.

Defense experts know that public statistics on arsenals, decommissioned armaments including nuclear warheads, ballistic missile reloads, dual-use capabilities, prolonged warfighting reserves, weapons production, deployments, military manpower, and readiness, as well as judgments about combat effectiveness can be seriously misleading. There is a façade of transparency provided by various "authoritative" sources like the International Institute for Strategic Studies' Military Balance that serves

---

[10] The doctrine of MAD is usually associated with US Defense Secretary Robert McNamara and has various countervalue and counterforce interpretations. It can be claimed that MAD was never America's sole deterrent strategy. See National Archives and Records Administration, RG 200, Defense Programs and Operations, LeMay's Memo to President and JCS Views, Box 83. Secret.

[11] Estonia, Latvia, and Lithuania.

sundry purposes, but there are also many deep secrets and conflicts of opinion. However, there is no dispute about the shift in correlation of forces under Putin's watch appraised from the standpoint of rising Kremlin military power. Moscow's military modernization and rearmament programs, as well as improved readiness, have been successful enough for Russia to credibly employ non-lethal and lethal coercion (soft power and hard power) against it neighbors and to capture strategically significant territorial assets through the deft use of hybrid warfare (Charap 2015/2016).[12] This would have been impossible under Yeltsin. The Kremlin has limited itself thus far mostly to proxy warfare,[13] but it could have just as easily seized Crimea with its own forces accepting the risk of a Western counterstrike (Kipp 2014).

North Atlantic Treaty Organization

This success has been primarily the Kremlin's doing, facilitated by a huge contraction in Western defense spending, particularly in the development, deployment, and maintenance of forces needed to counter Russia's challenge.[14] Official statistics on Europe's defense spending undistorted by

---

[12]Military Balance, *International Institute for Strategic Studies*, 115(1), 2015. Hybrid warfare is a military strategy that blends conventional warfare, irregular warfare (guerrilla warfare), and cyberwarfare. This is a Western definition. The Russians only use the term *gibridnaia voina* when they refer to the Western debate. For a discussion of the nature of Russian military strategy in Ukraine and against NATO more generally, see Samuel Charap (2015/2016).

[13]Stephen Blank contends that 9,000 people have been killed in Ukraine, including many by Russian forces. Personal correspondence, January 4, 2016.

[14]Techau (2015). "The members of the North Atlantic Treaty Organization (NATO) pledged in 2014 to increase their defense spending to 2 percent of their gross domestic products by 2024. It is unrealistic to assume that this goal will ever be reached by all 28 allies, and yet the 2 percent metric persists — and it has assumed a significance beyond its face value. It is about addressing Europe's growing security vacuum and defining who will be in charge of European security. The reduction of the U.S. security footprint in Europe and Europeans' dramatic loss of military capability since the 1990s have created a security vacuum in Europe. NATO's 2 percent metric is one instrument to address that. As a way to measure an increase in military capability, the 2 percent metric is barely useful. It does not measure spending in real terms or actual output. The target has had some success in stimulating

America's out-of-theater military activities declined from US$314 billion to US$227 billion between 1990 and 2015, computed in constant 2010 dollars (NATO 2015), even though NATO membership has nearly doubled. According to the International Institute for Strategic Studies, Germany's defense spending has fallen by 4.3% since 2008. In the same period, the United Kingdom has reduced its defense spending by 9.1% and Italy by 21%. This has led to a sharp drop in military capabilities in bigger and more exposed NATO member states, and it has made the already uneven burden-sharing in the alliance more lopsided. Jan Techau contends that the reduction together with America's diminished security footprint in Europe (the permanent US troop presence in Europe has been very substantially reduced since the 1990s) has created a security vacuum with scant prospects for swift reversal. Its declaratory goal is to increase the defense spending to 2%, but the Europeans have yet to reallocate funds from civilian to military purposes. The glaring discrepancy between NATO's rhetorical posture and its budgetary actions has not been overlooked in Moscow and must surely fortify Putin's resolve.

NATO has not been feckless. It has adopted a Readiness Action Plan (RAP) that encompasses a full array of military steps designed to enhance the deterrent value of NATO's military posture on its Eastern border. NATO has reassured the populations of Central and Eastern Europe that it will come to their aid under Article 5, if Russia attacks them. The pledge has been reinforced by land, sea, and air exercises focused on collective defense and crisis management on NATO's eastern flank. RAP has initiated "adaptation measures," i.e., longer-term changes to NATO's forces and command structures, including tripling the strength of the NATO Response Force, creating a Very High Readiness Joint Task Force deployable on short notice, and enhancing standing naval forces. Toward this end, six NATO Force Integration Units — small headquarters — are being established in Central and Eastern Europe, along with a headquarters for

---

debate on European security. It has become an important gauge of who is and who is not politically committed to NATO's core task: Europe's security."

"Europeans underestimate the political significance of 2 percent in the U.S. debate over security commitments to Europe. Americans overestimate the political significance of 2 percent among Europeans struggling with austerity and divergent threat perceptions, which make it difficult to increase their defense commitments."

the Multinational Corps Northeast in Szczecin, Poland, and a standing joint logistics support group headquarters (The Readiness Action Plan 2015). All these actions have real deterrent value, but will soon be overwhelmed by Russia's fast-paced arms buildup because readiness in the intermediate term is an inadequate substitute for large-scale, fifth-generation, conventional forces deployed on the periphery, including Novorossiya.

Moreover, bold talk and a willingness to employ force are two very different things. European governments find it difficult to maintain political support, not only for defense spending but also, and more fundamentally, for conceptualizing security as both territorial defense and expeditionary interventionism. Germany for one has made it clear enough that it would not fight in Novorossiya to reverse Crimea's annexation. The United Kingdom, France, and Italy would not participate in air, sea, or land assaults on Russian soil or the Luhansk People's Republic either.[15] NATO is not a paper tiger, but neither is it a daunting foe, if Putin is patient enough to expand the Kremlin's sphere of influence, gradually allowing the creation of a succession of "new normal" *status quos* that increase Russia's reach while the West persistently temporizes. This is the strategy Stalin used to build his postwar Eastern and Central European satellite system in the early postwar era, and there seems little to prevent the ploy from succeeding today. Indeed, the opportunity for Putin is better than it was for Stalin because the strategic vacuum created by Europe's unwillingness to adequately defend itself and America's gradual withdrawal from the continent invite the Kremlin to fill the void. The West, from a military perspective, is in retreat precisely at the moment Putin has chosen to launch his project for the restoration of Russia's great power, suggesting that Moscow's pressure would not evaporate of its own accord.

Theaters of Military Operation

Russia and the West both desire to expand their spheres of influence on each other's turf. The West's preferred tactic is pressing color

---

[15] "Eastern Europe Fears Closer French-Russian Ties Amid Ukraine Crisis," *Economic Times*, November 23, 2015, available at http://economictimes.indiatimes.com/articleshow/49888340.cms?utm_source=contentofinterest&utm_medium=text&utm_campaign=cppst.

revolutions, regime change ("Putin must go"),[16] accession to the EU and NATO, and foreign direct investment. Russia employs analogous methods plus hybrid warfare, and in the Crimean case added annexation. How might shifts in the military correlation of forces, given recent trends, affect the outcomes of spheres of influence tussles during the remainder of Putin's years in power? Consider two carefully crafted hypothetical cases that could occur just prior to his likely fourth presidential term in 2018 that leave ample time for the Kremlin to conquer, annex, and consolidate gains before Russia's legislative elections in 2020.[17] Both are concordant with Russia National Security Strategy and the latest version of its military doctrine (Katri 2015). In the first scenario, the West is the transgressor. It manages to entice a country in Russia's neighborhood (Finland, Ukraine, Moldova, Transnistria, Armenia, Georgia, South Ossetia, Azerbaijan, or Belarus) to join NATO, provoking the Kremlin to retaliate by seizing and/or annexing territory. Call this the "West's Greater Europe gambit." In the second scenario, Russia is a blue skies aggressor. It uses uniformed Russian troops to wrest territory without provocation from a neighboring sovereign state (Finland, Estonia, Latvia, Lithuania, Ukraine, Moldova, Armenia, or Georgia) that is a neutral, an EU accession candidate, or an EU-NATO member. Classify this as a "Greater Russia re-conquest initiative." Will a pattern of gradual NATO diminishment and rapid Russian weapons growth allow the Kremlin to prevail in one or both scenarios, holding other aspects of the correlation of forces constant?

---

[16] Michael McFaul and Anders Aslund have publicly expressed this view. Anders Aslund, group e-mail, December 12, 2011. "Has Putin Come to the End of His Regime?" "On Saturday, December 10, the spell of the Vladimir Putin regime was broken. Today, the key questions that many are asking are how fast he will lose power and what will come in his place. Peaceful mass demonstrations took place all over Russia. In Moscow, probably 80,000 gathered on Bolotnaya Ploshchad near the Kremlin to protest against Putin and what they and most observers say were the stolen elections of December 4. I had argued before these protests that if more than 50,000 came, the regime would be seen as finished. This was the biggest and most important demonstration in Russia since August 1991. Demonstrations took place in at least 15 Russian cities throughout the country, so this is a national phenomenon and not limited to Moscow."

[17] Russia switched from a four-year to a six-year presidential cycle in 2012.

The West's Greater Europe Gambit

The Greater Europe gambit (scenario one) assumes that the Kremlin continues modernizing its strategic and tactical nuclear forces, opts to reintroduce nuclear-armed intermediate range ballistic missiles,[18] and continues to gradually escalate its nuclear saber-rattling, making it relatively safe for Russia to wage conventional war in NATO's European periphery. This is a fundamental aspect of assured nuclear deterrence — making the world free for conventional warfighting. Assume further that Moscow substantially increases the share of combat-effective fifth-generation weapons in its conventional forces (sixth-generation jet fighter technology would not be available in America until the 2025–2030 time frame) Echevarria (2005),[19] improves its rapid deployment capabilities, and increases the readiness both of its active troops and prolonged warfighting reserves (Baev 2015; Gorenburg 2010, 2015; Norberg 2015).[20] Finally, assume too that NATO, in an environment of shrinking

---

[18]Persson (2015): "Makhmut Gareev, influential military theorist and a veteran of the Second World War, stated in July 2013 that the destruction of the intermediate-range ballistic missiles in the late 1980s and 1990s was a mistake. 'Now also the highest leadership of the Russian Federation recognizes this mistake,' he wrote."

[19]Military theorists often conceptualize weapons technologies and styles of warfighting in terms of generation. William Lind introduced the idea in 1989. See Echevarria (2005). First-generation warfare refers to battles fought with massed manpower, using line and column tactics with uniformed soldiers governed by the state. Second-generation warfare is the tactics used after the invention of the rifled musket and breech-loading weapons and continuing through the development of the machine gun and indirect fire. Third-generation warfare focuses on using speed and surprise to bypass the enemy's lines and collapse its forces from the rear. Essentially, this was the end of linear warfare on a tactical level, with units seeking not simply to meet each other face to face, but to outmaneuver each other to gain the greatest advantage. Fourth-generation warfare is characterized by a return to decentralized forms of warfare, blurring of the lines between war and politics, combatants and civilians due to nation-states' loss of their near-monopoly on combat forces, returning to modes of conflict common in premodern times. Fifth-generation warfare emphasizes the impact of precision-guided weapons and advanced electronic technologies on all prior forms of warfighting.

[20]For a knowledgeable discussion of the difficulties the Kremlin faces in achieving its military modernization goals, see Baev (2015). Cf. Gorenburg (2010, 2015). Norberg (2015): "Russia's Armed forces in the four years 2011–2014 trained to launch and fight largescale joint inter-service operations, i.e., launching and waging interstate

European military budgets, fails to develop credible rapid-reaction air, sea (operating in the Black Sea), and ground forces capable of defeating Russia in a sustained war in the territories of Ukraine, Moldova, Transnistria, Armenia, Georgia, South Ossetia, Azerbaijan, or Belarus. What would NATO do in this realistic environment if Putin responded to a Greater Europe gambit by swiftly conquering part or all of a target country?[21] Would NATO's members, including Germany, France, Italy, and Turkey, commit themselves to a full-scale war in Russia's backyard over the organization's "right" to attract new recruits from the Kremlin's sphere of influence?

Polls show that Germany's electorate today opposes any kind of armed intervention in Ukraine. No information is available regarding the attitude of Germans toward high-intensity "boots on the ground" operations in Moldova, Transnistria, Armenia, Georgia, South Ossetia, Azerbaijan, or Belarus, but there are no reasons to suppose there would be a groundswell for war. It therefore can be plausibly inferred that Russia's arms buildup is not only improving the military correlation of forces from Moscow's perspective, but is also providing Russia with a credible defense of its realms from what it considers Western provocations, even if American and EU leaders believe that the Kremlin is unjustified in feeling provoked by color revolutions, regime change, and accession to the EU and NATO. Faith in the

---

wars." "Russian Armed Forces carried out at least one joint inter-service exercise each year in the three years 2011–2013. This enabled senior Russian military and political decision makers to exercise in a scenario where Russia was fighting two operations at the same time. In 2011 and 2012, smaller parallel joint inter-service exercises took place simultaneously. In 2013, the parallel exercise was a Navy exercise, but probably coordinated with the annual strategic exercise. In 2014, the size of the annual strategic exercise, 155,000 men, made parallel exercises redundant. In 2013 and 2014, the Russian Armed Forces also carried out surprise inspections to check and develop combat readiness, both in separate functions in the Armed Forces and in systemic tests in entire military districts. Altogether, these exercises related to Russia's collective ability to launch and wage interstate wars in all of Russia's strategic directions." Available at www.foi.se/russia.

[21] It is difficult to ascertain what Putin deems a *casus belli*. He appeared to tolerate Ukraine's democratization, its aspiration to join the EU Union, and the more remote prospect of NATO accession before striking Crimea. His judgment about red lines should be expected to be on a case-by-case basis.

righteousness of its cause cannot shield the West from being forced to stand down or incur a humiliating defeat in scenario one.

Greater Russia Re-conquest Initiative

Now suppose alternatively, given the same core assumptions that applied in the first scenario, that Putin decides to wrest territory from a neighboring sovereign state (Finland, Estonia, Latvia, Lithuania, Ukraine, Moldova, Armenia, or Georgia), a neutral, EU–NATO member, or an EU accession candidate. He is nakedly aggressive. There is no Western provocation. What would be the prospects for the Kremlin's success in the period of high vulnerability, 2018–2020?

The answer is great. The Kremlin will have a distinct advantage because of asymmetries in the deployment, command, control, and communications in theaters of military operation under consideration in scenario 2, even if Russia fails to cultivate fifth columns in the victim's territory. Putin has ample time to prepare limited "shock-and-awe" wars by 2018 that would simultaneously achieve valuable objectives and discourage the onset of World War III by encouraging Western leaders to place their faith in strategic patience (Ullman and Wade 1996). He could wager on strategic surprise, confronting Washington, Berlin, and Brussels with a *fait accompli* like his Crimean annexation by prepositioning, rapidly deploying massive combined armed forces, and striking quickly, while simultaneously threatening out-of-theater targets to stretch NATO's retaliatory assets. The ploy should be effective because, by assumption, the West would not pay for the readiness needed to credibly retaliate and NATO was not designed for swift responses to Greater Russian re-conquest initiatives. It was created to close the barn door after Stalin seized his Eastern and Central European empires in 1947 — not to dislodge a nuclear superpower arguably on its own turf.

Surgical shock-and-awe tactics are apt to work better in some countries than others. They can be employed in Moldova, Armenia, or Georgia, but this would be overkill. There does not appear to be any pressing reason to conquer Finland, and attacking Estonia, Latvia, or Lithuania would invoke Article 5 of the founding 1949 NATO Treaty, although this paper pledge is not the ironclad guarantee many suppose. Insiders know that Article 5 is more a hope and prayer than a promise for the Baltics.

The Washington Treaty clearly states that an attack on any member shall be deemed an attack on the collective, but the assistance entailed is vague, allowing members broad wiggle room to decide whether and to what extent to fight.[22] The political calculation would necessarily require delicate judgment, but it would hardly be unreasonable for Putin to conclude that he could launch an invasion from Narva or Kaliningrad to seize and annex a large chunk of Estonia, Latvia, and Lithuania, and then gull the West gradually into accommodating the new normal.

The most lucrative target of opportunity from multiple perspectives, however, continues to be the eastern, southeastern, and Donbas regions of tsarist Novorossiya. There are considerable strategic military and economic advantages to annexing the northern coast of the Black Sea, including Mariupol and Odessa, as a gateway to Moldova and beyond. Russia would not only gain valuable natural resources, but could also more effectively project forces against Ukraine, Turkey, and the Middle East. The West would be enraged, but also toothless in the face of the carefully planned 2018 strike hypothesized in scenario 2 that overcame existing obstacles to conquest. The presence of superior, entrenched Russian military forces and the exorbitant military costs of physically dislodging Kremlin armies might well daunt Western leaders.

Scenarios 1 and 2 do not preclude alternatives or serve as reliable predictors of the shape of things to come because military power is only

---

[22] Washington Treaty (1949). "The Parties agree that an armed attack against one or more of them in Europe or North America shall be considered an attack against them all and consequently they agree that, if such an armed attack occurs, each of them, in exercise of the right of individual or collective self-defense recognised by Article 51 of the Charter of the United Nations, will assist the Party or Parties so attacked by taking forthwith, individually and in concert with the other Parties, such action as it deems necessary, including the use of armed force, to restore and maintain the security of the North Atlantic area."

"Any such armed attack and all measures taken as a result thereof shall immediately be reported to the Security Council. Such measures shall be terminated when the Security Council has taken the measures necessary to restore and maintain international peace and security."

one component of the correlation of forces. Nonetheless, both scenarios illustrate that the Kremlin's investment in military strength can be construed as a strategically opportunistic, rational response to the drift in Western security policy, and that Russia's drive to restore its great power is unlikely to fade quietly into the night under Putin's watch unless the economy falters.

Guns and Butter

Soviet power was undermined by the Kremlin's dystopic economic system which criminalized private property, markets, and entrepreneurship. Russia's "structurally militarized" communist economy (Shlykov 2001, 2003, 2005, 2006a, 2006b, 2008) was good enough to sustain military superpower, but failed to provide Russia's people with a Western standard of living (Rosefielde 2007b). Most Soviets accommodated themselves to their Spartan standard of living, but powerful members of Gorbachev's entourage gradually found life without butter unbearable. They craved *la dolce vita*, and dynamited both the economic and political system under the pretext of what Mikhail Gorbachev described as "new thinking" (*novoe myshlenie*), democratization (*demokratizatsiya*), openness (*glasnost*) and radical economic reform (*perestroika*) (Gorbachev 1987). The rest is history (Rosefielde and Hedlund 2008).

Are Western leaders justified in assuming that this time will be the same; that Russian military power in the post-Soviet age must eventually be undone by the shortcomings of the Kremlin's economic system? It could happen, but there are solid grounds for expecting Russia's new economic system to substantially outperform its Soviet predecessor. First and foremost, there has been a "transition" from plan to market. Russia's civilian sector is now privatized and market-driven. It has modernized and is integrated into the global economy. Second, while Russia's defense–industrial complex (VPK) has been renationalized, it has been redesigned to harness the benefits of market competition (see section on "VPK Policy, Institutional, and Incentive Reforms").

The World Bank Group considers the transformation of Russia's civilian economy successful enough to have generated rapid economic growth between 1998 and 2007. It is now predicting further moderate rates of advance after 2017 (Rosefielde 2017). The rapid economic growth achieved during Putin's first two presidential terms was almost all "butter." Weapons production was negligible. This pattern changed in 2010 as Russia's arms modernization program gathered momentum. Consumption growth decelerated as weapons production surged, but never turned negative, suggesting that if the WBG forecast for 2017 is on target, the Kremlin should be able to continue modernizing its armed forces without impoverishing the nation, even if natural resource prices remain at their current depressed levels. Future windfall gains from rising natural resource prices will be the icing on the cake but will not fundamentally alter the sobering prospect that the outcome of Cold War II might not be the same. Putin has a chance to outplay his Soviet mentors.

Conclusion

Western leaders appear to want to change the subject. They do not want Crimea's annexation, hybrid warfare in Novorossiya, across Russia's periphery and Syria (Cordesman 2015), and the expansion of the Kremlin's sphere of influence to crowd out other domestic and foreign agendas (including the Middle East). They are hoping that Putin will go away (democratic revolution) or that punitive economic sanctions, high occupation costs in Crimea, Luhansk, and Donetsk, and plummeting natural resources prices will deflate Moscow's aspirations. These hopes do not constitute an adequate response to the Kremlin's challenge. Putin has been assiduously pursuing the restoration of Russia's great power since he came to office in 2000. He is constructing the forces and strategies to achieve his goals[23] and is unlikely to be deterred by NATO's build down or a faltering economy.

---

[23] Roger McDermott, "Russia's Strategic Mobility and Its Military Deployment in Syria," RUFS Briefing, No. 31, November 12, 2015, available at foi@nyhetsbrev.foi.se: "Russia's ability to project power beyond its immediate border has been questioned since the dissolution of the Soviet Union. On 30 September 2015, Russia launched its first out-of-area military operation since the Soviet-Afghanistan War. It witnessed remarkable speed and sophisticated planning advances to support the reinforcement of the Tartus naval depot and form a de facto forward operating airbase in Latakia. Such movements of air assets and military hardware and weapons also aimed at boosting military-technical aid to

The message for Western policymakers is simple. Wake up and shoulder the costs of deterring Putin in key TVDs. This means matching the scale, quality, and readiness of Russia's conventional armed forces. The goal can be partially accomplished by ramping up exercises in frequency and scale and by adequately supplying NATO troops with armor. A clear signal should also be given to Russia that substrategic nuclear weapons are impermissible, even though NATO is unlikely to retaliate under the threat of mutually assured destruction.[24]

Donald Trump's muscular rhetoric suggests that he may increase America's conventional and nuclear deterrents sufficiently to prevent Russia expansion in the Baltic states and Novorossiya, but it is premature to judge whether his advisors understand the situation well enough to take the requisite countermeasures.

References

Adamsky, Dima (2016), "The current state of Russian strategic thought in the nuclear realm," Paper presented to the American Foreign Policy Council Conference on "The Russian Military in the Contemporary Perspective" held May 9–10, in Washington, D.C.

Baev, Pavel (2015), "Russian air power is too brittle for brinksmanship," Ponars, Policy Memo 398, November.

Barabanov, Mikhail (2014), "Testing a 'new look', the Ukrainian conflict and military reform in Russia," in Centre for Analysis of Strategies and Technologies (CAST), available at www.cast.ru/eng/?id=578 — online on December 18, 2014.

Baumol, William (1959), *Business Behavior, Value and Growth*, rev. ed., New York: Macmillan.

the Syrian government and sustaining Russia's air campaign was made possible by recent advances in Russia's combat service support system. The pre-existing logistics and supply system was reformed in 2010 into Materiel-Technical Support (materialno-tekhnicheskogo obespechniia — MTO); additional improvements resulted from testing the MTO during strategic-operational military exercises and in conducting service level exercises. In this case, Moscow has overcome traditional reliance upon railway infrastructure, geographically impossible in its Syria intervention, and greatly enhanced its use of sea lines of communication (SLOCs) and air lines of communication (ALOCs)."

[24] Johan Norberg suggested these policy prescriptions.

Bender, Bryan (2016), "The secret U.S. army study that targets Moscow," *Politico*, April 14, available at http://www.politico.com/magazine/ story/2016/04/moscow-pentagon-us-secret-study-213811.

Birman, Igor (1978), "From the achieved level," *Soviet Studies*, 30(2), 153–172.

Charap, Samuel (2015–2016), "The ghost of hybrid war," *Survival*, 57(6), 53–57.

Cooper, Julian (2016), *Russia's State Armament Programme to 2020: A Quantitative Assessment of Implementation 2011–2015*, FOI, FOI-R—4239—SE, March, 13, 28–31.

Cordesman, Anthony (2015), "Russia in Syria: Hybrid political warfare," CSIS, September 23, available at http://csis.org/publication/russia-syria-hybrid-political-warfare.

Echevarria, Antulio (2005), *Fourth-Generation War and Other Myths*, US Army War College: Strategic Studies Institute.

Ellman, Michael (2015), "Russia's current economic system: From delusion to glasnost'," *Comparative Economic Studies*, 57(4), 693–710.

Giles, Keir (2016), *Russia's "New" Tools for Confronting the West: Continuity and Innovation in Moscow's Exercise of Power*, Chatham House: The Royal Institute of International Affairs.

Gorbachev, Mikhail (1987), *Perestoika i Novoe Myshlenie*, Moscow: Politicheskie Literatury.

Gorenburg, Dmitry (2010), "Russia's State Armaments Program 2020: Is the third time the charm for military modernization?" *PONARS Eurasia Policy Memo* No. 125, October.

Gorenburg, Dmitry (2015), "Russian naval shipbuilding: Is it possible to fulfill the Kremlin's grand expectations?" *PONARS Eurasia Policy Memo* No. 395, October.

Gressel, Gustav (2015), "Russia's quiet military revolution, and what it means for Europe," *European Council on Foreign Relations (ECFR)*, December 31, available at http://www.isn.ethz.ch/Digital-Library/Articles/Detail/?id= 195415.

Howe, James (2016), "Future Russian strategic nuclear and non-nuclear forces: 2022," Paper presented to the American Foreign Policy Council Conference on "The Russian Military in the Contemporary Perspective" held May 9–10, in Washington, D.C.

Izyumov, Alexei, Leonid Kosals, and Rosalina Ryvkina (2001a), "Privatisation of the Russian defense industry: Ownership and control issues," *Post-Communist Economies,* 12(4), 485–496.

Izyumov, Alexei, Leonid Kosals, and Rosalina Ryvkina (2001b), "Defense industrial transformation in Russia: Evidence from a longitudinal survey," *Post-Communist Economies,* 12(2), 215–227.

Katri, Pynnoniemi (2015), "Analysis of the signals and assumptions embedded in Russia's adjusted security doctrines," *Russian Analytical Digest* No. 173, October 12, available at http://www.css.ethz.ch/publications/pdfs/Russian_Analytical_Digest_175.pdf.

Kipp, Jacob (2014), "Putin's Ukrainian gambit," Conference on Challenges to the European Union, University of North Carolina, Chapel Hill, September 18–20.

Kogan, Eugene (2016), *Russian Military Capabilities*, Tiblisi Georgia: Georgian Foundation for Strategic and International Studies.

Lipsey, Richard and Kelvin Lancaster (1956), "The general theory of second best," *Review of Economic Studies*, 24(1), 11–32.

Liu, Yiyi and Steven Rosefielde (2016), "Public private partnerships: Antidote for secular stagnation?," in: Rosefielde, S., M. Kuboniwa, S. Mizobata and K. Haba (eds.), *EU Economic Stagnation and Political Strife: Lessons for Asia*, Singapore: World Scientific Publishers.

McDermott, Roger (2015), "Russia's strategic mobility and its military deployment in Syria," RUFS Briefing, 31.

Meade, James (1955), *Trade and Welfare*, London: Oxford University Press.

Metz, Steven and James Kievit (1995), "Strategy and the revolution in military affairs: From theory to policy, US Army War College, June 27," available at http://www.strategicstudiesinstitute.army.mil/pubs/summary.cfm?q=236.

Military doctrine of the Russian Federation (2010), *Voyennaya doktrina Rossiyskoy Federatsii"* Военная доктрина Российской Федерации [*Military doctrine of the Russian Federation*]. scrf.gov.ru (in Russian). Moscow: Security Council of the Russian Federation. 2010-06-25 (presidential decree 2010-06-25).

NATO (2015), "Defense expenditures data for 2014 and estimates for 2015," press release, June 22, available at www.nato.int/cps/en/natohq/news_120866.htm.

Norberg, Johan (2015), "Training to fight — Russia's major military exercises 2011–2014," FOI-R–4128 — SE, December.

Ogarkov, N.V. 1982, "Vsegda v golovnosti k zashchite Otechestva," *Moskva*, 31.

Ogarkov, N.V. 1985, "Istoriya Uchit vditel'nosti," *Moskva*, 41.

Persson, Gudrun (2015), "Russian strategic deterrence — beyond the brinkmanship?" FOI, RUES Briefing 29, September 17.

Polina, Sinovets and Renz Bettina (2015), "Russia's 2014 military doctrine and beyond: threat perceptions, capabilities and ambitions," Research Paper, Rome, IT: NATO Defense College, Research Division.

The Readiness Action Plan (2015), "NATO," September, available at http://www.nato.int/cps/en/natohq/topics_119.

Renz, Bettina (2014), "Russian military capabilities after 20 years of reform," *Survival*, 56(3), 61–84.

Rosefielde, Steven (2007a), *Russian Economy from Lenin to Putin*, New York: Wiley.

Rosefielde, Steven (2007b), *Russian Economics from Lenin to Putin*, London: Blackwell.

Rosefielde, Steven (2007c), "Russian rearmament: Motives options and prospects," in: Jan, L. and F. Westerlund (eds.), *Russian Power Structures: Present and Future Roles in Russian Politics, FOI-R-2437-SE*, 71–96, Stockholm.

Rosefielde, Steven (2015), "Economic theory of the second worst," *Higher School of Economics Journal* (HSE), 19(1), 30–44.

Rosefielde, Steven (2016), *Kremlin Strikes Back: Russia and the West after Crimea's Annexation*, Cambridge: Cambridge University Press.

Rosefielde, Steven (2017), *The Kremlin Strikes Back: Russia and the West after Crimea's Annexation*, Cambridge: Cambridge University Press.

Rosefielde, Steven and Stefan Hedlund (2008), *Russia since 1980: Wrestling with Westernization*, Cambridge: Cambridge University Press.

Rosefielde, Steven and Ralph W. Pfouts (2013), *Inclusive Economic Theory*, Singapore: World Scientific Publishers.

Techau, Jan (2015), "The Politics of 2 Percent: NATO and the Security Vacuum in Europe," Carnegie Europe, September 2, available at http://carnegieeurope.eu/ 2015/08/31/politics-of-2-percent-nato-and-security-vacuum-in-europe/ifig?mkt_ tok=3RkMMJWWfF9wsRogva3BZKXonjHpfsX56OsvXqGg38431UFwdcjK Pmjr1YUDTcZ0aPyQAgobGp5I5FEIQ7XYTLB2t60MWA%3D%3D.

Schneider, Mark B. (2016), "Russian nuclear weapons policy and programs, the European security crisis, and the threat to NATO," Paper presented to the American Foreign Policy Council Conference on "The Russian Military in the Contemporary Perspective" held May 9–10, in Washington, D.C.

Selten, Reinhard (2002), "What is bounded rationality?" in: Gigerenzer, G. and S. Reinhard (eds.), *Bounded Rationality The Adaptive Toolbox*, Cambridge, MA, MIT Press.

Shlykov, Vitaly (2001), "Chto Pogubilo Sovetskii Soiuz? Amerikanskaia Razvedka o Sovetskiskh Voennykh Raskhodakh" ("What destroyed the Soviet Union? American intelligence estimates of Soviet military expenditures"). *Voenny Vestnik*, 8.

Shlykov, Vitaly (2002), "Russian defense industrial complex after 9-11," Paper presented at Russian Security Policy and the War on Terrorism, U.S. Naval Postgraduate School, Monterey, CA, June 4–5.

Shlykov, Vitaly (2003), "Russian defence industrial complex after 9-11," Paper presented at the Russian Security Policy and the War on Terrorism conference, U.S. Naval Postgraduate School, Monterey, CA, June.

Shlykov, Vitaly (2005), "Globalizatsiia voennoi promyshlennosti-imperativ XXI veka," *Otechestvennye zapiski*, 5, 98–115.

Shlykov, Vitaly (2006a), "Nazad v budushchee, ili Ekonomicheskve uroki kholodnoi voiny," *Rossiia v Global'noe Politike* 4, 2, 26–40.

Shlykov, Vitaly (2006b), "Nevidimaia Mobilizatsii," *Forbes*, 3, 1–5.

Shlykov, Vitaly (2008), "The Military reform and its implications for the modernization of the Russian armed forces," in: Leijonhielm, J. and F. Westerlund (eds.), *Russian Power Structures*, Stockholm: FOI, Swedish Defense research Agency, January, pp. 50–60.

Simon, Herbert (1982), *Models of Bounded Rationality*, Cambridge, MA, MIT Press.

Simon, Herbert (1991), "Bounded rationality and organizational learning," *Organization Science*, 2(1), 125–134.

Solow, Robert (1956), "A contribution to the theory of economic growth," *Quarterly Journal of Economics,* 70, 65–94.

Solow, Robert (1957), "Technical change and the aggregate production function," *Review of Economics and Statistics,* 39, 312–320.

Sprenger, Carsten, (2008), "State-owned enterprises in Russia" Presentation at the OECD Roundtable on Corporate Governance of SOEs," Moscow, October 27, available at https://www.oecd.org/corporate/ca/corporategover-nanceprinciples/42576825.pdf.

Swan, Trevor (1956), "Economic growth and capital accumulation," *Economic Record,* 32, 334–361.

Ullman, Harlan and James Wade (1996), *Shock and Awe: Achieving Rapid Dominance*, National Defense University, Institute for National Security Studies.

Washington Treaty (1949), Article 5, August 24, available at www.nato.int/cps/en/natolive/official_texts_17120.htm.

Zakheim, Roger (2016), "Clinton and trump both offer more of the same for the military," *AEI*, September 2, available at http://www.aei.org/publication/clinton-and-trump-both-offer-more-of-the-same-for-the-military/?utm_source=paramount&utm_medium=email&utm_content=AEITODAY&utm_campaign=090616.

Chapter 7

Military Industrial Potential

Masaaki Kuboniwa

Introduction

A Hollywood action motion picture series "Mission: Impossible," starring Tom Cruise, assumes a fictional, heroic agency named "IMF (the Impossible Mission Force)." This fictional IMF may remind some economists of actual IMF (the International Monetary Fund). In fact, the actual IMF appeared in Moscow, just like the fictional IMF, immediately after the collapse of the Union of Soviet Socialist Republics (USSR). Their mission was to stabilize Russian economy through liberalization of prices, foreign trade, and foreign exchange with structural reforms such as privatization. They implemented a series of measures for this mission just as quickly in 1992, which is called a shock therapy. In 1993, they thought their mission would be completed within a short period, say three months (author's interview with an economist at the IMF Moscow office). However, budget deficits continued. Employing short-term treasurer bonds with high returns to compensate for the deficits induced speculations involving world-leading investment organizations relying on the actual IMF. This finally led to the 1998 financial crisis. Unlike the movie, the actual IMF's mission was not completed, and they did not explain their failures.

Then, Mr Putin appeared as a heroic president, like Tom, armed with a natural gift or oil windfalls due to continuing increase of international oil prices during 1999–2008. These long-run oil shocks or adverse oil shocks were the historical events that we have never experienced. Nevertheless, thanks to oil windfalls, Putin could successfully reorganize or recentralize key industries, including oil and gas, passenger cars, and military production, reimbursing international debts succeeded from the USSR. People could also enjoy the boost of imports based on increasing wages and pensions with the appreciating ruble. Oil bubbles were gone with the Lehman shock in 2008–2009 even though international oil prices revived again after 2010. Again, oil prices largely fell in 2015, and remained at a lower level in 2016. Putin's mission of diversification of the economy to be independent of oil, supported by the second fictional IMF, that is to say, increasing international oil prices, was not completed. Conversely, it may be stated that present-day Russia made its Soviet legacy of oil dependency much stronger.

However, looking at the growth of gross domestic product (GDP) and manufacturing for the period 2011–2015, it is worth investigating whether there was some countervailing power against falling oil prices, including the impact of military outputs and exports, which is expected to be the third IMF. Military goods with strong competitiveness and product differentiation are, indeed, another Soviet legacy for present-day Russia.

Long-Run Relationships between Economic Growth and Oil Prices in Russia

As Kuboniwa (2012) showed, most of the economic variables in Russia have been exposed to changes in international oil prices. We can confirm these facts by an estimation of canonical cointegrating regression (CCR).

Figure 7.1 displays Russia's real GDP growth with the Urals oil prices for the period 1995Q1–2016Q2. Data on real GDP were seasonally adjusted by the so-called Census X-13.

Using CCR for sample (adjusted) 1995Q3–2016Q2, we have the following long-run cointegrating equation:

$$gdp = 0.176oil + C + 0.006t \quad \text{(annualized trend rate of 2.4\%)},$$
$$[3.311] \ [27.73] \ [3.807] \qquad \text{adj. } R^2 = 0.972, \tag{7.1}$$

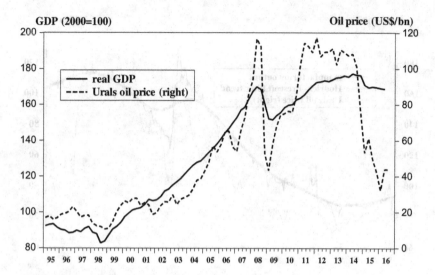

Figure 7.1   Russian GDP Growth and Oil Prices for the Period 1995Q1–2016Q2.

Source: Author's calculations based on Rosstat (CEIC) and Bloomberg–Thomson–Reuters.

where *gdp* = log(real GDP), *oil* = log(oil price), *t* = time trend, *C* = constant, and [.] = *t*-statistic. All coefficients are at the 1% significance level.

Equation (7.1) implies that, in the long run, a 10% increase (decrease) in oil prices would lead to 1.8% growth (contraction) of real GDP. Underlying trend rate, which, in Russia, equals total factor productivity in production function, is about 2.4%.

When we carefully look at recent movements in Figure 7.1, we find that, for the period 2014Q3–2014Q4, Russian growth decline compared to the previous period was only 0.1% despite a large decrease in international oil prices, 25%. Moreover, for the period 2015Q2–2016Q1, the Russian growth decline was merely 0.3% in spite of a marked fall in international oil prices, 47%. This suggests that some factor might have checked further declines of GDP growth as a countervailing power against huge drops in oil prices.

Figure 7.2 shows Russian growth of monthly manufacturing output with international oil prices. Monthly manufacturing output is seasonally adjusted by X-13.

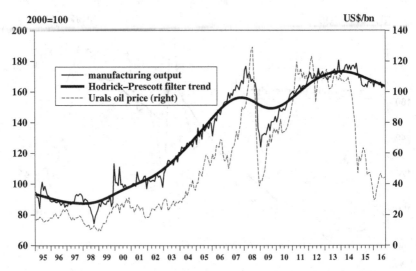

Figure 7.2   Russian Manufacturing Output and Oil Prices for January 1995–September 2016.

Source: Author's calculations based on Rosstat (CEIC) and Bloomberg–Thomson–Reuters.

Employing CCR for sample (adjusted) 1995M03–2016M09, we have the following long-run cointegrating equation:

$$manu = 0.205oil + C + 0.0016t \quad \text{(annualized trend rate of 2.0\%),}$$
$$[7.950] \; [53.66] \; [6.522] \qquad \text{adj. } R^2 = 0.942, \qquad (7.2)$$

where *manu* = log(real manufacturing output). All coefficients are significant at the 1% level.

From Equation (7.2), we see that a 10% increase in international oil prices would result in 2% growth of manufacturing output with underlying trend rate of 2%. Oil elasticity of manufacturing is slightly higher than that of GDP, while the underlying trend of manufacturing is slightly smaller than that of GDP. It is noteworthy to learn that, unlike the Dutch Disease, Russia, suffering the Russian Disease, showed a strong growth under favorable external conditions simply because most of manufacturing goods, except for refined oil and military goods, were not for export but for domestic use.

As demonstrated by recent movements, depicted in Figure 7.2, we also find that, for the period 2014M09–2014M12, seasonally adjusted decrease in the growth rate compared to the previous period was only 1%, despite a large decrease in international oil prices, 36%. Furthermore, for the period 2015M09–2015M12, there was only 0.5% decrease in spite of an oil price decrease of 22%. Since 2013M12, Russian manufacturing output has fallen by 6%, with an oil price drop of 60%. These facts may suggest that manufacturing itself has checked a further slowdown of GDP and that some factors might have bolstered up manufacturing output.

Investigating what this factor is, we find that an industrial sector shows irregular movements for these three years.

As is shown in Table 7.1, "other transport equipment," including ships, aircraft, spacecraft, locomotives, and others, showed remarkable developments in December of 2014 and 2015. As a result, annual average growth rate of this sector in 2014 was 29% higher than overall manufacturing growth, while despite a 55% growth of the sector compared to the previous month in December 2015, its annual average growth showed a

Table 7.1   Growth of "Other Transport Equipment."

	Overall manufacturing	Machinery and equipment	Electrical, electronic and optical equipment	Transport equipment	Other transport equipment (ships, aircraft, space crafts and others)
Monthly growth rate % (to previous month)					
Dec. 2013	1.8	1.4	−1.6	11.3	21.3
Dec. 2014	9.2	29.8	13.3	41.6	50.9
Dec. 2015	8.4	26.3	9.0	41.8	55.2
Annual average growth rate %					
2013	0.6	−3.5	−1.0	2.2	4.8
2014	2.1	−7.9	−3.4	12.7	29.2
2015	−5.4	−13.0	−10.2	−19.8	−17.3

Note: Monthly growth is not seasonally adjusted.
Source: CEIC (Rosstat) database.

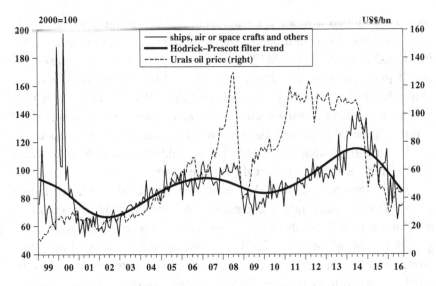

Figure 7.3   Russian "Other Transport Equipment" Output and Oil Prices for January 1999–September 2016.

Source: Author's calculations based on Rosstat (CEIC) and Bloomberg–Thomson–Reuters.

marked decline of 17% overall in 2015. This "other transport equipment" is likely to be dominated by military transport outputs as will be discussed below.

Figure 7.3 demonstrates movements of the "other transport equipment" sector and its trend with oil prices. Growth of this sector was seasonally adjusted by X-13.

Similarly, CCR yields the following cointegrating equation:

$$militr = 0.178oil + C,$$
$$[3.385]\ [18.14] \qquad adj.\ R^2 = 0.275, \tag{7.3}$$

where *militr* = log (real "other transport equipment" output). All coefficients are significant at the 1% significance level. Phillips–Ouliaris test rejects null hypothesis: series are not cointegrated at the 1% significance level. Oil elasticity of Equation (7.3) is similar to that of Equation (7.1), while Equation (7.3) is not supported by a linear trend and its goodness-of-fit is rather poor. Regardless, military transport equipment or "other transport equipment" has also been exposed to changes in oil prices in the long run.

Russian Military Goods in the National Accounting

On April 4, 2016, Rosstat released a new series of overall current GDP at market prices as well as sectoral value-added at basic prices on their website.[1] They made large upward revisions of current GDP and sectoral value-added for the period 2011–2015. When we look at the disaggregated version of data on sectoral value-added, we witness an interesting change that Rosstat reclassified two disaggregated sectors. Russian sector classification code, introduced in 2003, follows an international code (NACE version 1.1). Two of the Russian disaggregated sectors prior to April 4, 2016, were the following: (A1) other transport equipment (code 35) and (A2) other manufacturing (codes 37 + 23.3 + 24.61 + 29.6), where

Code 35:   Manufacture of other transport equipment includes:

   35.1: building and repairing of ships and boats,
   35.2: manufacturing railway and tramway locomotives and rolling stock,
   35.3: manufacturing aircraft and spacecraft,
   35.4: manufacturing motorcycles and bicycles, and
   35.5: manufacturing other transport equipment and not elsewhere classified;

Code 23.3:   processing of nuclear fuel;
Code 24.61: manufacturing explosives (gunpowder etc.);
Code 29.6:   manufacturing weapons and ammunition; and
Code: 37:   recycling.

These are reclassified into following new sectors: B1 (codes 35 + 23.3 + 24.61 + 29.6) and B2 (code 37). Obviously, goods of codes 23.3, 24.61, and 29.6 are military goods. Code 35 can also be considered as military goods even though 10% to 20% of the goods of code 35 are for civilian

---

[1] Cooper (2016) provides an outline of Russian military developments for these 25 years. However, he did not show any new evidence for the military goods in the national accounting.

Table 7.2   Value-added of Russian Military Goods.

	Current GDP or values-added: in current bn rubles				
	2011	2012	2013	2014	2015
Military goods (B1)					
1. Current-value-added	453.9	589.1	658.7	838.9	944.0
2. % real change	—	11.73	7.58	7.61	−4.85
3. Share in GDP %	0.8	0.9	0.9	1.1	1.2
4. Share in manufacturing value-added %	6.6	7.7	8.0	9.1	9.2
5. Contribution to GDP growth rate %	—	0.09	0.07	0.07	−0.05
6. Contribution to manufacturing value-added growth rate %	—	0.78	0.58	0.61	−0.44
7. Current GDP	59,698	66,927	71,017	77,945	80,804
8. % real change	4.26	3.52	1.28	0.71	−3.73
9. Current manufacturing value-added	6,830	7,693	8,282	9,209	10,245
10. % real change	6.28	5.44	4.40	0.58	−5.06
11. Budgetary defense expenditure (% GDP)	2.5	2.7	3.0	3.2	3.9

Note: Value-added is in basic prices, excluding net taxes on products, while GDP is in market prices.

Source: Author's calculations based on Rosstat (www.gks.ru) as of April 4, 2016.

use. Thus, the new classification clearly aggregates the military goods into a single sector (B1), while non-military recycling is classified into another sector (B2). This may imply that Russian authorities recognize the important role and position of the military goods in the national accounting and economic growth and that they would like to reveal the presence of their respectable competitive goods with better product differentiation.

Table 7.2 presents data on the military goods (sector B1) in the newly released national accounting of GDP.

As is shown, the share of value-added of the military goods sector at basic prices in the overall GDP showed increases from 0.8% in 2011 to 1.1% in 2014 and 1.2% in 2015, much larger than the share of automobiles. If we measure its value-added at market prices, the share would be

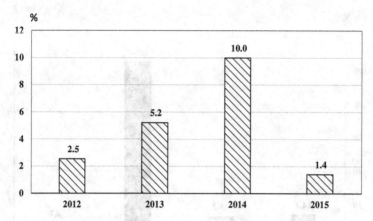

Figure 7.4   Share of Military Goods Contribution in GDP Growth Rate (%).

Source: Author's calculation based on data of Rosstat website as of April 4, 2016.

over 2%. The share in overall manufacturing value-added at basic prices amounted to 7% in 2011 and increased to 9% in 2014 and 2015. The military goods value-added in real terms showed rather high growth from 12% to 8% for the period 2012–2014 and showed a contraction of 5% in 2015.

Figure 7.4 demonstrates the share of the military goods value-added growth contribution in the overall GDP growth, while Figure 7.5 shows that the share of the military goods value-added growth contribution in the overall manufacturing value-added growth.

Figure 7.4 shows that the military goods contribution share in GDP growth increased from 2.5% in 2012 and, indeed, to a large contribution of 10% in 2014. In 2015, its contribution to GDP contraction was rather small, 1.4%. Figure 7.5 demonstrates large contributions of the military goods sector to overall manufacturing. The growth rate of 0.6% of manufacturing value-added in 2014 was entirely brought about by the military goods sector. However, the military goods contribution to the contraction of 5% of manufacturing in 2015 was not so large. The slowdown of GDP and manufacturing growth was checked by the military goods expansion, while their further slowdown could not be bolstered up.

Table 7.3 shows Russia's defense revenue derived from defense revenues of Russian military enterprises ranked in Defense News' world top 100 military enterprises.

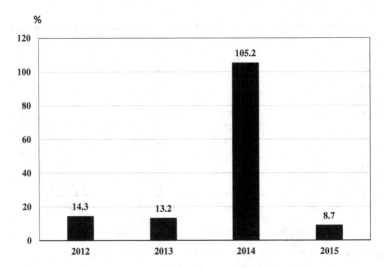

Figure 7.5   Share of Military Goods Contribution in Growth Rate of Manufacturing Value-Added (%).

Source: Author's calculation based on data of Rosstat website as of April 4, 2016.

Table 7.3   Russia's Defense Revenue.

	2011	2012	2013	2014	2015
Defense revenue in million US$ of which:	12,626	15,797	21,404	24,054	18,866
Almaz-Antey	3,552	5,754	8,326	9,210	6,966
Russian Helicopters	2,644	3,489	3,406	3,960	3,194
Defense revenue % GDP	0.6	0.7	1.0	1.2	1.4
Real growth rate %					
Defense revenue of which:	—	13.1	22.2	12.1	5.3
Almaz-Antey	—	46.4	43.7	12.7	1.5
Russian Helicopters	—	19.2	−3.0	18.4	8.3
Common deflator %	—	16.2	3.9	18.4	18.3

Note: Concern Radioelectronic Technologies' revenue (US$1,618) is excluded in this table for in 2015 because of lack of data of this company in 2014.

Sources: Current defense revenue: Defense News World Top 100 military enterprises for 2013–2016 (http://people.defensenews.com/top-100/).
Common deflator: Author's calculation from Rosstat data on military goods for 2011–2015.
Annual growth rate: Author's calculation from current revenue and deflator.

Table 7.4   Russian Military Exports.

	2010	2011	2012	2013	2014	2015
Military exports in billion US$	8.7	10.7	12.9	13.2	13.2	14.5
% in total exports	2.0	1.9	2.2	2.2	2.4	3.7
% in total GDP	0.6	0.5	0.6	0.6	0.6	1.1

Note: Exports for 2010–2012 are Rosoboronexport's exports.

Sources: Reuters, World News, March 29, 2016 (www.reuters.com) (http://www.reuters.com/article/us-russia-arms-idUSKCN0WV1TB); (http://sputniknews.com/trend/russian_arms_export/); (http://www.linkedin.com/pluse/russian-defence-indusrty-enjoys-bumper-year-despite-steve-macvi car?articleId=8389760618103443891#comments-8389760618103443831&trk=sushitopicposts guest).

"Revenue" in Table 7.3 may mean sales which are much larger than value-added. However, the trend of GDP share in Table 7.3 well corresponds to data in Table 7.2. According to our estimates, the growth rate of the defense revenue for 2012–2014 is much larger than that of the military goods value-added in Table 7.2. In 2015, the defense revenue might have shown positive growth.

Russian major defense enterprises are export-oriented for Asia (India, China, etc.), Latin America, and Africa. Therefore, some watchers saw Russian defense industry's bumper years, despite sanctions and oil price falls.

Table 7.4 shows Russian military exports. As can be seen, Russian military goods exports in current US dollar terms increased for the period 2010–2015. If these figures reflect the actual situation of the Russian military industry, the share of the military goods value-added at market prices would be much larger than that shown in Table 7.2, say higher than 2%. Some fragmentary information shown here suggests some possibility that the Russian military industry is still growing despite falling oil prices. Needless to say, as Federal budget revenue heavily depends on oil prices, a reduction in defense spending is today's task for Mr Putin. In this context, state orders (*goszakaz*) for military goods cannot be raised under falling oil prices. Mr Putin has to expect only developments in military exports with keeping Russian own procurements for local conflicts. Unless some countries such as China need a large amount of procurements from Russia at non-subsidized prices for their local conflicts,

Russia cannot expect Japanese or Taiwanese experiences supported by booming procurements for Korean War or Vietnamese War. Therefore, it is rather difficult to say that the military expansion can be IMF for V-shaped economic growth under falling international oil prices. The Mission is unlikely to be completed without rising oil prices.

Concluding Remarks

I studied movements of the military goods sector and its impact on growth of GDP and manufacturing. I demonstrated that the military expansion strongly checked further growth retardation in Russia for 2012–2014, while it was likely to insufficiently bolster up Russia's growth in 2015. Lack of the 2011 benchmark disaggregated input–output system with supplementary tables for distribution margins and net taxes on products, at this moment, it is rather difficult to capture the whole picture of the military goods sector. For example, we do not know whether the foreign trade revenues of the military giant, *Rosoboronexport* under the State Corporation *ROSTEC*, monopolizing defense exports, are recorded as trade margins or the military production sector's value-added. We do not know the export tax system of the military goods, either. As in the case of GDP of the oil and gas sector, we should investigate the full size of GDP of the military goods using disaggregated input–output data with supplementary tables. Regardless, Putin's plan for the structural reform for exports, raising machinery export share up to more than 20% in 2020, is insufficiently implemented only in the defense industry. However, unlike Toyota or Apple, the defense industry cannot involve massive consumers all over the world. Therefore, the military expansion would not finalize its mission of V-shaped recovery of the Russian economy. The Mission will be not completed.

References

Cooper, J. (2016), "The military dimension of a more militant Russia," *Russian Journal of Economics*, 2, 129–145.

Kuboniwa, M. (2012), "Diagnosing the 'Russian disease': Growth and structure of the Russian economy," *Comparative Economic Studies*, 54(1), 121–148.

Chapter 8

Macroeconomic Challenges

Torbjörn Becker

Introduction

This chapter makes two simple but important points, first, Russia's oil addiction runs much deeper than most understand, and second, close ties with the European Union (EU) will remain Russia's best hope to change this for the foreseeable future.

Although Russia's oil dependence is the topic of many discussions of the Russian economy, few understand just how deep this runs and what it means to the income of Russia both in the short and the long term.[1] This chapter will show how striking the correlation between international oil prices and the income of Russia is. This correlation goes far beyond what can be expected from sectoral statistics or regular growth accounting and should once and for all lay to rest any claims that "oil" is not so important for the economic development of Russia.

Similarly, the power of economic geography or strength that countries can derive from having prosperous neighbors should not be underestimated.[2] Russia is of course an enormous country with many

---

[1]Becker (2014) provides some quantitative estimates on the relationship that are less detailed than what is presented later on in this chapter. Cf. Rosefielde (2016).

[2]There is a long list of papers that estimate and theoretically explain how and why gravity models, where distance, size, and development of markets, are important for bilateral trade

neighbors, but the most accessible and prosperous of the markets in their neighborhood are still the countries that are part of the EU (despite its inability to deal with the aftermath of the financial crisis and even after the United Kingdom leaves the Union).[3] Instead of making these countries part of a problem that includes sanctions and poor political and business relations, Russia need to rethink its approach towards the EU. This may be hard for a military superpower, but should be easy for any policymaker focused on economic prosperity.

The chapter first details exactly how important international oil prices are for the economic fate of Russia. The subsections in the first part deal with how difficulties in forecasting oil prices spill over to forecasts of Russian income; if Russia would be better off without oil; and how Russian policymakers learnt an important lesson on how to deal with falling oil prices in the global financial crisis in 2008/2009. The chapter then describes the strong and important economic ties that exist between Russia and the EU despite recent sanctions before moving on to what needs to be done in the short and longer term to secure economic growth in Russia moving forward. Finally, there are some concluding remarks that sum up the discussion in the chapter.

Russia's Macroeconomic Legacy

Russia's macroeconomic performance since the breakup of the Soviet Union in 1991 has had several ups and downs, but overall, per capita income has grown significantly. There are many descriptions of what caused the ups and downs as well as the increase in income, ranging from the effects of shock therapy to the political leadership or the pace of economic reforms in general.[4] Although they are all important factors, there is a much simpler "model" of what has been behind much of the ups and downs and the significant increases in income — the rise and volatility of

---

and investments, see, for example, Anderson (2010) or Kleinert and Toubal (2010). Becker (2016) takes a closer look at the investments between Sweden and Russia.
[3] Becker (2015) details the trade links between Russia and the EU.
[4] For different accounts of Russia's economic development, see, for example, Rosefielde (2007), Ofer (2010), Popov (2010), or Åslund (2012).

international oil prices. Most scholars, analysts, and policymakers would acknowledge that "oil" plays an important role in Russia's economic development. However, not everyone understands the truly fundamental role *international* oil *prices* have had in explaining both short-term fluctuations and long-term growth in income. The fact that it is international oil prices rather than Russian decisions on how much oil to produce and sell is extremely important since it means that the fate of the Russian economy is in the hands of the international oil market rather than Russian policymakers (regardless of whether or not they renationalize Russian oil companies).

A common argument against the importance of "oil" for the Russian economy is that only around 10% or so of real activity is related to the oil industry and therefore it simply cannot be so important. This argument has several shortcomings; first, the purely statistical issue of measuring the oil sector is not trivial, since it will always involve more or less arbitrary boundaries between sectors; are the IT services used in the oil sector recorded in the IT sector or the oil sector; are the houses built to accommodate oil workers part of the real estate sector or the oil sector and so on. This problem of boundaries between sectors is neither unique to the oil sector nor to Russia, but the point is that simple sector statistics are not always useful for understanding macroeconomic dynamics, and in the case of Russia and its oil sector statistics, it is extremely misleading.

The world's simplest macro "model"?

A central hypothesis in this chapter is that international oil prices have governed Russia's macroeconomic performance for a long time. This hypothesis can be tested empirically. In this section, we will explore just how far this hypothesis takes us in understanding Russian income dynamics over the last couple of decades. An even longer-term hypothesis would be that international oil price fluctuations were also a key determinant of the fate of the Soviet Union, but this will not be considered here.[5]

Figure 8.1 provides the first evidence of the strong correlation between international oil prices and Russian incomes measured both in

---

[5] See, for example, Gaidar (2010).

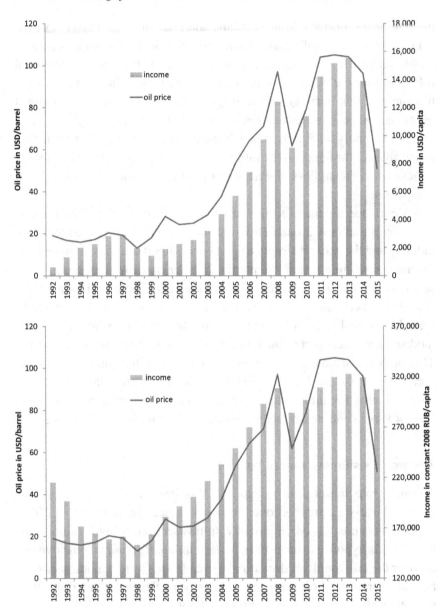

Figure 8.1   Oil Prices and Gross Domestic Product (GDP) Per Capita.

Source: International Monetary Fund (IMF) (2016a).

terms of current US dollars and constant (2008) rubles. For the readers who prefer income measured in purchasing power parity (PPP) terms, it can be noted that such a chart would be somewhere in between the two versions shown, but closer to the 2008 RUB chart than the US dollar chart. The extremely close comovement between dollar income and international oil price is of course due to both changes in real ruble incomes and the exchange rate between the ruble and the dollar. The latter may not sound too important to readers who live in countries that have their own stable convertible currencies, but for many Russian citizens, dollar income was what mattered for a long time (and for some, still is).

The variables shown in Figure 8.1 have strong trends, and we can suspect that they are not stationary from a statistical point of view. Formal unit root tests of the variables cannot reject the null hypothesis of a unit root in all of the plotted series. Furthermore, statistical tests indicate that oil prices and income measured in US dollars are cointegrated, while oil prices and real ruble income are not.[6] The detailed account of these more technical time series considerations are omitted here but we use this insight in the statistical analysis that follows.

Table 8.1 contains descriptive statistics of three series: international oil prices, Russian income measured in US dollars, and Russian income measured in constant 2008 rubles. The statistics for the series are shown in levels, first differences and growth rates, where the two latter are common transformations used when running regressions on time series that are not stationary in levels. The first observation from Table 8.1 is how volatile oil prices were between 1992 and 2015, ranging from a low of US\$13 per barrel to US\$105 per barrel. This volatility can also be seen in income measured both in US dollar and real ruble terms. Although average income measured in levels, differences, and growth rates for both dollar and rubles have been higher in 2000–2015 compared with 1992–2015 (with one exception), volatility has remained high in both the longer and shorter samples.

Although we could estimate vector error correction models with a cointegration relationship, we settle for simple bivariate ordinary least square regressions on first differences or percent growth rates given the

---

[6]The tests are based on Johansen (1991).

Table 8.1   Descriptive Statistics on Oil Price and Income.

	Levels			First differences			Percent growth rates		
	oil price	USD income	2008 RUB income	oil price	USD income	2008 RUB income	oil price	USD income	2008 RUB income
1992–2015									
min	13.1	614	153,239	-45.5	-4,848	-25,093	-47.2	-34.7	-12.8
max	105.0	15,531	322,599	25.9	2,826	23,037	57.0	115.0	10.5
average	48.8	6,379	236,968	1.4	367	4,006	7.8	16.6	1.8
median	33.3	3,783	224,797	1.3	563	10,174	7.9	24.6	4.2
st. dev.	33.4	5,095	62,234	16.0	1,782	14,337	26.3	32.1	6.4
2000–2015									
min	24.3	1,893	180,814	-45.5	-4,818	-24,330	-47.2	-34.7	-7.9
max	105.0	15,531	322,599	25.9	2,826	23,037	57.0	37.9	10.5
average	64.4	8,612	268,863	2.1	477	8,977	10.6	14.6	4.1
median	63.0	9,094	288,578	5.4	794	12,516	13.2	24.7	5.1
st. dev.	30.4	4,854	49,689	19.2	2,110	12,556	28.0	21.8	4.9

Source: Author's calculations based on IMF (2016a) data.

limited number of observations (but still acknowledging the non-stationarity of the series in levels). This "model" lacks many standard variables that can be included in growth regressions, but again, the limited number of observations is a good reason to not add a long list of explanatory variables that may or may not be exogenous. The international oil price is however an exogenous variable, and the direction of causality is not an issue in the regressions presented below. Nevertheless, the regression results should only be regarded as a way to provide relatively reasonable quantifications of the relationships between Russian income and international oil prices that we see in Figure 8.1 and not interpreted as a full-fledged macro-model of Russia.

Table 8.2 shows one-variable regressions of US dollar or 2008 ruble income on international oil prices in first differences and growth rates for the full sample (1993–2015) and the more recent sample (2000–2015). The more recent sample has the advantage of omitting the rather unstable initial part of Russia's transition process and also coincides

Table 8.2   One-Variable Regressions of Income on Oil Price.

Dep. Vars.	First differences		Percent growth rate	
	USD income	2008 RUB income	USD income	2008 RUB income
1993–2015				
oil price (same trans.)	105.03**	596.68**	0.4311*	0.1653**
constant	221.96*	3182.44	13.20*	0.4646
Adj. *R*-sq	0.88	0.42	0.08	0.43
# Obs	23	23	23	23
2000–2015				
oil price (same trans.)	105.72**	553.27**	0.6862*	0.1399**
constant	260.23	7842.61**	7.32**	2.64**
Adj. *R*-sq	0.92	0.69	0.77	0.62
# Obs	16	16	16	16

Notes: * indicates statistical significance at 10% level.
** indicates statistical significance at 1% level.
Source: Author's regressions based on IMF (2016a) data.

with the current political leadership's tenure in the highest political offices. Although the regression coefficients based on growth rates are easier to interpret, it does not necessarily produce the most accurate or powerful relationships from a statistical point of view, but the difference in explanatory power between the model of first differences and growth rates is not substantial. Instead, all the regressions except one generate high or very high adjusted R-squares and the coefficients on changes in international oil prices are significant at the 1% level in all but one regression for which the R-square is also low. This is the regression using percent growth rates and US dollar income, and the result is due to a very large outlier in the first year of the regression.

In short, changes in international oil prices explain between one-half and two-thirds of the variation in income changes or growth. In the extreme case of first differences of US dollar income, the adjusted R-square is over 90%, i.e., less than 10% of the variation in dollar income is left unexplained once changes in international oil prices are included in this one-variable regression. This is nothing short of a remarkable one-variable macro "model" for any country or time period.

Definitely, factors other than international oil prices impact Russian income growth, but it is undeniable that no other single factor would come close to the importance oil prices has had on economic growth over the last decades. One could be tempted to say that this strong relationship between income and oil prices means that Russia has a very simple model at hand to forecast its economic future, but as we will see in the next section, this is not the case.

Or not so simple?

Although the estimated macro "model" only includes one variable, the variance in international oil prices implies that growth forecasts also have very large variances. In other words, a significant share of Russia's macroeconomic volatility comes from oil prices, and so Russian economic policymakers are "hostage" to the international oil market to a very substantial degree when they make plans for their own economy. Of course, most modern, open economies are subject to external shocks, but the concentrated exports of a single set of commodities with very volatile prices makes the

Russian situation particularly difficult. Russian policymakers are of course not unaware of this situation, and talks of diversification have been around forever in Russia, and a few words on this will come later in this chapter.

Figure 8.2 illustrates the extent to which policymakers are in the hands of international oil markets when making their forecast of the Russian economy. In particular, the scatter plots show the IMF's WEO forecasts of oil prices and real growth of Russian GDP. The two top panels show the one-year ahead forecast and the bottom panels show the two-year ahead forecasts. Data are available since 1999, and the one-year ahead forecast is thus available for 16 years. However, the two-year ahead forecasts are only available for six years, but they are still included here as an illustration that, if anything, the relationship grows stronger with the forecast horizon. The scatterplots all indicate the importance of international oil prices for Russian income dynamics. Between 65% and 95% of all the forecast errors of Russian GDP can be derived from changed forecasts of international oil prices. Even if policymakers know that oil prices are important for the Russian economy, these are staggering numbers that imply that Russian policymakers have not really been in charge of their country's economic fate for a long time. This does not automatically imply that Russia would have been better off without oil and some counterfactuals are simulated below to illustrate this point.[7]

Russia without oil-driven growth

In addition to the above discussion of the volatility international oil price fluctuations bring to the forecasts and outcomes of Russian income, there is a large amount of literature on the so-called natural resource curse.[8] In short, the presence of natural resources and the rents they provide may prevent countries (read political leaders or special interests) from developing proper institutions and strategies that would allow non-extractive parts of the economy to prosper because this could make it harder to control

---

[7] Rosefielde (2016, 2017).

[8] Sachs and Warner (2001) discuss how natural resources crowd out other exports and Boschini *et al.* (2007) show how institutional quality interact with different types of natural resources to sometimes reverse the curse.

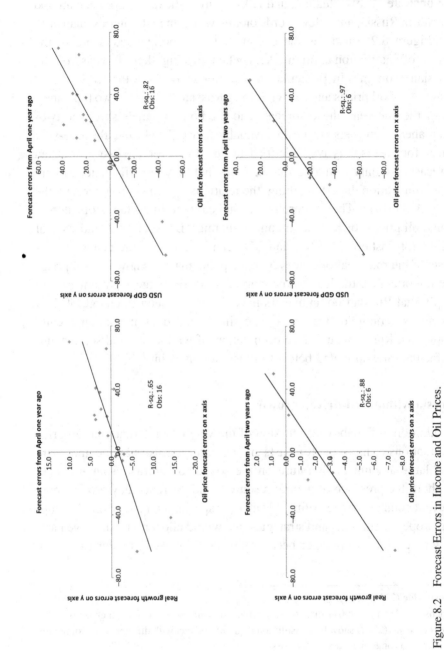

Figure 8.2   Forecast Errors in Income and Oil Prices.

Source: Author's calculations based on IMF (2016b), World Economic Outlook (WEO) data from all vintages from April 1999 to April 2016.

resource rents. The rigidity impedes institutional development and income growth by transforming what should be a blessing into a curse.

We do not have a counterfactual to what Russia's growth would have been without oil or how that would have generated a different set of institutions, economic policies, or growth over the past couple of decades. However, we can run alternative growth scenarios for the past 15 years by using one of the models estimated above and by using other countries' growth experiences over the same time period to illustrate how Russian income would have developed with different growth paths. Since we know that there is a significant difference in the growth trajectories for US dollars and real (2008) ruble income, we do the same exercise based on both real growth in domestic currency terms and in terms of US dollars.

There are two groups of countries that seem relevant as the basis for alternative Russian growth scenarios. First, we have the set of successful transition countries that like Russia emerged after the collapse of communism and the breakup of the Soviet Union. This group of countries is here illustrated by the Polish and Lithuanian growth experience — Poland being a slower and steady example and Lithuania a high-growth, high-volatility example among the transition countries in Eastern Europe. Second, we have the BRIC countries that Russia is often bunched together with for the simple reason that they are the four largest countries that are not among the high-income group of countries and despite the fact that the BRIC countries differ in many other important dimensions, including per capita GDP. This latter note is particularly important if we believe in catch-up growth or income convergence.

Figure 8.3 provides the counterfactual simulations of how Russian real ruble and US dollar income would have developed if we apply the path of growth rates of the countries mentioned above to the common starting point of Russia in the year 2000. In addition to the different countries, the left panel also includes the prediction generated by the models estimated in Table 8.2 if we take out the impact of changes in oil prices. This simply amounts to using the estimated constants as the yearly growth rate. For the simulation of real ruble income, we use the real growth rates of the respective countries and regression and similarly for US dollar growth rates. It is important to understand that real domestic currency and US dollar growth rates differ quite significantly for the countries, and it

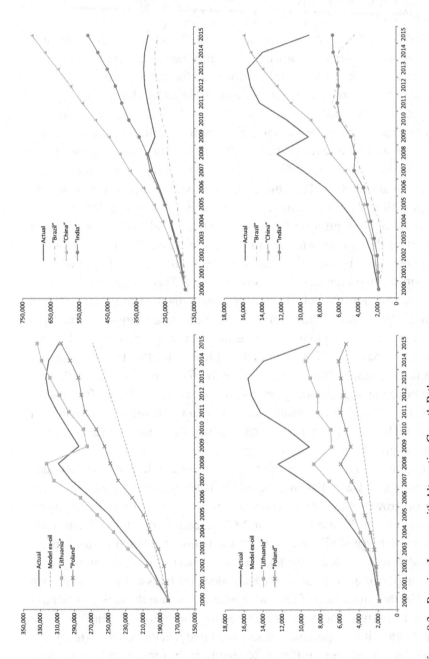

Figure 8.3   Russian Income with Alternative Growth Paths.

Source: Author's calculation based on IMF (2016a).

highlights the importance of exchange rate policies in connection with growth discussions.

In the top left panel, Russia's actual real ruble income is compared to the hypothetical cases of Lithuanian and Polish growth as well as the model-predicted growth had oil prices not changed over the period. It is rather striking how similar Russia's actual growth path is to the simulated Lithuanian counterfactual, with very strong growth prior to 2008, then the collapse at the time of the global financial crisis, and subsequent return to more modest growth. This is in stark contrast to the Polish counterfactual, where the slow initial growth picks up and remains steady over the 2008/2009 years. In 2015, the Polish tortoise caught up with the Russian hare and basically ended up in a dead race, while the Lithuanian high-growth, high-volatility path came in first place. The Russian model counterfactual without changes in oil prices generates a growth rate that (of course) is steady but too slow to match the other growth paths.

Turning to the same countries but looking at US dollar income in the lower left panel of Figure 8.3, the effect of exchange rates becomes very evident. Russia experienced a much higher growth path until 2013 when income in US dollar terms was dramatically higher than it would have been for the other growth paths. Then the ruble halved its value relative to the US dollar, and in a very short time period, this growth path was only marginally above the Lithuanian counterfactual (while still well ahead of the income level that would have resulted with Polish US dollar growth or the model without oil price changes).

In the right-hand panels of Figure 8.3 we turn to counterfactuals based on Russia's BRIC peers. Here the importance of exchange rates and what income to focus on becomes even starker. Looking first at real ruble income, had Russia experienced Chinese growth rates over the period, real incomes would have been 130% higher than the actual Russian real income level in 2015, while Indian growth would have led to 68% higher income in 2015. Only the other natural resource-rich BRIC country, Brazil, falls behind in income.

However, comparing how US dollar income develops paints a very different picture. According to this metric, Russia outpaced all the other BRIC countries, including China, through 2013, but was overtaken by China in 2014 and 2015 when the ruble exchange rate plummeted. It is interesting to note how steady the Chinese growth rate is compared to the other BRIC countries both in terms of real local currency and US dollar.

This comparison of different counterfactual growth paths leads to a number of conclusions. First, the currency used when comparing income and growth paths matters much more than most would expect. When income levels in US dollars are compared, only China is ahead of Russia in 2015, but for most of the period, Russia was the leader of the pack. Focusing instead on real domestic currency incomes, Russia is a long way behind the Chinese and Indian growth experience and is more or less at par with the steady but not so fast growing Polish experience. The second observation is that the even slower and steadier model without changes in oil prices is far behind the actual Russian income level. In other words, the volatility in income that changes in oil prices bring has at least generated a higher average growth rate, so there has been some sort of reward for the added uncertainty. This is of course a result of looking at a period when oil prices on average have increased, which has not always been the case and is a very uncertain proposition for the long run given the shift to other energy sources.

In short, this exercise suggests that it is far from clear that Russia would have been better off in terms of income without its oil in the past couple of decades. At the same time, it also points to the vital role proper exchange rate management has in mitigating the international oil price-induced volatility on real income. Russia has two recent falls in real income with rather different management of the exchange rate that will serve to illustrate this further in the next section.

Crisis management 2008/2009 versus 2014/2015

Figure 8.4 summarizes how the key macrovariables developed from January 2008 to December 2009 and contrast this with how they moved in the same months of 2014 and 2015. It is clear that Russian policymakers learned important lessons on how to manage the exchange rate in the 2008/2009 crisis. This was of great importance in the more recent downturn. The key policy difference between the two recent crises was to let the exchange rate adjust more rapidly and in line with market

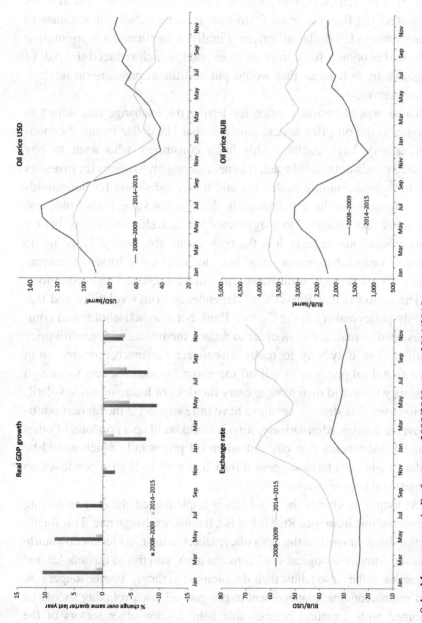

Figure 8.4 Macroeconomic Performance 2008/2009 versus 2014/2015.

Source: Author's calculations based on CBR (2016) and IMF (2016a) data.

forces to keep international oil prices measured in rubles more or less constant. This helped preserve international reserves at the Central Bank and protect the fiscal account from deteriorating rapidly in response to a sharp drop in US dollar oil prices. Finally, it facilitated a reorientation of the real economy from imports to exports, which reduced the risk of a negative trade balance that would put additional pressure on international reserves.

There was of course a price for letting the exchange rate adjust in response to the oil price shock, which is that US dollar incomes experienced a very large decline. This hurts consumers who want to buy imported goods or travel abroad, it generates negative returns for investors who do their accounting in dollars, and it increases costs for households and companies that have borrowed in dollars. For some households and companies, this amounted to a significant loss in welfare or profits, but for the macroeconomy at large it is the only sustainable policy. Propping up an overvalued exchange rate could have led to massive losses of international reserves at the Central Bank and a more depressed real economy.

The lesson is that Russia's oil dependence brings volatility and that not only policymakers at the Central Bank but also households and companies need to realize this in order to reduce the impact of future oil price volatility. The only way to really disconnect the macroeconomy from international oil prices is to sell off the natural resource assets to foreign investors who would then have to carry the risks of future oil price volatility. However, this strategy seems to have little support at the highest political level in Russia. Alternatively, Russia could build up a portfolio of other financial instruments that pay out when oil prices fall, which would be similar to what has been suggested for Chile with its high dependence on international copper prices.

As long as neither of these policies is implemented, the only remaining macroeconomic insurance Russia has is a flexible exchange rate. This finally seems to have dawned on the key policymakers in the most recent downturn. However, some pedagogical work remains to explain this to households and companies so they also adjust their decisions accordingly. For the longer run, good macroeconomic management to mitigate oil price volatility should be combined with structural policies that help develop other sectors of the economy. In short, this is the old diversification solution to the problem, and here the EU can play a positive role if Russia lets it. And the economic links and importance of the EU is the topic of the next section.

Why EU Links are Important for Russia

Geography is an important determinant of trade and investment flows between countries. Moreover, large markets tend to generate more flows than smaller ones. These are some of the relatively straightforward conclusions from standard gravity models that are used to predict both trade and investment flows. This is also the case for Russia that has a very large share of its trade with the countries that make up the EU. EU countries are also home to the major foreign investors in Russia, although investment data are complicated to interpret for reasons that we will discuss later. If Russia is serious about diversifying its economy away from oil, the EU offers both the prospect of a future market for new Russian exports as well as a source of investments that can bring both money and knowledge that can be used to develop these new export goods.

Trade patterns

Figure 8.5 shows how the destination and source of Russian exports and imports have changed over the past three years. The EU's position as Russia's major trading partner is unthreatened despite significant declines in the share of exports and imports to and from the EU that has come with the different sanctions both the EU and Russia have introduced. In 2013, the EU accounted for 54% of exports and 43% of imports to Russia, and two years later this was down to 48% and 38%, respectively. This is still well ahead of China that accounted for 19% of imports and only 8% of exports in 2015, or the Commonwealth of Independent States (CIS) countries that together accounted for around 12% of both imports and exports. Russian trade with the United States and Japan in contrast only ranges from 2% to 6% of imports and exports.

Figure 8.5 also lays bare the massive drop in trade that Russia experienced from 2013 to 2015 due to the fall in oil prices (that affected

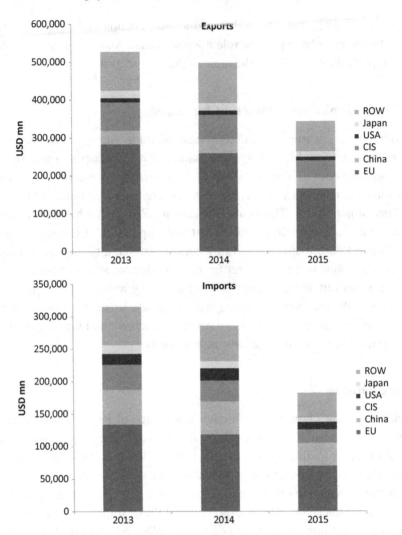

Figure 8.5   Russian Trade by Country.

Source: Author's calculations based on IMF (2016c).

exports), massive currency depreciation (that reduced imports), and sanctions. From 2013 to 2015, total exports declined by 35% and imports by 42%. Since the sanctions between Russia and the EU happened at the same time as the general macroshock of falling oil prices, it is hard to disentangle the more precise effect sanctions have had on trade, but the reduced share of trade with the EU indicates that sanctions have mattered, but Russia and the EU are far from shutting down trade completely.

However, when we look more closely at how much exports and imports have declined with different trading partners, it is noteworthy that the decline in trade with EU is basically matched by the decline in trade with CIS countries. This suggests that the trading partners' own macroeconomic situation also contributes to the changes in trade with Russia, and some of the decline in trade with the EU can be the result of the macroeconomic difficulties some EU countries have experienced. This comes back to the value of having prosperous neighbors when geography matters to trade. A stagnant EU is not in the interest of Russia any more than a stagnant Russia is of interest to the EU from an economic perspective or the welfare of the citizens both in Russia and the EU.

Capital flows, foreign direct investment, and knowledge transfers

The other important economic connection between the EU and Russia is in terms of capital flows and investments. During the years of high and ever-increasing oil prices, Russia did not really need extra inflows of foreign exchange, but there was still ample scope to import ideas and know-how to support more wide-ranging economic development. Now, with relatively low oil price and an even stronger need to find new products to export to diversify the economy, attracting foreign investments should be high on the agenda for Russian policymakers. Figure 8.6 shows that EU countries have been the prime source of foreign investments in Russia, although the data on the source of investments are of mixed quality since much of international capital flows go through tax havens. We know that Russian companies and individuals often place assets in tax havens in general and Cyprus in particular. It is therefore no surprise that Cyprus is the country with the largest recorded foreign direct investment (FDI) stock in Russia. However, the flows from Cyprus are not likely to come with much foreign know-how, but simply bring back Russian money that has been parked outside the country until a suitable investment opportunity has appeared. Much of the investment from the Netherlands can

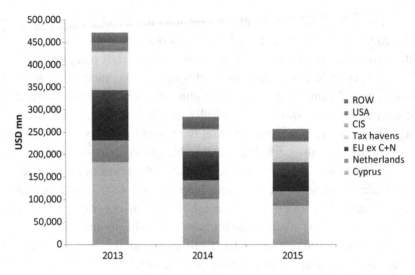

Figure 8.6   Source Countries of FDI Stock in Russia.
Source: Author's calculations based on CBR (2016).

also be expected to be a result of using offshore havens, and there is also a large part that comes from what we all think of as tax havens outside of the EU. When these flows are parsed, EU countries emerge as the largest foreign investors in Russia, often in the form of mid-sized German companies or multinationals. These types of investments can bring both new technologies and management practices with the money to the Russian market and help modernize the economy and make it more competitive on international markets.

Russian companies and individuals also make investments abroad as can be seen in Figure 8.7. The motives for outward FDI from Russia has been discussed by Liuhto (2015) and Fortescue and Hanson (2015). Tax havens seem to also dominate the list of destinations for such flows. Nevertheless, the haven countries are in many cases EU countries and destinations Russian investors trust with their money. If sanctions and other policies make economic transactions more uncertain for Russian investors, this carries a cost to all investors who want to do business in Russia. Although it is hard to quantify the costs associated with this uncertainty, we can be sure that the mere discussion of sanctions contributed to an increase in uncertainty for any transaction that involved Russian entities.

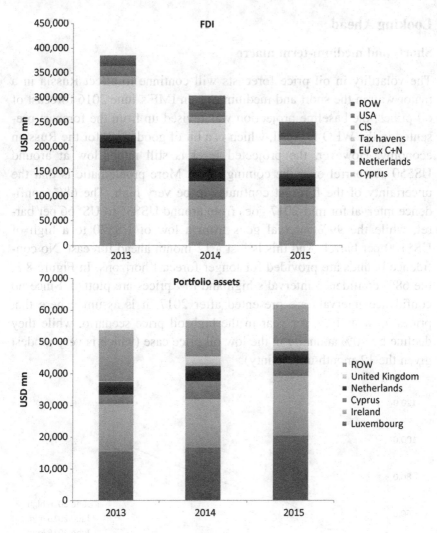

Figure 8.7   Russia's Foreign Investment Stocks Abroad.

Source: Author's calculations based on CBR (2016).

Recorded outward FDI stocks of around US$250 billion in 2015 are significantly higher than the 60 billion or so stock of portfolio assets, but there is a stark difference in trends between 2013 and 2015; FDI stocks have declined by 35%, while portfolio assets have increased by 15%. The reason is not obvious, but it could possibly be the case that the increased uncertainty has led to a shift to assets that are easier to move on short notice.

Looking Ahead

Short- and medium-term macro

The volatility in oil price forecasts will continue to affect Russia in a major way in the short and medium run. In IMF's June 2016 forecast of oil prices, the baseline projection was revised up from the forecast presented in the WEO in April, which is a bit of good news for the Russian economy. However, the projected level is still rather low at around US$50 per barrel over the coming years. More problematic is that the uncertainty of the forecast continues to be very high. The 68% confidence interval for mid-2017 goes from around US$35 to US$66 per barrel, while the 99% interval goes from a low of US$20 to a high of US$100 per barrel. And this is just a 12-month ahead forecast. No confidence bounds are provided for longer forecast horizons. In Figure 8.8, the 68% confidence interval's high and low prices are plotted. Since no confidence intervals are presented after 2017, it is assumed here that prices grow at 10% per year in the high oil price scenario, while they decline by 10% annually in the low oil price case (which is very modest given the 12-month uncertainty).

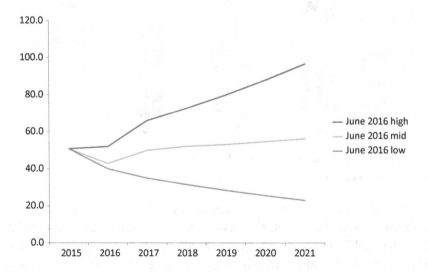

Figure 8.8   Oil Price Forecast for Mid-2016.

Source: Author's calculations based on IMF (2016a).

The different oil price paths can be translated into real GDP growth projections by using the estimates of the one-variable model presented in Table 8.2 based on growth rates of real income and oil prices over the past 16 years. The three oil price paths thus generate three paths for real income as is shown in Figure 8.9.

None of these scenarios imply that the Russian economy implodes, but the income level is 18% lower in the low oil price scenario compared to the high oil price scenario. In the low oil price scenario, the real GDP growth rates is around 1%, while the high oil price scenario leads to growth of a bit more than 4% per year. The 3% difference in average growth adds up to a cumulative 18% difference by 2021. To put this in perspective, an 18% increase in PPP income today would correspond to Russia moving up from ranking 48th in international income rankings to match Slovakia in 39th place, while an 18% drop would move Russia down to Romania (59th place).

These scenarios do not include the very sharp swings in oil prices we have seen over the past decade, and it will be important that Russian policymakers stay the course on flexible exchange rates in the event of future gyrations of oil prices. The political leadership should back this

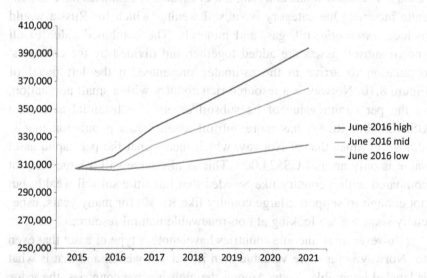

Figure 8.9 Model Forecast of Real Income in 2008 Ruble.
Source: Author's calculations based on IMF (2016a).

policy as well and educated households and companies should not expect to be saved every time the exchange rate moves in an unfavorable direction.

A flexible exchange rate is of course not a way to completely offset the real effects of low oil prices, and the government should make sure that fiscal priorities are toward spending that help growth both in the short and long run. This would suggest that spending on human capital (education, research, and health) rather than military spending should be protected in times of declining real revenues. These short-run considerations should be complemented by structural reforms that generate long-term growth, and some possible areas are discussed below.

Long-term structural reforms needed

Russia's natural resources have been an important growth driver for a long time and contribute significantly to the country's wealth. However, Russia's natural resource wealth is in itself not enough for Russia to become a high-income country. Figure 8.10 shows some of the sources of wealth different countries possess as compiled by the World Bank (2011). The study looks at a long list of resources countries have to generate income. One category is subsoil wealth, which for Russia would include, *inter alia*, oil, gas, and minerals. The combined value of all known subsoil assets are added together and divided by the countries' population to arrive at the estimates presented in the left panel of Figure 8.10. Norway is a resource-rich country with a small population, so the per capita value of its subsoil assets is substantial at around US$100,000. Russia has more subsoil assets but a population that is almost 30 times that of Norway, which means that the per capita asset value is only around US$24,000. This is of course still a large amount compared with a country like Sweden that has little subsoil wealth, but not enough to support a large country like Russia for many years, especially since we are looking at non-renewable natural resources.

However, high-income countries have another type of asset that even for Norway is far more valuable than its subsoil wealth and that is what is labeled intangible assets. Among the high-income countries, the value of this is between US$400,000 and US$600,000 per capita. Resource-rich

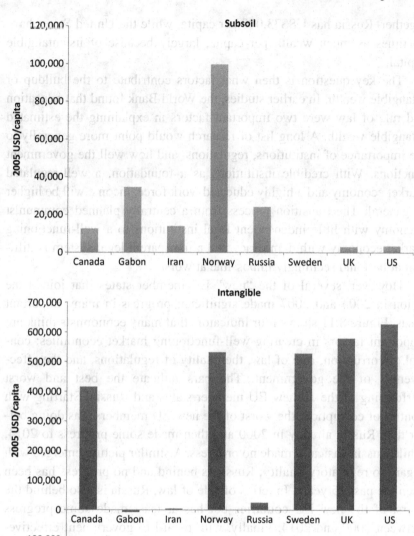

Figure 8.10   Sources of the Wealth of Nations.

Source: World Bank (2011).

Gabon, Iran, or Russia, on the other hand, have very low estimated levels of intangible assets compared the high-income countries. It is interesting to note that for Russia, intangible wealth of US$24,000 is almost exactly the same as subsoil wealth. When all the sources of wealth are added together, Russia has US$73,000 per capita, while the United States have 10 times as much wealth per capita, largely because of its intangible capital.

The key question is then what factors contribute to the buildup of intangible wealth. In earlier studies, the World Bank found that education and rule of law were two important factors in explaining the estimated intangible wealth. A long list of research would point more generally to the importance of institutions, regulations, and how well the government functions. With credible institutions as a foundation, a well-regulated market economy and a highly educated work force, income will be higher in general. The transition process from a centrally planned communist economy with little independent legal institutions to a well-functioning market economy with democracy and a transparent legal system is difficult at best and seemingly impossible at worst.

However, several of the "new" EU member states that joined the union in 2004 and 2007 made significant progress in many important areas. Figure 8.11 shows four indicators that many economists think are important factors in creating well-functioning market economies: control of corruption, rule of law, the quality of regulations, and the effectiveness of the government. The bars indicate the best and worst performing of the 10 new EU member states and Russia. Starting with control of corruption, the worst of the new EU members was doing better than Russia already in 2000 and then made some progress to 2014, while Russia basically made no progress. A similar picture emerges with regard to regulatory quality; Russia is behind and no progress has been seen the past 15 years. In terms of rule of law, Russia is also behind the worst of the new EU countries but has at least made some progress between 2000 and 2014. Finally, with regard to government effectiveness, Russia made significant progress over the past 15 years but is still behind the worst of the new EU countries. Note that these countries are also transition countries, so there is really no reason why Russia should not be able to do what these countries did if its policymakers made it a priority. We can only imagine how attractive Russia would be to foreign investors if it set itself a goal to reach the *best*-performing new EU country rather than playing catch up with the worst performers in terms of institutional reforms.

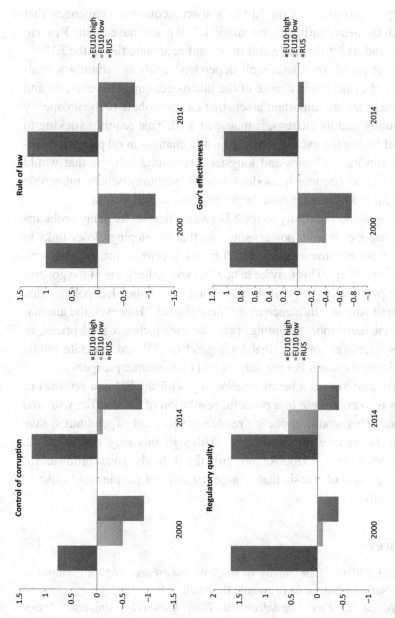

Figure 8.11   Governance Indicators: Russia versus EU Transition Countries.

Note: EU10 hi and EU10 lo is the best and worst of the 10 transition countries that joined the EU in 2004 and 2007.

Source: World Bank (2015), Worldwide Governance Indicators (WGI), and author's calculations.

Concluding Remarks

This chapter has focused on Russia's macroeconomic challenges that come with the heavy influence international oil prices have on the Russian economy, and its (still) strong and important economic ties to the EU.

When it comes to Russia's oil dependence, this is certainly a challenge for policymakers in charge of the macroeconomy. However, oil and natural resources are important assets that can contribute to the prosperity of the country and its citizens, if managed well. That requires sticking to a policy of letting the exchange rate adjust to changes in oil prices to manage short-run macro issues and long-term structural reforms that would allow Russia to become a modern market economy where intangible wealth is an order of magnitude larger than its subsoil wealth.

Its geographic proximity to the EU (which despite its many problems still is a major economic power) suggests that developing closer links in terms of trade and investments should be a top priority for Russia's economic policymakers. This may be in conflict with other parts of the government and political system that do not appreciate various EU policies that seek to limit Russia's influence in its "near abroad." However, the alternatives do not seem more tempting: pray for ever-increasing oil prices, or waste resources on conflicts that look good on TV and generate public support the next quarter but are detrimental to economic prosperity.

A first step toward a better relationship with the EU and removal of sanctions is to contribute to a peaceful resolution of the conflict with and in Ukraine. This would in one go reduce government expenditures, save lives, and boost investor confidence. Although this may not be in the standard economics textbooks on growth, it holds great promise for the future growth of Russia that a large majority of people would like to see materialize.

References

Anderson, J. (2010), "The gravity model," *Working Paper* 16576, Cambridge, MA: National Bureau of Economic Research.

Åslund, A. (2012), *How Capitalism Was Built*, Cambridge University Press. New York.

Becker, T. (2014), A Russian Sudden Stop or Just a Slippery Oil Slope to Stagnation? *BSR Policy Briefing* 4/2014, Turku: Centrum Balticum.

Becker, T. (2015), "Russia's economic troubles — a perfect storm of falling oil prices, sanctions and lack of reforms, SIEPS," *European Policy Analysis*, 9, May, 1–12.

Becker, T. (2017), "Investment relations between Sweden and Russia," in: Liuhto, K., Sutyrin, S. and J.-M. F. Blanchard (eds.), *The Russian Economy and Foreign Direct Investment*, Routledge Studies in the Modern World Economy, London, pp. 80–102.

Boschini, A. D., J. Pettersson and J. Roine. (2007), "Resource curse or not: A question of appropriability," *Scandinavian Journal of Economics*, 109(3), 593–617.

CBR (2016), Central Bank of Russia, Statistics, available at http://cbr.ru/Eng/statistics/ (accessed on October 14, 2016).

Fortescue, S. and P. Hanson (2015), "What drives Russian outward foreign direct investment? Some observations on the steel industry," *Post-Communist Economies*, 27(3), 283–305.

Gaidar, Y. (2010), *Collapse of an Empire*, Brookings Institution Press, Washington, D.C.

IMF (2016a), International Monetary Fund, World Economic Outlook, April 2016 database, available at http://www.imf.org/external/pubs/ft/weo/2016/01/weodata/download.aspx.

IMF (2016b), International Monetary Fund, World Economic Outlook, databases from 1999 to 2016, available at http://www.imf.org/external/ns/cs.aspx?id=28.

IMF (2016c), International Monetary Fund, Direction of Trade Statistics database, available at http://data.imf.org/?sk=9D6028D4-F14A-464C-A2F2-59B2CD424B85.

Johansen, S. (1991), "Estimation and hypothesis testing of cointegration vectors in Gaussian vector autoregressive models," *Econometrica: Journal of the Econometric Society*, 59(6), 1551.

Kleinert, J. and F. Toubal (2010), "Gravity for FDI," *Review of International Economics*, 18(1), 1–13.

Liuhto, K. T. (2015), "Motivations of Russian firms to invest abroad: How sanctions affect the Russian outward foreign direct investment?," *Baltic Region*, 26(4), 4–19.

Ofer, G. (2010), "Twenty years later and the socialist heritage is still kicking: The case of Russia," WIDER *Working Paper* No. 2010/59, 1–33.

Popov, V. (2010), "The long road to normalcy: Where Russia now stands," WIDER *Working Paper* No. 2010/13, 1–31.

Rosefielde, S. (2007), *The Russian Economy: From Lenin to Putin*, Wiley-Blackwell, New Jersey.

Rosefielde, S. (2016), *Kremlin Strikes Back: Russia and the West after Crimea's Annexation*, Cambridge University Press, New York.

Rosefielde, S. (2017), "Russia's military industrial resurgence: Evidence and potential," in: Stephen, B. (ed.), *The Russian Military in Contemporary Perspective*, Carlisle Barracks, PA: Strategic Studies Institute, US Army War College.

Sachs, J. D. and A. M. Warner (2001), "The curse of natural resources," *European Economic Review*, 45(4–6), 827–838.

World Bank (2011), The Changing Wealth of Nations data, available at http://data.worldbank.org/data-catalog/wealth-of-nations.

World Bank (2015), Worldwide Governance Indicators (WGI) data, available at http://info.worldbank.org/governance/wgi/index.aspx#home.

Chapter 9

Sanctions

Iikka Korhonen

Introduction

In this chapter, the author will review some economic effects of the recent sanctions and countersanctions introduced by the United States, European Union (EU), Russia, and other countries, following Russia's unlawful annexation of Crimea and continuous Russian military presence in Eastern Ukraine. The restrictive measures of various parties in the conflict have been very asymmetrical, the United States and EU mostly limiting some Russian entities' access to market finance (as well as export of some technologies), while Russia banned import of, for example, many agricultural goods from various countries.

It is argued that so far economic effects of sanctions are relatively small, although Russian inflation would have been clearly lower (and consequently Russians' economic welfare higher) without Russian import bans.[1] For Russia, oil price collapse has been clearly much more important in explaining the current crisis.

---

[1] In this section, the author will neither consider Russia's ban on imports of foodstuff from Turkey nor consider ban on the Russian travel agencies to arrange charter tours to Turkey. These measures followed the downing of a Russian fighter plane in Turkish airspace on November 25, 2015. There is a reason to believe that ban on food imports increased prices on these products in the Russian market, of course.

However, if sanctions are kept in place for a longer period, their cumulative effect may very well be significant, especially if they compound various structural problems in the Russia economy.

This chapter is structured as follows. In the second and third sections, the author will briefly describe various sanctions imposed by different countries, and in the fourth section some evidence on their economic effects are offered. The fifth section concludes and offers some speculation on the future of sanctions.

Brief Summary of US and EU Sanctions

In this section, the author will briefly describe what kinds of sanctions Russia faces as a result of its military aggression in Ukraine. In the fourth section, the author reviews how these sanctions and Russia's own sanctions have so far affected Russian economy. We will see that in the short run, sanctions related to capital markets seem to have the largest effect on Russian economy.

After the annexation of Crimea and start of military operations in East Ukraine, many Russian entities (as well as persons) have been subjected to several waves of economic and financial sanctions by the EU, United States, as well as other countries such as Canada and Australia. Initially sanctions included restrictions on travel and asset freezes as well as restrictions on doing business with entities based in Crimea and Sevastopol, unless Ukrainian authorities issued a certificate of origin.[2] Typically different political and economic actions were deemed to be "undermining Ukraine's territorial integrity" (which they of course were), and persons and institutions involved in such actions were added to the sanctions list. Initially only one financial institution was added to the sanctions list: the Russian National Commercial Bank established in Crimea to handle banking business in the annexed peninsula. It is wholly owned by the regional government of Crimea.

The downing of Malaysian Airlines flight MH-17A caused a definite sea of change in the scale of sanctions. This event spurred the EU

---

[2] For comprehensive and up-to-date listing of EU's restrictive actions, see http://europa.eu/newsroom/highlights/special-coverage/eu_sanctions/index_en.htm#3.

countries to take a much firmer stance toward Russian entities and the so-called People's Republics, and many institutions as well as many individuals were added to the sanctions list on July 30, 2014. In addition to energy and defense companies, Russian banks were also targeted, even if they had no direct involvement with the fighting in Donetsk and Luhansk regions. Investors in the EU were forbidden to provide long-term financing to Sberbank, VTB, Gazprombank, Rosselkhozbank (Russian Agricultural Bank), and VEB. Initially this meant financing with maturity longer than 90 days in addition to equity financing, but later (September 12, 2014) the maturity threshold was dropped to 30 days.[3] Generally the EU and the United States have been able to coordinate their actions reasonably well, but the United States did not include Sberbank in its own list as quickly as the EU.

While it is clear that sanctions have severely affected targeted Russian banks' ability to raise financing from abroad, it is conceptually difficult to pinpoint exactly how large this effect is. The problem here is that general uncertainty concerning Russia's economy has been mounting for quite some time, partly also for political reasons, and this affected banks' access to external financing (and the price of said financing). In the latter half of 2014 and during 2015, drop in the price of crude oil — by far the most important determinant of Russia's terms-of-trade — also greatly contributed to heightened uncertainty in the Russian economy.

The most obvious result from general uncertainty and financial sanctions has been that many Russian companies have been unable to refinance or roll over their foreign liabilities. Instead, they have been forced to draw down currency reserves. Figure 9.1 shows the evolution of Russia's corporate foreign debt and Bank of Russia's foreign currency reserves. It should be noted that Russia's emerging market peers (e.g., India, Brazil, Mexico, and Malaysia) did not see similar

---

[3] Often, such stipulations are relatively difficult to interpret in advance, and, for example, Sberbank's daughter banks in the EU were exempt from the ruling. However, the EU has tried to ensure they are not used to circumvent financing ban. Also, initially, syndicated loans were not included in the EU sanctions. Russian banks have traditionally been very active in the market for syndicated loans, but the amount of loans taken by Russian banks in this market declined already by 45% year-on-year in the first half of 2014 with almost no new issuance since May of that year.

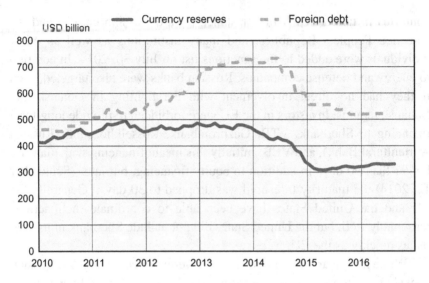

Figure 9.1   Foreign Debt of Russia's Corporate Sector and Foreign Currency Reserves of Bank of Russia (US Dollar in Billion).

Source: Bank of Russia.

drastic increase in capital outflows in 2014 and 2015, which suggests that Russian companies were at least relatively unique in paying back their foreign loans.

A similar drop in Russian companies' foreign indebtedness occurred in late 2008 and in 2009 in the aftermath of the global financial crisis. Obviously, that period corresponded to a sharp drop of oil price too, which peaked in July 2008 at over US$140 per barrel, before plummeting to slightly more than US$30 per barrel in January 2009. However, at that time, recovery of oil price was substantial and relatively rapid.

Sanctions imposed by the EU are regularly reviewed every six months and their continuation requires renewed support from all the 28 member countries. Therefore, in principle, this sanction regime is relatively fragile; any member country can end EU sanctions. In practice, this has not happened. The first set of sanctions related to annexation of Crimea was renewed again in September 2016, and the larger, arguably more effective, set in July 2016. For an insightful assessment of various criteria on designing sanctions against Russian entities, see Christie (2016).

Brief Summary of Russian Sanctions

Very soon after the EU and United States imposed their sanctions on Russian entities in July 2014, Russia retaliated. On August 6, 2014, Russia imposed a ban on imports of farm produce and foodstuffs from the EU, United States, Norway, Canada, and Australia.[4] The ban includes poultry, pork, beef, fish, dairy products, fruits, vegetables, and some processed foods (BOFIT 2014). For many product categories, the banned imports constituted a significant portion of Russia's consumption of those goods. For example, some 30% of fruits and almost 30% of cheese consumed in Russia before the ban came from the EU countries.

Originally the food import ban was designated to be in effect for a year, but it has now been extended. In June 2016, President Vladimir Putin issued a decree extending the import ban to the end of 2017, i.e., well past the current validity of the EU's sanctions. This gives cause to suspect that the import ban is not merely meant as a countermeasure for the EU and US sanctions, but also serves to boost domestic food production.[5]

Effects of Sanctions on Russia

In this section, the author will review some evidence on the economic effects of sanctions on Russia. At the outset, it should be noted that trying to estimate effects of sanction is fraught with difficulties, especially in a situation where price of energy, Russia's most important export product, has also collapsed.

It is illustrative to start with forecasts of the International Monetary Fund (IMF) for Russian economy. Figure 9.2 shows two vintages of forecasts, first from October 2013 and the second from July 2016 (forecasts for 2018–2020 are actually from April). Obviously, in October 2013, both the price of oil and expectations about its future path were very different from

---

[4] Other countries have been added to the list later.

[5] It should be noted that Russia has, at various points in time, halted food imports from various countries for various reasons. Often, concerns over phytosanitary conditions are cited, but sometimes analysts have expressed doubts about the true causes of such actions, e.g., when Russia banned pork imports from the EU in January 2014 or when Russia banned wine imports from Moldova and Georgia in March 2006.

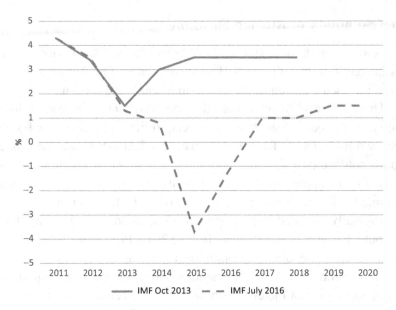

Figure 9.2   IMF Forecasts for Russia's GDP Growth Rate.

Source: IMF World Economic Outlook Database, versions October, 2013, and April, 2016, as well as July, 2016 update.

what actually happened and very few people expected Russia to annex Crimea. The IMF expected cyclical recovery in 2014 and the growth rate to remain at 3.5% between 2015 and 2018. However, Russia's gross domestic product (GDP) declined by 3.7% in 2015, and growth is expected to converge to 1.5% in 2019 and 2020, implying a drastic downward revision in the long-run growth potential. For the year 2018 (end point of 2013 forecasting round), the difference between levels of GDP implied by these two forecasting rounds is 21%. This serves as an indicator of the total GDP loss caused by lower oil prices, increased general uncertainty, sanctions, etc.

Despite the aforementioned difficulties in separating effects of sanctions from all the other factors on Russia's GDP growth, some attempts have been made. IMF (2015) reports that sanctions and (Russia's) countersanctions could initially reduce Russia's real GDP by 1% to 1.5%. In the medium term, Russia's cumulative output loss could be as high as 9%. It should be noted that such a large loss in the level of GDP presupposes lower level of investment and lower level of productivity growth (as

Russia's own inward-looking policies lead to lower level of competition). Taking this at face value, one could perhaps say that, without any sanctions, the IMF's estimates imply that Russia's GDP in 2015 might have declined only by 2.5% instead of 3.7%.

There have been some other attempts to estimate the effects of sanctions on Russia's economic performance. For example, Citibank (2015) estimated a small macroeconomic model of Russia and found that in it some 90% of observed decline could be explained by drop in oil prices. Therefore, only 10% of the output decline was left to be explained by sanctions and everything else that might be happening in and around Russia in 2014–2015.

Gurvich and Prilepskiy (2015) gauge the effects of financial sanctions on the availability of finance for Russian companies. They find that financial sanctions do reduce the amount of finance available. However, this effect is mitigated by the fact that Russian companies have been able to run down their foreign assets as well. Looking forward, Gurvich and Prilepskiy formulate four different scenarios for different combinations of sanctions regimes and oil price. They find that cumulative effect of sanctions on Russian GDP between 2014 and 2017 is 2.4 percentage points, i.e., without sanctions level of GDP would be 2.4% higher at the end of 2017. However, negative effects of low oil prices are some three times larger than this, reinforcing the preeminent role played by oil prices in the Russian economy.

As macroeconomic effects of sanctions are difficult to estimate directly because of, e.g., concurrent drop in the price of oil, Crozet and Hinz (2016) take a somewhat different approach. They utilize difference-in-difference methodology to see how exports from the countries placing sanctions on Russia reacted to the introduction of sanctions. They calculate that decline in sanctioning countries' exports to Russia was approximately 30% larger than non-sanctioning countries' export drop from August 2014 onwards. However, this is overwhelmingly explained by Russia's own sanctions. More curious is the fact that for those goods that Russia did not sanction, non-sanctioning countries' exports[6] declined by

---

[6] However, even list of "other" countries is far from complete. For example, China and Korea are excluded because of data limitations. Korean exports, consisting overwhelmingly of capital goods, have been among those hurt most by Russia's economic downturn.

more than 10% (again, in comparison to non-sanctioning countries' exports) already in March 2014. More importantly, this effect did not increase in August 2014. As the sanctions that were introduced in March 2014 were mostly travel bans and asset freezes of individuals and certain organizations, it is hard to argue that these measures could have affected exports already in March 2014. It is more likely that countries like Germany that exported predominantly machinery and equipment to Russia suffered disproportionally from the drop in investment and extreme uncertainty in Russian financial markets that followed the annexation of Crimea. In a short note, Gros and Mustilli (2016) show that sanctioning countries' market share in Russian imports has not changed since July 2014, i.e., after introduction of tighter sanctions.

Concluding Remarks

It seems certain that sanctions imposed by the EU, United States, and other countries have damaged Russian economy. Trade-destroying barriers necessarily do this in competitive market theory. However, in recent times effects of lower oil price and general uncertainty (partially caused by Russia's aggression in Crimea and East Ukraine) have been much more important drivers of Russia's GDP decline. If sanctions are in place for a longer time, at least the IMF (2015) believes their effect will become larger, as e.g., investment activity remains lower than it otherwise would have been.

Exports of, e.g., EU countries to Russia have declined drastically since the annexation of Crimea. However, taking into account, e.g., composition of exports, sanctioning countries' exports have not decreased more than other countries', i.e., they have maintained their market shares in Russian imports. In those foods sanctioned by Russia itself, this does not hold true, of course.

References

BOFIT (2014), *BOFIT Weekly* 33, Russia, http://www.suomenpankki.fi/bofit_en/seuranta/viikkokatsaus/Documents/w201433.pdf (accessed on July 1, 2016).

Christie, Edward Hunter (2016), "The design and impact of western economic sanctions against Russia," *The RUSI Journal*, 161(3), 52–64.

Crozet, Matthieu and Julian Hinz (2016), "Collateral damage: The impact of the Russia sanctions on sanctioning countries' exports," *CEPII Working Paper* 2016-16.

Gros, Daniel and Federica Mustilli (2016), "The effects of sanctions and counter-sanctions on EU-Russian trade flows," CEPS Commentary, July 5, 2016, available at https://www.ceps.eu/publications/effects-sanctions-and-counter-sanctions-eu-russian-trade-flows.

Gurvich, Evsey and Ilya Prilepskyi (2015), "The impact of financial sanctions on the Russian economy," *Russian Journal of Economics*, 1(4), 359–385.

International Monetary Fund (IMF) (2015), *Russian Federation: 2015 Article IV Staff Report*, available at http://www.imf.org/external/pubs/ft/scr/2015/cr15211.pdf.

Chapter 10

Finance

Victor Gorshkov

Introduction

There is ample support in the academic literature for the claim that financial sectors play an important role in advancing sustainable economic growth. The construction of efficient financial markets is a key task for many emerging and developing economies because they lack sufficient growth-promoting financial resources. Financial sectors spur economic growth by facilitating efficient factor allocation and lowering information and other transaction costs. Long-term finance is particularly crucial for this purpose.

The development of Russia's financial sector has been a government priority for years. It has liberalized the financial sector and forged deep links with the international financial system, but the results have not lived up to expectations. Financial reform in some instances has been

The first draft of this paper was presented on March 9, 2016 at the International Conference on "EU Economic Stagnation and Political Insecurity for Asia" organized by the Institute of Economic Research, Kyoto University and co-organized by KIER Joint Usage and Research Center Project and KIER Foundation. The author would like to thank Professor Bruno Dallago for his valuable comments regarding the first manuscript of his research work. The second draft of this paper was presented on May 28, 2016 at the 164th Regular Research Seminar on Macroeconomics and Economic systems. The author would like to thank Professor Mizobata and Professor Anna Kovalova for their valuable suggestions. He is particularly indebted to Professor Steven Rosefielde for his constructive critiques and effective suggestions for the final draft of this paper. All remaining errors and omissions are full responsibility of the author.

counterproductive by making the economy more vulnerable to external shocks. Moreover, some scholars, with the financial crisis of 2014–2015 in mind, contend that Russia's financial system operates primarily for the benefit of foreign investors seeking exorbitant speculative returns in currency markets (Glaz'ev 2015a, 2015b, 2015c; Glaz'ev *et al*. 2015).

The aim of this chapter is twofold. First, it provides a short overview of Russia's financial sector, focusing on its ability to provide long-term financing essential for modernization. Second, it surveys financial sanctions levied by the West against Russia, spotlighting their long-term repercussions at home and abroad. The survey shows that while there is abundant evidence that the short-term impact of the West's trade sanctions have been ineffectual,[1] the long-term impact of financial sanctions may be more pronounced in an era of low petroleum prices — Russia's "new reality" (Medvedev 2015).

Brief Overview of Russia's Financial Market

Growing financial globalization in recent years has augmented Russia's access to external credit, increased the volume of cross-border transactions, and stimulated competition among major financial centers. Russia has beneficially participated in the process, but was also drawn into the financial crises of 2008 and 2014–2015.

The net costs have been higher than anticipated. According to the data of *The Global Competitiveness Report 2015–2016*, gains have been unspectacular. Russia ranks 45th out of 140 countries in overall competitiveness; 100th in terms financial institutional competitiveness; and 95th in terms of the quality of its financial markets.[2] The depth and level of Russia's financial sector are even lower.

---

[1] The term "financial sanctions" generally includes the following: decrease or termination of foreign aid; decrease, termination, or restrictions of financing; freeze or confiscation of foreign banking assets; bans on interest rates and other payments; decline in refinancing or rescheduling the loan repayment schedule; and control or termination of cross transfer of capital (Zagashvili 2015, p. 67).

[2] *The Global Competitiveness Index* in detail (financial market development): availability of financial services (71st place), affordability of financial services (69th), financing through local equity market (86th), ease of access to loans (56th), venture capital availability (61st place), soundness of banks (118th), regulation of securities exchanges (91st place), and legal rights index (113th) (World Economic Forum 2015).

Table 10.1 Investments into Fixed Assets by Sources of Financing (in Percentage).

	1995	2000	2005	2010	2015
Investments into fixed capital by sources of financing, total	100	100	100	100	100
Equity (internal sources of financing including retained profits)	49.0	47.5	44.5	41.0	51.1
Debt financing (external (acquired) sources of financing)	51.0	52.5	55.5	59.0	48.9
— Bank loans (including foreign bank loans)		2.9 (0.6)	8.1 (1.0)	9.0 (2.3)	7.8 (1.9)
— Loans and credits from other companies		7.2	5.9	6.1	5.7
— Foreign investments					0.9
— Budget funds	21.8	22.0	20.4	19.5	16.5
— Financial resources of affiliated companies and financial groups			10.6	17.5	10.5
— Issuance of corporate bonds			0.3	0.01	1.6
— Emission of stocks		0.5	3.1	1.1	0.5
— Other sources		19.9	7.1	5.79	5.4

Source: Compiled by author with reference to Federal State Statistic Service data, available at http://www.gks.ru.

Long-term financing is provided in Russia by a variety of domestic and foreign institutions.[3] Pertinent data on the financing of new fixed capital are provided below.

Table 10.1 shows that new fixed capital formation is funded mostly by equity financing (51.1%). This dependency, which prevailed throughout the period 1995–2015, is unusual. Bank loans traditionally are the most important source of long-term finance, but were surpassed in Russia by

[3] Some of the sources of long-term financing include the following institutions: commercial banks and non-bank intermediaries; bond markets; stock markets; institutional investors (insurance companies, pension funds, and sovereign funds); hedge funds, venture capital funds, and private capital funds; international capital markets (foreign direct investments [FDI], bank loans, portfolio investments, international syndicated loans for project financing, and foreign currency international bond markets); and state-owned financial intermediaries (development banks) (World Bank Group 2015, pp. 26–27).

state and municipal financing (16.5%) and affiliated companies and financial groups (10.5%). The subordinate role of banks in financing new capital formation is confirmed by related statistics.

While the total amount of domestic credit to private sector is estimated as 40.1% of gross domestic product (GDP), the share of bank loans financing new capital formation in 2015 was only 7.8%, a figure even lower than the 11.8% figure that prevailed during the crisis period 2008–2009. Bank loans provided by foreign banks have also decreased from 3.2% in 2009 to 1.9% in 2015. The amount of financing provided from other sources such as new corporate bonds, stocks, and foreign investments remains insignificant. Modernization consequently is extraordinarily dependent on the magnitude of corporate-retained profits and the willingness of managers to investment in upgrading enterprise plant and equipment.

The present structure of financing is to a great extent explained by Russia's financial market architecture. It is a bank-based financial system, heavily dependent on bank financing instead of stock and insurance markets, non-government pension funds, and mutual funds. As of January 2016, the share of the total banking assets in GDP amounted to 103.2% — the share of capital (equity) was 11.2%. The share of bank credit provided to the corporate sector (non-financial enterprises) and households in GDP amounted to 54.7% (Bank of Russia 2016, p. 2). All of these indicators are low by international standards.

Russia's financial system is distinguished by the following: the limited scope for individual participation in financial markets; a shift in preferences of the households toward services provided by credit institutions offering both banking services and services on the stock market; and low public trust in financial intermediaries. Russia's investment level is low due in part to high interest rates paid on safe bank deposits protected by the Deposit Insurance Agency.[4] Nevertheless, the share of deposits by

---

[4] Deposit Insurance Agency is a state non-profit organization established in 2004 to provide deposit insurance in Russia. At the end of 2014, the president of Russia signed a law binding the government to provide RUB 1.1 trillion to the Deposit Insurance Agency to support the level of capitalization (liquidity) of banks facing troubles caused by the financial crisis and the imposition of sanctions. However, these measures are believed to have a temporary effect (Daskovkij and Kisilev 2016, p. 16). Bank deposits also receive preferential tax treatment on interest rates and foreign currency deposits.

households in GDP remains low. In January 2016, it amounted to 28.9%, a figure which is lower than those prevailing in other emerging economies (Bank of Russia 2015a, p. 18).[5] In addition, the level of investments is low due to a low household savings rate — in the first quarter of 2015, it amounted to only 13.6% (Bank of Russia 2015a).

Banking sector

Idiosyncratic features of Russia's banking sector are its oversegmentation, strong state participation, concentration in large-size banks, a large number of small banks, undercapitalization of the banking sector, regional dispari-ties in the distribution of banking services, unbalanced revenue structure (high proportion of revenue from foreign exchange operations), chronic problems with long-term financing, low efficiency, restricted competition, fragmentation of the banking sector and strong dependence on external financial markets, low level of transparency of credit institutions, offshori-zation of the banking sector, and Russia's economy itself (Gorshkov 2015).

As of January 2016, 733 banks were operating in Russia including many directly and indirectly controlled by the state; banks with foreign capital participation; large private banks; small- and medium-sized banks of the Moscow region; and regional small- and medium-sized banks (Figure 10.1). The number of banks has been steadily declining since the beginning of 2000s due to stricter capitalization requirements. Russia is gradually trying to introduce Basel principles; thus, banks lacking sufficient capital are com-pelled either to merge with larger credit institutions or terminate their opera-tions. Nonetheless, the decline in the number of banks in 2014–2016 was extraordinary. After the West's imposition of economic and financial sanc-tions (see "International Sanctions Targeting Russia's Financial Sector" section below), the Bank of Russia revoked almost 200 licenses.

Geographical disparities in banking service accessibility are pro-nounced. About 60% of banks are located in the Central Federal District (431 bank), followed by the Volga (85 banks), North-West (59 banks), and Siberian (40 banks) federal districts. Other regions have fewer banks, with

---

[5] The share of deposits by households in GDP for selected economies in 2012: Chile, 47.6%; South Africa, 39.9%; Indonesia, 33.6%; and Mexico, 27.5% (Bank of Russia 2015a, p. 18).

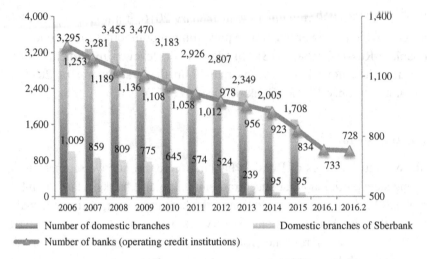

Figure 10.1   Number of Credit Institutions and Their Domestic Branches in Russia in 2006–2016.

Source: Compiled by author with reference to Bank of Russia.

Far-Eastern (17 banks) and Crimea (5 banks) federal districts the least representative. State-owned Sberbank has the most domestic branches in Russia (Table 10.2). Concentration in the banking sector is extremely high. For instance, Sberbank accounts for 45% of all household deposits, and the share of top 5 banks in assets of the banking sector is about 55%, while top 200 banks control 97% of the total capital of the banking sector.

As of January 2016, the average interest rate for bank loans to private sector with maturities of 1–3 years was 14% in rubles, 6.73% in US dollars, and 7.45% in euro, which makes it difficult for many companies to borrow. State-controlled and large private banks provide approximately 90% of long-term credit to the private sector.

Western investors adjusted their business plans in Russia after their governments imposed financial sanction in 2014. The number of banks with foreign capital participation decreased from 251 to 212 in 2014–2015. Their share in total charter capital fell from 26.15% in 2008 to 14.71% in December 2015.

The number of foreign banks with 100% foreign capital participation fell by 5, leaving a residual of 71. Banks with foreign capital participation accounted for 13.1% share of non-resident bank loans, while for the state-controlled banks' share was 2.7%. It was just 1.5% for large private banks.

Table 10.2   Shares of Different Groups of Banks in Deposits and Loans (in Percentage).

Share in %	Household deposits	Firm deposits	Household loans	Corporate loans	ROA (2014)	ROE (2014)
State banks	60.4	62.2	57.4	64.2	1.2	10.2
Banks with foreign capital participation (foreign share of more than 50%)	6.6	9.2	15.5	7.7	1.6	11.1
Large private banks	28.2	27.3	24.1	25.0	0.1	1.2
Small- and medium-sized banks in the Moscow region	2.3	0.8	1.4	1.7	1.1	6.2
Regional small- and medium-sized banks	2.5	0.6	1.6	1.4	1.6	9.6

Source: Compiled by author with reference to Bank of Russia (2015b).

Small- and medium-sized banks have no financial resources from international markets.

Instability on the market caused by the imposition of sanctions and deteriorating economic conditions compelled some banks to borrow to maintain adequate liquidity. State-controlled banks and large banks, respectively, purchased 53.5% and 38.4% of these bonds and promissory notes, comprising the majority of financial resources acquired from the Bank of Russia. Many banks employed repo agreements with the Bank of Russia to solve their liquidity problems. They used bonds and promissory notes in the Bank of Russia's Lombard List as collateral.

The interbank lending market focused on domestic transactions, while non-resident banks' domestic loan share decreased from 5.3% to 4.0% in 2014 (Bank of Russia 2015b).

Capital market

Russia's capital (stock) market blossomed after 2000, in tandem with the nation's post-Soviet economic recovery. The Russian capital market is considered "emerging" because it offers rich investment opportunities accompanied by correspondingly high risks. The Moscow Exchange was established in December 2011 by merging the Moscow Interbank Currency Exchange and Russian Trading System (RTS). It is the largest stock exchange in Russia and deals in stocks, bonds, derivatives, foreign exchange, money, and precious metals market.

As of December 2015, shareholders holding 5% or more at the Moscow Exchange included the Bank of Russia (11.768%), Sberbank (9.992%), Vneshekonombank (VEB) (8.395%), European Bank of Reconstruction and Development (EBRD) (6.064%), and LLC "Russian Fund of Direct Investments Investment Management — 6" (5.261%). About 50.7% of shares on the Moscow Exchange are considered free-floating.

The Moscow Exchange can be subdivided into two large markets: equity (shares) and bond markets. Stocks and shares of Russian and foreign companies, depository receipts, and investment fund shares are traded at the stock (equity) market, while the bond market is a platform for transactions in federal loan bonds,[6] regional and municipal bonds, Russian corporate bonds nominated in both rubles and foreign currencies, as well as corporate Eurobonds and sovereign Eurobonds of Russia's government.

Stock (equity) market

The stock (equity) market in Russia evolved in tandem with the privatization of state-owned enterprises, but failed to become the principal source of corporate finance. The share of the stock market in financing new capital formation is extremely low (Table 10.1). The composition of the RTS Index that includes the stocks of top 50 companies in Russia is heavily weighted with companies in the natural resource sector. Petroleum and gas sectors comprise more than 50% in RTS Index, making it vulnerable to external market shocks. About 57% of Initial Public Offerings (IPOs) during 2005–2014 originated at the London Stock Exchange, while the Moscow Exchange's share amounted to 32%, mostly companies in the metals and mining (15), financial services (14), and oil and gas sectors (14) (PWC 2014, p. 2). Capitalization of the stock market in the first quarter of 2015 amounted to RUB 27.3 trillion (37.2% GDP), which is considerably lower than the world's average — 85.4%. Profit rates for companies listed on Russia's stock market are a quarter of those in the United States and half those in China (Bank of Russia 2015a, p. 24).

---

[6] *Oblgatsiyya Federal'nogo Zaima* — federal loan bond of Russia.

Deteriorating market conditions, growing geopolitical and economic risks aggravated by Western sanctions, and reduced credit ratings caused high price volatility on the Moscow Exchange in 2014–2015. In December 2014, RTS Index set a new record low at 629 (4/23/2016, 931). The number of IPOs declined and the market capitalization decreased.

Bond market

Russia's bond market includes the domestic private bond market, domestic public bonds market, international private debt securities market, and the international public debt securities market. The first two bond markets deal with internal (domestic) debt and the latter two deal with external (foreign) debt. Due to the dearth of domestic investors and high inflation rates, the bond market in Russia trades heavily in Eurobonds denominated in foreign currency, and foreign investors are the most important players. The share of bonds in financing new fixed capital formation is low (Table 10.1). The domestic private debt securities market is underdeveloped. The total volume of domestic debt securities is RUB 3.3 trillion, slightly more than 10% of total amount of debt financing to the corporate sector (Bank of Russia 2015a, p. 23). Despite the fact that government bonds are considered highly liquid, they play only a minor role in financing new capital formation.[7]

External borrowings of the corporate sector are US$128.4 billion. The non-financial share is US$58.4 billion. External financing has played a large role in funding the working capital of many Russian large corporations. Western financial sanctions have been particularly harmful in this regard.

Insurance market and pension funds as sources of the long-term financing

The insurance market is also underdeveloped. The share of life insurance in the total insurance premiums remains insignificant (about 10.3% in 2015), while it generally exceeds 50% in developed countries. The share

[7]Regulators worry that state loans to support private sector investment could be macroeconomically destabilizing even though according to the Bank of Russia domestic public debt is only RUB 12.9 trillion (17.6% GDP).

of life insurance premiums in GDP constitutes 1–15% in other economies, while in Russia this indicator is just 0.2%.

The allocation of pension funds is risk-averse. Pension savings in the first quarter of 2015 were about 6.3% of GDP, mostly invested in time deposits, rather than stocks or bonds. Pension funds consequently are not a significant source of long-term financing in Russia and are unlikely to become so in the short term.

Individual investors do not actively trade on the Moscow Exchange. Total assets of mutual investment funds to GDP amounted to 3.5%, substantially less than their peers in other developing economies. As of February 2016, there were 1.3 million registered individuals investors (1.7% of the labor force) on the Moscow Exchange. Active traders are even smaller (Bank of Russia 2015a, pp. 16–21).

International Sanctions Targeting Russia's Financial Sector

International sanctions have contributed to the collapse of the Russian ruble, harmed Russia's economy, and aggravated the financial crisis of 2014–2015. They have continued to exercise their negative impact in 2016 and, together with other factors, are an impediment to the long-term financing Russia needs in order to cope effectively with "the new reality" and foster rapid economic modernization.

While the first two rounds of sanctions (March — beginning of April 2014 and April 28, 2014) targeted specific individuals and did not impose financial restrictions, the third round did (July 17, 2014). Table 10.3 provides a selected chronological inventory of these financial sanctions. A list of sanctions directed specifically against banks is displayed in Table 10.4. The United States was the first to impose sanctions against Russian banks. Other countries, such as Canada, Japan, Australia, Norway, and Switzerland, soon thereafter imposed similar restrictions on Russia's financial entities and made it more difficult for them to obtain medium-term and long-term financing. The situation deteriorated when the US authorities announced that they would freeze VISA and MasterCard transactions for certain Russian banks (Stefanova 2015). The European Investment Bank and EBRD additionally halted new investment projects in Russia.

While there are slight discrepancies in the initial list of sanctions introduced by the United States and EU, sanctions were primarily imposed on the

Table 10.3 Chronology of Sanctions Imposed by the West.

Date	Country	Content of sanctions
July 17, 2014	United States	Transaction bans on two Russian banks, Gazprombank and VEB.
July 24, 2014	Canada	Sanctions on certain financial entities from Russia.
July 30, 2014	EU	Restriction on the issuance and trade of certain bonds, equity, and similar financial instruments with maturity over 90 days (30 days since September 2014). Ban on purchase of shares and bonds of Russian banks with more than 50% government participation and their affiliated juridical entities.
August 8, 2014	Japan	Freeze of funds for new projects in Russia provided within the framework of the EBRD.
August 12, 2014	Norway	Ban on mid-term and long-term financing by Russian state banks.
August 27, 2014	Switzerland	Sberbank, VTB, VEB, Gazprombank, and Rosselkhozbank required authorization to issue long-term financial instruments in Switzerland.
September 12, 2014	United States	Sanctions on Sberbank: limited access to the US debt markets.
September 24, 2014	Japan	Ban on the issuance of securities by Sberbank, VTB, Gazprombank, Rosselkhozbank, and VEB.
March 6, 2016	United States, EU	Extension of sanctions against targeted officials, businessmen, and state-owned companies for one more year.

Note: EU, European Union.

Source: Compiled by author with references to Zagashivili (2015), Stefanova (2015), and other sources.

Table 10.4   List of Banks Under Sanctions

United States	European Union
State-owned banks:	*State-owned banks*:
Sberbank (Bank of Russia — 50 + 1% shares)	Russian National Commerce Bank (Federal Agency for State Property Management — 100% shares)
VTB (Federal Agency for State Property Management — 60.93% shares)	Sberbank (Bank of Russia — 50 + 1% shares)
Rosselkhozbank (Federal Agency for State Property Management — 100% shares)	VTB (Federal Agency for State Property Management — 60.93% shares)
VEB (Russia's development bank)	Gazprombank
Gazprombank	VEB (Russia's development bank)
Bank of Moscow (VTB — 100% shares)	Rosselkhozbank (Federal Agency for State Property Management — 100 % shares)
Banks related to the "inner circle" of the president of Russia	
Sobinbank (Bank "Russia" — 100%)	
SMP Bank	
Invest Capital Bank (branch of SMP Bank)	
Bank "Russia"	

Source: Compiled by author with references to Stefanova (2015) and other sources.

two categories of banks: state-owned banks under direct and indirect government control and banks with shareholders and management that according to the US authorities comprise President Putin's the "inner circle." It is necessary to stress that Sberbank, VTB, and Gazprombank account for the lion's share of Russia's banking assets, capital, deposits, and loans outstanding. They, together with Russia's development bank VEB and Rosselhozbank (Russian Agricultural Bank), are key players and the imposition of sanctions on their activities potentially could be profoundly detrimental.

In March 2016, both the United States and the EU extended sanctions for another year targeted against officials, businessmen, and state-owned companies, freezing their assets and further prohibiting Western firms from transacting business with them (The World Bank 2016).

Impact of Financial Sanctions on Russia's Economy

Although the impact of financial sanctions and investment rating downgrades by Standard & Poor's and Moody's are difficult to estimate, some studies suggest that they have soured the investment climate, fueled inflation, decreased real incomes, aggravated capital outflows, impaired sovereign funds, complicated foreign debt service, and devalued the ruble.

The United Nations Conference on Trade in Development (UNCTAD) finds that sanctions have (1) increased foreign exchange market volatility and aggravated the depreciation of the ruble; (2) restricted access and increased transaction costs for external financing for certain Russian banks and companies; and (3) lowered domestic business and consumer confidence in future growth. UNCTAD stresses the difficulties encountered by Russian banks and large corporations in raising equity and borrowing abroad and infers that this has decreased inward and outward investments (UNCTAD 2015, *World Investment Report*, pp. 68–69).

UNCTAD judgment seems sensible. Russia traditionally has been a net FDI exporter, and this imbalance has worsened (Gorshkov 2013, 2015). FDI inflows to Russia in 2014 decreased by 69.7%, reducing Russia's world ranking to 16th, with a total value of US$21 billion (*World Investment Report* 2015).[8] Outward FDI, largely by Russian multinationals, decreased from US$87 billion in 2013 to US$56 billion in 2014 (sixth place in the world).[9] Low commodity prices and ruble devaluation reduced investments by Russian multinationals abroad (UNCTAD 2015, *World Investment Report*, p. 68). Some Russia multinationals with substantial foreign holdings have repatriated their assets, fearing intensified sanctions (Zagashvili 2015, p. 73). The threat of litigation in foreign courts is also prompting repatriation of Russian capital invested abroad (Glaz'ev 2015a, p. 16).

Financials sanctions, moreover, have inflicted losses on Russian bondholders (even firms excluded from the sanctions list) due to fears about closed access to bridge loans from European and American banks (Kvashnina and Obolenskij 2015, p. 74). Gurvich and Prilepskiy (2015) believe that the effect of Western financial sanctions on non-listed Russian firms is greater than on those explicitly targeted.[10]

---

[8] According to UNCTAD (2015), FDI inflows amounted to US$69 billion (5th place) in 2013. This decline was mitigated by "round-tripping."

[9] Almost 60% of the FDI outflow was directed to Cyprus, Switzerland, and Bermuda.

[10] Gurvich and Prilepskiy (2015) estimate the decrease of total capital inflow for 2014–2017 to be US$280 billion. The effect from sanctions is estimated to decrease GDP by 2.4% for the specified period. However, the impact from sanctions is still 3.3 times lower than the effect from declining crude oil prices.

Repayment of private debt outstanding in 2014 also explains a large proportion of Russia's capital outflow. According to the Bank of Russia, net capital outflow in 2014 was estimated to be US$150 billion, significantly exceeding the crisis year 2008 when it amounted to US$134 billion. Total foreign debt as of January 2016 was US$515.3 billion, down from its July 2014 peak of US$732.8 billion. Commercial banks account for 26% of this figure, government authorities — 8%, and other sectors — 66%.[11] More than 50% of foreign debt is intracompany debt against offshore regions and Special-Purpose Entities (SPEs) (Zagashvili 2015, p. 72). The debt-to-GDP ratio is relatively low in comparison to other developed and developing economies.[12]

Figure 10.2 demonstrates the dynamics of foreign debt, international reserves, and assets of the Reserve Fund and National Wealth Fund during 2008–2016. New foreign expenditures obviously are being financed from the international reserves and assets of the Reserve Fund and the National Reserve Fund. As of March 2016, international reserves declined to US$380.5 billion. The assets of the two sovereign funds were depleted and now stand at US$49.9 billion for the Reserve Fund and at US$71.3 billion for the National Wealth Fund, respectively. The funds of the Reserve Fund were halved in 2008–2016 and are likely to decrease further, as suggested in the *Plan of Government Actions for Stable Socio-Economic Development 2016* approved by the government in March 2016 which listed the fund as a source for fresh financing.

Ruble devaluation and growing food prices caused by Russia's countersanctions on agricultural imports fueled inflation (15% in 2015). This in turn prompted a renewed round of ruble devaluation.[13] The government

---

[11] Other sectors here include financial and non-financial corporations where government authorities have more than 50% shares. The share of foreign debt according to the extended definition of the public sector roughly accounts for more than 50% (Bank of Russia, www.cbr.ru).

[12] McKinsey Global Institute estimated Russian debt-to-GDP ratio (domestic and foreign debt obligations of the government, corporate sector, and households) in 2014 at 65%, which is a very moderate level compared to Japan (400%), United Kingdom (252%), France (280%), and China (217%). In Russia, outstanding public debt securities is lower than in the above-mentioned countries; however, the share of the private debt (primarily external borrowings of large Russian corporations) is substantially high.

[13] Foreign exchange average (US$/RUB) was 75.17 as of January 2016. In comparison to 2006, the ruble has depreciated by 2.7 times.

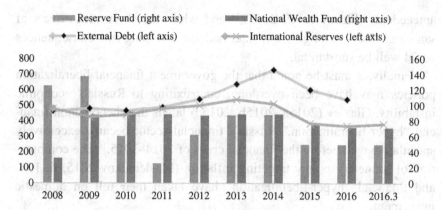

Figure 10.2 Dynamics of Foreign Debt, International Reserves, and Assets of the Reserve Fund and National Wealth Fund in 2008–2016 (US Dollar in Billion).

Source: Compiled by author based on the data of Bank of Russia, available at http://www.cbr.ru, and the Ministry of Finance, available at http://minfin.ru/ru/.

intervened, but this had to decrease its international reserve holding to do so (Figure 10.2). A rise in the prime rate aimed at supporting the ruble of course inevitably increased borrowing costs on the domestic investment market,[14] compelling companies to rely more heavily on retained profits for their working capital and modernization.

Nonetheless, the impact of financial sanctions should not be overestimated. Negative trends in Russia's economy started at the beginning of 2013 before the advent of Western sanctions. According to the World Bank data, annual GDP growth rate in 2012 was around 3.4%, while in 2013 it decreased to 1.3% and in 2015 plummeted to −3.8%. Russia's growth retardation after 2012 is partly attributable to unfavorable economic conditions on world commodity markets and to the decrease of investment activity of large Russian corporations. The underinvestment appears to be connected with Russia's monetary policy and deficient aggregate-effective demand. Western sanctions may have made a bad situation worse, but Russia's economic malaise has powerful domestic

---

[14] The key rate of the Bank of Russia was subsequently raised from 5.5% in March 2014 to a maximum of 17% in December 2014. The current rate of the key rate as of March 2016 is 11% (established since August 2015).

antecedents (Shirov *et al.* 2015),[15] and while the short-term effects of sanctions may be slight, the intermediate and long-run consequences could well be substantial.

Finally, it must be noted that the government financial liberalization policies may have been overdone, contributing to Russia's economic instability. Glaz'ev (2015a, 2015b, 2015c) labels the phenomenon financial "hyper-liberalization." Russia's financial sector became excessively speculative well before the financial crisis of 2014–2015.[16] The combination of monetary policy targeting inflation (Maslennikov 2015, p. 154) and financial "hyper-liberalization" have taken their toll on domestic investment.

Conclusion

Russia's financial sector has failed to facilitate optimal domestic investment and modernization. Companies are forced to self-finance instead of relying on least cost external credit. Russia's financial market is poorly capitalized, reflected in its internationally low share of debt financing to GDP. Stock and bond markets, investments, and pension funds activities are small. Moreover, the banking sector does not adequately service the financial needs of the real sector because of its institutional flaws, high domestic interest rates, and low national savings. The lion's share of the long-term financing is inefficiently provided by large state-owned and directly or indirectly state-controlled banks, while other private banks lack adequate capital ratios and are mostly engaged in short- and medium term lending. The banking sector's financial resources are too limited to foster vibrant corporate development. In some cases, banks even transfer credit resources to stock and currency markets for speculative purposes (Daskovkij and Kisilev 2016, p. 16).

Russian companies have traditionally obtained a substantial portion of their financing from the international capital markets, enticed further by low international lending rates. Russian banks themselves are active

---

[15] Illiquidity played an important role is the ruble's volatility (Shirov *et al.* 2015).

[16] Glaz'ev (2015a, p. 11) estimates 95% of transactions at the Moscow Exchange to be speculative.

borrowers of this cheap external financing. The dependency is better than being straitjacketed by limited domestic financial resources, but poses a potentially serious obstacle to long-run modernization, especially when exacerbated by Western financial sanctions. These sanctions force Russian firms to finance new capital formation from retained profits. Some large companies will be able to do so, but many small and medium enterprises will not (Shirov *et al.* 2015, p. 6). The diversion of scarce financial resources to speculative purposes poses an additional peril. Glaz'ev (2015a) estimates that about 75% of the monetary base in Russia is being circulated to provide foreign credits and foreign investments. The share of non-residents trading on the financial market is estimated to exceed 75%.

Western financial sanctions are more potent than casual observers might assume because of the shortcomings of Russia's financial system detailed in the Section on "Impact of Financial Sanctions on Russia's Economy." The government has managed to mitigate their negative impact by tapping its sovereign funds and depleting its international reserves. However, if negative market conditions persist in the long term, Russia may not be able to finesse the consequences. Galz'ev (2015a, p. 10) ominously warns that there is a danger of a "speculative funnel" diverting the economy's liquidity from long-term to short-term financing. If the Bank of Russia continues to make inflation-targeting its core policy, it may not be able to prevent rechanneling of bank funds into speculative transactions. Asian leaders therefore are well advised to closely monitor Russia's economy and its ability to expand great power presence in global affairs.

References

Bank of Russia (2015a), "Osnovnye napravleniya razvitiya i obespecheniya stabilnosti funktsionirovaniya finansovogo rynka Rossijskoj Federatsii na period 2016–2018 godov" ["Basic development prospects and stabilization support measures for the functioning of the Russia's financial market for 2016–18"] (in Russian).

Bank of Russia (2015b), "Otchet o razvitii bankovskogo sektora i bankovskogo nadzora v 2014 godu" ["Report on banking sector development and control in 2014"] (in Russian).

Bank of Russia (2016), "Obzor bankovskogo sektora Rossijskoj Federacii" ["Overview of the banking sector of the Russian Federation"], 161, March (in Russian).

Daskovkij, V. and V. Kisilev (2016), "Vzaimootnosheniya realnogo i bankovskogo sektorov ekonomiki" ["Interrelations of real and banking sectors of the economy"], *Ekonomist*, 1, 15–29 (in Russian).

Glaz'ev, S. (2015a), "O neotlozhnih merah po ukrepleniyu ekonomicheskoj bezopasnosti Rossii i vyvodu rossijskoj ekonomiki na traektoriyu operezhayushego razvitiya" ["On urgent measures to strengthen the economic security of Russia and leading Russian economy on the path of advanced economic development"], *Rossijskij ekonomicheskij zhurnal*, 5, 3–52 (in Russian).

Glaz'ev, S. (2015b), "Natsional'naya valyutno-finansovaya sistema: Destabiliziruyushie usloviya Zapada i mery po ih nejtralizatsii" ["National financial system: Destabilizing conditions of the West and measures on their neutralization"], *Rossijskij ekonomicheskij zhurnal*, 4, 34–43 (in Russian).

Glaz'ev, S. (2015c), "O neotlozhnih merah po vyvodu rossijskoj ekonomiki na traektoriyu operezhayushego razvitiya" ["On urgent measures to lead Russian economy on the path of advanced economic development"], *Svobodnaya Mysl'*, available at http://svom.info/entry/601-o-neotlozhnyh-merah-po-vyvodu-rossijskoj-ekonomiki (accessed on March 17, 2016) (in Russian).

Glaz'ev, S. *et al.* (2015), "Kluch k buduschemu: kak sdelat finansovuyu sistemu instrumentom razvitiya" ["Key to the development: How to make financial system to be the instrument of economic development"], *Svobodnaya Mysl'*, available at http://svom.info/entry/603-klyuch-k-budushemu-kak-sdelat-finansovuyu-sistemu- (accessed on March 17, 2016) (in Russian).

Gorshkov, V. (2013), "Foreign banking in Russia: An analysis of inward-outward expansion," *The Journal of Comparative Economic Studies*, 8, 77–107.

Gorshkov, V. (2015), "Inward foreign entry of banks into Russia's banking sector," *The Journal of Comparative Economic Studies*, 8, 183–202.

Gurvich, E. and I. Prilepskij (2016), "Vliyanie financovih sanktsij na rossijskuyu ekonomiku" ["The impact of financial sanctions on the Russian economy"], *Voprosy Ekonomiki*, 1, 5–35 (in Russian).

International Bank of Reconstruction and Development/The World Bank (2016), *Global Financial Development Report 2015/2016*, available at http://documents. worldbank.org/curated/en/2015/09/24944751/global-financial-development-report-2015-2016-long-term-finance (accessed on March 23, 2016).

Kvashnina, I. and V. Obolenskij (2015), "Vvoz i vyvoz kapitala: effekti dlya Rossii" ["Import and export of capital: Effects for Russia"], *Mirovaya ekonomika i mezhdunarodnye otnosheniya*, 1, 63–76 (in Russian).

Maslennikov, V. (2015), "Vliyanie sovremennoj denezhno-kreditnoj politiki Rossii na ekonomicheskij rost" ["Impact of contemporary monetary policy of Russia on economic growth"], *EKO*, 10, 153–165 (in Russian).

McKinsey Global Institute (2015), "Debt and (not much) deleveraging," available at http://www.mckinsey.com/global-themes/employment-and-growth/debt-and-not-much-deleveraging (accessed on March 31, 2016).

Medvedev, D. (2015), "Novaya realnost: Rossiya I globalnye vyzovi" ["A new reality: Russia and global challenges"], *Voprosy Ekonomiki*, 10, 5–29 (in Russian).

PWC (2014), "An overview of Russian IPOs: 2005 to 2014," available at http://www.pwc.ru/en/capital-markets/publications/assets/a4_brochure_ipos_eng_print.pdf (accessed on March 17, 2016).

Shirov, A., A. Yantovskij and V. Potapenko (2015), "Otsenka potentsialnogo vliyaniya sanktsij na ekonomicheskoe razvitie Rossii i Evropejskogo Souza" ["Evaluation of the potential impact of sanctions on economic development of Russia and the EU"], *Problemy Prognozirovaniya [Studies on Russian Economic Development]*, 4, 3–16 (in Russian).

Stefanova, N. (2015), "Vliyanie ekonomicheskih sanktsij na bankovskij sector Rossii" ["Impact of economic sanctions on Russia's banking sector"], *Aktual'nye problemi gumanitarnih i estestvennih nauk*, 4(1), 258–261, available at http://cyberleninka.ru/article/n/vliyanie-ekonomicheskih-sanktsiy-na-bankovskiy-sektor-rossii (accessed on September 29, 2017) (in Russian).

The World Bank (2016), "Russia Monthly Economic Developments," available at http://www.worldbank.org/en/country/russia/brief/monthly-economic-developments (accessed on March 31, 2016).

World Bank Group (2015), "Global Financial Development Report 2015–2016: Long-Term Finance," p. 189, available at https://openknowledge.worldbank.org/handle/10986/22543 (accessed on June 23, 2017).

World Economic Forum (2015), "The Global Competitiveness Report 2015–2016," available at http://www3.weforum.org/docs/gcr/2015-2016/Global_Competitiveness_Report_2015-2016.pdf (accessed on March 23, 2016).

UNCTAD (2015), "World Investment Report 2015." p. 253, available at http://unctad.org/en/PublicationsLibrary/wir2015_en.pdf (accessed on June 23, 2017).

Zagashvili, V. (2015), "Zapadnye sanktsii i rossijskaya ekonomika" ["Western sanctions and Russian economy"], *Mirovaya ekonomika i mezhdunarodnye otnosheniya [World Economy and International Relations]*, 11, pp. 67–77 (in Russian).

Chapter 11

Industry and Transport

Olga Bobrova

Russia with its unique position both in Europe and in Asia plays an important role in both worlds — East and West. Russia reinvented itself in 1991 after the fall of Communism and has been trying ever since to modernize in the new post-Soviet environment.

Industry and transport are important components of this modernization drive.[1] Their contribution to post-Soviet Russian modernization is the centerpiece of this investigation.

Russia has immense development potential. It has a rich resource base and abundant social capital. Its people are flexible and open-minded. They have good communication skills, are responsive to external competitive

---

[1] There are several motives and preconditions for sustainable business development in Russia:

- Global demand on many kinds of material and non-material resources which the country possesses;
- Dramatic changes on oil and gas world markets;
- Mentality (rooted in the Orthodox Christianity);
- Northern climate conditions;
- Encouragement from the state to keep enterprises working due to safety and security reasons;
- Social infrastructure of industrial enterprises and the Soviet heritage in general; and
- High society's expectations.

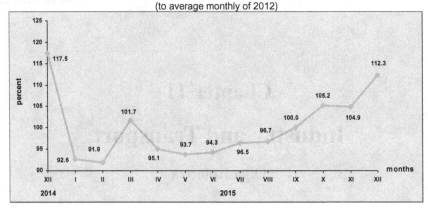

Industrial Production Index
(to average monthly of 2012)

Industrial production index is compiled by economic activity «Mining and quarrying», «Manufacturing», «Electricity, gas and water supply».

Figure 11.1   Russian Federation Industrial Production Index, % to Monthly Average 2012.

Source: Current Statistical Survey, No. 1 (96), Rosstat, 2016, p. 36.

pressures, and are excellent international partners in today's turbulent times. As Dmitry Mendeleev wrote more than 100 years ago, "For her well-being Russia has everything. Russia is just lacking free enterprise (business spirit)."

Russian industrial sector recently has been doing surprisingly well despite Western economic sanctions and the problems caused by plummeting natural resource prices. Figure 11.1 graphs the trend just before and after Crimea has returned to Russia.

Table 11.1 reports the structure of industrial output in 2014 for Russia and the Central and Northwest regions.

Machine-building, together with electric, electronical, and optical equipment, give 20.8% of industrial output in Russia as a whole, and almost 30% in the Northwest. It means the presence of a significant part of complicated manufacturing with meaningful added value among all industries. The contribution of manufacturing in Russian gross domestic product (GDP) is more significant than mining and extracting, but almost not rising after the world economic crisis of 2008–2011 (see International Monetary Fund (IMF), which provides statistical data about structure of economy of many countries).

Table 11.1   Structure of Industrial Output of Central and Northwest Regions of Russian Federation in 2014.

	Russia as a whole	Central Federal district	Northwest Russia
Food stuffs and Tobacco	16	18.5	17.4
Light industries	1	1.5	1.1
Timber and wood-working	1.3	1	2.6
Pulp paper	2.7	3.6	5
Fuels, chemicals, and plastics	33.5	35	27.4
Non-metal mineral products	4.2	4.2	3.1
Metallurgy	15.2	9.5	10.9
Machine-building	15.1	12.3	23.0
Electrical, electronical, and optical equipment	5.7	7	6.6
Others	5.2	7.4	2.9

Russian's federal government wants to build on these achievements and has established a set of appropriate guidelines called "Core areas of activity of the Russian Federation Government" (CAAG).[2]

The set includes the following goals:

- Increase the rates of growth of GDP up to 3.5–4% (but not less than a worldwide average ones);
- Increase a share of investments' volume into GDP up to 21–22%;
- Increase a share of a non-energy export by up to 45%;
- Decrease the share of imports in the retail sector by up to 30%.

The government believes that the key to success lies in increasing national competitiveness and has taken concrete steps toward this end through its National Entrepreneurship Initiative, tax reductions, and exemptions. The government also encourages industrial import substitution and regional development. It has created special economic zones,

[2] See http://economy.gov.ru/en/home/activity/sections/strategicplanning/2015251106 (accessed on July 3, 2017). On May 14, 2015, the Russian Federation Government approved CAAG for the period up to 2018.

although in some cases they malfunctioned — in Kaliningrad region in April 2016 some of the tax and customs relief were rescinded.

The Ministry of Economic Development summarized its intentions as follow:

> A comprehensive implementation of strategic planning instruments of the Russian Federation is the main mechanism of increasing the efficiency of public administration. Principles, priorities, goals and tasks of country's development, the priorities of industrial and regional development will be internally integrated, complex correlation between development of the system of urbanized regions (settlement network) and development and allocation of economic and social sphere objects will be made, allocation of large investment projects and their infrastructure supply will be justified, a content of macro-regions of Russia will be justified and the process of preparation of their strategies will be launched as a result of implementation of the state strategic management system.[3]

The financial crisis that beset Russia in 2014 has complicated the endeavor. The government has responded by

- supporting import substitution and export on wide nomenclature of non-energy commodities with state subsidies for payments of interest on credits or financing of companies' activity. Defense plants and producers of high-technology goods are top priorities;
- providing vulnerable citizens (retired persons, families with several children) with supplementary income to offset inflation;
- increasing the banking system's stability and creating of bailout mechanism for systemically important organizations; and
- optimizing budgetary expenditures.[4]

The government is also continuing structural reforms in healthcare and education. It is succeeding. The business climate is improving gradually. The taxation system has stabilized. The pension system was placed under

---

[3] See http://economy.gov.ru/en/home/activity/sections/strategicplanning/2015251106 (accessed on July 3, 2017).

[4] See http://economy.gov.ru/en/home/activity/sections/strategicPlanning/2015251107 (accessed on July 3, 2017).

the Federal Tax service's supervision in 2017. Nonetheless, the efficiency of public administration and large business still needs improvement.[5]

Sanctions have caused further difficulties.[6] Access to foreign imports has been hampered, creating temporary opportunities for profitable import substitution (Truel and Pashchenko 2016). Russian agro-business and IT industry appear to be principal beneficiaries. The agro-industrial complex has grown rapidly during the sanction years 2014–2016.[7]

Table 11.2 provides statistics on Russian subsector food production growth for the period 2015–2016, with significant growth.

Growing internal demand for Russian food also aided the agricultural machinery sector. The St. Petersburg Tractor Plant increased 2016 sales by 30%.[8]

Federal assistance is required to exploit other opportunities, but the level of aid has been modest.[9]

Perhaps, Donald Trump will relax or terminate sanctions.[10] If he does, Russian industrial modernization should accelerate.

Industrial Policy

Russia introduced its first industrial policy law on December 31, 2014 (Federal Law No. 488), building on lessons learned from other countries and Russia's own Skolkovo experiment. It governs

— manufacturing,
— industrial parks,

---

[5] See Federal Law No. 87-FZ dated April 20, 2015, "On the report of the Russian Federation Government and the Information of the Central Bank of the Russian Federation about realization of the first priority action plan securing stable development of the economy and social stability in 2015."

[6] Russia spent 18 years in the negotiation process to enter World Trade Organization (WTO), but in 2014 after only two years of the participation in that organization it lost a great part of the advantages of being a member of WTO because of economic sanctions and contrasanctions which appeared because of the Ukrainian crises.

[7] See data on agricultural development published by Rosstat.

[8] See http://kirovets-ptz.com/rus/s/16/profily_kompanii.html (accessed on July 3, 2017).

[9] The European Union faces similar adjustment issues. See Debra Johnson and Colin Turner "Strategy and Policy for Trans-European Network."

[10] President Tramp's announcement that United States is going to leave Trans-Pacific Partnership means more opportunities for Russia to strengthen trade ties in Asia and across Pacific Ocean.

Table 11.2   Production of Selected Food Products.

	2015			2016	
	I half	9 months	Year	I quarter	I half
	Percent of corresponding period of previous year				
Meat and by-products of slaughter bearing	113.2	114.2	113.0	111.4	114.3
Meat and subproducts of poultry	111.4	110.2	109.6	105.9	105.8
Sunflower-seed not refined oil and its fractions	91.7	87.4	91.0	97.0	103.2
Whole milk products (in milk equivalent)	101.4	101.0	101.2	103.6	102.8
Butter and buttery pastes	105.8	104.7	102.5	96.2	96.8
Flour of grain, green and other; their mixtures	101.9	102.3	102.1	101.8	100.0
Grouts, seconds and grains, never else classified	94.8	94.4	93.9	101.3	105.0
White beet sugar in solid state	36.1	103.9	111.9	227.5	202.9
White cane sugar in solid state	98.0	94.0	92.7	27.1	37.6

Source: Current Statistical Survey, No. 2 (97), Rosstat (2016, p. 44).

— industrial clusters, and

— engineering centers.

The law creates an industrial information system and provides funds for industrial development. The government is now empowered to issue special investment contracts to private businesses. The law's goals are to develop a hi-tech, competitive industry, facilitating the transition of Russia's economy from a raw materials exporter to an innovation-driven economy; to assure the country's defense; to provide employment; and to increase the nation's standard of living.

"Effective application of all developed instruments of industrial policy, first and utmost for securing of import substitution and export support including attraction of significant volumes of direct foreign investments (project financing, guarantees, economic support fund, industrial parks, state purchasing, public-private partnership)."[11]

---

[11] See http://economy.gov.ru/en/home/activity/sections/strategicPlanning/2015251107 (accessed on July 3, 2017).

Maxim Oreshkin, Russia's new minister of economic development will use a matrix of diverse indicators to monitor progress under Federal Law No. 488.[12]

Russia's industrial policy emulates best foreign practices — that of the European Union, Japan, and the United States. Many enterprises nonetheless are still hesitant to modernize. They consider the state not as partner but as an enemy. Progress requires sector-by-sector mutual understanding between business and government. The most promising sectoral opportunities are in the following.

Shipbuilding. In 2015, in the Northwestern Federal District, the United Shipbuilding Corporation (USC) became the sixth-largest among the top 250 businesses in the region. Its total sales were RUB304 billion with profits of RUB20 billion. The corporation includes around 40 shipbuilding companies and organizations: main shipbuilding and ship repair yards, and leading design bureaus. Currently, USC has consolidated most of the domestic shipbuilding industry. USC enterprises and organizations employ more than 80,000 people. USC is a leader of shipbuilding in Russia and plays an important role in industrial development of the country.

Energy sector. This sector is developing rapidly. It is a vital input for industrial growth. An Organization for Economic Co-operation and Development (OECD) research published in 2013 highlights the following needs in the area: "In industry, energy management systems and techniques should be more widely employed, especially in energy-intensive industries. Efforts to improve data and statistics collection should be also pursued, especially on the energy demand side, a complex effort which involves all sectors of the economy".[13]

Transport. Two important transport projects are in progress — modernization of the Trans-Siberian Railway and activation of the North Marine Way. Table 11.3 provides basic information on Russian investment in the transport sector.

Railway transport is a significant share of total investments. In 2014, Vladimir Yakunin, former head of Russian Railways, published an integrated Eurasian development plan. The mega project's centerpiece is

---

[12] See http://kommersant.ru/doc/3186798 (accessed on July 3, 2017).
[13] See https://www.oecd.org/russia/Russia-Modernising-the-Economy-EN.pdf (accessed on July 3, 2017).

Table 11.3   Investments in Fixed Assets, Billion Rubles.

Type of transport	2010	2011	2012	2013	2014	2015
Transport as a whole	1471.0	2048.3	2063.6	1999.9	1871.6	1862.5
Railway	364.6	403.1	443.4	413.9	328.4	339.3
Buses	12.3	18.9	16.2	24.4	12.8	11.5
City electric transport	56.4	80.5	111.6	218.6	102.9	82.1
Automobile cargo transport	10.5	19.3	25.1	28.0	18.9	20.6
Pipes	624.5	949.9	836.2	643.0	714.6	715.4
Marine transport	4.6	13.3	3.4	6.2	7.0	3.3
Inland water transport	2.7	12.3	9.1	4.5	5.2	2.7
Air transport	18.9	17.8	26.4	33.1	44.5	57.6

Source: Transport and connection in Russia. Statistical survey, Rosstat (2016, p. 18).

the modernization of the Trans-Siberian Railway, designed to support a public–private partnered Eurasian industrial development belt. Russia will build railway lines to 18 industrial zones covering more than 4,600 km by 2030, jointly funded by state and private sources.

The top management of Russian Railways changed in 2015. Oleg Belozerov, the new head has outlined his vision:

Ratified by the government in June 2008, the Strategy for Developing Rail Transport in the Russian Federation up to 2030 envisages a significant expansion of Russia's rail network in two stages. The first involves a period of modernisation (2008–15) to ensure the necessary capacity on key routes, a fundamental renewal and upgrading of existing infrastructure and the beginning of planning and surveying work for expansion, as well as a start on the construction of some high-priority lines… The second stage from 2016 to 2030 involves large-scale expansion. This will create the infrastructure needed to develop new areas of economic growth across Russia's vast territory, achieving a world-class level of technology and improving the competitiveness of the country's rail system on the global market.[14]

---

[14] See http://eng.rzd.ru/statice/public/en?STRUCTURE_ID=7.

There are two versions of the strategy: minimum and maximum. The minimum version envisages the construction of 16,017 km of new route by 2030, while the maximum scenario calls for 20,730 km.

The minimum strategy focuses on full modernization of the existing rail infrastructure and development of the necessary capacity on key freight corridors to meet the needs of the economy and population. It will serve new development zones, with some freight-only and high-tech lines constructed.

The maximum version will employ world-class infrastructure to end capacity bottlenecks across the entire rail network. It will ensure state-of-the-art infrastructure all the way to Magadan, offering green field natural resource access.

Both alternatives encourage competitive domestic and foreign private investments in a venture that will link the Pacific to Europe's frontier. They will allow fast container freight trains to move across Russia in a week, an average of more than 1,000 km per day, facilitating trade with Europe and Korea, Japan, and Northeast China.

Air travel is also becoming increasingly popular and has grown rapidly since 2000. Figure 11.2 shows that it accounts for half of the passenger turnover (billions of passengers/kilometer). Railways remain popular for short distance travel, but Russians now prefer to fly longer distances.

Sustainability

Development under Federal Law No. 488 will be internally and externally sustainable for enterprise managers and stakeholders. The socioeconomic dimension will be monitored to assure relationships remain harmonious and that enterprises in the development zone are competitive enough to continuously attract essential investment.

Sakhalin Energy provides a good example of self-monitoring.[15] It voluntarily adopted an ISO26000 internal self-audit in 2012 and applies Corporate Social Responsibility (CSR) activity protocols in everyday practice.[16]

---

[15] Sakhalin Energy pays more that 60% of Sakhalin's regional tax bill.
[16] Sakhalin Energy publishes a humorous brochure called: "If you don't know how to use ISO26000, ask me!"

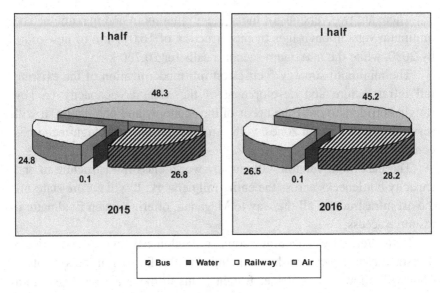

Figure 11.2   Passenger Turnover by Transport Modes (Percentage of Total).

Enterprise management researchers mostly concern themselves with financial sustainability. Corporate social responsibility advocates urge them to take account of the social side of sustainable development, including ecological aspects. Market sustainability and sustainable relations with stakeholders also deserve attention. An inclusive approach is best for the wholesome development of Russia's manufacturing industrial services, transport, munitions manufacturing, pharmaceutical industry, chemistry, agriculture and food industry, and energy and transport machinery sectors.

Conclusion

Russia is committed to developing its industrial prowess in the national interest, guided by Federal Law No. 488. It wants to work within a global framework in Eurasia, without compromising its spheres of influence. Russia's national interest has and will continue to take precedence over globalizing. Russia is able to balance its national and global interests through constructive participation in the Commonwealth of Independent

States, Shanghai Cooperation Organization, and BRICS. Russian industrial development has made great inclusive strides during the new millennium and appears poised to build further on its past accomplishments.

References

Johnson D. and C. Turner (2007), *Strategy and Policy for Trans-European Networks,* Berlin: Springer.

Truel, J.L. and Y. Pashchenko (2016), "Under which conditions can an import-substitution policy be a driver for re-industrialization?," *Review of Business and Economic Studies*, (1), 68–74.

Chapter 12

Innovation

Anna Kovaleva*

Introduction

Western economic sanctions and plunging natural resource price have adversely affected Russia's budget and the government's ability to incubate innovation. The federal budget of Russia was RUB 1 trillion 945 billion 99.5 million in the red in 2015, or 2.6% of gross domestic product (GDP). The share of state budget financing in expenditures on science, education, and innovation has correspondingly decreased in recent years. Despite the budgetary duress, the Russian government continues its initiatives to improve the country's innovative infrastructure as part of its drive to shift the economy from an efficiency focus to an innovation-driven system (The Global Competitiveness Report 2014).

After the collapse of the Union of Soviet Socialist Republics (USSR), the Russian Federation launched new initiatives to protect and support the further development of science and technology, particularly in activities linked to the military–industrial complex. The Russian government devised a new system for encouraging innovations that promoted stakeholder participation. At the same time, the country's political and economic systems

*The author expresses a special gratitude to Professor Steven Rosefielde. Errors and oversights are the sole responsibility of the author.

changed dramatically post 1991 and new actors appeared (e.g., special state entities promoting innovation — Russian Venture Company (RVC)[1]), without altering the main features of Soviet's science, technology, and innovation (STI) policy.

This chapter surveys government innovation policy to identify key innovation initiatives shaping Russian STI policy and related government regulation.

One of the main goals of the Soviet system was to narrow the gap between science and the adoption of research and development (R&D)-generated innovation in manufacturing. It relied on hierarchical methods that are now inappropriate. Flexible and decentralized technology management institutions are essential today for integrating science, education, and high-tech manufacturing (Karlik and Platonov 2015). These institutions are the focus of our concern.

Background

Experts agree that innovations are the main drivers of modern economies (Karlik *et al.* 2013). A great deal has been written about the best techniques for boosting creativity in business and higher education organizations. Russia is trying to integrate itself into international scientific networks, paying great attention to the development of the global innovation networks, while coping with the consequences of the collapse of the USSR in 1991, economic sanctions, and declining natural resource prices. This effort has been particularly vigorous in the military–industrial complex.

Key features of Soviet science such as strict government regulation, insularity, and a strong ideological bias still hamper Russian science and technology policy. Scientists of the Soviet epoch (both humanitarian and natural scholars) thought "out of the box." They were supported by institutions like the Houses of Young Technicians and publications such as "Science and Life" ("Nauka i Zhizn"). The Russian government today has launched various projects to safeguard Soviet intellectual traditions in creative science via competitions, festivals, and programs,

---

[1] See http://www.rvc.ru/en/. The official website of the Russian Venture Company.

preserving aspects of the Soviet legacy, including the prioritization of defense industry and persistence of "shadow" science (informal protocols like those for resolving conflicts of research interest in laboratories).

Russia's innovation policy development has been energetic under Vladimir Putin, May 2000–May 2016. These initiatives form the center-piece of our inquiry.[2]

Approaches to Innovations

Russia is exploring two basic strategies for nurturing innovation.

The first establishes innovation codes and priorities based on documentary information generated at the international, national, and local levels. Standard sources are "The Model Innovation Code for the CIS" (Model Innovation Code 2014) and "The Strategy for the Innovation Development of the Russian Federation until 2020" (The Strategy of Innovative Development 2011).

The second assembles recommendations from expert sources like the Oslo Manual (2005), "Bridging the Innovation Gap in Russia (2001),"[3] and "Measuring Design and Its Role in Innovation" (Galindo-Rueda and Millot 2015). Traditional expert sources for improving quality, processes, markets, organization, and external relations are also available (Oslo Manual 2005, p. 46). They focus on product, process, organizational, and marketing innovation (*Oslo Manual* 2005, p. 16).

The concept of innovation in the Russian legislative documents is similar to the *Oslo Manual*: "innovations are new or improved product (service) or process, new marketing or organizational method in the business practices, workplace organization or external relations" (The Federal Law 1996).

---

[2] "The policy framework of the Russian Federation in the field of science and technology for the period up to 2010 and beyond," approved by order of the President on 30.03.2002 No. Pr-576, available at http://www.consultant.ru/document/cons_doc_LAW_91403/.

[3] "Bridging the innovation gap in Russia. The Helsinki seminar," OECD Proceedings. March 2001, available at http://www.oecdbookshop.org/en/browse/title-detail/?k=5LMQ CR2KMP46.

The last approach stresses company business practice. It provides an alternative, non-academic perspective.

Innovation is a diffuse concept. The specifics are essential (Borrás and Edquist 1996). The crucial aspect is how innovation-driven organizations operate on the national, regional, and local levels (Aoki 1990, 2013), particularly their network-centricity (Nambison and Sawhney 2011) and information-sharing (Kovaleva and Platonov 2010).

The merit of innovation initiatives is judged from their content (documents), stakeholders, and resource-based (RBV) analyses (Grant 1991; Eliseeva and Platonov 2014; Karlik and Platonov 2013). The latter deals with ownership and asset control conflicts (Bronwyn and Rosenberg 2010).

Problems and Responses

The author's investigation reveals that investment and innovation activities of Russian organizations have been hampered by financial crises. These crises compelled many small and big companies in Russia to wind down investment and innovative projects (Kovaleva and Varzina 2012).[4] Companies have cut innovation budgets with three consequences:

1. Innovative companies have been forced to maintain no-frills innovative projects to preserve their competitive advantages awaiting better times.
2. Small and medium enterprises (SMEs) have taken the niches abandoned by big companies. SMEs often adapt more easily to market changes.
3. The Russian government set up new academic and educational institutions to mitigate damage to Russian domestic innovation. The Russian government encourages general and policy-specific innovation initiatives (The Strategy of Innovation Development

---

[4] Boldyrev V. N., S. V. Ovsyannikov and M. A. Shatalov (2009), "Features of the mechanism of enterprise investment policy under conditions of crisis" (in Russian), available at http://www.lerc.ru/?part=bulletin&art=28&page=7; V. Mau (2010), "The Russian economy does not perceive innovation," March 16, available at http://www.forbes.ru/node/46400.

2011). Different programs have been developed under the Putin regime. The government created its generic policy for preserving the Soviet science and enterprise heritage. It supported small scientific and technical enterprises.

The government of Russia devised more specific initiatives aimed at supporting a dialogue among the government, academia, and business (Kovaleva and Shevstsova 2013; Dezhina and Simachev 2012).[5] These include "Guidelines for implementing cluster policies in the Russian Federation" and the Government Resolution No. 219 of April 9, 2010, "On state support of innovation infrastructure in the federal educational institutions of higher education." They have been platforms for opening competition among Russian universities seeking special funding and can be viewed as applications of Henry Etzkowitz Triple Helix concept (Etzkowitz 2003).

Available statistics indicate that triadic patent families[6] and government research have increased in Russia since 1986,[7] even though gross domestic spending on R&D has fallen from 2.032% of GDP in 1990 to 1.133% in 2013, attributable to expenditures volatility during the period 2007–2016 (Figure 12.1). Education expenditures however have been largely unchanged.

Figure 12.2 shows that government support for applied research was significant during the period 2007–2016, with a spike in 2014.

Data collected by the author between 2014 and 2016 in St. Petersburg provide further insights.

First, government innovation organizations strictly comply with Moscow's budget and strategy, despite intraorganization disagreements about research priorities.

---

[5] The Concept of Long-Term Social and Economic Development of the Russian Federation Until 2020, approved by the Government Executive Order dated November, 17, 2008, No. 1662-r, available at http://government.ru/.

[6] A patent for the same invention obtained by the same applicant or inventor at the European Patent Office, the US Patent and Trademark Office and the Japan Patent Office.

[7] Triadic Patent Families (indicator), available at doi: 10.1787/6a8d10f4-en; Government Researchers (indicator), available at doi: 10.1787/c03b3052-en; Gross Domestic Spending on R&D (indicator), available at doi: 10.1787/d8b068b4-en.

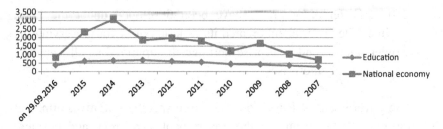

Figure 12.1   Federal Budget Expenditures in Russia in Education and National Economy (Billion Rubles).

Source: Compiled by author with reference to the single portal of the Russian budget system "Electronic Budget," available at http://budget.gov.ru/.

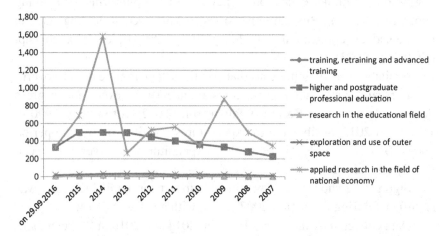

Figure 12.2   Federal Budget Expenditures in Russia in National Economy and Education, Billion Rubles.

Source: Compiled by author with reference to the single portal of the Russian budget system "Electronic Budget," available at http://budget.gov.ru/.

Second, compliance is sometimes a problem in elementary schools. OJSC Rusnano tried to improve the situation by creating a "School League Rusnano" to stimulate communication among schools, universities, businesses, and other organizations about nanoscience and nanotechnologies developments.[8]

---

[8]Project "School League RUSNANO," official site, available at http://schoolnano.ru.

Third, stakeholders often hold conflicting opinions that require central adjudication (The Strategy for Innovation Development 2011).

Summary

The Russian government under Vladimir Putin's watch has tried to incubate innovation to compensate for the private sector's lack of initiative and investible funds.[9] It has made a credible institutional and financial effort.

Russia has pursued a policy path that includes the creation of institutions for the development of innovations, and the integration of Russia into the global innovation network.

Russia tries to blend best global innovation practices with Soviet science and technology tradition.

Russia's innovation strategy is forward-looking, paying special attention to large firms.

Insufficient demand, however, has driven many Russian startups to move abroad (National Report on Innovations in Russia 2016).

Russia is coping with innovation issues common to transitioning counties. Its experience therefore should be instructive for Asian nations at a similar stage of development (National report on innovations in Russia 2016).

Russia needs to pay more attention to innovation principals' and stakeholders' motivations.[10]

Western economic sanctions are likely to be rescinded soon. The government should be prepared to modify its innovational priorities, taking account of prospects for the emergence of a mature private self-regulating

---

[9] Decree of the Russian Government dated March 21, 2016 No. 475-p in accordance with the Federal Law. "On procurement of goods, works and services of certain kinds of legal entities" approve the attached list of the specific legal entities mentioned in paragraph 2 of Article 1 of the Federal Law, and we are required to carry out the procurement of innovative products, high-tech products, including the subjects small and medium-sized businesses, available at GARANT.RU: http://www.garant.ru/products/ipo/prime/doc/71258530/#ixzz4RtidsYuW.

[10] According to the empirical research conducted at the Saint-Petersburg State University of Economics and Finance, top-management mainly of big companies do not want to implement innovations in their companies due to its suppose additional transformation in the business processes.

innovation market. This will expedite its initiative to make Russia an innovation-driven economy.

References

Aoki, M. (1990), "Toward an economic model of the Japanese firm," *Journal of Economic Literature*, 28(1), 1–27.

Aoki, M. (2013), " 'Individual' social capital, 'social' networks, and their linkages to economic game," in: *Comparative Institutional Analysis: Theory, Corporations and East Asia: Selected Papers of Aoki Masahiko*, 250–266, Cheltenham, UK: E. Elgar.

"Bridging the Innovation Gap in Russia, The Helsinki seminar," OECD Proceedings, March 2001, available at http://www.oecdbookshop.org/en/browse/title-detail/?k=5LMQCR2KMP46.

Borrás and Edquist (1996), "Conceptual underpinnings for innovation policy design — indicators and instruments in context," available at https://www.oecd.org/sti/019%20-%20Borras-Edquist%20Blue%20Sky%20SUBMIT-TED%2025th%20July.pdf.

Bronwyn, H. H. and N. Rosenberg (2010), *Handbooks in Economics of Innovation*. Volume 1. Amsterdam: Elsevier.

Dezhina, I. and Y. Simachev (2012), "Partnering universities and companies in Russia: Effects of new government initiative," available at http://mpra.ub.uni-muenchen.de/43622.

Eliseeva, I. and V. Platonov (2014), "Dinamicheskij potencial — nedostayush-chee zveno v issledovanii innovacionnoj deyatel'nosti. Finansy i biznes" ["The dynamic potential as the missing link in the innovation research"], *Finance and Business* No. 6, 102–110 (in Russian).

Etzkowitz, H. (2003), "Innovation in innovation: The triple helix of university–industry–government relations," *Social Science Information*, 42(3), 293–337.

The Federal Law (1996), The Federal Law of August 23, 1996 No. 127-FZ "On Science and State Scientific and Technical Policy" (as amended on and in force at the date of June 03, 2016).

Galindo-Rueda, F. and V. Millot (2015), "Measuring design and its role in innovation," OECD Science, *Technology and Industry Working Papers*, 2015/01, OECD Publishing, available at http://dx.doi.org/10.1787/5js7p6lj6zq6-en.

The Global Competitiveness Report 2014–2015 (2014), by World Economic Forum, available at http://www3.weforum.org/docs/WEF_GlobalCompeti-tivenessReport_2014–15.pdf.

Grant, M. (1991), "Robert the resource-based theory of competitive advantage: Implications for strategy formulation," *California Management Review*, 33(3), 114–135.

Karlik, A., A. Kovaleva, V. Platonov *et al.* (2013), *Upravlenie intellektual'nymi resursami innovacionno-aktivnyh predpriyatij* [*Management of Intellectual Resources of Innovation-Active Enterprises*], SPb: Publishing House of SPbSUEF (in Russian).

Karlik, A. and V. Platonov (2013), "Analiticheskaya struktura resursno-orientirovannogo podhoda" ["Analytic structure of resource-based approach"], *Problemy teorii i praktiki upravleniya* No. 6, 26–37 (in Russian).

Karlik, A. and V. Platonov (2015), "Organizatsionno-upravlencheskie innovatsii: rezerv povysheniya konkurentosposobnosti rossijskoj promyshlennosti" ["Organizational and managerial innovations: A reserve to increase the competitiveness of the Russian industry"], *Ehkonomicheskoe vozrozhdenie Rossii*, 3, 34–44 (in Russian).

Kovaleva, A. and J. Varzina (2012), "Innovative mechanisms for financial recovery in the macro-and micro-economic instability," in: *Economic and Organizational Aspects of Intellectual Development and Innovation*, 80–91, SPb: Publishing House of SPbSUEF (in Russian).

Kovaleva, A. and V. Platonov (2010), "Izuchenie vzaimodejstviya aktivnyh predpriyatij v ramkah setevogo podhoda" ["The study of the interaction innovation-driven enterprises within framework of the network approach"], in: Gorelova N. A. and S.V. Kuznecova (eds.), *Mezhvuzovskij sbornik nauchnyh trudov. Vypusk* No. 8 / pod red., 145–149, SPb: Publishing House of SPbSUEF (in Russian).

Kovaleva, A. and O. Shevstsova (2013), *Sovremennye aspekty potrebleniya konsaltingovyh i obrazovatel'nyh uslug v mezhdunarodnoj srede* [*Modern Aspects of the Consumption of Consulting and Educational Services in the International Environment*], 68–74, Izvestia of SPbUEF. SPb: Publishing House of SPbSUEF, (in Russian).

The Model Innovation Code (2014), "Model'nyj innovatsionnyj kodeks dlya gosudarstv-uchastnikov SNG" (Prinyat v g. Sankt-Peterburge 28.11.2014 Postanovleniem 41–23 na 41-om plenarnom zasedanii Mezhparlamentskoj Assamblei gosudarstv-uchastnikov SNG) iz informatsionnogo banka "Mezhdunarodnoe pravo" [The model innovation code for the CIS member nations], available at http://www.consultant.ru/cons/cgi/online.cgi?req=doc;base=INT;n=32143;frame=4294967295.

Nambison, S. and M. Sawhney (2011), "Orchestration processes in network-centric innovation," *Academy of Management Perspectives*, 25(3), 40–57.

National report on innovations in Russia (2016), "Open Innovations Forum — Supporting materials," October 26, available at http://www.rvc.ru/upload/ iblock/6c5/20161025_2200_Forum_OI_eng.pdf.

O'Brien, J. (2011), "Hard vs. soft power in global and national politics: Innovative concepts of smart power and cultural diplomacy in an age of interdependence, digital revolution, and social media," The International Symposium on Cultural Diplomacy. Berlin, Mai 11–15, available at http://www.culturaldiplomacy.org/ academy/content/pdf/participant-papers/2011-symposium/Hard-Vs.-Soft-Power-in-Global-and-National-Politics-Innovative-Concepts-of-Smart-Power--Josiane-Martin-O'BRIEN.pdf.

Oslo Manual (2005), *Guidelines for Collecting and Interpreting Innovation Data*, 3rd ed., Paris: OECD.

Porter, M. E. M. Ketels and C. Delgado (2007), "The microeconomic foundations of prosperity: Findings from the business competitiveness index," available at http://www.forumdaliberdade.com.br/fl2009/apresentacao_arquivos/ Chapter2.pdf.

Russia: Focus on Innovation (2013), "Russia: Focus on innovation," Public Analytical Report on the Implementation of the Strategy for Innovative Development of The Russian Federation for The Period until the Year 2020. Release I. 2013.

The Strategy of Innovative Development (2011), The Strategy of Innovative Development of the Russian Federation until 2020, approved by the Government Executive Order Dated December 8, 2011 No 2227-r.

Part III
China

Chapter 13

Rising Red Star

Steven Rosefielde

Economy

China claimed that communist economy is superior from the day Mao Zedong seized power on October 1, 1949. Official statistics show that annual gross domestic product (GDP) growth has oscillated around a mean of 10% since 1950, tapering off to 7% after 2010. These results which span both the Mao and post-Mao market communist eras are impressive and, if true, imply a bright future for contemporary China's rising red star, despite blemishes like one-party political rule, ethnic unrest, unequal development, congestion, pollution, income inequality, high indebtedness, speculative excesses, wage pressure, inflation, and unemployment. Perhaps, "the East will be red."[1]

But is the impression imparted by official data reliable? The Soviet Union reported similar accomplishments during 1921–1928 and 1950–1968. Its official statistics were notoriously unreliable for diverse reasons, including hidden inflation and free invention (Bergson 1953,

---

[1] The "East Is Red" is a song that was the *de facto* anthem of the People's Republic of China during the Cultural Revolution in the 1960s. Today in China the song is considered by some to be a somewhat unseemly reminder of the cult of personality associated with Mao. Its official use has largely been replaced by the "March of the Volunteers," whose lyrics mention neither the Communist Party nor Mao.

1972, 1975; Rosefielde 2005b, 2010; Harrison 2000). The Union of Soviet Socialist Republics (USSR) did industrialize enough to defeat Nazi Germany in World War II and hold its own in the Cold War until 1989, but it no longer exists. Its red star has fallen.

Specialists have long understood that Chinese economic statistics also are unreliable; that they greatly exaggerate accomplishments (Koch-Weser 2013; Rawski 2001).[2] There are many arcane explanations for the distortion, and free invention is doubtlessly part of the mix.[3] The Central Intelligence Agency (CIA) and RAND corporation decades ago unofficially tried to deal with the ambiguity by arbitrarily halving Chinese GDP growth claims for their internal assessments. The rule of thumb is imprecise, but compatible with China's physical achievements, index number issues, and a deep understanding of "forced substitution."[4]

China's big picture can be gleaned by focusing on the basics, despite the fog. Official Chinese economic statistics are computed in domestic

---

[2] Koch-Weser (2013):

> China's national output figures are not as reliable as those of the United States and Europe. Although alternative indicators and internal consistency checks are imperfect methods, they serve to cast doubt on the quality of data. A closer analysis of China's statistical work sheds light on some of the underlying problems facing China's statistics. These problems stem in part from the lack of reform since the 1990s. With the exception of certain breakthroughs, such as seasonally adjusted growth, there has not been any deeper reform. The lack of reform of statistical work appears to follow a broader pattern during the decade-long administration of President Hu Jintao: a wide range of reforms, from corporate ownership to social welfare, were less ambitious than under the preceding government of President Jiang Zemin.

"Are Chinese GDP statistics reliable?," *BOFIT*, April 13, 2016, available at http://www.bofbulletin.fi/en/2016/1/are-chinese-gdp-statistics-reliable/.

[3] The author was in teaching in Nanjing during the severe acute respiratory syndrome epidemic. The country was closed down for months, but there was no trace of the disruption in the official data.

[4] Authoritarian countries confront consumers with numerous "take it or leave it" option. Purchases and sales are recorded, but consumers are compelled to buy things that they do not prefer or do not want. The transactions are entered in GDP as if they were competitively efficient, overstating value added.

prices. GDP series provide an impression of mean real economic growth between 1950 and 2016 to be in a range between 4.5% and 10% per annum, depending on the degree of statistical exaggeration assumed. This means that China's GDP grew rapidly, above America's long-term historical rate, regardless of whether one prefers the unofficial CIA judgment or China's official series. China's red star definitely is rising, but most likely more slowly than Beijing's data indicate, and appears to be gradually diminishing as the advantages of relative economic backwardness wane (Rosefielde *et al.* 2012). A recent Congressional research report predicts that China's growth rate will asymptotically converge to America's 2% rate by 2050 (Morrison 2015b).

It might seem to follow on the principle of transitivity that China's growth rate also exceeds America's long-term rate measured in dollars, but this may not be so. Differences between quality-adjusted dollar prices and yuan prices could reduce China's growth rate as the CIA perceives it below American's long-term trend. This is the index number relativity problem made famous by Moorsteen and Powell (1966) and Moorsteen (1962).

Moreover, comparative economic size estimates of China's and America's GDPs are surprisingly sensitive to the method used to convert yuan to dollars. China's 2015 GDP is almost 40% less than America's, using the official market-based exchange rate, but China's GDP exceeds 2015 US GDP measured with purchasing power parities.[5] America's 2015 GDP was US$17.95 trillion. China's 2015 purchasing power parity (PPP) GDP was US$19.39 trillion, but the figure using the market exchange rate was only US$10.98 trillion.

The CIA contends that the PPP adjustments it reports are reliable.[6] Perhaps, but it should be appreciated that PPP calculations are a dark art, sometimes bordering on the occult (Bergson 1961). When PPP coefficients are periodically adjusted, the revised conversion rates usually differ drastically from the old benchmarks. It is wise therefore to take comparative size measures with a grain of salt.

---

[5] CIA World Factbook (2016), available at https://www.cia.gov/library/publications/the-world-factbook/geos/ch.html.

[6] The World Bank Group and OECD develop the PPP numbers that the CIA reports in its World Factbooks. The Agency computes special PPP for other purposes like building block-based defense statistics.

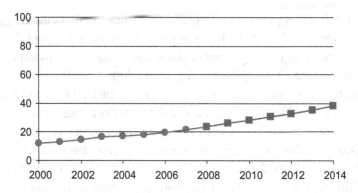

Figure 13.1   China Per Capita GDP Growth, US = 100.

Note: Observations 2000–2009 were computed by Angus Maddison. Statistics 2008–2014 are IMF projections. West Europe includes Austria, Belgium, Denmark, Finland, France, Germany, Italy, Netherlands, Norway, Sweden, Switzerland, and the United Kingdom. GDP for West Europe and Russia is calculated in 1990 international Geary–Khamis dollars.

Source: Table 11.1. in Angus Maddison, *The World Economy: Historical Statistics*, OECD, 2003, pp. 558–563, p. 566; Angus Maddison, available at http://www.ggdc.net/maddison/Historical_ Statistics/horizontal-file_03-2009xls (accessed on March 2009).

Nonetheless, despite the statistical fog, several things appear certain. First, China has one of the world's largest GDPs. Second, whatever its true magnitude, China's GDP has grown much faster than America's and the European Union's after the 2008 global financial crisis (Figure 13.1). Third, China's per capita income remains a small fraction of the American standard (Morrison 2015a). Fourth, Chinese living standards are rapidly improving and moving toward those of the developed West. In short, China is not the Soviet Union. Beijing has the proven ability, which the Soviet Union never had, to sustain the growth of real per capita consumption by attracting direct foreign investment and outsourcers and by transferring technology (Rosefielde 2007). It is entrepreneurial, competitive, and integrated into the global economy with largely positive macroeconomic characteristics (see the indicative figures in Table 13.1). There are problems, but Xi Jinping is addressing them.[7]

---

[7]China's 12th Five-Year Plan (2011–2015) and the newly approved 13th Five-Year Plan (2016–2020) forcefully address these issues. They highlight the development of services and measures to address environmental and social imbalances, setting targets to reduce pollution, to increase energy efficiency, to improve access to education and healthcare,

Table 13.1   Key Indicators of China's Economic Performance During 2011–2015.

	2011	2012	2013	2014	2015
Population (million)	1,347	1,354	1,361	1,368	1,375
GDP per capita (US$)	5,575	6,260	7,037	7,569	7,808
GDP (US$ in billion)	7,511	8,476	9,576	10,352	10,736
Economic growth (GDP, annual variation in %)	9.5	7.8	7.7	7.3	6.9
Consumption (annual variation in %)	11.0	9.1	7.3	7.8	—
Investment (annual variation in %)	24.0	20.6	19.6	15.7	10.0
Industrial production (annual variation in %)	13.9	10.0	9.7	8.3	6.1
Retail sales (annual variation in %)	17.1	14.3	13.1	12.0	10.7
Unemployment rate	4.1	4.1	4.1	4.1	4.1
Fiscal balance (% of GDP)	−1.1	−1.6	−1.9	−1.8	−3.5
Public debt (% of GDP)	14.9	14.5	14.8	15.0	—
Money (annual variation in %)	13.6	13.8	13.6	12.2	13.3
Inflation rate (CPI, annual variation in %, end of period)	4.1	2.5	2.5	1.5	1.6
Inflation rate (CPI, annual variation in %)	5.4	2.6	2.6	2.0	1.4
Inflation (producers price index, annual variation in %)	6.0	−1.7	−1.9	−1.9	−5.2
Policy interest rate (%)	6.56	6.00	6.00	5.60	4.35
Stock market (annual variation in %)	−21.7	3.2	−6.7	52.9	9.4
Exchange rate (vs. US$)	6.29	6.23	6.05	6.21	6.49
Exchange rate (vs. US$, average over period)	6.46	6.31	6.15	6.16	6.28
Current account (% of GDP)	1.8	2.5	1.5	2.7	3.1
Current account balance (US$ in billion)	136	215	148	277	331
Trade balance (US$ in billion)	154	231	258	383	602
Exports (US$ in billion)	1,898	2,049	2,209	2,342	2,283
Imports (US$ in billion)	1,744	1,819	1,952	1,959	1,681
Exports (annual variation in %)	20.2	8.0	7.8	6.0	−2.5
Imports (annual variation in %)	25.0	4.3	7.3	0.4	−14.2
International reserves (US$)	3,181	3,312	3,821	3,843	3,330
External debt (% of GDP)	9.3	8.7	9.0	8.6	13.2

Source: *China Economic Outlook*, September 20, 2016, available at http://www.focus-economics.com/countries/china.

Defense

During the Cold War, CIA dollar estimates of Soviet comparative economic size were significantly overstated. They were substantially revised downward after the USSR collapsed (Rosefielde 1998; Rosefielde and Hedlund 2008). The bias is explained by strong domestic political pressures in the wake of the Helsinki Final Act for depicting the USSR as a soft power competitor capable of comanaging peaceful coexistence, together with liberal sympathy for the Bolshevik experiment (Morgan and Sargent 2016; Morgan 2016).

The Agency's estimate of the Soviet arms build-up was the reverse. CIA procurement series 1973–1990 were flat, while post-Soviet evidence confirms Department of Defense (DoD) estimates of weapons' double-digit growth (Rosefielde 1982, 1987, 2005a). The bias here is explained by political opposition to diverting funds from social programs to American defense on the part of those who did not believe that the Russians were coming or who did not care.

Washington's political management of Chinese economic and military performance statistics in its annual reports to the Joint Economic Committee of Congress have displayed the same biases for similar reasons. However, neither the CIA nor the DoD publish serial data on Chinese weapon production.[8] Assessments of the level and trend of China's armed forces are primarily shaped by budgetary data without disclosing the details assessable with the CIA's building block method.[9] Also, it should be noted that the Chinese do not disclose how their yuan-valued defense statistics are converted into dollars. If they use the official foreign exchange rate, this substantially understates dollar

---

and to expand social protection. The annual growth target in the 12th Five-Year Plan was 7% and the growth target in the 13th Five-Year Plan is 6.5%, reflecting the rebalancing of the economy and the focus on the quality of growth while still maintaining the objective of achieving a "moderately prosperous society" by 2020 (doubling GDP for 2010–2020). World Bank, September 14, 2016, available at http://www.worldbank.org/en/country/china/overview.

[8] These data are obtained by "national technical means" mostly controlled by the Defense Intelligence Agency. The data exist, but are not public divulged.

[9] Again, the data exist, but are not divulged. On the building block method see Rosefielde (1982, 1987).

defense spending on a PPP basis (Bitzinger 2015).[10] This opacity precludes precise measurement of China's arms build-up, but many analysts disregard the obvious and simply claim that Beijing is arming at a double-digit rate in line with the growth of the national budget.

The US "top line" 2015 defense expenditures before sequestration were US$560.4 billion (United States Department of Defense 2016). Chinese officially spent US$146 billion[11] or 26% of America's. This figures rises to 46% adjusted with the CIA's GDP PPP coefficient.[12]

No Western authoritative source accepts China's US$146 billion figure at face value. They all adjust it for what they believe are definitional differences in the scope of countable military activities. The US DoD claims that China actually spent US$180 billion on defense in 2015 using standardized definitions. The Stockholm International Peace Research Institute (SIPRI) places the figure at US$214 billion. The corresponding comparatives are 32% and 38%, which adjusted to a PPP basis rise to 56% and 67%, respectively.[13]

Judging by Soviet defense budgetary shenanigans, these high estimates are only the tip of the iceberg (Rosefielde 2005a). Full Chinese defense spending properly computed according to the CIA's building block method in PPP dollars could easily exceed American outlays. This might seem preposterously high to the uninitiated, but it is certainly in line with Soviet experience.

Beijing's military modernization initiative is across the boards. It is bolstering land, sea, air, missile, space, and combined arms capabilities.

---

[10] Official Chinese defense spending in 2015 was US$146 billion. The consistency of the figure can be assessed by dividing this figure by the CIA's alternative GDP estimates. The "defense burden" computed via the exchange rate is 1.3% and 0.75% with the PPP denominator. The CIA's own Chinese defense burden figure is 1.99%. CIA World Factbook (2016), "Caveat emptor!" available at https://www.cia.gov/library/publications/the-world-factbook/geos/ch.html.
Center for Strategic and International Studies, "What does China really spend on its military?" available at http://chinapower.csis.org/military-spending/.
[11] Center for Strategic and International Studies, "What does China really spend on its military?" available at http://chinapower.csis.org/military-spending/.
[12] The implied PPP dollar figure is 219.
[13] Center for Strategic and International Studies, "What does China really spend on its military?" available at http://chinapower.csis.org/military-spending/.

The details are not germane for our purposes.[14] China's nuclear modernization, however, deserves brief attention because it bears on Beijing's potential as a superpower. Statistics on China's nuclear inventory are a state secret. The American government is silent too, estimating "launchers" instead, and these numbers are low. Various Western institutions using DoD launcher statistics and some supplementary information put China's nuclear weapon inventory around 260 for delivery by nearly 150 land-based ballistic missiles, 48 sea-based ballistic missiles, and bombers (Kristensen and Norris 2016). The threat to America accordingly is small because only 45 missiles today are capable of hitting US targets, and Beijing has an official policy of no first use. China, therefore, unlike Russia, does not operate in a world of "mutually assured destruction" and is not a nuclear "superpower." Indeed, North Korea could someday have a larger nuclear arsenal *ceteris paribus*.

The Soviet experience however suggests that this official story is for public consumption only. The Soviet nuclear arsenal was seven times larger than the Federation of American Scientists' estimation,[15] despite the CIA's insistence that the USSR did not have enough fissionable material.[16] China has enough short-range nuclear capable missiles to support a figure of 1,500 nuclear weapons (United States Department of Defense 2016), and Farber's 3,000 estimate is not out of the question (Karber 2011). If these higher numbers are ultimately substantiated, China should be graduated from a great regional military power to a junior military superpower joining the magic circle with America and Russia.

Either way, the Western defense establishment prior to Donald Trump's election displayed no sign of alarm because political leaders did not believe that the Chinese were coming and military effectiveness and threat involved more than "bean counting." America's public posture reflected little serious concern for today, and limited wariness

---

[14] SIPRI Yearbook 2016.

[15] Available at http://fas.org/issues/nuclear-weapons/status-world-nuclear-forces/ The FAS number is 7,300 nuclear warheads. According to Viktor Mikhailov, head of MinAtom, the real figure was 52,000. Personal disclosure.

[16] After the Soviet Union collapsed, Russia agreed to sell more nuclear material to America than the CIA estimated it possessed.

about tomorrow (Office of the Secretary of Defense 2016). The Office of the Secretary of Defense (OSD) summarizes its assessment of China's military prospects as follows (Office of the Secretary of Defense 2016):

> The long-term, comprehensive modernization of the armed forces of the People's Republic of China (PRC) entered a new phase in 2015 as China unveiled sweeping organizational reforms to overhaul the entire military structure. These reforms aim to strengthen the Chinese Communist Party's (CCP) control over the military, enhance the PLA's ability to conduct joint operations, and improve its ability to fight short-duration, high-intensity regional conflicts at greater distances from the Chinese mainland. China's leaders seek ways to leverage China's growing military, diplomatic, and economic clout to advance its ambitions to establish regional preeminence and expand its international influence. Chinese leaders have characterized modernization of the People's Liberation Army (PLA) as essential to achieving great power status and what Chinese President Xi Jinping calls the "China Dream" of national rejuvenation. They portray a strong military as critical to advancing Chinese interests, preventing other countries from taking steps that would damage those interests, and ensuring that China can defend itself and its sovereignty claims.

Donald Trump distrusts American intelligence estimates intended for public consumption, and the numbers appearing in future annual reports to Congress prepared by the OSD may soon show a grimmer picture of the size and trajectory of Chinese defense activities.

Asian Superpower

The impact of the West's economic stagnation, social strife, and decline on Asia depends on whether China is, or soon will be, a military superpower. If America and Russia maintain their duopoly on assured nuclear destruction, the United States can stare down China in a crisis. The West's weakened condition permits Beijing to nibble and gradually dominate aspects of Asian regional relations, but not to cross critical red lines.

Alternatively, if Xi Jinping is concealing a big stick and bidding his time, or is secretly assembling the nuclear arsenal needed to join the superpower club, then the West's decline threatens Asia's independence.

References

Bergson, Abram (1953), "Reliability and usability of soviet statistics: A summary appraisal," *American Statistician*, 7(3), 13–16.

Bergson, Abram (1961), *The Real National Income of Soviet Russia since 1928*, Cambridge, MA: Harvard University Press.

Bergson, Abram (1972), "Soviet national income statistics," in: Treml, V. and J. Hardt (eds.), *Soviet Economic Statistics*, Durham NC: Duke University Press, pp. 148–152.

Bergson, Abram (1975), "Index numbers and the computation of factor productivity," *Review of Income and Wealth*, 4(3), 259–278.

Bitzinger, Richard A. (2015), "China's double-digit defense growth what it means for a peaceful rise," *Foreign Affairs*, March, available at https://www.foreign-affairs.com/articles/china/2015-03-19/chinas-double-digit-defense-growth.

Harrison, Mark (2000), "Soviet industrial production, 1928 to 1955: Real growth and hidden inflation," *Journal of Comparative Economics*, 28(1), 134–155.

Karber, Phillip (2011), "Strategic Implications of China's underground Great Wall," September 23, available at https://fas.org/nuke/guide/china/Karber_UndergroundFacilities-Full_2011_reduced.pdf.

Koch-Weser, Iacob N. (2013), "The reliability of China's economic data: An analysis of national output," U.S.–China Economic and Security Review Commission Staff Research Project, January 2, available at http://www.uscc.gov/sites/default/files/Research/TheReliabilityofChina'sEconomicData.pdf.

Kristensen, Hans M. and Robert S. Norris (2016), "Chinese nuclear forces, 2016," *Bulletin of the Atomic Scientists*, 72(4), 205–211, DOI: 10.1080/00963402.2016.1194054, available at http://www.tandfonline.com/doi/pdf/10.1080/00963402.2016.1194054.

Moorsteen, Richard (1962), *Prices and Production of Machinery in the Soviet Union, 1928–1958*, Cambridge, MA: Harvard University Press.

Moorsteen, Richard and Raymond Powell (1966), *The Soviet Capital Stock, 1928–1962*, Homewood, IL: Irwin.

Morgan, Michael Cotey (2016), "Confidence and distrust at the conference on security and cooperation in Europe (CSCE)," in: Klimke, Martin, Reinhild Kreis and Christian Ostermann (eds.), *Trust but Verify: The Politics of*

Uncertainty and the Transformation of the Cold War Order, 1969–1991, Palo Alto, CA: Stanford University Press.

Morgan, Michael Cotey and Daniel Sargent (2016), "Helsinki 1975: Borders and people," in: Reynolds, David and Kristina Spohr (eds.), *Transcending the Cold War: Summits, Statecraft, and the Dissolution of Bipolarity in Europe, 1970–1990*, Oxford: Oxford University Press.

Morrison, Wayne (2015a), "China's economic rise: History, trends, challenges, and implications for the United States," Congressional Research Service 7-5700, October 21, Table 1, p.9. The source is official Chinese data, available at www.crs.gov RL33534, https://www.fas.org/sgp/crs/row/RL33534.pdf.

Morrison, Wayne (2015b), "China's economic rise: History, trends, challenges, and implications for the United States," Congressional Research Service 7-5700, October 21, Figure 5, p. 8. The source is official Chinese data, available at www.crs.gov RL33534, https://www.fas.org/sgp/crs/row/RL33534.pdf.

Office of the Secretary of Defense (2016), "Annual report to Congress: Military and security developments involving the People's Republic of China 2016," April, available at http://www.defense.gov/Portals/1/Documents/pubs/2016%20China%20Military%20Power%20Report.pdf.

Rawski, Thomas (2001), "What is happening to China's GDP statistics?" *China Economic Review*, 12, 347–354.

Rosefielde, Steven (1982, 1987), *False Science: Underestimating the Soviet Arms Buildup*, Transaction, 1982 (expanded 2nd ed., 1987), New Brunswick, NJ.

Rosefielde, Steven (1998), *Efficiency and the Economic Recovery Potential of Russia*, Aldershot: Ashgate, 1998.

Rosefielde, Steven (2005a), *Russia in the 21st Century: The Prodigal Superpower*, Cambridge: Cambridge University Press.

Rosefielde, Steven (2005b), "Tea leaves and productivity: Bergsonian norms for gauging the soviet future," *Comparative Economic Studies*, 47(2), 259–273.

Rosefielde, Steven (2007), "The illusion of westernization in Russia and China," *Comparative Economic Studies*, 49, 495–513.

Rosefielde, Steven (2010), *Red Holocaust*, New York: Routledge.

Rosefielde, Steven and Stefan Hedlund (2008), *Russia since 1980: Wrestling with Westernization*, Cambridge: Cambridge University Press.

Rosefielde, Steven, Masaaki Kuboniwa and Satoshi Mizobata (2012), "East–West convergence and intra-Asian stratification," in: Rosefielde, Steven,

Masaaki Kuboniwa and Satoshi Mizobata (eds.), *Two Asias: The Emerging Postcrisis Divide*, Chapter 16, 421–437, Singapore: World Scientific Publishers.

United States Department of Defense (2016), "Fiscal year 2016, budget request," available at http://comptroller.defense.gov/Portals/45/Documents/defbudget/fy2016/FY2016_Budget_Request_Overview_Book.pdf.

Chapter 14

Belt and Road Strategy

Zhikai Wang

Introduction

Constructing the Silk Road Economic Belt and the Maritime Silk Route of the 21st century, which is also named as the "One Belt and One Road" strategy, is a step to promote globalization in China and other Asian countries. It is important for China as well as other Asian countries to play positive roles in the new round of globalization. The Silk Road Economic Belt will be based on nodes of inland China, including Xinjiang, Gansu, Qinghai, Shaanxi, and some other provinces, extending westward through Central Asia, the Middle East, across Russia, and finally reaching Western Europe. The 21st Century Maritime Silk Route will extend to the South Pacific, across the South China Sea, continuously across the Indian Ocean and the Mediterranean, and finally reaching Western Europe through Africa. Thus, both the Silk Road Economic Belt and the 21st Century Maritime Silk Route start from Asia, ending in Europe, and the "Belt and Road" will run through the Eurasian continent and Africa, which is expected to create the world's largest economic circle, drawing the outline of the global vision of China, Asia, and the world.

"One Belt and One Road" strategy is of benefit for the enhancement of the right of speech in developing countries and emerging market economies in the context of globalization, shaping a fair and reasonable new order of global governance. Multilateral investment and financing system of AIIB would be an important guarantee for the implementation of the "One Belt and One Road" strategy. This chapter examines the strategy of the "Belt and Road," explores the missions of AIIB, and traces the participatory role of private capital and private enterprise participation in the Chinese/Asian strategy of the "Belt and Road" and the operation of AIIB. Finally, the chapter will discuss how the strategy of "Belt and Road" and AIIB innovate the global governance and promote global win–win development.

Globalizing Era and the Limitations of Existing Global Governance

Along with the improvement in transportation facilities, world trade has been continuously expanding, global economic cooperation has been constantly deepening, and the concept of globalization has become the trend of world development since the middle of the last century. The essence of globalization is a kind of economic and political phenomenon, in which a national economy has become increasingly open to the international economy and politics beyond the given country and has been extending more and more influence to individual countries (Nicola 2001). Initiation of globalization was started with the internationalization of trade, FDI, and growth of multinational corporations, but the economic internationalization was/is not the complete globalization. Globalization also includes the blend of diverse cultures, coexistence of religions, political inclusiveness among the countries of the world, etc., and is not just the level of economic internationalization. And, in particular, today's efficient three-dimensional traffic and Internet is all over the world and has been deeply implanted in economic production, culture, and education, as well as in our social lives. Today, the earth is really a small village, and we can conclude that every country or region in the world has actively become a member of or is passively involved in the globalization of the world.

Although globalization is not just about economic internationalization, globalization, which started from economic internationalization, has always been affected by the process and trend of internationalization. The essence of globalization discussed today encompasses a greater range of economic internationalization. Most analysts' understanding of globalization and internationalization is consistent. Namely, globalization and internationalization are a kind of idea or concept, and the two are compatible with each other and non-exclusive. In fact, the internationalization of the economy is the liberalization of trade, wherein the status and role of import and export have been enhanced in the national economy, FDI has been increasing, these were/are important contents of the economies of western countries after World War II. Along with the advancing of the western countries of economic internationalization, currency and capital began to freely flow across borders, and it has become a fact that the western countries lead the globalization trend. International organizations established after World War II, such as the World Bank (WB), International Monetary Fund (IMF), and other regional organizations, have become more conscious of the importance of the role of global governance. The architecture of these organizations has determined the leading role and dominant position of the developed Western countries in the global governance.

Globalization is mainly economic liberalization. In fact, it can be said that the market is becoming more open. Market liberalization and integration will allow the productive factors and resources to flow into the areas with high market returns, forming the Matthew effect, and leading to the strong getting stronger and the weak becoming weaker. And the world has been shaped as a structure of coexisting developing countries' economies and developed countries' economies in the process of economic globalization, which is the typical phenomenon of the coexistence of globalization and regional economic integration (Wang 2003). This pattern of globalization lacks balance and equivalence. In fact, the developed countries occupy the market and technology advantages, robbing resources from the developing countries and operating market monopoly, and thus developing countries have to rely heavily on developed countries. Like African and South American countries, these countries too have been providing resources to North America and Western Europe (now as EU) for quite a long period of time. This was and is the reason why South America and Africa have not been able to achieve their own development, thereby further initiating frequent events such as "South–South Cooperation" and "North–South Dialogue." In fact, in today's globalization, the financial and market innovations of western developed economies have been developing at a considerably advanced level, and room for further economic growth of the developed countries tends to be saturated. The globalization dominated by the western developed countries has not brought about sustained growth capacity to the developing countries. In today's globalization, Central Asian countries, Southeast Asian countries, Central and Eastern European countries, African countries, Central and South American countries, etc., seriously lack growth.

In the existing era of globalization and the current governance system, the West has a vested interest as the globalization leader; they do not want to take the initiative to break the unfairly balanced development of global economy in this present saturated state. China has been integrated into the economic internationalization and globalization since 1990s, but in the context of western-dominated globalization, China almost has no voice in the globalizing world and can only play a limited role in international community, just like that of other developing countries and regions. This turn of Asian economic integration promoted by the "One Belt and One Road" strategy advocated by China, which in fact is Asian globalization, is the new wave of globalization launched and stimulated by China (China Economic Net 2014). China is leading Asian integration and globalization, which can innovate system of global governance, enhance China's right to speak, and improve the status of the developing countries through the process of globalization.

The Strategy of "One Belt and One Road" is a New Round of Globalization for Innovating Global Governance

Since modern globalization is driven by the Western society, the non-Western countries will be of great importance for the new round of globalization. The strategy of "One Belt and One Road" is the Chinese, and Asian, concept of globalization; it is a practical measure to promote regional integration in Asia. The planning vision of "One Belt and One Road" is to connect Asia, Europe, and Africa as a whole, and it is expected to create the world's largest Eurasian–African economic circle. The new round of globalization promoted by the strategy of "One Belt and One Road" will create common interests, shared institutions, and effective conflict resolution mechanisms among member countries, pushing forward mutual development. "One Belt and One Road" is China's initiative, but not China's one-man show. All countries and regions along the "One Belt and One Road," including countries outside the "Belt and Road," are all welcome to participate in the cooperation of construction and development, sharing the win–win prosperity. Xi Jinping said that Asia is the world's Asia, and only when Asian countries put themselves in the world could they accurately self-position. China is willing to become an engine of growth so as to safeguard the prosperity of the Asian–European Continent; its ultimate goal is to create a new system for global economic governance.

At the end of the last century and the beginning of the 21st century, the WB and the IMF, including the main western countries, were talking about the future truth that the 21st century would be Asia's century, and would be the century of China, and that China and other Asian countries would be the driving force of the new round of globalization (Xinhua International 2011). Asia currently accounts for one-third of the total global economy, with 60% of the world population. This region has the highest economic vitality and growth potential, dominative leaders, and a new engine for today's and future globalization. The construction of infrastructure and interconnection of infrastructure facilities would be the key initiatives of globalization pushed forward by the Asian countries' cobuilding and cooperation for the "Belt and Road." Due to the lack of economic growth, Asian countries always fall short of construction funds. Inadequate rail and road networks in some of the Asian regions, especially in Central and Southeast Asia, makes Asia's economic growth one of the lowest in the world. Asian countries need US$8 trillion for infrastructure investment for 2010–2020 to make further development or maintain the existing economic growth, which means Asian countries require US$800 billion investment annually when we calculate the yearly average investment for a period of 10 years (China Business Network 2015). Asian Development Bank (ADB) has a capital of about US$160 billion, and the WB has only US$223 billion. ADB and WB normally provide about US$20 billion for Asian countries annually. The development planning, projects, and funding of "One Belt and One Road" will be provided together, and it will bring about the grand vision of globalization to be expected for Asia.

The vast majority of Asian countries, including Japan, have very close relations of trade and economic cooperation with China; many countries have become the essence of the common interests' community of economic cooperation and trade with China. The strategy of "One Belt and One Road" can increase the investment and trade cooperation in Asian countries, promoting the level of economic development of Asian countries and further enhancing exchanges of economy and trade of Asian countries with the rest of the world, stimulating the better growth of the global economy. The strategy of "One Belt and One Road" can promote the national economic prosperity and regional economic cooperation of countries along the line of "Belt and Road," improving Asian countries' infrastructure and investment environment, laying a good foundation for Asian countries to attract international investment and cooperate with developed countries from Europe and America and the whole world.

In fact, Asia and China have a decisive role today in the healthy and sustainable development of the global economy. The whole world knows this; when the subprime mortgage crisis was at its peak in the US during 2008 and 2009, the US and EU, and in fact the whole world, trusted China to restore the global economic growth. China timely adopted an expansionary fiscal policy and active monetary policy, which made China's economy the first one to walk out of the recession during 2008–2009 global economic crisis and quickly achieve high economic growth. Indeed, in the effort of the world response to the global economic crisis caused by the US subprime mortgage crisis in 2008–2009, China made a great contribution in helping the world economic recovery and growth. Even in 2014, when China encountered a marked decline in the economic growth, the IMF statistics concluded that the contribution rate of China's economy to the world economic growth was 27.8% (World Wide Network 2015), China was/is still the country which provides the largest contribution annually for the world economic growth.

Due to China's contribution to the stability of the growth of world economy in 2009–2010, IMF said in 2010 that China should be given a substantial increase in voting rights. IMF planned to let China rise to the top three in votes at the IMF and had China's voting power increased from about 3.65% to 6.07%, which is more than that of Germany, France, and Britain, respectively, and only behind that of the United States and Japan, so as to achieve the expansion of China's voice in the IMF. Indeed, China's voting rights in IMF had long been very small, and of course, it was because of China's limited share in the IMF. The increase of the voting rights of China in IMF would mean an increase of China's voice in the world. At that time, the increase of voting rights promised by IMF for China was not the newly added voting rights, but the dispensing of other members' voting rights in IMF. At the time, the EU said they could alienate three voting rights for China, and Canada could pass over one voting right to China; if that did happen, China should have the IMF's four voting rights (Sina Finance and Economy 2009). China was very excited and anticipated the hospitality of increase of voting rights offered by the western world and the IMF, which would be the direct embodiment of China's global influence. The IMF was instrumental in increasing China's voting power in the IMF, which indicated that China's influence and role in the process of globalization was getting important.

But unfortunately, until November 2015, China did not obtain one more voting right from IMF. Regarding the increase of voting rights for China in the IMF, it was supported by all IMF member countries except the US, which opposed and voted against. Thus, we clearly understood China lacks the right of the voice of international community in China's participation in the governance of globalization, which was the result of the existing global governance system dominated by the western countries but excluded the developing countries and emerging market economy countries to the side. Then again, we the Chinese recently proposed that we wanted to have our currency RMB listed as one of the special drawing right (SDR) currencies of IMF, but the Obama administration said that it was too early to list Chinese RMB in SDR currencies. The US said that Chinese marketization of RMB was not yet mature. All in all, the US was reluctant to let China play the dominant role in the global economy. On November 30, 2015, the decision of including RMB into SDR was finally passed in the second ballot of IMF.

Therefore, China's "One Belt and One Road" initiative, which is about promoting economic integration in Asia, promotes economic and trade cooperation in Asia, Europe, and Africa, thus injecting vitality into the new round of world globalization. China and Asia's globalization, set up by the strategy of "One Belt and One Road," will form the common interests, shared institution, and effective mechanism for conflict resolution within Member States and their regions. Asia is the world's Asia, and China has assumed the role of an engine in the new round of globalization led by Asia. China works for the prosperity of Asia, Europe, and Africa, and even the whole world, and the new round of globalization will build a new system of global governance, enhance the developing countries' voice and influence in the process of globalization, and promote the balanced development and better growth of global economy.

AIIB is the Safeguard for the Implementation of the "Belt and Road" Strategy

Investment and trade cooperation are key to "One Belt and One Road" construction. Relevant countries should eliminate trade and investment barriers and build a good business environment in the region. China should actively coestablish free trade areas with countries and regions along the "Belt and Road," trigger and release the potential for cooperation, thus creating better cooperation "cake." China and other Asian, European, and African countries should broaden the field of trade, and optimize the trade structure, mining new trade growth point and promoting trade balance. All countries should innovate the mode of trade, develop cross-border e-commerce, establish and improve the promotion system of service trade, consolidate and expand the traditional trading, and vigorously develop modern service trade. All member countries have to organically integrate the investment and trade into cooperation, drive the trade development through investment, accelerate investment facilitation and remove investment barriers, strengthen agreement of bilateral investment protection, consult the agreement of double taxation avoidance, and protect investor's legitimate rights and interests. Undoubtedly, Chinese and Asian internationalization, promoted by the strategy of "One Belt and One Road," will bring about large-scale development of investment and trade, which requires a lot of infrastructure investment, and thus it essentially needs the support of AIIB and Silk Road Fund.

AIIB is the multilateral cooperation bank for Asia infrastructure construction and investment. In October 2013, Xi Jinping proposed the initiation of AIIB to the Indonesian President in Jakarta, and in the same month, Premier Li Keqiang proposed this initiation of "The Silk Road Fund" at the ASEAN-China (10 + 1) Meeting. On the morning of November 4, 2014, Xi Jinping chaired the eighth meeting of the central leading group of financial work, studying the planning of Silk Road Economic Belt and the 21st Century Maritime Silk Road, and initiated the establishment of Asian Infrastructure Investment Banking (AIIB) and the establishment of the Silk Road Fund. AIIB was launched by China as a multilateral cooperation bank in investment and financing, and to date there are 57 founding members. Members include countries in Asia, Europe, Africa, Latin America, and Oceania (except Japan and the United States), and AIIB is open. AIIB will still accept other countries and regions to join as general members, and its extensive international influence is self-evident (Financial News Net 2015). AIIB is China's international financial institute outside of the WB dominated by the US and the ADB dominated by Japan. The establishment and operation of AIIB marks the fact that China has come to participate in dominating the world economic rules, which is an important guarantee for China and Asia to promote the new round of world globalization.

AIIB has closely tied the interests of many founding members together, such as Central Asia. Southeast Asia will be benefited directly from the globalization strategy of "One Belt and One Road" secured by AIIB, and many Asia–Europe countries and the world member countries will obtain the win–win common interests. As most countries in Asia have become founding members of AIIB, these countries will certainly choose AIIB in their infrastructure constructions, rather than the WB and the ADB. AIIB is led by China, and China is the largest investor of AIIB. The headquarters of AIIB is located in Beijing, and the RMB has become the common currency accepted by everyone for reserve and trading in Asia; thus, the Chinese RMB could be used for lending and balance in AIIB financing. In Asia and other places, we can use RMB but not the USD as a reserve currency or trading currency, which would greatly reduce the cost of investment and financing in Asia, improving the efficiency of capital and currencies in the Asian market.

While we actively promote the organizational operation of AIIB and Silk Road Fund, China has to deepen international financial cooperation, promoting the establishment of a stable Asian monetary, investment, and financing system, as well as credit system, expanding the scope and scale of bilateral exchange of currencies, balancing currencies among member countries along the "Belt and Road." China should work together with member countries along the "Belt and Road" and other countries participating in AIIB, promoting the openness and development of Asian bonds market, while pushing forward the establishment of AIIB and the BRICS Development Bank. China should cooperate with Shanghai Cooperation Organization member countries and work together to build Shanghai Cooperation Organization Bank, accelerating the formation and operation of Silk Road Fund, providing a solid financial intermediation for the construction of the "One Belt and One Road" (Eastern Wealth Network 2015). For further financial cooperation, it is essential for AIIB to deepen cooperation with China–ASEAN Bank Consortium and Shanghai Cooperation Organization Bank, operating multilateral financial cooperation with syndicated loans, bank credit, and in other ways.

Of course, it is essential to prevent and control risks in AIIB's projects and capital operation. For effective operation of AIIB, we must solve three problems: the first is that the mechanism of risk evaluation and after-investment project control has to be established as soon as possible; the second is that most Asian "Recipient" countries have poor credit, and so there will be projects with no return of investment, to the embarrassment of debt service violation. The third is that the status and roles of AIIB in the international financial market have to be integrated; we have to acknowledge that the global financial supervision, evaluation, and service system dominated by western countries has become the standard of the financial industry. Even if the operation of AIIB does not need to completely adapt to the international financial system led by western countries, we still need to draw experience from western service operation. Therefore, China should take reference from experience of the WB, ADB, and other international agencies in the project assessment, risk control, and investment management, making efforts to solve the three problems discussed above and achieve healthy and safe operation of project funding of the AIIB and Silk Road Fund.

Supporting Private Capital' Participation in the Operation of AIIB and Construction of the "Belt and Road" Strategy

The investment of China's state-owned capital in the Middle East, Africa, and Russia has begun to take shape, but the investment is mainly focused in the mining production and construction project investment. This kind of investment expansion of state-owned capital has, in fact, many limitations, and failings of overseas' investment of state-owned capital are often seen. The legal relationship of duties and obligations between persons who take responsibility for the state-owned capital and the owners who entrust agent of responsible persons is not clear, and the initiative, enthusiasm, sense of competition of the state-owned capital's foreign investment and expansion is far less than that of private capital. Of course, the competition principle of market economy has determined the nature of capital running for benefits, and only private capital is of the most competitive power and expansion efficiency. In terms of overseas' investment, although we cannot say the private capital has been repressed, compared to the state-owned capital enjoying a lot of policy support and convenience in overseas' investment, it is very difficult for private capital to take overseas' investment. From the view of the "One Belt and One Road" investment trends and strategies, Chinese government does first support the scaled state-owned capital for overseas' investment; private capital is apparently still being marginalized.

Encouraging and supporting private enterprises to participate in the construction of "Belt and Road," and operation of AIIB, is an important measure for us to push forward the new round of globalization led by China and Asia. How much money will be invested in the strategy of "One Belt and One Road"? It is hard to say now; when will the construction of the "Belt and Road" be finished? In fact, there is no timetable. But the strategy of the "Belt and Road" will need tens of trillions of investment. It is relatively clear that the "Belt and Road" will be a long-term strategy. Tens of trillions of investment demand is unlikely to solely rely on money supply of multilateral investment and financing system composed by credits of member countries of AIIB. The huge investment strategy of "Belt and Road" has to be cosupported by social capital, especially the participation of private capital. In the operation of private capital participation in the construction of "Belt and Road" and AIIB, we are aware that China's private capital has had such conditions and capacities after 20 years' development, and the future work is how to stimulate the enthusiasm of private enterprises' investment into the "Belt and Road" construction and AIIB, which is very important.

Encouraging private enterprises' and the state-owned enterprises' (SOEs) coparticipation in the "Belt and Road" would be much more effective. The open development of "Belt and Road" strategy has to be supported by the financial sector, and the development of private enterprises has long been lacking the financial support compared with state-owned enterprises. Therefore, China has to let the private enterprises play an important role in participating in "Belt and Road" construction, encouraging private enterprises to go out; the state-owned commercial banks and policy banks should give support and assistance to the private enterprises. China should gradually expand the scope of cross-border trade denominated in RMB by making use of the economic and trade zones created by private enterprises in the surrounding countries; when the domestic enterprises try their efforts to go global, it can drive private firms groups to go global as well (Sina Finance and Economics 2015). In order to support and encourage private enterprises to participate in the "Belt and Road" strategy and the operation of AIIB, China has to make full use of existing financial instruments, including the traditional credit, securities, credit and leasing, trust and means, etc., and China also needs to rapidly develop financing lease, further develop cross-border Internet banking, actively explore cross-border insurance business, and provide escort for China's private enterprises to go global.

Social capital and private enterprise participation in AIIB and in the construction of "Belt and Road" conforms to the market rules and international practice, and this national strategy of open development can often be achieved through civil cooperation. For example, in the process of enterprise's going global and participating in the cross-border mergers and acquisitions (M&As) of "Belt and Road" construction, private enterprises and private capital have great advantages, which means private enterprises and private capital can achieve their international M&A targets through legitimate competition in the market. Instead, if the state-owned enterprises and state-owned capital participate in global transnational M&A, it might provide people an excuse that China's M&A is an act of unfair competition behavior, and then relevant partner could take the excuse to refuse China's M&A activity. When Petro-China intended to acquire Yugansk oilfields of Yukos after 8 months' hard negotiation, when the acquisition was just to be reached, the United States judged that Petro-China's involvement in buying Yugansk oilfields of Yukos oil was unfair competition. The reason was that the Petro-China is a state-owned enterprise, which was supported by Chinese government. As Russia's largest private oil company, when Yukos Oil Company was disposed by Russian Federal Government in 2004, Yukos turned to the US Federal Court and launched application for bankruptcy protection; this is because the US government bankruptcy protection spans the world. Yukos made this move to avoid its main oil producing company — Yugansk oilfields — from being auctioned (Ministry of Commerce of China 2004). However, at that time, we the Chinese were bewildered by the international cross-border M&As. Now, in the face of many problems in our construction of "Belt and Road," Chinese government should take effective measures, via effective strategies and methods, and vigorously support the private capital participation in major investment projects of "Belt and Road" construction. For example, although mixed ownership is not easy, the government could initiate the establishment of mixed investment funds with government involvement but not share-holding to help the mixed investment funds participate in the optimistic "Belt and Road" projects.

If so, the West will not have an excuse to accuse Chinese M&A activities in the international market as government behavior or unfair competition, and therefore the door for Chinese enterprises' participation in international M&A will not be closed by the international community.

References

China Business Net (2015), "2009 Asian Development Bank and Asian Development Bank Institute released the report on Asian infrastructure construction," available at http://finance.china.com.cn/roll/20150203/2942741. shtml (accessed on September 3, 2015).

China Economic Net (2014), "Xi Jinping proposed strategic idea: 'Belt and Road' opening 'Cherish Dream Space,'" available at http://news.xinhuanet.com/fortune/2014-08/11/c_1112013039.htm (accessed on May 7, 2015).

Ministry of Commerce (2004), "Yukos applied for bankruptcy protection to the United States Court," available at http://www.mofcom.gov.cn/article/i/jyjl/1/200412/20041200320765.shtml (accessed on September 13, 2015).

Eastern Wealth Network (2015), "Constructing the 'Belt and Road' strategy so as to achieve common development and common prosperity," available at http://finance.eastmoney.com/news/137120150205475384468.html (accessed on February 5, 2015).

Financial News Net (2015), "The list of the 57 intention founding members of the Asian Infrastructure Investment Bank is to be out of the oven," available at http://finance.caixin.com/2015-04-15/100800470.html (accessed on May 13, 2015).

Sina Finance (2009), "IMF President: Voting rights of China will gain the greatest increase," available at http://finance.sina.com.cn/world/gjjj/20090927/0221 6797481.shtml (accessed on April 23, 2015).

Sina Finance (2015), "China encounters the greatest opportunity since the Han Dynasty," available at http://finance.sina.com.cn/zl/china/20150803/115822861084.shtml (accessed on August 3, 2015).

World Wide Network (2015), "IMF: China became the largest contributor to the economic increment," available at http://world.huanqiu.com/hot/2015-01/5356074.html (accessed on September 5, 2015).

Xinhua International (2011), "Foreign media: The 21st century belongs to Asia," available at http://news.xinhuanet.com/world/2011-11/19/c_122305133.htm (accessed on May 3, 2015).

Yeates, Nicola (2001), *Globalization and Social Policy*, London: Sage Press.

Wang, Zhikai (2003), Western welfare economic system in the era of globalization, *Journal of Zhejiang University* (Humanities and Social Sciences Edition), 33(6), 64–73.

Chapter 15

Public–Private Partnerships

Yiyi Liu

It is commonly believed that multilateral disagreements are caused by conflicting participant preferences. This chapter shows that conflicts may arise when participants have the same goal. This may happen when the action of any individual participant is insufficient to assure that the common goal is efficiently achieved. This chapter explains why Public–Private Partnerships (PPPs) could be superior to traditional government owned and operated public service enterprises. The point is proven with an example where two government regulators working separately to achieve the same goal fail to jointly optimize, impairing contact efficiency. Losses of this sort can be avoided by a single authority with full decision-making power in principle, but it is shown more generally that the comparative merit of traditional and PPP public services depends heavily on particularities and context. PPP could help revitalize China's flagging growth, but should be viewed as a panacea.

Introduction

Fifty countries signed the article of agreement for the Asian Infrastructure Investment Bank (AIIB) on June 29, 2015, signifying a new wave of worldwide multilateral public service cooperation. It strives to overcome obstacles thwarting the achievement of the Paris Agreement's environment goals and other objectives. Government regulators need guidance from the AIIB, World Bank, International Monetary Fund (IMF), and the Asian Development Bank on how to choose public–private partners and conduct postcontract renegotiations.

Public service infrastructure contracting takes two forms: concessions and public–private cooperation. This chapter analyzes how the behavior of regulators may affect contract efficiency and assesses policy implications, using a water treatment concession as an example.

The construction regulator chooses the contractor to build facilities and the environmental protection regulator establishes operational criteria. Contracts can be either traditional concessions (separate construction and operations contracts) or a PPP contract, i.e., Build Operate Transfer (BOT). In a BOT contract, the concessionaire constructs and operates the plant for a specific period, after which the facility reverts to the government.

This chapter compares the efficiency of traditional and PPP contracts. It examines the trade-off between bureaucratic efficiency and fairness, highlighting the point that traditional government contracts create a common agency problem even when regulators desire the same final outcomes.[1] The chapter underscores the importance of transparency and complete disclosure of private information for achieving desirable results and probes subtle aspects of regulatory mal-coordination.

The section "background" provides a brief introduction to the subject of public services. The section on institutional designs and public service efficiency elaborates the concept of PPPs and discusses its relationship to standard practices. The conclusion shows how incomplete information disclosure impairs public service efficiency in traditional government

---

[1] There is a potential direct efficiency loss due to the two-department institutional setup. In the literature, common agency problems are often due to rivalry concerns among principals (Martimort and Stole 2002). In such an environment, each principal partially affects the agent's utility, and thus the agent has an extended message space with strategic concerns. Both factors lead to the failure of indexing the principal's strategy with the agent's type, and therefore the failure of the revelation principle application. It is easy to suspect a causal relationship between the strategic concerns among rivalry principals and such failure. However, the new common agency problem in this model indicates that there is a possibility of failing to apply the Revelation Principle even with preference-aligned principals.

concessions. It discusses the insufficiency of full information disclosure for ensuring contract efficiency and provides detailed comparison of traditional and PPP contracts. The appendix offers policy suggestions.

Background

State-provided public services

The state traditionally plays a dominant role in providing public services because private markets fail to capture externalities. Unlike regulated natural monopolies operated by private entities, public service enterprises are state owned and operated. Fees are administratively fixed instead of being set by competitive equilibrium. The costs of state public services are budget financed (from taxes and debt). State enterprises tend not to finance themselves from net sales and do not maximize profits. These practices cause inefficiency.

The inability of private markets to measure the externalities of public goods and services is intrinsic. Public services are rival, but non-excludable. In this sense, public services are like common goods. They have no private alternatives. No one owns common natural resources, while the benefits to users are zero-sum over all consumers. For example, everyone is entitled to fish in the sea, but two people cannot catch the same salmon. This induces people to over-fish to society's detriment.

Coase's theorem provides a partial solution by assigning property rights to common goods and quantifying externalities. Once the property rights are defined, tradeoffs become explicit. Coase contends that the government's role in common goods markets should be limited to regulation in a double sense. But public goods are different. The state holds the freehold property right in its entirety.

Private–public service property rights do not exist *ex ante,* and there is no legal foundation for their *ex post* allocation. Public service externalities are opaque, allowing some users to free ride more benefits than they pay in taxes. This poses a conundrum. Should government regulators apply Pareto principles to link burdens and rewards, or invoke other normative principles to achieve best outcomes and resolve the externalities problem? The answer is a matter of policy judgment.

Collaboration

PPPs are a device for introducing aspects of Pareto efficiency into public services. They tailor responsibilities to comparative advantage by allowing the state to contract for selective private service.

PPP contracts are bargains between the state and private companies. They provide private entities the right to operate government-owned monopolies for specified periods in return for funding construction and operating costs. This arrangement differs from standard leasing by requiring private operators to pay some or all project construction costs, even though the government retains the full freehold right. Investors recoup their principal from project profits. The government for its part reduces its regulatory reach to improve public service effectiveness.

PPPs combine leasing (rental) contracts with an equity kicker. The private partner provides the initial equity, but does not own it. Private companies cannot buy and sell the government's asset. However, they can recoup their initial investment and earn a competitive return by selling monopoly public services on market principles during the tenure of their lease. PPPs are hybrid institutions not only because the private sector provides capital, but also because monopoly leases permit services to be sold competitively, instead of being state rationed.

The government's ability to separate ownership from usage rights adds competitiveness while still leaving space for beneficial regulation on the public's behalf. The services of some public assets like toll roads and water treatment plants can be sold to customers on a usage basis. This allows the state to price services in accordance with individual demand, while permitting access for the needy on a free or subsidized basis.

Partnership or privatization

Privatization has its virtues, but is not always a panacea. Externalities often justify retaining a public presence. There was a wave of privatization of water services in the 1990s in developing countries. The tariff on improved water quality and sanitation, however, sometimes made access unaffordable for the poor. In Europe, privatization of water service in Paris was terminated in 2009. Water usage was reduced by 5–10% the following year. Privatization of monopoly public services can be problematic because it often creates anticompetitive rent-seeking and power-seeking opportunities. The same principle, however, does not apply to the privatization of firms with competitive market potential. Dong Xiaoping's *"Gaige Kaifang"* ("reforms and openness") program, which led to leasing privatization in the 1990s, greatly enhanced China's economic efficiency.

PPPs are different from privatization because the government retains freehold ownership and only permits private operation of state facilities. Private companies cannot freely buy and sell their usage rights.

Public or private financing

The virtue of PPP partly depends on the possibilities of self-financing. There is no general rule. Empirical evidence is mixed. Governments may use PPP to decorate their budgets. Alternatively, the state may benefit because the private sector saves on construction costs by acquiring low-cost financing. "The advantages of PPPs must be weighed against the contractual complexities and rigidities they entail."[2]

Market-based public services

Before 1980, almost all public services/goods were owned and operated by the state. This created huge public debts that enticed governments to adopt PPP as a device allowing public projects to grow without increasing public debt. It was soon recognized however that PPP had another important virtue. It enhanced efficiency. The Rion-Antirion Bridge linking the northwest region of Peloponnese to southwest mainland in Greece is a case in point. The bridge is "amongst the largest and most needed transport projects ever undertaken in Greece. Efficient transport networks are particularly important for countries such as Greece, whose peripheral location is a challenge for European integration ... to stimulate economic activity through large infrastructure financing."[3] By separating and privatizing the usage right, the government introduced aspects of market competition that offer superior consumer services.

---

[2] Public Sector Research Center (2008).

[3] This is the quote from European Investment Bank Vice President P. Gennimatas, EIB support for the Rion-Antirion Bridge in Greece, 1997-061-E.

Vulnerabilities

Responsible governments face three accountability problems in grappling with public goods. They must be natural monopolies. Public goods and services must be as efficient as possible in an anticompetitive environment, and adequate attention must be paid to externalities. The first issue is political. Governments should not compete with the private sector to placate insiders. The second problem is administrative. The state may find it difficult to supply the right services with the right characteristics to the right recipients on terms that acceptably approximate least marginal cost using administrative, bureaucratic, planning, and not-for-profit incentives. Third, the non-market methods employed by state public service providers may fail to adequately account for externalities. The magnitude and distribution of externalities is always subject to dispute among rival claimants. There is no market mechanism to adjudicate claims on a Paretian basis, allowing insiders to choose and manage public programs on capricious normative grounds. Coase's Theorem cannot resolve this problem.

Political, administrative and non-market vulnerabilities can turn public projects into fiascos. PPP is not necessarily better than the traditional public procurement. It should be employed only when market and government boundaries are clearly defined. Even then, there is no guarantee that PPP contracts will succeed.

The Cross City Tunnel located in Sydney, Australia, provides an illuminating example. It was supposed to provide users with self-financing benefits, but low traffic forced the agency into insolvency. Taxpayers had to bear the full cost. No official or stockholder was held accountable, as is typically the case for not-for-profit enterprises funded by government revenues. Is there a solution? Can public authorities directly or indirectly be made more diligent by making decision-makers partly financially accountable in return for profit shares?

Institutional Designs and Public Service Efficiency

The institutions adopted by states for building and providing public services depend on whether ownership and control are wholly the responsibility of states, or are mixed government/private activities. Institutional specifics vary and affect efficiency. This section investigates and compares the optimal institution design for traditional concessions (where the state permits private parties to operate government-owned facilities without equity participation) and BOT contracts (where facilities are financed and built by private companies, who are then permitted to operate facilities for a fixed term).

Traditional public service providers do not concern themselves with optimality either in construction or operations. They typically rely on partial information to make a few critical decisions. PPP providers by contrast are supposed to operate with full and transparent information.

Construction and environment protection regulators jointly determine both traditional concessions and BOT contracts. In a traditional concession, contractors report decision-relevant costs to construction and environmental regulators separately. In a BOT contract, contractors by contrast report full costs data to both regulators.

The choice criteria employed in traditional and BOT institutional setups differ and affect outcomes. They can be formally modeled. Proposition 1 summarizes the impact of traditional and BOT institutions on the environmental protection choice making. Propositions 2 and 3 summarize their effects on construction decision makers. The section on information disclosure in two different contracts analyzes efficiency losses associated with each contract type. It is followed by the issue of government integrity.

Setup

The government grants a concession for a water treatment plant. There is a construction contractor with private information (F_i) and facility operator concerned with environmental cost (c_j). The government's construction and facility regulators make independent decisions without communicating with each other, but share the same objective function. When the same agent is contracted to build and operate a project that ultimately reverts to the government, the relationship is a BOT contract.

Construction regulators have two instruments: monetary transfer (payments) T_i and construction probability P_i. The instruments employed by public service facility regulators (henceforth "operation regulator" to save space) are monetary transfer O_j and phasing t_j.

The project's lifespan n, has a stable revenue flow during the operation stage: R if operated by the private contractor and s if operated by the government.

The private information held by the contractor is its cost structure, including its operation and construction cost (c_j, F_i) and the prior of such type is α_{ji}; the contractor is either a high (H) or low (L) efficiency type on both cost dimensions.

Regulators have two different reporting requirements: (1) payoff-relevant information or (2) a complete report of all the private information. When the contractor only reports decision-relevant costs, this refers to traditional concession. The government institution is fairness-oriented.

The timing of the two-stage game is as follows: the construction regulator announces the contract (T_i, P_i) and the contractor reports its payoff-relevant construction cost F_i (or full report (c_j, F_i)); the operation regulator announces the operation contract (t_j, O_j, Q_j) (Q_j is the probability the contractor (c_j, F_i) will be awarded the contract (t_j, O_j)). The contractor reports the payoff-relevant operation cost c_j (or full report (c_j, F_i)).

The government's problem

The government's utility under these schemes is analyzed in this section. The investigation reveals that the construction regulator can do better with full private information reported even though the operation cost is irrelevant for construction and the construction regulator cannot affect decisions at the operation stage.

Operation regulato

The operation regulator's problem can be assessed with backward induction. The solution depends on the construction regulator's optimal contract (T_i, P_i) and the operation regulator's beliefs about it.

In the case of full reporting, these beliefs are:

$$\alpha^H = \frac{\sum_i P_i \alpha_{Hi}}{\sum_i \sum_j P_i \alpha_{ji}} \quad \text{and} \quad \alpha^L = \frac{\sum_i P_i \alpha_{Li}}{\sum_i \sum_j P_i \alpha_{ji}}$$

In the case of partial reporting (decision-relevant information only), the operation regulator's beliefs are:

$$\alpha^H = \frac{\sum_i \alpha_{Hi}}{\sum_i \sum_j \alpha_{ji}} \quad \text{and} \quad \alpha^L = \frac{\sum_i \alpha_{Li}}{\sum_i \sum_j \alpha_{ji}}$$

Recall, Q^j is a random probability of choosing different operation stage contracts. The private operator's program is

$$\max_{(t, O, Q)} \sum_{j \in \{H, L\}} \alpha^j \left[Q^j (n - t^j) s + (1 - Q^j) n \cdot s - O^j \right]$$

s.t.

$\forall j, k \in \{H, L\}$

$Q^j [t^j (R - c^j) + O^j] \geq Q^k [t^k (R - c^j) + O^k]$ ⠀⠀⠀⠀⠀⠀⠀(IC)

$Q^j [t^j (R - c^j) + O^j] \geq 0$ ⠀⠀⠀⠀⠀⠀⠀⠀⠀⠀⠀⠀(IR)

$$0 \leq t^j \leq n$$

$$0 \leq Q^j \leq 1.$$

Proposition 1. *Given the beliefs α^H and α^L, the operation regulator may choose to let either high- or low-cost operators participate if they are more efficient than the government, that is, $R - s > c^L + \frac{\alpha n^H (c^L - c^H)}{\alpha^L}$; otherwise they are excluded sequentially as the relative efficiency $(R - s)$ shrinks.*

The operation regulator solves his/her problem the same way in both reporting schemes. He/she assesses the contractor's relative operational efficiency. Assessments differ across the reporting schemes.

The optimal solution for the entire two-stage game is obtained by inserting the operation regulator's optimal program back into the construction regulator's objective function.

The condition is more complicated when the relative efficiency of the government and the private contractor converge. The efficiency lost from restricted information is assessed initially for the case where the government can choose both low- and high-efficiency operators.

Construction regulator

The construction regulator's program:

$$\max_{(P, T)} \sum_{i \in \{H,L\}} \alpha_{ji} \left[-T_i + Q^j(n - t^j)s + (1 - Q^j)n \cdot s - O^j \right] P_i$$

s.t.

$\forall i, m \in \{H, L\}$

$$[t^{j*} (R - c^j) + O^{j*} + T_i - F_i] \, Pi \geq [t^{k*} (R - c^j) + O^{k*} - T_m - F_i] P_m \quad \text{(IC)}$$

$$[t^j (R - c^j) + O^j + T_i - F_i] \geq 0 \quad \text{(IR)}$$

$$0 \leq P_i \leq 1.$$

Under the full reporting scheme, we have

Proposition 2. *When the prior probability of* (c^L, F_L) *is low and the information rent on the operation dimension is high:*

$$\alpha_{LL} \left\langle \frac{F_L - F_H}{n(R - c^L) - F_H} \quad \text{and} \quad n(c^H - c) - (F_L - F_H) \right\rangle 0,$$

the optimal construction contract satisfies:

- *The type* (c^L, F_L) *is excluded from the contract,* $P(c^L, F_L) = 0.$
- *The monetary transfers paid to different types are:* $T(c^j, F_i) = F_H$, *$j = H, L; i = H.$*

Under the restricted information disclosure scheme, where only payoff-relevant (for the construction regulator) is reported, we have

Proposition 3. *The construction regulation agency's optimal decision depends on the expected value of the project* $\alpha_L (n \cdot s - F_L)$ *after the rent concerns* $\alpha_H (F_L - F_H)$, *where* $\alpha_i = \sum_j \alpha_{ji}$ *with* $i, j = H, L$:

- *When the value of the project is large enough,* $\alpha_L (n \cdot s - F_L) - \alpha_H$ *$(F_L - F_H) > 0$: all types are asked to construct,* $P(c^j, F_i) = 1$; *every type receives the same compensation:* $T(c^j, F_i) = F_L.$

- *When the value of the project is low, $\alpha_L (n \cdot s - F_L) - \alpha_H (F_L - F_H) < 0$, the low type(s) on the construction dimension are excluded from the contract, $P(c^j, F_L) = 0$, high constructional efficient type receive zero rent $T(c^j, F_H) = F_H, j = H, L$.*

Propositions 2 and 3 depict the construction operators optimal contract when the contractor is more operationally efficient than the government (i.e., the inequality on Proposition 1 holds: $R - s > c^L + \frac{\alpha n^H (c^L - c^H)}{\alpha^L}$;

Propositions 2 and 3 also tell us that the operation regulator will let choose the constructor for type ji, $Q^j = 1$ if and only if $P_i > 0$.

When the builder only reports constructions cost F_i to the construction regulator, type (c^L, F_L) is chosen if $(\alpha_{LL} + \alpha_{HL})(n \cdot s - F_L) > (\alpha_{LH} + \alpha_{HH})$ $(F_L - F_H)$. This implies that the benefit of including the low construction efficient type is greater than the cost of paying the information rent. Yet, when the contractor reports a full summary of its private information, type (c^L, F_L) is chosen if $n(R - c^L) - F_L > (1 - \alpha_{LL})(n(R - c^L) - F_H)$ because the construction regulator is forward looking. It considers rent-paying on both dimensions.

In the full-report scheme, two things affect the construction regulator's decision. First, it knows who will operate the facility. Second, the construction and operation regulators have identical preferences. Knowing that the operation regulator will play a best response, the best that the construction regulator can do is to ration out the type (c^L, F_L) when $n(R - c^L) - F_L > (1 - \alpha_{LL})(n(R - c^L) - F_H)$ does not hold.

Define $n \cdot s - F_L$ (the government operates the facility on its own and the private contractor constructs it) as the minimum of the project value the government expects to realize by hiring a contractor (c^j, F_i). The construction regulator is able to do better by rationing the type (c^L, F_L) to save construction information rent with full knowledge of the private sector cost structure (the shaded region). In particular, if α_{LL} is "small" and α_{LH} is "large" (the contractor is more likely to be a type (c^H, F_L) and unlikely to be (c^L, F_L)), it is not optimal for the construction regulator to pool the contracts for types (c_L, F_L) and (c^L, F_H). If the contractor only needs to report partial cost structure to different agencies, types (c^L, F_L) and (c^L, F_H) cannot be distinguished. This shows that the effect of partial information disclosure on contract design in the BOT model is significant because it attracts inefficient private contractors to the partnership instead of encouraging efficient small businesses.

Information disclosure in two different contracts

The revelation principle fails to hold in the traditional government concession because it reduces the information conveyed to the regulator. This precludes the best outcome. Constructing an infeasible equilibrium that cannot be attained in an optimal truthful contract proves this. This means that regulators cannot achieve best results merely by retaining the traditional mechanism.

Government regulators are satisfied to receive incomplete reports on contractors' cost structures in the traditional process.

The construction regulator only requires construction costs, and the operation regulator only needs information about operating expenses. This impairs the contract design when agent reports are incomplete or only partly true. Both regulators screen types more coarsely than they would with full reporting. Restricted information prevents the government from filtering out unqualified contractors.

This section shows that untruthful equilibria can generate better results than the optimal truthful outcomes when information is restricted.

In a communication game with competing principals, individual principals cannot index their strategies with a full range of agent types. The message space in these instances is enlarged by market information, which is composed of other principals' contracts. The principal unable to properly use the revelation principle, may resort to payoff equivalent menu games. If principals coordinate, the revelation principle could conceivably be applied without strategic concerns. The two-regulator concession game with restricted reporting, however, suggests otherwise.

For preference-aligned government regulators (they have the same objective function) with restrictive reports on the private sector's cost structure, indexing their strategies constrains regulators to a subset of the entire communication game whenever only decision-relevant private information applies. Therefore, discovering partial truth in a traditional concession is weakly strategically dominated.

The completeness of the reported information is key for the regulators to seek optimal concession contracts. Reporting games like auctions in government's concessions require truthful reporting. With a constrained report of private information, the truth does not guarantee the government an optimal outcome by using revelation principle. While the partial truths may seem sufficient, undisclosed information show that the surmise is mistaken. Under such circumstances, government regulators should focus on the payoff equivalent menus to achieve the best outcome achievable and therefore eliminate the negative effect of the restricted messaging.

Integrated decision power

Another source of inefficiency in water treatment plant concessions is the partial control over contractors' utility. Split decision-making processes impair regulators' ability to offer optimal incentives to private contractors, even if there is full information. A sole agent can always be punished, but blame becomes ambiguous if there are multiple participants.

The naive assumption that two regulators always work together as one is false. Although some believe that the central government is inferior because it is susceptible to corruption,[4] there may be countervailing virtues. Central governments are capable of making integrated decisions. Decisions made by central governments (integration-oriented government institution) may or may not weakly dominate models with dispersed decision-making authority. The tradeoff between two approaches is a matter of political judgment. Transparency-oriented government institutions trade the optimality of concession contract (in terms of inability to implement some optimal concession contract that is viable under the

---

[4] "…At another level corruption may be intrinsic to the way power is exercised and may be impossible to reduce through lawmaking alone. In the extreme case state institutions may be infiltrated by criminal elements and turned into instruments of individual enrichment… The dynamic of corruption in the public sector can be depicted in a simple model. The opportunity for corruption is a function of the size of the rents under a public official's control, the discretion that official has in allocating those rents, and the accountability that official faces for his or her decisions…" (The World Bank Group, Helping Countries Combat Corruption: The Role of The World Bank, http://www1.worldbank.org/publicsector/anticorrupt/corruptn/cor02.htm).

integration-oriented government) for the prospect of reduced corruption. Integration-oriented governments sacrifice efficiency by raising the risks of corruption and rent-seeking.

These tradeoffs are unavoidable; nonetheless, social costs may be mitigated by flexibly adapting to circumstances.

Conclusion

Government institutions are important because they determine concessionary rules and welfare distributions. The government's role is either restricted to regulator in a traditional concession contract or project organizer in PPP contracts. Neither role is complete. This chapter has analyzed the subtleties.

It has been shown that government institutions may have direct and indirect effects on the optimality of infrastructure contracts. In dual regulatory concession games, the rules of private information disclosure affects regulators' selection criteria. When the information disclosed is incomplete, regulatory judgment is impaired. Transparency and informational completeness is necessary and sufficient for optimal contracting. However, even with complete information, the dual regulatory setup still has a direct effect on optimal concession contract design. Limited regulatory contract control affects perspectives. Regulators treat contractual aspects outside their jurisdictions as constants rather than variables subject to optimization.

This conclusion follows from scrutinizing the assumptions underlying the Revelation Principle. Preference-aligned regulators, who are only capable of extracting partial truths, should not use the Revelation Principle because the equilibrium path cannot be completely mapped. Moreover, even with complete truth, constrained preference-aligned regulators may not be able to implement best contracts because they are unable to provide sufficient incentives. Under these conditions, institutional designers must choose between the effectiveness of a central regulator and collaboration between regulatory agencies. The Revelation Principle fails because of the incompatibility of jurisdiction and regulatory strategy (game structure).

Jurisdictional barriers to optimal collaboration appear to be a fact of life. Even with preference-aligned regulators, attention must be paid to maximizing social welfare. This insight illuminates the subtleties affecting the choice between concession methods and PPP contracts. AIIB reflects the perceived benefits of public funding. However, the popularity of government infrastructure programs does not guarantee their merit. BOT has had successes and failures[5]; the debate over the pluses and minuses of private financing remains inconclusive.[6]

We demonstrate using simple models that PPP contracts may be inferior if regulators do not have integrated decision power, or a complete understanding of private contractor costs. The operational efficiency of the private sector appears to be a key reason why governments are attracted to BOT. If this premise is wrong, BOT loses its luster, especially when private companies are overcompensated.

An important attraction of BOT contracts is the recoupment of construction costs from monopoly operation rights. This implies that project risks should not exceed alternative private sector investments unless appropriate compensation is built into the project.

The potential benefit of a powerful unitary PPP regulator under ideal circumstance deserves attention, but is not decisive because the efficiency gain may be countervailed by diminished transparency. Corruption costs may be exorbitant. Tradeoffs should be carefully weighed in choosing best concessionary regimes. Whatever the choice, welfare losses can be reduced by mandating full disclosure of contractors' costs, and benefits enhanced by independently scrutinizing results instead of relying on contractors' self-evaluations. Strengthening interagency transparency and cooperation also should be constructive.

Appendix: A Lagrangian Decomposition Perspective

If there is only one regulator, finding an optimal BOT contract is equivalent to a two-dimensional screening problem. The dimensionalities of

---

[5] South Bay Expressway, http://www.fhwa.dot.gov/ipd/p3/default.aspx.
[6] Klein, Michael U. Infrastructure Finance — The Core Debates, http://www.pwfinance.net/document/researchr exports.

the private information are the same as the number of regulatory allocation instruments. The problem is modeled by decomposing the two
sectors because the natural ordering in multidimensional space is
unknowable. The decomposition has two different aspects: timing of
the game as well as information disclosure, both affected by the games
setup.

In a BOT contracting environment, the private information of the
contractor, including construction and operation costs, is a binary distribution on two dimensions. The government has two allocation instruments
(construction and operation decisions). We can translate the two-dimensional
BOT screening problem into two subscreening problems on each dimension to facilitate analysis.

The decomposition represents the extreme case and can be softened to
accommodate mixed restrictions. The institutional setup postulates two
regulators working cooperatively, but independently. The timing of the
game is sequential where the construction regulator makes the first decision and the operation regulator follows. The setup allows the information
disclosure to be one-dimensional from the private entity to the corre-
sponding regulator.

I prove that this decomposition cannot be translated into multiple
one-dimensional screening problems without coarsening the contractors'
selection criterion. Keeping both the institutional setup and the game's
limitation the same, but changing information during the process, we
prove that better outcomes are achievable when jurisdictional barriers are
eliminated.

Propositions 1, 2 and 3 compare two Lagrangian decomposition methods with the only difference being the information disclosed.

In the section "Information disclosure in different contracts", the
paper uses game theoretic theory to explain how restricted information
affects the optimality of contract design. In the appendix, we tie the
mathematical idea to our game theory concepts. We use Lagrangian
decomposition methods to find the optima of the problems. The
Revelation Principle fails to apply in incomplete information disclosure
because the decomposition in a pseudo-combinatorial optimization
problem is invalid.

The operation regulator's problem is

$$\max_{(t,O,Q)} \quad \sum_{j\in\{H,L\}} \alpha^j \left[Q^j(n-t^j)s + (1-Q^j)n\cdot s - O^j \right]$$

s.t.

$\forall j, k \in \{H, L\}$

$$Q^j [t^j (R - c^j) + O^j] \geq Q^k [t^k (R - c^j) + O^k] \qquad \text{(IC)}$$

$$Q^j [tj (R - c^j) + O^j] \geq 0 \qquad \text{(IR)}$$

$$0 \leq t^j \leq n$$

$$0 \leq Q^j \leq 1.$$

First, it is established that the objective function is concave (linear) in all the choice variables, and that the constrained set is convex. Then the Lagrangian for the operation regulator is presented. The proof's logic is explained immediately after presenting the first-order conditions and complementary slackness conditions to avoid confusion.

Two different methods are used to prove that the objective function is concave (linear): principal minors and the eigenvalue of the Hessian Matrix.

The objective function is concave in all choice variables. The determinant of the Hessian is

$$D^2 f = \begin{matrix} 0 & 0 & 0 & 0 & a & 0 \\ 0 & 0 & 0 & 0 & 0 & b \\ 0 & 0 & 0 & 0 & c & 0 \\ 0 & 0 & 0 & 0 & 0 & d \\ e & 0 & f & 0 & 0 & 0 \\ 0 & g & 0 & h & 0 & 0 \end{matrix}$$

A matrix is negative definite if all its kth order leading principal minors alternate in sign, starting from negative and for semidefiniteness, we replace the strict inequalities with weak inequalities.

$$a = -\alpha^H s + \lambda_2 (R - c^H),$$
$$b = -\alpha^L s + \lambda_1 (R - c^L) - \lambda_2 (R - c^H),$$
$$c = -\alpha^H + \lambda_2,$$

$$d = -\alpha^L + (\lambda_1 - \lambda_2),$$
$$e = -\alpha^H s + \lambda_2 (R - c^H),$$
$$f = \lambda_2 - \alpha^H,$$
$$g = -\alpha^L s + \lambda_1 (R - c^L) - \lambda_2 (R - c^H),$$
$$h = -\alpha^L + \lambda_1 - \lambda_2.$$

Therefore, the objective function is a concave.

Alternatively, we can also prove that the objective function is concave (linear) by changing variables. I find the eigenvalues after the change of variables. Redefine $Q^j * t^j = t^j$, where $j = H, L$.

The operation agency's objective function can be rewritten as

$$\alpha^H [(n - t^H)s - O^H] + \alpha^L [(n - t^L)s - O^L],$$

using Mathematica to find the eigenvalues for the Hessian matrix. They are $[0, 0, 0, 0]$. Therefore, the objective function of the operation agency is concave (linear).

The constraint set is convex. The Hessian of the constraint set is

0	0	0	0	$R-c^H$	0
0	0	0	0	0	$-(R-$
0	0	0	0	1	0
0	0	0	0	0	-1
$-c$	0	1	0	0	0
0	$-(R-c^H)$	0	-1	0	0

$D^2 g = R$

$\text{Det2nd} = \text{Det3rd} = \text{Det4th} = \text{Det5th} = \text{DetD}^2 g = 0.$

Therefore, the constraint set is convex.

For the operation sector, the Lagrangian is

$$L = \alpha^H \{n \cdot s - Q^H [t^H s + O^H]\} + \alpha^L \{n \cdot s - Q^L [t^L s + O^L]\}$$
$$+ \lambda_1 Q^L [t^L (R - c^L) + O^L]$$
$$+ \lambda_2 \{Q^H [t^H (R - c^H) + O^H] - Q^L [t^L (R - c^H) + O^L]\}$$

$$+ \lambda_3 \, t^H + \lambda_4 \, t^L$$
$$+ \lambda_5 \, (n - t^H) + \lambda_6 \, (n - t^L)$$
$$+ \lambda_7 \, Q^H + \lambda_8 \, Q^L$$
$$+ \lambda_9 \, (1 - Q^H) + \lambda_{10} \, (1 - Q^L).$$

F.O.Cs:

$$Q^H \, [\lambda_2 \, (R - c^H) - \alpha^H \, s] + \lambda_3 - \lambda_5 = 0,$$
$$Q^L \, [\lambda_1 \, (R - c^L) - \lambda_2 \, (R - c^H) - \alpha^L \, s] + \lambda_4 - \lambda_6 = 0,$$
$$[\lambda_2 - \alpha^H] Q^H = 0,$$
$$[\lambda_1 - \lambda_2 - \alpha^L] Q^L = 0,$$
$$-\alpha^H \, (t^H \, s + O^H) + \lambda_2 \, [t^H \, (R - c^H) + O^H] + \lambda_7 - \lambda_9 = 0,$$
$$-\alpha^L \, (t^L \, s + O^L) + \lambda_1 \, [t^L \, (R - c^L) + O^L] - \lambda_2 \, [t^L \, (R - c^H) + O^L]$$
$$+ \lambda_8 - \lambda_{10} = 0,$$
$$(\lambda_5 - \lambda_3) t^H - \lambda_9 = 0,$$
$$(\lambda_6 - \lambda_4) t^L - \lambda_{10} = 0.$$

The complementary slackness

$$\lambda_1 \, Q^L \, [t^L \, (R - c^L) + O^L] = 0,$$
$$\lambda_2 \, \{ Q^H \, [t^H \, (R - c^H) + O^H] - Q^L \, [t^L \, (R - c^H) + O^L] \} = 0,$$
$$\lambda_3 \, t^H = 0,$$
$$\lambda_4 \, t^L = 0,$$
$$\lambda_5 \, (n - t^H) = 0, \, \lambda_6 \, (n - t^L) = 0, \, \lambda_7 \, Q^H = 0,$$
$$\lambda_8 \, Q^L = 0,$$
$$\lambda_9 \, (1 - Q^H) = 0,$$
$$\lambda_{10} \, (1 - Q^L) = 0.$$

Idea of the proof: Recall, the government optimally chooses contract (t^j, O^j) with a random probability Q^j.

Phase t^j is the allocation variable for the operation regulator; O^j is the monetary transfer at the operation stage; and Q^j is a random instrument. Therefore, there are nine categories available for the operation regulator in the allocation space indicated by $\{t^H = 0, 0 < t^H < n,$

$t^H = n\} \times \{t^L = 0, 0 < t^L < n, t^L = n\}$. It can be proven that only three of the nine categories will be considered. The rest are not optimal contracts candidates.

Lemmas 1 and 2 exclude five categories involving interim solutions of the allocation (t^H, t^L), implying that any non-monotone arrangement of allocation (t^H, t^L) is not rational because the high operational efficiency type would always be able to mimic the low efficiency type.

Lemma 1. $0 < t^H < n$ *will not be a category that is included in the optimal contract.*

Proof. Based on the organized F.O.Cs, we have

$$\lambda_2 Q^H t^H (R - c^H - s) = 0,$$

with $0 < t^H < 1$, there are two possible conditions.

Either $Q^H = 0$ or $\lambda_2 = 0$.

If $Q^H = 0$, for optimal contract $(t^{H*}, t^{L*}, O^{H*}, O^{L*})$ where $t^{H*} \in (0, 1)$, the government picks it with probability zero.

If $\lambda_2 = 0$, according $\lambda_2 Q^H = \alpha^H Q^H$, therefore either $Q^H = 0$, then we arrive at the above conclusion. Or $\lambda_2 = \alpha^H = 0$, therefore according to $\lambda_2 Q^H O^H - \lambda_9 - \lambda_5 n = 0$, since $\lambda_5 = 0$ because this is the multiplier for complementary slackness condition for $t_H = n$, therefore $\lambda_9 = 0$ and it is the multiplier for complementary slackness condition for $Q^H = 1$, then $Q^H \leq 1$.

Since $\alpha^H = 0$ means that the operation regulator's updated expectation for locating a high operational efficient type contractor is zero, issuing a contract to this type of operator is contradictory.

Lemma 2. $0 < t^L < n$ *will not be a category in the optimal contract.*

Proof. Suppose $0 < t^L < n$, $t_H = n$.

Then based on the assumption, $\lambda_5 \geq 0$ and $\lambda_6 = \lambda_4 = 0$,

$$(\lambda_5 - \lambda_3)t^H - \lambda_9 = 0,$$
$$(\lambda_6 - \lambda_4)t^L - \lambda_{10} = 0.$$

If $\lambda_{10} = 0$, then $t_L = 0$, which contradicts the assumption.

If $\lambda_{10} > 0$, then $Q^L = 1$. Therefore, $(\lambda_6 - \lambda_4)t^L - \lambda_{10} = 0$ and there is no t^L that can satisfy the above function.

Under the assumption that $0 < t^L < n$, $t^H = 0$, it would not be sensible because the high efficiency type would always be capable of mimicking the low-efficiency type.

The optimal allocations of the three categories $t^H = n$, $t^L = n$, $t^H = n$, $t^L = 0$, $t^H = 0$, $t^L = 0$ consequently are limited by Lemmas 2 and 3. Given these allocations, the operation regulator uses the random instrument Q^j to improve utility if improvement is possible.

Lemma 3. *($t^H = n$, $t^L = n$) is one of the operation regulator's optimal allocations with no randomization.*

Proof. First, $Q^H = 1$, $0 < Q^L < 1$ is not viable.

Based on the assumptions, $\lambda_7 = 0$, $\lambda_8 = 0$, $\lambda_{10} = 0$, $\lambda_9 \geq 0$.

Since $Q^H = 1$, $\lambda_2 = \alpha^H$ and $\lambda_1 = \alpha_H + \alpha_L$

and $-\alpha^L (n \cdot s + Q^H) - \alpha^L [n(R - c^L) + O^L] - \lambda_2 n(c^L - c^H) - \lambda_{10} = 0$,

$$\lambda_{10} = \alpha^L n(R - c^L - s) - \alpha^H (c^L - c^H)n = 0.$$

Hence, there is a contradiction.

Second, $0 < Q^H < 1$ and $Q^L = 1$ is not viable.

Based on the assumptions, $\lambda_7 = 0$, $\lambda_8 = 0$, $\lambda_9 = 0$, $\lambda_{10} \geq 0$.

Since $Q^L = 1$, $\lambda_2 = \alpha^H$ and $\lambda_1 = \alpha_H + \alpha_L$

and $-\alpha^H [n \cdot s + O^H] + \alpha^H [n(R - c^H) + O^H] - \lambda_9 = 0$.

Therefore, $\lambda_9 = \alpha^H n(R - c^H - s) = 0$, and again there is a contradiction.

Third, $0 < Q^H < 1$ and $0 < Q^L < 1$ is not viable.

Based on the assumptions, $\lambda_7 = 0$, $\lambda_8 = 0$, $\lambda_9 = 0$, $\lambda_{10} = 0$.

$\alpha^H = \alpha^L = 0$ which contradicts the assumption that the operation regulator will grant positive operation phase to the contractor.

Lemma 4. *If the allocation ($t^H = n$, $t^L = n$) is chosen, it means each will receive a contract with $Q^H = Q^L = 1$.*

Proof. We know that ($t^H = n$, $t^L = n$) is chosen with $Q^H = Q^L = 1$ and the conditions for its optimality can be discovered.

In order for this to be a legitimate solution, $\lambda_{10} > 0$ and $\lambda_p > 0$ must hold simultaneously, requiring $R - c^H - s > 0$ and $\alpha^L n(R - c^L - s) - \alpha^H (c^L - c^H)n > 0$ making $\alpha^L (R - c^L - s) - \alpha^H (c^L - c^H) > 0$.

Construction Regulator's Solution

This section proves Propositions 2 and 3. Those two propositions provide alternative ways for decomposing a multidimensional screening problem for a single regulator using two instruments. A legitimate Lagrangian decomposition is identified by comparing results. A theoretical explanation is provided at the end of this section.

The construction regulator's program:

$$\text{Max } \alpha ji \, [-T_i + Q_j (n - t_j)s + (1 - Q_j)n \cdot s - O_j]P_j$$

(P,T).

$$\Sigma$$

$i \in \{H, L\}.$

$\forall i, j, m, k \in \{H, L\}$

s.t.

$[t_j^* (R - c_j) + O_j^* + T_j - F_j]P_i \geq [tk^* (R - c_j) + Ok^* - Tk - F]Pk \quad \text{(IC)}$

$Pi \, [t \, (R - c) + O + T_i - F_i] \geq 0 \quad \text{(IR)}$

$0 \leq P_j \leq 1,$

where

$$\alpha^H = \frac{\sum_i P_i^H \alpha_{Hi}}{\sum_i \sum_j P_i^j \alpha_{ji}},$$

$$\alpha^L = \frac{\sum_i P_i^L \alpha_{Li}}{\sum_i \sum_j P_i^j \alpha_{ji}}.$$

Proof. When $R - s > c_L + \dfrac{\alpha \Delta c}{\alpha^L}$ and $n \, \Delta c > \Delta F$:

$\lambda_1 = 0, \, \lambda_2 = \alpha_H, \, \lambda_3 = \alpha_L, \, \lambda_4 = 1,$

$\lambda_5 = \lambda_6 = 0$

$\lambda_7 = \alpha_H, \, \lambda_8 = 0, \, \lambda_9 = 0, \, \lambda_{10} = 0, \, \lambda_{11} = 0,$

$$\lambda_{12} = \lambda_{13} = \lambda_{14} = \lambda_{15} = 0,$$
$$\lambda_{16} = \alpha_H \left[ns + (d^H - s)t^{H*} - F_H \right],$$
$$\lambda_{17} = \alpha_H \left[ns + (d^H - s)t^{H*} - F_L \right],$$
$$\lambda_{18} = \alpha_H \left[ns + (d^L - s)t^{L*} - F_H \right],$$
$$\lambda_{19} = 0,$$
$$\lambda_{20} = \lambda_{21} = 0,$$
$$\lambda_{22} = \alpha_H \left(nd^L + nd^H - {}_2 F_H \right),$$
$$\lambda_{23} = \alpha_L \left(nd^H - F_L \right),$$

$$H = P_H P_L = 1,$$
$$P_L = 0,$$
$$T_L^H = F_{H'}$$
$$T_H^j = F_{H'}$$

And the solution is consistent with the expectations of the operation sector: If α_{LL} is small and

$$\alpha^H = \frac{\alpha_{HH} + \alpha_{HL}}{\alpha_{HH} + \alpha_{HL} + \alpha_{LH}}$$

$$\alpha^L = \frac{\alpha_{LH}}{\alpha_{HH} + \alpha_{HL} + \alpha_{LH}}$$

If α_L is big with a full pooling for every type.

By observing the first-order conditions of Q's above:

$$\alpha^H Q^H ns + \lambda_5 n = \lambda_9,$$
$$\alpha^L Q^L ns + \lambda_6 n = \lambda_{10}.$$

Assume that the operation sector will grant the project to the contractor with a positive probability $0 < Q^H < 1$.

Then, according to the complementary slackness conditions:

$$\lambda_9 = 0,$$
$$\lambda_5 \geq 0.$$

The above equation holds only when $Q^H = 0$, which is contradictory. The same logic can be used to show Q^L.

First-order conditions:

$$\alpha_H \left[P_H \left(ns - F_H \right) \right] + \lambda_1 - \lambda_3 = 0,$$

$$P_L \left[\alpha_L \left(ns - F_L - \alpha_H \Delta F \right] + \lambda_2 - \lambda_4 = 0.$$

$$\lambda_1 = \lambda_2 = \lambda_3 = \lambda_5 = \lambda_6 = \lambda_9 = \lambda_{11} = 0,$$

$$\lambda_4 = 3\alpha_L + \alpha_H,$$

$$\lambda_7 = \alpha_H, \lambda_8 = \alpha_L, \lambda_{10} = \alpha_L,$$

$$\lambda_{12} = \lambda_{13} = \lambda_{14} = \lambda_{15} = 0,$$

$$\lambda_{16} = \alpha_H \left[ns + (d_H - s)t^{H*} - F_H \right],$$

$$\lambda_{17} = \alpha_L \left[ns + (d_H - s)t^{H*} - F_L \right],$$

$$\lambda_{18} = \alpha_H \left[ns + (d_L - s)t^{L*} - F_H \right],$$

$$\lambda_{19} = \lambda_{20} = \lambda_{21} = \lambda_{23} = 0,$$

$$\lambda_{22} = \alpha_H \Delta c,$$

$$H = P_H = P_L = 1,$$

$$P_L = 0,$$

$$T_L = F_L - n\Delta c,$$

$$T_H = F_H.$$

It also can be proven for Proposition 3 that the construction agent's objective function is actually a concave (linear) function with eigenvalues of its Hessian Matrix being [0, 0, 0, 0]. This is a basic one-dimensional screening problem. The "standard" approach to finding the "optimum" can then be employed, with the IR constraint binding for the low-efficiency type and the IC binding for the high-efficiency type. Once this optimum is obtained, its monotonicity is confirmed.

References

Martimort, David and Lars Stole (2002), "The Revelation and Delegation Principles in Common Agent Games," *Econometrica*, 70(4), 1659–1673.

Public Sector Research Center (2008), *The Value of PFI: Hanging in the Balance (Sheet)?*" New York: Price WaterhouseCoopers, p. 22.

Chapter 16

Housing

Wenting Ma

Introduction

Recent extreme fluctuations in China's stock market and the secondary aspects of this volatility have caused concern in many countries. Since the 1980s, the Japanese and Chinese export-led economies displayed similar cyclical characteristics. Both had blooms and asset bubbles. Many investors worried that China might follow in Japan's footsteps.[1] Under international pressure, China's central bank, the People's Bank of China, cut China's prime interest rate by 25 basis points and decreased reserve ratios by 50 basis points in order to stimulate the economy, causing domestic share prices and housing prices to increase.[2] This study measures the impacts of the expansionary policies implemented in 2008 and 2012 for future reference.

Due to the 2008 financial crisis, China's GDP growth rates fell sharply from 14.2% in 2007 to 9.22% in 2009. Approximately two-thirds of the Chinese stock exchange market value was wiped out by the end

---

[1]"China Crisis covers tracks of Japan," http://www.reuters.com/article/global-markets-china-parallels-idUSL4N1112R720150830.
[2]*The New York Times*, "China's Housing Market Shows Signs of Hope," https://www.nytimes.com/2015/05/19/business/international/chinas-housing-market-shows-signs-of-hope.html.

of 2008. China's exports plummeted by about 17% in 2009.[3] Housing prices of first, second, and third-tier cities fell by 13.82%, 4.36%, and 3.52%, respectively during the 2008 crisis.[4] Due to the 2010 European debt crisis and the Chinese government's contractionary polices implemented in 2010 and 2011, similar patterns occurred in the most recent crisis. China's GDP growth rates fell from 10.6% in 2010 to 7.8% in 2012, stock prices fell by approximate 30% by the end of 2011, and prices for the three tiers of China's housing started dropping again in the middle of 2011.

Although Chinese housing prices initially dropped in 2008 and 2011, they rebounded rapidly. Fang *et al.* (2015) claim that the strong government intervention helped China's housing markets recover from the 2008 recession. But their study did not quantify the impact of these interventions. This chapter estimates the magnitude and timing of the impacts of China's expansionary policies implemented in 2008 and 2010 on its residential housing market in order to answer the following two questions:

Question 1: Did housing markets in different tiers of cities respond differently to China's central government expansionary policies in 2008 and 2012?

Question 2: Did government intervention increase the rates of return in China's housing sector compared with counterpart investments in the Shanghai stock market, the American housing market, the Japanese housing market, or the international housing market?

Event studies and excess return analysis are utilized to answer these questions. The approach assumes that policy change announcements are promptly reflected in asset prices (MacKinlay 1997). This information is

---

[3] *Economist*, "Fear of the Dragon — China's Share of World Markets Increased During the Recession," http://www.economist.com/node/15213305, 2010.

[4] It is common in China to separate cities into three tiers based on population. The methodology used in this paper to differentiate between China's first, second, and third-tier cities follows the methodology used in Fang *et al.* (2015) to determine the tiers for each city studied since the housing price indices they built are the primary data resource for this work. The first tier includes four big cities which have the largest populations and the largest economic impact in China. The second tier includes 35 key industrial or commercial cities. The third tier includes 85 smaller cities. The detailed list of cities in each tier is shown in Appendix I.

readily available. In this chapter, event studies are conducted on each tier's housing market to measure the deviation of the actual returns from the market's prior expectation, and the results can be used to answer Question 1.

For answering Question 2, event study is not applicable. A market portfolio, which includes the China's housing market as the objective asset, is required to estimate the market's prior expectation on this asset's return. However, due to data limitation, such market portfolio is not available. Instead, analyzing the excess returns made from investments in Chinese housing market will help us evaluate the impacts of the government interventions, the results from which can be used to answer Question 2.

A similar study was done by Ding (2013). Although Ding (2013) also tries to measure the impact of government intervention in the Chinese housing market by conducting an event study, she used real estate firms' stock prices as the measure of the housing market performance since the housing price indices were not available. Instead of examining the heterogeneity in the impacts of an expansionary policy on different tiers' housing markets, Ding (2013) mainly focused on examining the heterogeneity in the impacts of a contractionary policy on the value of different types of firms, instead of different tiers' housing markets.[5]

The main findings from this study can be briefly summarized into following points: (1) In terms of timing, housing markets in each tier of cities respond differently to an announcement of expansionary policy; (2) the magnitude of an announcement's impact on each tier of cities is different, but the difference is significant only between the first and third tiers; (3) investments in the Chinese housing market earned higher returns than did investments in the other four markets, but the difference is not significant between the returns from investments in the Chinese and American housing market. The first two points are brief answers for Question 1 and the last point is a brief answer for Question 2.

Answering these questions is even more important for the currently slowing Chinese economy in which property fuels up to 15% of GDP and

---

[5]There are three main types of firms in China: private firms, central state-controlled firms, and local state-controlled firms.

the value of the property market underpins the banking system.[6] Answers may help policymakers understand the impact and effectiveness of previous expansionary polices on the housing market and shed light on what kind of stimulus plans should be made for a specific tier of city size. The effectiveness of these policies is not only closely related to the well-being of Chinese households who own their houses,[7] but it is also an important information for potential homebuyers who are making investment decisions. Meanwhile, as real estate has strong linkages to several upstream and downstream industries, such as banking, concrete, and glass (Liang *et al.* 2006), whether the real estate market can again be bolstered has significant ramifications for related industries.

This chapter is organized as follows: The section on institutional background reviews the development of China's housing market and government intervention between 2008 and 2012. Next, government policies and housing market provides a review of the literature regarding government interventions in housing markets in order to provide the theory underpinning the empirical results from the later sections. In the succeeding section, the data set used in this chapter is reviewed. The next two sections introduce the empirical methodologies and analyze the empirical results for Questions 1 and 2, respectively. The last section draws conclusions.

Institutional Background

In accordance with the chronology listed in Table 16.1, this section reviews the major events related to the development of the Chinese housing market since 1997, focusing on measuring the impact of the expansionary policies implemented in 2008 and 2012, briefly summarized in Tables 16.2 and 16.3.

First housing market boom, 1997–2008

In July 1997, a financial crisis originating in Thailand spread throughout Asia. Rapid currency devaluations caused several Asian banking systems

---

[6] *Economist*, "The Great Fall of China," http://www.economist.com/news/leaders/21662544-fear-about-chinas-economy-can-be-overdone-investors-are-right-be-nervous-great-fall.
[7] According to the China Household Finance Survey, 89.7% Chinese households own their houses.

Table 16.1 Chronology of Major Events Related to Chinese Housing Market Development, 1997–2012.

Date	Major events
July 1997	Asian financial crisis started in Thailand
November 1997	Real estate commercialization
Housing prices took off	
October 2004	Housing price controls started
September 2008	US and worldwide financial crisis
Housing prices dropped down and returns became negative	
Expansionary policies started (see more details in Table 16.2)	
March 2009	Housing prices went up and returns went back to positive
January 2010	Housing price controls started
Late of 2010	European debt crisis
Expansionary policies started (see more details in Table 16.3)	
January 2012	Housing prices dropped down and returns became negative
April 2012	Housing prices went up and returns went back to positive

to collapse. As the crisis ricocheted through Asia, the economic development of each affected country slowed. Although China's financial system was not affected as badly as were the financial systems of many other Asian countries, slowing exports caused China's GDP growth rate to fall sharply. As shown in Figure 16.1, China's GDP growth rate fell from 9.23% in 1997 to 7.62% in 1999. In order to reduce its heavy reliance on exports, China decided to fully commercialize its domestic housing market in November 1997 so that its housing industry could become one of the key drivers for the economy. This implied that homes would have to be purchased rather than rationed on a welfare basis.[8] The newly commercialized housing market also attracted many domestic and foreign investors,

---

[8] In the welfare housing system, the housing allocation involves two stages: the state allocated public rental housing to work units, then the work units distributed the housing to individual households. In this system, social status, rather than economic contribution, merit, and need, serves as the determining factor in housing distribution (Chen and Yang 2014).

Table 16.2   Events Announced in 2008.

Event date	Effective date	Event	Monetary policy	Fiscal policy
15-Sep-08	16-Sep-08	Required reserve ratio for small banks decreased by 1%	1	
		Primary lending rate decreased by −0.27%	1	
9-Oct-08	15-Oct-08	Required reserve ratio for large banks decreased by 0.5%	1	
		Required reserve ratio for small banks decreased by 0.5%	1	
12-Oct-08	31-Oct-08	Tax on deed decreased to 1% for houses less than 90 square meters		1
		Eliminate stamp duty and land value increment tax Primary		1
		lending rate decreased by 0.58%	1	
		Provident fund lending rate decreased by 0.27%	1	
9-Nov-08		Announced four-trillion RMB (US$586 million) stimulus package		1
26-Nov-08	28-Nov-08	Required reserve ratio for large banks decreased by 1%	1	
		Required reserve ratio for small banks decreased by 2%	1	
22-Dec-08	23-Dec-08	Primary lending rate decreased by −0.27%	1	
		Required reserve ratio for large banks decreased by 0.5%	1	
		Required reserve ratio for small banks decreased by 0.5%	1	

causing housing prices to rise steadily between 2000 and 2008.[9] This is illustrated by the national price indices (Figure 16.2) derived from urban housing price indices complied by Fang *et al.* (2015).[10] The aggregate

---

[9] According to data from National Bureau of Statistics of China (NBSC), 24.1% of foreign direct investment was invested in real estate sector in the first half year of 2007.

[10] The national price indices are constructed by three different methods. The details about these methods can be found in Appendix II.

Table 16.3 Events Announced in 2012.

Event date	Effective date	Event	Monetary policy	Fiscal policy
18-Feb-12	24-Feb-12	Required reserve ratio for large banks decreased by 0.5%	1	
		Required reserve ratio for small banks decreased by 0.5%	1	
12-May-12	18-May-12	Required reserve ratio for large banks decreased by 0.5%	1	
		Required reserve ratio for small banks decreased by 0.5%		
5-Jun-12	8-Jun-12	Primary lending rate decreased by −0.25%	1	
5-Jul-12	6-Jul-12	Primary lending rate decreased by −0.31%	1	
		Primary deposit rate decreased by 0.25%	1	

Note: For the monetary policy column, value 1 represents the event is monetary policy. For the fiscal policy column, value 1 represents the event is fiscal policy.

Source: People's Bank of China, Xinhua Net (http://www.xinhuanet.com/english/china/) and People. cn(http://www.people.com.cn/).

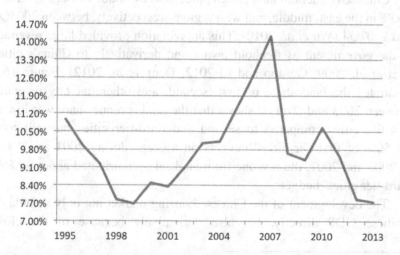

Figure 16.1 GDP Growth Rate of China (Annual %).
Source: World Bank.

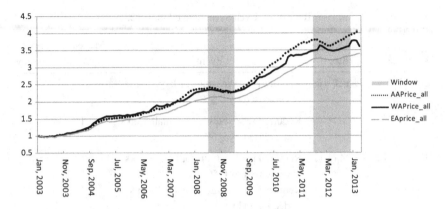

Figure 16.2   National Price Indices.

Note: This study uses three different methods to construct the national housing price indices based on the data provided by Fang *et al.* (2015). The details about these methods can be found in Appendix II. Each of these three lines represents a national price index (market price) for the Chinese housing market constructed by a specific method. Shaded areas represent two periods during which Chinese central government were more activate in implementing expansionary policies.

Source: Constructed based on the data provided by Fang *et al.* (2015).

price index for first and second-tier cities constructed by Wu *et al.* (2010) rose by approximately 100% between 2000Q1 and 2008Q2.[11]

Chinese residential land price appreciated by about 150%, 125%, and 100% in the east, middle, and west regions, respectively, between 2004Q1 and 2007Q4 (Wu *et al.* 2010). This appreciation provided large revenues to the government as freehold owner and derivatively to China's cities (Cai *et al.* 2009; Gordon and Li 2012; Deng *et al.* 2012). Figure 16.3 illustrates the land share of first, second, and other tier city revenues between 2003 and 2011. It shows that the land revenue share was low in first-tier cities compared to second and third-tier cities but still took 20–50% of first-tier cities' budgets on average during 2003 and 2008. In 2003 and 2007, the revenue from land sales contributed about 90% of third-tier cities' budgets.

The development of the Chinese housing market not only stimulated Chinese GDP directly, but also derivatively because of the close

---

[11] This index is computed as the weighted average of the local market series, with transactions volume between 2000 and 2008 as the fixed weight.

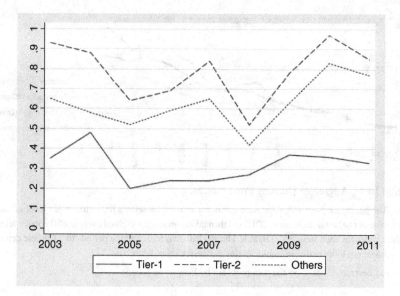

Figure 16.3   Share of Land Revenue in City Budget.

Source: Fang *et al.* (2015). Data were collected from China Municipal Statistical Yearbook and China National Land Resource Year Book.

connection between Chinese real estate industry and 60 other downstream and upstream industries (Liang *et al.* 2006). As a result, China's GDP and its growth rate increased rapidly since 1990 (Figure 16.1).

First housing market downturn and expansionary policies, 2008–2009

The global financial crisis of 2008 adversely affected China (Liang *et al.* 2011).[12] China's GDP growth rates decreased sharply from 14.2% in 2007 to 9.22% in 2009. During October and November 2008, China's export growth rate fell sharply from 20% to negative 2.2%. China's exports fell

---

[12]As argued by Zhang Ming, a government think tank in Beijing, there is always a higher degree of risk for the creditor when sovereign debts become massive. See more details at   http://www.smh.com.au//business/china-tops-us-govt-foreign-creditor-list-20081119-6bin.html.

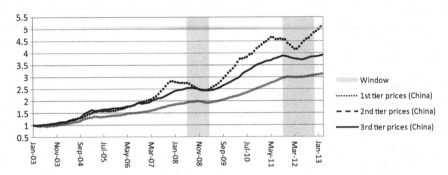

Figure 16.4   Aggregate Housing Price Indices.

Note: The aggregate price index for each tier is constructed by setting the initial index level of each city in that tier to be one at January 2013 and then taking an equal weighted average of the index levels of these cities for each subsequent month. The shaded areas represent the periods that Chinese central government are more active in implementing expansionary policies.

Source: Constructed based on the data provided by Fang *et al.* (2015).

by about 17% in 2009.[13] The 2008 crisis also hit China's financial market. The People's Bank of China data show that total household loans dropped by a third between March and July of 2008. About two-thirds of the Shanghai Stock Exchange (SSE) market value was wiped out. Many people tried to sell houses to raise money to pay for leveraged positions in the stock market, and people became more cautious in housing investment because they were fearful of a housing market crash.

In this environment, many people expected that China's housing prices would drop significantly.[14] However, the data suggest China's housing prices only dropped by 3.26% on average from July 2008 to March 2009.[15] Housing prices in first-tier cities were affected most significantly by the crisis (Figure 16.4). First-tier cities had an average housing price decrease of 13.82%. Average housing prices in second and third-tier cities only dropped by 4.36% and 3.52%, respectively (for details see Table 16.4, panel 1). The price correction was brief.

---

[13] *Economist*, "Fear of the Dragon — China's Share of World Markets Increased During the Recession," http://www.economist.com/node/15213305, 2010.

[14] *The New York Times*, "Real Estate Woes Spread to China," http://www.nytimes.com/2008/09/11/business/worldbusiness/11y.

[15] This is calculated with the value-weighted national housing price index which is constructed by method two described in Appendix II.

Table 16.4 Aggregate Change Rate of China's Housing Prices, 2007–2009 and 2011–2012.

Tier	Reduction period	Aggregate change rate of prices
Panel 1: First Housing Market Downturn		
1	12.2007–03.2009	−13.82%
2	08.2008–03.2009	−4.36%
3	10.2008–02.2009	−3.52%
Panel 2: Second Housing Market Downturn		
1	05.2011–04.2012	−6.92%
2	10.2011–06.2012	−4.30%
3	12.2011–04.2012	−0.53%

Source: Calculated based on housing price indices built by Fang *et al.* (2015).

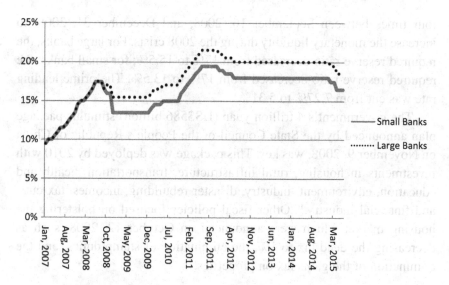

Figure 16.5 Required Reserve Ratio in China, 2007–2013.
Source: The People's Bank of China.

Government expansionary measures are credited for the rapid price recovery (Fang *et al.* 2015; Barth *et al.* 2012). These policies are summarized in Table 16.3. As shown in Figures 16.5 and 16.6, the People's Bank of China cut the required reserve ratios and the prime lending rate

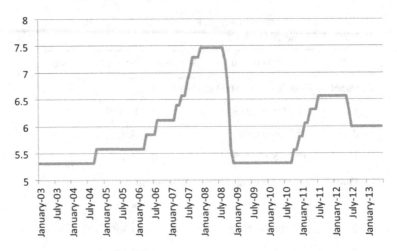

Figure 16.6   Primary Lending Rate, 2003–2013.

Source: The People's Bank of China.

four times between September 16, 2008, and December 31, 2008, to increase the monetary liquidity during the 2008 crisis. For large banks, the required reserve ratio decreased from 17% to 15.5%; for small banks, the required reserve ratio decreased from 17% to 13.5%. The prime lending rate was cut from 7.27% to 5.31%.

The government's 4 trillion yuan (US$586 billion) stimulus package plan announced by the State Council of the People's Republic of China on November 9, 2008, was key. This package was deployed by 2010 with investments in housing, rural infrastructure, transportation, health and education, environment, industry, disaster rebuilding, incomes, tax cuts, and financial industry.[16] Other fiscal policies focused on bolstering the housing market which were announced on October 12, 2008, such as decreasing the deed tax to 1%, the elimination of stamp duties, and the elimination of the gains tax on properties.

Second housing market boom, 2009–2011

The second housing market boom started in early 2009. As shown in Figures 16.5 and 16.6, the required reserve ratio and prime lending rate

---

[16] http://news.xinhuanet.com/english/2008-11/09/content 10332422.htm.

were kept at low levels in 2009 in order to help the Chinese economy recover. During this period of time, lower borrowing costs attracted housing investors. Data show that the sale of residential housing floor space increased by about 75% in 2009. Although low borrowing costs also attracted housing suppliers, it took longer to actually increase housing supply due to construction lags. Figures 16.2 and 16.4 confirm that Chinese housing prices went up rapidly in early 2009.

The explosive increase in housing prices in 2009 triggered expectations of housing inflation and created speculative opportunities. Some housing developers kept houses off the market hoping for higher future profit. Households stretched to pay high prices in expectation of even higher prices in the future. Speculation caused the Chinese housing market to overheat in 2010.[17]

Second housing market bust and expansionary policies, 2011–2012

In order to cool the overheated housing market, the Chinese government implemented a series of contractionary policies during 2010 and 2011, including an increase in the prime lending rate, an increase in the down payment percentage, and property-purchasing limitations.[18] These contractionary policies lowered housing investors' expectations and discouraged them from speculating in the housing market.

Around the same time, the European debt crisis hit the world. The depreciation of the euro plus the shrinkage of the European market led to a slump in China's exports, which negatively impacted the growth.[19]

---

[17]VOX, "On the Chinese house-price bubble," http://voxeu.org/article/china-s-housing-bubble-new-evidence.

[18]On January 2011, the State Council issued eight guidelines to curb housing prices of major cities, one of which prevents residential families with two or more houses in a major city from buying any more in that city. Non-residential families are only allowed to buy one house.

[19]*Bloomberg*, "China's Exports to Europe 'Falling Off Cliff': Chart of the Day," http://www.bloomberg.com/news/articles/2011-11-29/china-s-exports-to-europe-falling-off-cliff-chart-of-the-day.

Weakening housing demand was exacerbated, and housing prices started to drop in late 2011.

By the end of 2011, many Chinese and foreign investors worried that the housing bubble was about to burst. However, the national housing price index only dropped 4.53% between November 2011 and April 2012.[20] Table 16.4, panel 2 demonstrates that housing prices of first, second, and third-tier cities only had 6.92%, 4.3%, and 0.53% drops, respectively.

It appears that central government's expansionary policies, primarily monetary measures implemented at the start of 2012, were successful (Table 16.3). The required reserve ratio decreased from 21% to 20% for large banks and from 19% to 18% for small banks between February 24, 2012, and May 12, 2012. The prime lending rate was lowered from 6.56% to 6% between June 2012 and July 2012. Meanwhile, to avoid overheating the housing market again, the central government prohibited local governments from easing the property purchase constraints.

Government Policies and Housing Market: Theory

There is a rich academic literature on government intervention in housing markets. It shows that (1) expansionary policies boost housing prices; (2) housing prices adjust slowly to shocks; and (3) different regions respond differently to the same policy. This section elaborates these findings to provide context for empirical results reported later in this chapter.

(1) Expansionary policies boost housing prices. The Discount Cash Flow model (Fisher 1930; Williams 1938) states that asset price can be estimated by the summation of the discounted future cash flows. Mathematically, the present housing price (P_0) (present discounted value of the expected net revenue steam) can be estimated as:

$$P_0 = \frac{R_1}{1+r} + \frac{R_2}{(1+r)^2} + \cdots + \frac{R_{t-1}}{(1+r)^{t-1}} + \frac{R_t}{(1+r)^t}, \tag{1}$$

---

[20]This refers to the value-weighted national price index. See more details about the methodology for constructing this index in Appendix II.

where R_t is the net rent of the house at time t, P_t is the expected housing price at time t, and r is the interest rate.

If we assume that R_t remains constant in short run, then a decrease in r or an increase in P_t would cause an increase in the current housing price P_0. Therefore, we should expect *ceteris paribus* that P_0 will increase after a central bank cuts interest rates and the expected price P_t will rise under expansionary policies. Harris (1989) and Bernanke and Gartler (1995) explain that when interest rates drop, increased affordability stimulates housing demand, and financial leverage works to the advantage of buyers.

Tax cuts and stimulus packages augment housing demand and growth further (Alesina and Ardagna 2010; Afonso and Sousa 2011). Fang *et al.* (2015) contend that expected household income growth rate determines buyer's willingness to pay. Similarly, housing price growth in current period is positively related to prior income growth (Case and Shiller 1980; McCarthy and Peach 2002). Expansionary policies therefore should bolster housing prices.

(2) Housing prices adjust slowly to shocks. If housing prices could adjust to shocks immediately, then the equilibrium housing price $P*$ could be fixed by the intersection of the housing demand and supply curves. However, the majority of the literature argues that housing prices cannot respond to the shocks that quickly (Fair 1972; Rosen and Smith, 1983; DiPasquale and Wheaton 1994; McCarthy and Peach 2002). McCarthy and Peach (2002) incorporate a wedge between actual price and equilibrium price from the last period into the housing demand equation for short run to take slow price adjustment into account:

$$\Delta P_t = \lambda(P_{t-1} - P^*_{t-1}) + \beta_0 + \beta_1 \Delta C_t + \beta_2 \Delta U_t + \beta_3 \Delta W_t + \beta_4 \Delta W_t + \beta_4 \Delta R_t + \varepsilon_t,$$

(2)

where Δ is the first difference of a variable. C_t and U_t are consumption and user cost at time, respectively. W_t and R_t represent wealth and rental price at time t, respectively. The wedge, $(P_{t-1} - P^*_{t-1})$ represents excess supply if it is positive.

One of the results from estimating Eq. (2) with US data from 1975Q1 and 2000Q3 shows that λ is significantly negative. It indicates that excess supply reduces home price inflation, and thus it takes a while for the actual housing price to reach the equilibrium price. Therefore, we should expect that expansionary policies would have lagged effects on housing price growth if there exists excess supply in the housing market.

(3) Regional housing prices respond differently to the same policy. Carlino and DeFina (1998 and 1999) suggest that the impact of monetary policy on the US economy can differ across regions and that the sensitivity of different regions to monetary policy shock may vary. This implies that housing markets of different cities may respond diversely to the same monetary policy. The differences may be caused by city-specific characteristics, such as export growth, population, level of excess supply, and so on (Liu and Shen 2004).

Data and Summary Statistics

City level housing price indices and returns

City-specific data are needed to measure the heterogeneous effects of central government housing focused policies. The NBSC regularly reports two types of city-level house price indices: "Average Selling Price of Newly-Built Residential Buildings"[21] and "Price Indices for Real Estate in 70 Large and Medium-sized Cities."[22] Deng *et al.* (2012, 2013) however do not recommend their use for three reasons. First, the "Average Selling Price of Newly-Built Residential Buildings" index does not reflect the differences in housing quality across cities. Second, the "Price Indices for Real Estate in 70 Large and Medium-sized Cities" inadequately captures the appreciation and volatility in housing prices. For example, the nominal housing price at the national level only increased by 1.5% in 2009 compared with the previous year according to these indices, even though the general public and the Chinese government were highly concerned with

---

[21] "Average Selling Price of Newly-Built Residential Buildings" for new housing units in each city equals total sales divided by total size of housing unit transacted.

[22] The first step of constructing "Price Indices for Real Estate in 70 Large and Medium-sized Cities" is calculating the average sales price of new units each month by housing complex. The next step is taking value-weighted averages across complexes using the transaction volume of each complex as the weight.

the rapid growth of housing prices in 2009.[23] Third, these two sets of price indices are weakly correlated despite being constructed by same agency.

This study therefore substitutes the monthly city-level housing price indices constructed by Fang *et al.* (2015) for the official series. Their data set covers the housing prices for 101 Chinese cities from January 2003 to March 2013.[24] Fang *et al.* (2015) constructed these indices using a hybrid approach[25] that takes into account the following features of Chinese housing market: (1) there were few repeat sales; (2) new homes are condos; (3) condos in same development project have similar characteristics (number of rooms, square feet, lot size, quality of construction, and so on), while condos across development projects differ; (4) sequential sales of condos in the same development are observed over time. The Fang *et al.* (2015) indices not only cover more cities and a longer time span, but also do a better job of capturing the fluctuation of Chinese housing prices. In order to calculate abnormal returns and excess returns for empirical analysis in the subsequent section, monthly city-level returns of investments in city *i*'s housing market in month *t* (R_{it}) are calculated by $R_{it} = (P_{it} - P_{it-1})/P_{it-1}$, where P_{it} is the housing price index for city *i* in month *t*.

National housing price indices and market returns

There are three different methods to construct the national housing prices: AAPrices, WAPrices, and EAPrices. The detailed descriptions of these methodologies are provided in Appendix II. Monthly provincial-level floor space statistics obtained from Datastream are used to construct value weighted market prices (WAPrices).[26]

---

[23] *China Daily*, "Doubts over Increase in Property Price," http://www.chinadaily.com.cn/business/2010-02/27/content_9513379.htm.

[24] Originally, this data set included price indices for the 123 cities which are listed in Appendix I. However, 19 cities are excluded from the sample since these cities do not have enough data to cover estimation windows or event windows.

[25] A hybrid of hedonic approach (Kain and Quigley 1970) and repeated-sales approach (Case and Shiller 1987). See more details about the hybrid approach at Fang *et al.* (2015), pp. 10–13.

[26] Since this data set only goes back to January 2004, I assume that the monthly floor space of buildings sold in each province of each month in 2003 is as the same as the floor space sold in the same month in 2004.

Table 16.5   Summary Statistics of National Housing Price Indices.

Market Prices	Obs	Mean	Std. Dev.	Min	Max
AAPrices	123	2.331962	0.9705026	0.9788852	4.083398
WAPrices	123	2.256537	0.8612361	0.9820329	3.790621
EAPrices	123	2.057851	0.7687944	0.966965	3.401857

Table 16.6   Summary Statistics of National Housing Market Returns.

	Obs	Mean	Std. Dev.	Min	Max
Returns AAPrices	123	0.0116642	0.0114872	−0.0139414	0.0418515
Returns WAPrices	123	0.0106801	0.0151389	−0.0439907	0.0632659
Returns EAPrices	123	0.0101335	0.0098014	−0.0174114	0.0460579

Note: Returns AAPrices represents national housing market returns calculated with AAPrices. Returns WAPrices represents national housing market returns calculated with WAPrices. Returns EAPrices represents national housing market returns calculated with EAPrices.

Figure 16.2 reports alternative national housing price indices constructed by different methods. Equally weighted average housing prices show the lowest rates of inflation. Using equal weights overstates the contribution of third-tier cities. Summary statistics shown in Table 16.5 reveal that average Chinese housing prices of each tier more than doubled across time.

National housing market return in month t (R_{mt}) is calculated by $R_{mt} = (P_t - P_{t-1})/P_{t-1}$, where P_t is the housing market price in month t. The summary statistics are reported in Table 16.6. The mean of the returns are very close across methods, but the returns calculated with WAPrices are more volatile than the returns calculated with other market price indices.

Aggregate housing price indices and returns for different tiers

Aggregate price indices provide a good impression of real estate inflation across urban tiers, obviating the need to scour price indices for 101 separate cities. The aggregate housing price index for each tier is constructed by setting the initial index level of each city in that tier to be one in January 2013 and then taking an equal weighted average of the index levels of these cities for each subsequent month. These indices are plotted

Table 16.7   Summary Statistics of Aggregate Housing Price Indices.

Tier	Obs	Mean	Std. Dev.	Min	Max
First Tier	123	2.689675	1.284707	0.9807981	5.198798
Second Tier	123	2.402784	0.9559655	0.9962644	3.919827
Third Tier	123	1.903428	0.6795168	0.9420629	3.131568

in Figure 16.4. The graph shows that housing prices of first-tier cities are higher than the ones of other tier cities beginning in 2007. Prices in first-tier cities were more adversely affected by crisis and contractionary policies in early 2008 and late 2011. Table 16.7 summarizes the aggregate price indices of each tier. The third column shows that the average housing price of first-tier cities is higher than the other two tiers, and the fourth column shows that housing prices of first-tier cities are more volatile.

The aggregate return for tier g in month t (R_{gt}) can be calculated as $R_{gt} = (P_{gt} - P_{gt-1})/P_{gt-1}$. The aggregate returns for various tiers are plotted in Figure 16.8. However, differences in the returns across tiers over time are imperceptible in the graph. The summary statistics of aggregate returns in different periods for three tiers are shown in Table 16.8. Panel 1 describes aggregate returns across the whole sample period and shows that returns from investments in first-tier cities are generally greater and more volatile than those in other tier cities. Panels 2 and 3 describe aggregate returns during the two periods in which government was more active in implementing expansionary polices. Two facts are worth noting: (1) regardless of the period, the aggregate returns in first-tier cities are more volatile than in other tiers; (2) on average, aggregate returns in each tier varied but all were negative during September 2008 and March 2009 even though Chinese central government have implemented a series of expansionary policies. These facts illuminate Question 1: Did different tiers' housing markets respond diversely to the announcements of central government expansionary policies in 2008 and 2012?

Price indices and returns of other markets

The overall performance of the Chinese housing market can be judged with four benchmarks: the Chinese stock market, the American

Table 16.8   Summary Statistics of Average Returns.

Tier	Obs	Mean	Std. dev.	Min	Max
Panel 1: Feb. 2003–Mar. 2013					
1	122	0.0137	0.0176	−0.0360	0.0542
2	122	0.0116	0.0123	−0.0146	0.0727
3	122	0.0101	0.0092	−0.0213	0.0475
Panel 2: Sep. 2008–Mar. 2009					
1	6	−0.0076	0.0139	−0.0228	0.0148
2	6	−0.0064	0.0055	−0.0146	−0.0018
3	6	−0.0037	0.0070	−0.0116	0.0070
Panel 3: Feb. 2012–Oct. 2012					
1	9	0.0106	0.0184	−0.0259	0.02870
2	9	0.0009	0.0071	−0.0070	0.0102
3	9	0.0022	0.0042	−0.0043	0.0081

Source: Calculated based on housing price indices built by Fang *et al.* (2015).

housing market, the Japanese housing market, and the international housing market.

The performance of the Chinese stock market can be measured by the SSE index. Monthly SSE index data from January 2003 to March 2013 is collected from *Yahoo Finance*. The stock return in month t ($R_{stock,\,t}$) is calculated by $R_{stock,\,t} = (P_t - P_{t-1})/P_{t-1}$, where P_t is the Shanghai stock market price in month t.

The performance of the American housing market is generally measured by the S&P/Case–Shiller US national home price index (CS index). This index seeks to measure changes in the total value of existing single-family housing stock.[27] Monthly CS index from January 2003 to

---

[27] See more details at http://us.spindices.com/indices/real-estate/sp-case-shiller-us-national-home-price-index.

March 2013 is available from FRED. Return from investments in US housing market in month t $(R_{us, t})$ is calculated by $R_{us, t} = (P_t - P_{t-1})/P_{t-1}$, where P_t is the CS index in month t.

Considering how poorly the American housing market performed during 2008, it may be more edifying to evaluate the performance of Chinese housing market by comparing it with the Japanese and international housing markets.

The monthly national residential property index of Japan (JRPPI) is downloaded from the website of Japan's Ministry of Land, Infrastructure, Transport and Tourism (MLIT). Under the requirement of the International Monetary Fund (IMF), MLIT complied this price index based on the actual transaction data of residential property (approximately 300,000 transactions every year), with the quality of each property adjusted by using the Hedonic Approach.[28] Return from investments in Japan's housing market in month t $(R_{japan, t})$ is calculated by $R_{japan, t} = (P_t - P_{t-1})/P_{t-1}$, where P_t is the JRPPI in month t.

Currently, IMF uses international house price index produced by the Federal Reserve Bank of Dallas for tracking the developments in housing markets across the world on a quarterly basis. This index is the average of the housing price indices of 23 countries weighted by their IMF purchasing power parity-adjusted GDP shares in 2005.[29] This study uses the same index to measure the performance of the international housing market. Quarterly international housing price index data between 2003Q1 and 2013Q1 are downloaded from the website of the Federal Reserve Bank of Dallas.

Return from investments in international housing market in quarter q $(R_{global, q})$ is calculated by $R_{global, q} = (P_q - P_{q-1})/P_{q-1}$, where P_q is the international home price in quarter q. Recall that the Chinese housing price index is available on a monthly basis. In order to compare the performance of the Chinese housing market with the performance of international housing

---

[28] See more details about the methodology of the price index at http://tochi.mlit.go.jp/english/wp-content/uploads/2015/03/Methodology-of-JRPPI.pdf. Notice that JRPPI is only available between April 2008 and November 2015. However, it does not impact my later analysis, since the earliest month I need for calculating the excess returns is May 2008.

[29] The 23 countries include Germany, Denmark, Spain, Finland, France, UK, Ireland, Italy, Japan, South Korea, Luxembourg, Netherlands, Norway, New Zealand, Sweden, US, South Africa, Croatia, and Israel.

market without losing the information between months, it is necessary to convert quarterly international housing returns into monthly data. This study assumes that months in the same quarter have same data as the quarter.

Empirical Analysis for Question 1

This section is focused on answering Question 1: Did different tiers' housing markets respond diversely to the announcements of central government's expansionary policies? The methodology, event study, for answering this question is introduced in the first subsection. The second subsection evaluates the issue econometrically and briefly discusses about it.

Methodology for Question 1: Event study

Event studies have been conducted in many economic and finance studies. For example, Ding (2013) used the method to show that contractionary policy significantly decreased real estate firms' values. Taylor (2009) demonstrated that government actions prolonged and worsened the financial crisis. The event study method is used here to analyze the impact of government policy on China's tiered housing market. The Chinese central government's expansionary policies are the pertinent events (Cf. MacKinlay 1997). Tables 16.2 and 16.3 summarize the details of these policies.

The announcement month ($\tau = 0$) marks the start of each event. As shown by the following timeline, a benchmark event window for this study includes three months before and four months after the event month.

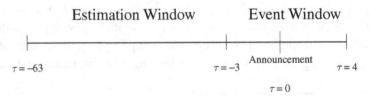

Several event windows were tested.[30] The 3 + 4 window (three months before and four months after the month in which an announcement has

---

[30] The event windows which are tested are 3 + 3, 3 + 4, 4 + 3, 4 + 4, 5 + 4, 5 + 5 and 5 + 6. See all results in the log file produced by Stata.

been made) was selected as the benchmark since this window is the most stringent one which can fully capture the difference of each tier's housing market performances before and after an event.

The impact of the event is assessed by abnormal returns over the event window. For each event j, the abnormal return of investments in the housing market of city i in month $(AR_{i\tau})$ is defined by:

$$AR_{i\tau,j} = R_{i\tau,j} - E(R_{i\tau,j} \mid X_{\tau,j}), \tau \in \text{event window for event } j, \qquad (3)$$

where $R_{i\tau,j}$ is the actual *ex post* return of city i's houses in month τ; $E(R_{i\tau,j} \mid X_{\tau,j})$ is the normal return for city i's houses in month τ predicted based on market information $X_{\tau,j}$ using market-adjusted returns model:

$$R_{i\tau,j} = \alpha_{i,j} + \beta_i R_{m\tau,j} + \varepsilon_{i\tau,j}, \tau \in \text{estimation window for event } j, \qquad (4)$$

$$E(\varepsilon_{i\tau,j}) = 0, \quad Var(\varepsilon_{i\tau,j}) = \sigma_\varepsilon^2,$$

where $R_{m\tau,j}$ is the actual market return in month τ, and the estimation window for event j is the 60-month before its event window. Abnormality is judged against returns in the preceding period.

It is cumbersome to compare the impacts of each announcement across 101 cities. It is more interesting to compare the impacts across the three tiers. This requires aggregating abnormal return observations. Two types of aggregation are considered in this study: cross-sectional aggregation and time-series aggregation.

Cross-sectional aggregation helps us to track the average changes of housing investor wealth across the event window. This type of aggregation for each tier is labeled cross-sectional average abnormal return and is calculated first by taking average of abnormal returns across all cities in the tier by event first and then taking the average across 10 events announced in 2008 and 2012. Mathematically, tier g's cross-sectional average abnormal return in month $\tau(AAR_{g\tau})$ can be expressed as:

$$AAR_{g\tau} = \frac{1}{10} \sum_{j=1}^{10} \frac{1}{N} \sum_{i=1}^{N} AR_{i\tau,j}, \qquad (5)$$

where N is the number of cities in the tier g^{31} and $i \in g$.

Time-series aggregation helps us to quantify the average of cumulative impacts of all announcements on each tier's housing market and to examine the housing investor wealth changes around an event. This type of aggregation for each tier g, average cumulative abnormal return (ACARg), is calculated by

$$ACAR_g = \frac{1}{10} \sum_{j=1}^{10} \frac{1}{N} \sum_{i=1}^{N} CAR_{i,j}, \tag{6}$$

where CAR_{ij} is the cumulative abnormal return of city i's housing market for event j. It can also be defined by

$$CAR_{ij} = \sum_{\tau=-3}^{4} AR_{i\tau,j}, \quad \tau \in \text{ event window for event } j. \tag{7}$$

In order to check the significance of the heterogeneity abnormal returns in different tiers, it is helpful to run the following regression with all observations

$$CAR_i = \beta_1 + \beta_2 D_2 + \beta_3 D_3 + \varepsilon, \tag{8}$$

where D_2 and D_3 are dummy variables for second and third-tier cities. β_1 is actually the average cumulative abnormal return of first tier (ACAR$_1$). β_2 can be interpreted as the difference of the magnitudes of the government interventions' impacts on housing markets of first and second-tier cities. To test whether the average of cumulative impacts of all announcements on the first tier's housing market (ACAR$_1$) differs from the second tier's housing market (ACAR$_2$), the null hypothesis H_0: $\beta_2 = 0$ must be tested. If the null hypothesis is rejected, then ACAR$_1$ and ACAR$_2$ are significantly different. Similarly, β_3 represents the difference of abnormal returns in the housing markets of first and third-tier cities. We can test whether ACAR$_1$ and ACAR$_3$ are significantly different by testing the null hypothesis H_0: $\beta_3 = 0$.

---

[31] For first tier, $N = 4$; for second tier, $N = 29$; for third tier, $N = 68$.

Empirical results for Question 1

This section empirically assesses whether abnormal returns varied across housing market tiers in response to China's government policies.

Cross-sectional aggregation

Figure 16.7 illustrates the average abnormal returns across housing market tiers estimated with different market price. Each plot tracks tier changes over the event window. The x-axis represents the benchmark event window for a policy which was announced in month $\tau = 0$. The trends of the average abnormal returns are similar.

Figure 16.7(a) shows that the average abnormal investment returns in the first tier's housing market significantly increased 2-months prior to the announcement. Figure 16.7(b) reveals that the average abnormal investment returns in the second tier's housing market significantly increased right after the announcement was made. The third-tier housing market responded most slowly to the expansionary policies. As shown by Figure 16.7(c), the average abnormal investment returns in the third tier's housing market did not go up until 2 or 3 month after the announcement. This establishes that the speed of adjustment to government policies is tier dependent.

Why did the first tier anticipate the policy announcement? There are two possible explanations: (1) Beijing and Shanghai insiders were given early notice. (2) Large populations and in-migration make first-tier housing demand relatively inelastic. Data show that populations of first-tier cities are all above 10 million. In the last decade, the annual increase of the resident population was about 400,000–500,000 in each first-tier city.[32] The strong inelasticity of housing demand in the period investigated is consistent with the longer trend. Table 16.9 reveals that excess demand was also present in first-tier cities between 2001 and 2012, but even more pronounced between 2011 and 2012. As a result, the abnormal

---

[32] See more details at http://news.xinhuanet.com/politics/2014-09/04/c1112351522.htm (in Chinese).

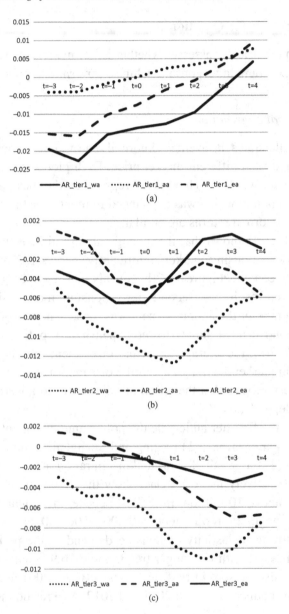

Figure 16.7   Average Abnormal Returns.

Note: *AR tierg wa* represents the average abnormal returns of tier *g* which is estimated with value-weighted average market prices (WAPrices); *AR tierg ea* represents the average abnormal returns of tier *g* which is estimated with equally weighted average market prices (EAPrices); *AR tierg aa* represents the average abnormal returns of tier *g* which is estimated with average–average market prices (AAPrices); See Appendix II for more details about different market prices.

Table 16.9   Supply–Demand Ratio.

	2011–2012	2001–2012
Nation	109.08%	91.21%
Beijing	47.21%	79.34%
Shanghai	30.95%	71.84%
Guangzhou	38.71%	81.40%
Shenzhen	15.63%	68.02%

Note: Supply-demand ratio is calculated by units of supply/units of demand.
Source: Wu *et al.* (2015).

returns of investments in first-tier housing markets rose more rapidly after a crisis.

McCarthy and Peach (2002) state that housing price inflation is reduced if there is an excess housing supply from the last period. A glut of housing in second and third-tier cities appears to explain their muted price response to the government's stimulatory policies. Figure 16.9 shows that there were significant increases in the Chinese housing inventories in 2007–2008 and 2010–2013, especially in second and third-tier cities.

The glut was driven by speculation. During the boom periods of China's housing market, 2003–2007 and 2009–2011, the central bank increased interest rates and prime lending rates (Figures 16.5 and 16.6). Many housing developers fled into second tier and third-tier housing markets where land prices are relatively cheaper. Vast tracts of new houses were developed blindly during these booming periods, but speculators fled when demand weakened creating "ghost cities."

Excess supply was especially acute in the third-tier housing market between 2010 and 2013. Third-tier cities had the highest vacancy rate. It averaged 23.8% by the 2013.[33] This could be caused by the property purchasing restrictions which were implemented in first tier and

---

[33] http://econweb.tamu.edu/gan/Urbanization-Nov-6-2014.pdf.

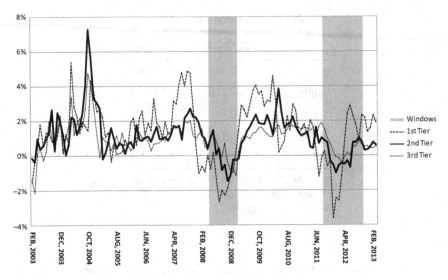

Figure 16.8   China's Housing Market Returns.

Note: The shaded areas represent the periods that Chinese central government are more active in implementing expansionary policies.

Source: Calculated based on price indices provided by Fang *et al.* (2015).

second-tier cities between 2010 and 2014 to prevent housing prices from going up too fast.[34] These restrictions moved the attention of housing speculators from first tier and second-tier cities to third-tier cities in 2011 and 2012. The glut was also abetted by local governments encouraging real estate developers in order to help central government achieve GDP growth targets.

Time-series aggregation

Table 16.10 shows each tier's average cumulative abnormal returns (ACAR$_g$) estimated using different market prices.[35] On average, each tier

---

[34] These restrictions require that local residents in the covered cities are only allowed to purchase at most two houses per family and citizens from other cities are only allowed to purchase one house per family in that city. The covered cities are listed in bold in Appendix I.

[35] See more details about different market prices in Appendix II.

Table 16.10 Average Cumulative Abnormal Returns.

Market price	First tier	Second tier	Third tier
WAPrice	−0.0923***	−0.0703***	−0.0574***
	−0.019	−0.0065	−0.003
AAPrice	0.0087	−0.0241**	−0.0217***
	−0.011	−0.0081	−0.0038
EAPrice	−0.0403*	−0.024***	−0.0147***
	−0.0214	−0.0077	−0.0037

Note: Average cumulative abnormal returns reported in this table are measured over an 8-month event window (3 months before announcement and 4 months after) using market model. The first column represents the type of market price used in market model estimation. For estimating the normal return, an estimation window is the 60-month period before each event window. Robust standard errors are in parenthesis. ***$p < 0.01$, **$p < 0.05$, *$p < 0.1$.

Table 16.11 Heterogeneity in ACAR's Across Tiers.

	Cons.	D_2	D_3
Coefficient	−0.0923	0.022	0.035*
(Std. error)	(0.0188)	(0.022)	(0.0190)

Note: ***$p < 0.01$, ** $p < 0.05$, *$p < 0.1$.

of cities has significant negative cumulative abnormal returns over the event window.[36] This indicates that the central government's expansionary polices did not restore full profitability, even though they did have positive countercyclical effects.

If we look at the ACAR's estimated by WAPrice, which takes into account the difference of transaction values across three tiers, the housing market of first-tier cities seems to have had the worst performance over the event window. According the Table 16.11, which reports the estimation results of the regression (8), ACAR's of second and third-tier housing markets are 2.2% and 3.5% higher than the one of first-tier housing

---

[36] Although ACAR1 estimated by AAPrice is positive, it is not significant.

markets, respectively. But only the difference between first tier and third-tier housing markets is significant.

The negative cumulative abnormal returns for first-tier cities may be partly explained by Chinese export growth. Wu *et al.* (2015) found that a one-standard deviation decrease in expected export growth is associated with a 0.15-standard deviation higher rate of local house price deflation. China's exports declined in 2009. The electronics and high-tech industries were hit especially hard.

Empirical Analysis for Question 2

Did China's expansionary policies in 2008 and 2012 enable housing market investors to earn higher rates of return than those achieved in the SSE, the US housing market, the Japan housing market, or the international housing market? Excess return analysis sheds light on the issue. The following two subsections introduce the methodology and empirical results, respectively.

Methodology for question 2: Excess return analysis

To evaluate the overall performances of the Chinese housing market under the government's interventions in 2008 and 2012, this study analyzes the excess returns surrounding the announcement month ($\tau = 0$). Excess investment returns are the differences between the returns of investments in the Chinese housing market and the returns of investments in a benchmark market. For event j, the excess return in month τ ($ER_{\tau,j}$) can be expressed as

$$ER_{\tau,j} = R_{\text{China}\tau j} - R_{\text{benchmark}\tau j}, \tau \in \text{ window for event } j, \qquad (9)$$

where $R_{\text{China},\tau j}$ is the Chinese housing market return in month τ, which is constructed using value weighted average prices (WAPrices). $R_{\text{benchmark},\tau j}$ is month τ's market return of SSE, US housing market, Japan housing market, or international housing market. The policy window is the period of 2 months before and 3 months after the announcement. This window is the most stringent one which can fully capture the difference of Chinese housing market performance before and after an announcement.

Instead of reporting 10 sets of results for each comparison, the aggregate results of 10 events for each comparison will be reported here.

Similarly, two types of aggregation are used in this study: cross-event aggregation and time-series aggregation. For each month, cross-event aggregation for each comparison is measured by the average of excess returns (AER$_\tau$)

$$\text{AER}_\tau = \frac{1}{10}\sum_{j=1}^{10}\text{ER}_{\tau,j}, \tag{10}$$

where 10 represents the 10 events. Cross-event aggregation helps us to track the changes of excess returns over the window on average.

For each comparison, time-series aggregation is measured by the average of the cumulative excess returns (ACER)

$$\text{ACER}_\tau = \frac{1}{10}\sum_{j=1}^{10}\text{CER}_{\tau,j}, \tag{11}$$

where CER$_j$ represents the summation of excess returns across the window for event j, and it
    can be expressed as

$$\text{CER}_\tau = \sum_{\tau=-2}^{3}\text{ER}_j. \tag{12}$$

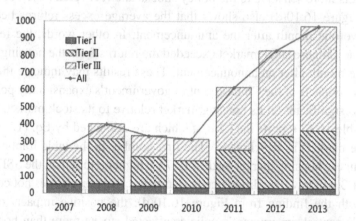

Figure 16.9   Chinese Residential Housing Inventory (in millions of square meters), 2007–2013.

Source: Chivakul *et al.* (2015).

Time-series aggregation approximates the cumulative impacts of Chinese government's expansionary policies.

Empirical Results for Question 2

Graphs in Figure 16.10 plot the average of excess returns across 10 events and help us track the changes of excess returns around the announcements. The x-axis represents the 2 + 3 window (2 months before and 3 months after an announcement) around a policy which was announced in month $\tau = 0$. The y-axis represents the level of average excess returns.

Figures 16.10(a)–16.10(c) show that, compared with the US, Japan, or international housing markets, respectively, the excess returns made from the Chinese housing market increased significantly one month before an announcement. The significant increases in excess returns imply that the Chinese housing market performed better than the US, Japan, and international housing markets.

Figure 16.10(d) shows that excess returns kept falling over the window if the benchmark market was the domestic stock market, the SSE. This is not surprising since the Chinese stock market was also under the support of the Chinese government's expansionary polices during the same periods. This result indicates that, compared with China's housing market, the stock market is more sensitive to the policy shocks and recovered faster. In addition, Figure 16.10(d) also shows that the average excess returns became negative one month after the announcement. In other words, the returns from the Chinese stock market exceeded the returns from the housing market one month after an announcement. These results may indicate that the positive impacts of the Chinese central government's expansionary policies are less significant on its housing market relative to its stock market.

Table 16.12 reports the CER's, which are calculated by Eq. (12) using diverse markets as benchmark. The first number in the table implies that the Chinese housing market made a 12.73% higher return than the SSE over the 2 + 3 window. The difference is significant. This result does not contradict with the finding from Figure 16.10(d): the positive impacts of the China's central government's policies affected stocks more than housing. The housing market reflects the market information more slowly than does the stock market because housing is relatively illiquid. Housing sellers

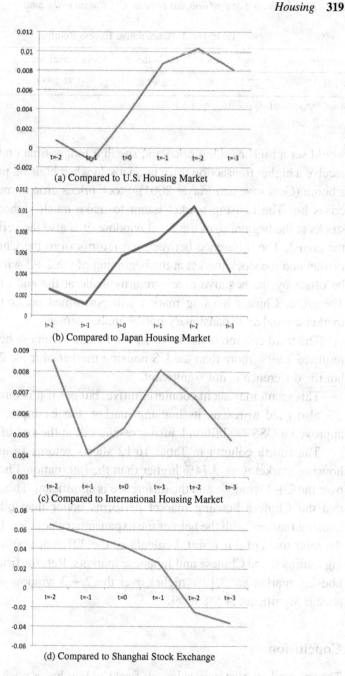

(a) Compared to U.S. Housing Market

(b) Compared to Japan Housing Market

(c) Compared to International Housing Market

(d) Compared to Shanghai Stock Exchange

Figure 16.10   Average Excess Returns.

Table 16.12   Cumulative Excess Returns.

Compared to	Shanghai stock	US housing	International housing	Japan housing
CER	12.73% **	2.99%	3.74%***	3.12 %**

Note: ***$p < 0.01$, **$p < 0.05$, *$p < 0.1$.

would set a higher asking price and spend a longer time on the market to receive a higher transaction price upon a sale when housing prices fall after a boom (Genesove and Mayer 2001). Stock prices drop immediately when crises hit. The housing market is apt to make much higher returns than stocks at the beginning of the 2 + 3 window (it is also the period right after the crisis). The difference between the returns from the Chinese housing market and the stock market at the beginning of the 2 + 3 window were not be offset by the negative excess returns made at the end of the window. Therefore, China's housing market still performed better than its stock market around an expansionary policy announcement.

The third column in Table 16.12 implies that Chinese housing market returned 2.99% more than the US housing market over the 2 + 3 window, but the difference is not significant.

This result may seem counterintuitive, but not if it is remembered that US also tried to rescue its housing market. For example, US Congress approved a US$300 billion housing rescue bill at the end of July 2008.

The fourth column in Table 16.12 shows returns from the Chinese housing market were 3.74% higher than the international housing market over the 2 + 3 window, and the difference is significant. This result implies that the Chinese housing market performs better than other countries' housing markets with the help of the expansionary policies. In order to test the robustness of this result, I calculated the difference between the housing returns in the Chinese and Japanese markets. Returns from the Chinese housing market are 3.12% higher over the 2 + 3 window and the difference is significant at 5% level.

Conclusion

Theory predicts that expansionary fiscal policy has a positive impact on income and housing prices. Expansionary monetary policies tend to lower the real cost of borrowing, and housing investors earn higher returns than they would have earned under contractionary policies. We did see from the empirical results that the abnormal returns of each tier's housing market became less negative around an announcement of expansionary policy.

China's expansionary policies implemented in 2008 and 2012 affected housing market tiers differently. Housing markets in first-tier cities responded to expansionary polices approximately two months prior to the announcement. Housing markets in second-tier cities responded almost immediately. The average abnormal returns in the third tier's housing markets did not increase until 2 or 3 months after the announcement. Thus, the third-tier cities responded most slowly on average. Meanwhile, the magnitude of an announcement's impact on each tier of cities is different, but the difference is significant only between the impacts on first and third-tier cities.

Although abnormal returns became less negative over the event windows, the cumulative abnormal returns are significantly negative indicating that central government's expansionary policies were weak in short run.

This chapter also analyzed the government policy's impact on overall performance of the Chinese housing market under the government's inventions in 2008 and 2012. It was found that China's housing market yielded higher returns than the Shanghai stock market and the American, Japanese, or international housing markets. The excess returns increased significantly one month before an announcement. Compared with the Chinese stock market, the excess returns in the Chinese housing market continued to fall during the time surrounding expansionary policy announcements.

Cumulatively, investments in the Chinese housing market earned 12.73% more than the SSE, 3.31% more than the investments in the American housing market, 4.87% more than investments in the international housing market, and 3.12% more than investments in the Japanese housing market. However, the differences between the cumulative returns made from the Chinese housing market and the US housing market are not significant. This implies the Chinese housing market did not perform significantly better than the US housing market in 2008 and 2012.

This study is the first to conduct an event study using monthly city level Chinese housing price indices to examine the impacts of Chinese expansionary polices on diverse tiers of cities. The results may help policymakers understand the impact and effectiveness of previous expansionary policies on the Chinese housing markets and shed light on how to better craft stimulus policies for a specific urban tiers.

Appendix I: List of Cities by Tiers

First tier includes: Beijing, Shanghai, Guangzhou, and Shenzhen

Second tier includes the following 35 cities: Beihai, Changchun, Changsha, Chengdu, Chongqing, Dalian, Fuzhou, Guiyang, Haikou, Hangzhou, Harbin, Hefei, Hohhot, Jinan, Kunming, Lanzhou, Nanchang, Naijin, Nanning, Ningbo, Qingdao, Sanya, Shenyang, Shijiazhuang, Suzhou, Taiyuan, Tianjin, Urumqi, Wenzhou, Wuhan, Wuxi, Xi'An, Xiamen, Xining, Yinchuan, and Zhengzhou.

Third tier includes the following 85 cities: Xuancheng, Fuyang, Chuzhou, Huangshan, Anqing, Bengbu, Wuhu (from Anhui province); Ningde, Zhangzhou, Quanzhou (from Fujian province); Jieyang, Zhongshan, Dongguan, Qingyuan, Yangjiang, Heyuan, Shanwei, Huizhou, Zhaoqing, Jiangmen, Foshan, Shantou, Shaoguan (from Guangdong province); Hengshui, Langfang, Zhangji-akou, Baoding, Xingtai, Qinhuangdao, Tangshan (from Hebei province); Jiamusi, Qiqihar (from Heilongjiang province); Zhumadian, Nanyang, Luohe, Xuchang, Puyang, Xinxiang, Luoyang, Kaifeng (from Henan); Changde (from Hunan province); Xilingol, Baotou (from Inner Mongolia); Jiangyan, Suqian, Zhenjiang, Yancheng, Huai'an, Lianyungang, Nantong, Changzhou, Xuzhou (from Jiangsu province); Fuzhou, Shangrao, Yichun, Xinyu, Jiujiang, Pingxiang, Jingdezhen (from Jiangxi province); Songyuan, Jilin (from Jilin province); Wuludao, Chaoyang, Tieling, Panjin, Yingkou, Dandong, Anshan (from Liaoning province); Liaocheng, Dezhou, Rizhao, Zaozhuang (from Shandong province); Yuncheng (from Shanxi province); Dazhou, Nanchong, Leshan, Mianyang, Deyang, Luzhou (from Sichuan province); Changji (from Xinjiang); Taizhou, Jinhua, Shaoxing, Huzhou, Jiaxing (from Zhejiang province).

Note: Twenty-three cities are excluded from the sample since either some of them do not have enough data over estimation periods to predict normal returns or some of them do not have enough data over event window.[37] The cities are listed in bold were under property-purchasing restrictions between 2010 and 2014.

Appendix II: Constructions of Market Price Indices

This study uses three methods to construct market indices for the whole Chinese housing market.

Method 1 takes average of housing prices across cities in each tier and then takes average of the average prices across each tier. By using this method, the market price in month t (AAPrice_$\overline{all}_t$) is defined as:

$$\text{AAPrice\_all}_t = \frac{1}{3} \sum_{g=1}^{3} \text{AvgPrice}_{g,t},$$

where AvgPrice$_{g,t}$ is the average housing price for tier g in month t and it is defined as:

$$\text{AvgPrice}_{g,t} = \frac{1}{N_g} \sum P_{i,t},$$

where N_g is the number of cities in tier g; $P_{i,t}$ is the housing price in month t for city i which belongs to tier g.

Method 2 takes average of housing prices across cities in each province[38] and then takes weighted average across provinces by using the value of area sold in each province as the weight. By using this method, the market price in month t (WAPrice_all_t is defined as:

$$\text{WAPrice\_all}_t = \sum W_{j,t} \text{AvgPrice}_{j,t}$$

---

[37] Brown and Warner (1980) show although the data requirements introduce a bias towards including only surviving cities, none of their simulation results suggest that the bias is of importance.

[38] The reason for calculating average prices for provinces is the data for calculating the weights is only available for province level.

where $W_{j,t}$ and $\text{AvgPrice}_{j,t}$ are the weight taken by province j in month t and the average housing price for province j in month t, respectively. They are defined as:

$$\text{AvgPrice}_{j,t} = \frac{1}{N_j} \sum P_{i,t},$$

$$W_{j,t} \left(\frac{\text{AreaSold}_{j,t} * \text{AvgPrice}_{j,t}}{\sum (\text{AreaSold}_{j,t} * \text{AvgPrice}_{j,t})} \right)$$

where N_j is the number of cities in province j; $P_{i,t}$ is the housing price in month t for city i, which belongs to province j; $\text{AreaSold}_{j,t}$ is the total square meters of housing has been sold in province j in month t.[39]

Method 3 takes equally weighted average of housing prices across all cities in the sample. By using this method, the market price in month t (EAPrice_allt) is defined as:

$$\text{EAPrice\_all}_t = \frac{1}{N} \sum_{i=t}^{N} P_{i,t},$$

where N is the number of cities in the sample; $P_{i,t}$ is the housing price in month t for city i. The market price indices constructed by these three methods are plotted in Figure 16.2.

References

Alesina, Alberto and Silvia Ardagna (2010), "Large Changes in Fiscal Policy: Taxes versus spending," *NBER Working Paper* No. 15438.

Afonso, Antonio and Ricardo Sousa (2011), "The macroeconomic effects of fiscal policy," *Applied Economics*, 44(34), 4439–4454.

Akerlof, George and Robert Shiller (2009), *Animal Spirits: How Human Psychology Drives the Economy, and Why It Matters for Global Capitalism*, Princeton: Princeton University Press.

Barth, James, Michael Lea and Tong Li (2012), *China's Housing Market: Is a Bubble about to Burst?* Working Paper.

Bernanke, Ben and Mark Gartler (1995), "Inside the black box: The credit channel of monetary policy transmission," *Journal of Economic Perspectives*, 9(4), 27–48.

Brown, Stephen and Jerold B. Warner (1980), "Measuring Security Price Performance," *Journal of Financial Economics*, 8(1980), 205–258.

Brunnermeier, Markus and Christian Julliard (2006), "Money Illusion and Housing Frenzies," *The Review of Financial Studies*, 21(1), 135–180.

Cai, Hongbin, J. Vernon Henderson and Qinghua Zhang (2013), "China's Land Market Auctions: Evidence of Corruption," *The RAND Journal of Economics*, 44(3), 488–521.

Carlino, Gerald and Robert DeFina (1998), "Monetary Policy and the U.S. and Regions: Some Implications for European Monetary Union," *Regional Aspects of Monetary Policy in Europe*, 1, 45–67.

Carlino, Gerald and Robert DeFina (1999), "The Differential Regional Effects of Monetary Policy: Evidence from the U.S. States," *Journal of Regional Science*, 39(2), 229–358.

Case, Karl and Robert Shiller (1990), "Forecasting Prices and Excess Returns in the Housing Market," *Real Estate Economics*, 18(3), 253–273.

Chen, Jie and Yang Zan (2014), "Housing Affordability and Housing Policy in Urban China". Springer-Briefs in Economics.

Chivakul, Mali, Waikei Lam Xiaoguang Liu Alfred Schipke and Wojciech Maliszewski (2015), "Understanding Residential Real Estate in China," *IMF Working Paper WP15/84*.

Deng, Yongheng, Joseph Gyourko and Jing Wu (2012), "Land and House Price Measurement in China," in: A. Heath, F. Packer and C.Windsor (eds.), *Property Markets and Financial Stability*, Reserve Bank of Australia.

DiPasquale, Denise and William Wheaton (1994), "Housing Market Dynamics and the Future of Housing Prices," *Journal of Urban Economics*, 35, 1–27.

Deng, Yongheng, Hongyu Liu and Jing Wu (2013), "House Price Index Construction in the Nascent Housing Market: The Case of China," *The Journal of Real Estate Finance and Economics*, 48(3), 522–545.

Ding, Wenjie (2013), "Evaluating Housing Policy Interventions in China Using Stock Market Data," *Publicly Accessible Penn Dissertations Paper 629*.

Fair, Ray C. (1972), "Disequilibrium in Housing Models," *Journal of Finance*, 27(2), 207–221.

Fang, Hanming, Quanlin, Gu Wei Xiong and Li-An Zhou (2015), "Demystifying the Chinese Housing Boom," *NBER Working Paper* No. 21112.

Fisher, Irving (1930), *The Theory of Interest*. New York: The Macmillan Co.

Geneosve, David and Christopher Mayer (1997), "Equity and Time to Sale in the Real Estate Market," *American Economic Review*, 87(3), 225–269.

Geneosve, David and Christopher Mayer (2001), "Loss Aversion and Seller Behavior: Evidence from the Housing Market," *Quarterly Journal of Economics*, 116(4), 1233–1260.

Gordon, Roger and Wei Li (2013), "Provincial and Local Governments in China: Fiscal Institutions and Government Behavior" in *Capitalizing China*, Fan and Morck. University of Chicago Press.

Harris, Jack (1989), "The Effect of Real Rates of Interest on Housing Prices," *The Journal of Real Estate Finance and Economics*, 2(1), 47–60.

Kain, F. John and John F. Quigley (1970), " Measuring the Value of Housing Quality," *Journal of the American Statistical Association*, 65(330), 532–548.

Liang, Yunfang, Tiemei Gao and Shuping He (2006), "Empirical Analysis of Harmonious Development Between the Real Estate Industry and the National Economy in Transitional China," *Social Sciences in China*, 6: 75–85.

Liang, Priscilla, Thomas Willett and Nan Zhang (2011), "Global Contagion and the Decoupling Debate," *Frontiers of Economics and Globalization*, 215–234.

MacKinlay, A. Craig (1997), "Event Studies in Economics and Finance," *Journal of Economic Literature*, 35(1), 13–39.

McCarthy, Jonathan and Richard Peach (2002), " Monetary Policy Transmission to Residential Investment," *Economic Policy Review*, 139–157.

Rosen, Kenneth and Lawrence Smith (1983), " The Price-Adjustment Process for Rental Housing and the Natural Vacancy Rate," *The American Economic Review*, 73(4), 779–786.

Shen, Yue and Hongyu Liu (2005). "Housing Prices and Economic Fundamental: A Cross City Analysis of China for 1995–2002" (in Chinese), *Economic Research Journal*, 2004(06), 78–86.

Taylor, John (2009), "The Financial Crisis and the Policy Responses: An Empirical Analysis of What Went Wrong," *NBER Working Paper* No. 14631.

Wu, Jing, Joseph Gyourko and Yongheng Deng (2010), "Evaluating Conditions in Major Chinese Housing Markets," *NBER Working Paper* No. 16189.

Wu, Jing, Joseph Gyourko and Yongheng Deng (2015), "Evaluating the Risk of Chinese Housing Markets: What We Know and What We Need to Know," *NBER Working Paper* No. 21346.

Williams, John (1938), "The Theory of Investment Value," *Journal of Political Economy*, 47(2), 276–278.

Chapter 17
Budget Cycles

Pi-Han Tsai

Introduction

In democratic countries, periodic elections create a relationship of formal accountability between politicians and the general public. In order to increase the chances of being elected, politicians have the incentive to respond to the public and to satisfy the needs of voters. In other words, opportunistic politicians with career concerns who can be held accountable have a greater motivation to demonstrate their competence. Such incentives sharpen during election periods, resulting in the electoral cycles of changed economic and fiscal policies. There is, in fact, a great deal of literature regarding the changes of fiscal behavior of opportunistic politicians during election periods.

Traditional political budget cycle models suggest that incumbent politicians have inducements to manipulate budget resources, such as increasing government spending or reducing taxes, prior to elections in order to encourage economic expansion, thus, maximizing their chances of being reelected (Drazen 2001). The empirical results of such aggregate political budget cycles are widely discussed.[1] Additionally, instead of examining

---

[1] For less-developed countries, Block (2002) studies sub-Saharan African countries from 1980 to 1995, finding evidence of pre-electoral fiscal manipulations and postelectoral retrenchments in some cases. The empirical results are more ambiguous in more developed

aggregate budget cycles, some scholars focus on studying disaggregate budget cycles. For instance, Rogoff (1990) designs a signaling model, reconciling the political budget cycles model and rational voter theory, where he finds information asymmetries. Incumbents have private and temporary information on the amount of capital expenditure and their own competencies, whereas voters can only observe the capital expenditure with a one-period lag. Thus, observed pre-electoral fiscal manipulation serves as a signal of a politician's level of competency. The separating equilibrium of the signaling model suggests that competent incumbents have the incentive to shift public-spending toward more salient projects, at the cost of less salient ones, whereas incompetent incumbents reveal their true types. In Rogoff's model, current expenditures have higher public visibility, when compared to capital expenditures. The prediction of Rogoff's signaling model has been proved by many empirical works in both international comparisons and subnational case studies. As examples, this work can be seen in both Vergne (2009) and Tsai (2014). Additionally, by modifying Rogoff's signal model (1990), Drazen and Eslava (2010) propose a targeting model, under the condition that voters are able to observe the capital expenditure of incumbents without a one-period lag. The targeting model suggests that politicians use pre-electoral fiscal manipulation to help voters make inferences about their future policy directions. Prior to elections, in order to be elected, politicians prefer to shift public spending from non-targeted expenditure to targeted expenditure, so that they will more easily be able to target particular constituencies by geographical region. Targeted expenditures usually take the form of development and construction

---

countries. Alesina *et al.* (1992) find an electoral cycle in fiscal deficit in a set of 13 OECD countries; however, they state that there is little evidence of budget cycles in government spending or revenues. In the case of United States, an apparent electoral cycle in transfer was observed between 1961 and 1978, but disappeared afterward (Keech and Pak 1989). The mixed results in more advanced democracies may be attributed to voters having better information about fiscal outcomes and more experience with electoral politics, making them less likely to be "fooled" by politicians' pre-electoral fiscal manipulations (Brender and Drazen 2005). Also, a rational voter dislikes budget deficits and knows that he or she has to pay back after the election, so his or her voting decision is not particularly affected by his or her government's budget behavior prior to an election. These are the reasons why traditional budget cycles models are criticized for the inconsistency of rational and forward-looking voters' theory (Mccallum 1978).

activities, such as schools, mass transportation, and large infrastructure projects. Drazen and Eslava (2010), for instance, show these patterns of budget cycles associated with targeted and non-targeted expenditures in the elections of Colombian municipalities.

Most of the literatures devoted to finding the evidence of political budget cycles for not only aggregate expenditure but also disaggregated expenditure focus solely on democratic countries, presuming that fiscal cycles only exist in countries with direct elections. Even though the timing of changes may vary across different political institutions, the structural component of political decision-making in non-democratic countries should be similar to their democratic counterparts; this is because they come from the shared desire of most politicians to maximize political power and remain in office. For this reason, politicians have the incentive to manipulative budget resources in order to achieve their political goals.

To examine this situation in non-democratic countries, we can take China as an example. As a single-party state, the Chinese Communist Party (CCP) has the ultimate power and dominates the institution of the state. During the reform period in the 1980s, the Chinese central government made substantial efforts to transform the state from an inward-looking and centrally administered economy to a market economy, and to do so, handed over some economic control to subnational governments. Nonetheless, the procedures of elite recruitment and personnel management are still controlled by the CCP. In this system, instead of the bottom-up electoral checks that politicians in democratic countries faced, Chinese officials face a range of top-down checks from higher-level party authorities. Thus, a local official's incentive to hold onto power depends on satisfying the needs of the Central Committee of the CCP, rather than trying to please the general public in their jurisdiction. Taken together, the preferences of the Central Committee are known as the cadre management system, acknowledged as a performance-based, elite promotion system. Such a cadre management systems is decisive for a local official's political future, leading to their specific behavioral choices regarding economic and fiscal policies. Thus, the powerful career concerns induced by the cadre management system are considered a key driver in shaping local governments' policy directions. In the other words, through the tactics of promotion and demotion, the Chinese central government can ensure that local governments' fiscal incentives and policies correspond with the wishes of the central government. Thus, Chinese federalism is characterized by economic decentralization accompanied by strong political centralization (Persson and Zhuravskaya 2016).

The uniqueness of China's political system, with its absence of democratic elections, competitive national parties, and socialist market economy, has long been considered as essentially informal, especially regarding political turnover. While most political economy models focus on explaining the phenomenon of Western democracies, while precluding the possibility of their application to the Chinese case, China does share certain similar characteristics with the West. For instance, the top-down checks on Chinese leaders' careers incentivize them to manipulate fiscal policies in a somewhat similar manner as politicians' careers in democratic countries result from bottom-up checks (i.e., the voting booth). For this reason, similar fiscal distortion may be observed in China as well.

As an overview, this chapter is organized into five sections. In the following section, the author discusses how the Chinese central government devolved power from the central to local levels. The author also introduces the role of China's political institutions as they pertain to implement a limited, yet effective government that is conducive to economic growth. In addition, the author explores how political and fiscal institutions shape local Chinese governments' fiscal incentives. In "Career Concerns of Chinese Officials" and "Nationally Coordinated Cycles" sections, the author turns her attention to the question of how fiscal incentives lead to political budget cycles at different administrative levels in China. The author then concludes this, providing a summary of the situation as it stands today.

Institutional Background

Fiscal institutions

The political system in China is organized into a five-level administrative hierarchy: (1) central, (2) provincial, (3) prefecture, (4) county, and (5) township. Historically speaking, the fiscal assignments of the central and local governments have evolved over time. The series of fiscal reforms and fiscal systems that have been initiated recently can be seen in three distinct phases. In the first period, before the 1980s, China had a consolidated budget system. In the second period, from 1980 to 1994, the consolidated budget system was replaced by a fiscal contracting system. Then, in the third phase, tax-sharing reform was launched in 1994, and the fiscal design became a rule-based system of tax assignments. Over this whole period, most of the reforms in the 1980s and 1990s targeted the central–provincial fiscal relationship, and for this reason the discretionary power of subprovincial governments is ambiguous during these decades. Due to strong career concerns found in the cadre management system, some scholars believe that the fiscal assignments of subprovincial governments were primarily dependent on the decisions of upper-level authorities (Shen *et al.* 2012; Tsai 2016). Thus, in this section, the overview of fiscal reforms in China will focus mainly on the central–provincial fiscal relationship.

Prior to 1979, the fiscal system in China was a consolidated budget system. It is also now known as the country's "unified revenue and expenditure" period. In this era, all fiscal assignments were centrally planned. Even though provincial governments were responsible for collecting more than 80% of the proceeds, including taxes and profits from state-owned enterprises (SOEs),[2] they were required to remit all these proceeds to the central government. At the time, the central government prepared a consolidated budget for all governments at the various administrative levels, and subnational governments did not create their own separate budgets (Jin *et al.* 2005).

Such a centralized fiscal appropriation system in China was philosophically aligned with the socialists' idea of a centrally planned economy. However, this system was incompatible with the market-oriented reforms that began in 1978. The market-oriented economic reforms led to the greater political autonomy of local governments, which, in turn, led them to demand more fiscal decision-making power. The central governments also faced the rapid emergence of non-SOEs in the 1980s, resulting in a significant reduction of budgetary revenue (Shen *et al.* 2012). In addition, from an economic point of view, the central governments needed a new fiscal system with local governments incentives to increase efforts to

---

[2] SOEs were also part of a state finance (Lin and Liu 2000).

collect revenue and promote local prosperity (Lin and Liu 2000). Therefore, in the 1980s, the "fiscal contracting system" replaced the consolidated budget system. Under this new arrangement, provincial governments were only required to remit a certain share of their proceeds to the central government based on established revenue-sharing arrangements. As for expenditure assignments, provincial governments were then responsible for balancing their own budgets, giving them discretionary power over fiscal matters. The proceeds generated by the provincial governments included central-fixed revenue, in which all proceeds were sent to the central government, including customs duties and profits from centrally owned state enterprises; central–local shared revenue, in which the proceeds were divided between the central government and the provincial governments, including industrial and commercial taxes, as well as profits from large-scale enterprises under dual ownership by the central and local governments; and local-fixed revenue, in which the proceeds were kept by the local governments, and included profits from locally owned state enterprises and specific taxes of a local nature (Lin and Liu 2000). The central–provincial revenue-sharing rules, which varied across provinces and could change over time, were determined by the central government according to the historical records of revenue and expenditure of each province. For example, in the case of poor and remote provinces, the central government transferred money to them to cover those provinces' fiscal deficits.

Such revenue-sharing arrangements under the "fiscal contracting system" created a new incentive mechanism for provincial leaders to boost local economic growth, thus yielding greater revenue, both for themselves and for the central government. In addition to budgetary revenue, the dramatic increase in extra-budgetary revenue also demonstrated the growing autonomy of local authorities. Extra-budgetary revenue was developed in China in the 1950s but was not institutionalized as a practice until after the reforms of the 1980s. Different from the budgetary revenue process described above, extra-budgetary revenue was another channel that was open to local governments to finance their spending, and the money was not subject to sharing with the central government.[3] Using this

---

[3] The extra-budgetary revenue includes tax surcharges, service fees, and some retained profits from SOEs (Jin *et al.* 2005).

mechanism, provincial governments had complete control and authority over the determination of taxes and fees that fell into the category of extra-budgetary revenue (Jin *et al.* 2005; Shen *et al.* 2012). In China in 1990, total extra-budgetary revenue reached 270.86 billion yuan, which was approximately five times more than it was in 1980 (*China Statistical Yearbook* 2006).

The reforms of the 1980s increased the autonomy of local governments and incentivized them to raise local revenues while, at the same time, it reduced the money that was being transferred to the central government. This led to the waning fiscal control of the central government, as well as central revenue financial shortfalls. Additionally, local jurisdictional competitions also resulted in the abuse of taxation power by local governments. For example, in order to attract investment, local governments would grant tax exemptions to enterprises without proper central authorization. Eventually, starting in 1994, this unbalanced structure ushered in the period of the so-called tax-sharing reform. The "fiscal contracting system" was replaced by a rule-based system of tax assignments. Under the new system, in addition to localized tax authorities, central tax administrations were established in order to curb fiscal decline. Here, the central tax administrations collected both the central and central–local shared taxes, and they localized the tax administrations collecting the local taxes (Jin and Zou 2005). Major local taxes included income taxes from all enterprises, with the exception of central government enterprises; business taxes from the sales of services; and individual income taxes (Jin *et al.* 2005). However, with this system, the most profitable taxes were now collected by the central government, for example, the value-added tax and personal and corporate income taxes (Jin *et al.* 2005; Shen *et al.* 2012). The ultimate purpose of the 1994 fiscal reform was to recentralize the revenue upward and devolve the expenditure downward, thus strengthening the fiscal power of the central government to collect from local governments. At the same time, even though the local governments' sources of revenue had decreased, they were still responsible for balancing their own budgets. Each level of authority imposed fiscal responsibilities on lower levels of governments, resulting in dire financial straits for local governments and the rapid increase in local debt. Since the sources of local taxes had diminished after the reform, local governments had to rely heavily on intergovernmental transfers from the upper-level governments, intensi-fying fiscal and political dependence of subprovincial governments on upper-level authorities while simultaneously increasing the leverage of both central and provincial governments over lower-level governments (Wedeman 1999; Shen *et al*. 2012).

Figures 17.1 and 17.2 show the shares of subnational budgetary revenue and expenditure, demonstrating the time trend of fiscal decen-tralization between 1978 and 2014. Due to the 1994 reform, budgetary revenue earmarked for local governments, as a monetary share of the total given by the national government, plummeted dramatically, from 78% in 1993 to 45% in 1994. In the meantime, the central government's share increased, from 22% in 1993 to 55% in 1994 (Figure 17.1), demonstrating the effectiveness of the tax-sharing reform.

Meanwhile, even though the revenue system was centralized in 1994, the assignments of government responsibility in expenditure did not change: in national expenditure allocations, the central government was

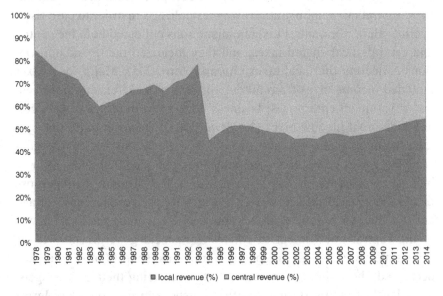

Figure 17.1   The Ratio of Subnational and Central Government to Total National Revenue.

Source: China Statistical Yearbook (2015).

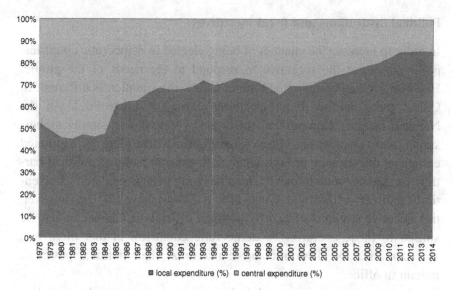

Figure 17.2   The Ratio of Subnational and Central Government to Total National Expenditure.

Source: China Statistical Yearbook (2015).

responsible for nationwide services, whereas subnational governments were responsible for all local public goods and services. Figure 17.2 shows the budgetary expenditure of local and central governments as shares of the total national expenditure between 1978 and 2014. Here, we see that in 2014, local governments were responsible for 85% of total expenditure, compared with 46% in 1980. Additionally, in 2014, local governments accounted for only 54% of total revenue, whereas in 1980, they had accounted for 75%. The mismatch of expenditure and revenue assignments shows the inherent burden in the decentralization of expenditure responsibilities on local governments. Yet, we can also see that the share of local budgetary expenditures has increased gradually since the 1980s, even during the beginning of the reform period in 1994, thus implying that the discretionary power of subnational governments has been unaffected by the reform. Politicians at the subnational level have been able to maintain sufficient discretionary authority over government money. In the following section, we will focus on how fiscal behaviors have been shaped by China's political structure.

Political institutions and fiscal incentives

In order to increase the chances of being elected in democratic countries, politicians have the incentive to respond to the needs of the public. However, in the People's Republic of China, the situation is different. In China, there are no direct elections above the township level; the National People's Congress, as the organ of state power, simply rubber-stamps party decisions (Lawrence and Martin 2013). Thus, as mentioned earlier, in the absence of both local elections and national political parties, vertical accountability in China has long been considered as essentially indirect or informal (Persson and Zhuravskaya 2016). However, the incentive structures faced by political officials in China can also be similar to those operating in democratic countries, in that there is a shared motive for all politicians to maximize their political power to remain in office.

As a single-party state with a dual-party government administrative system, the CCP has the ultimate power and dominates the institution of the state. The Central Committee of the CCP controls the procedures for elite recruitment and personnel management, and for this reason, the personnel preferences of the Central Committee are the ones that are decisive for a local official's political future. Thus, instead of satisfying the needs of voters, political officials in China have the inducement to respond to the needs of the party authority. This cadre management system, again referring to the decisions regarding appointments, transfers, promotions, or removals of any party or state, follows a *nomenklatura* system — the lists of political positions controlled by the different levels of the party (Manion 1985). All leadership changes require the approval of the party committee owning the *nomenklatura* at the next higher level. The details regarding the implementation and procedures of China's *nomenklatura* system are found in Manion (1985). Such a cadre management system has institutionalized personnel evaluations and personnel reshuffling decisions by the CCP. The personnel control system not only provides the official evaluation criteria for the different levels of cadres to follow but also helps the CCP retain its ultimate power by controlling those cadres. In the meantime, the system creates a paramount career concern for local officials, providing them sufficient incentive to adhere to the centrally proclaimed goals of the government. This system, then, is the main driving mechanism for shaping politicians' behaviors and policies. For this reason, any shifts in the cadre management system over time not only reflect the preferred changes by the CCP's Central Committee but also correspond to the behavioral shifts of local officials.

Prior to the 1980s reform era, the only criterion for cadre evaluation was political obedience and party loyalty to the CCP. However, since 1979, beyond political loyalty, the Central Committee has begun to emphasize more quantitative performance standards, such as sustaining the country's gross domestic product and generating foreign investment, as well as demonstrating expertise in administrative management. Furthermore, personal characteristics, such as the age and education levels of local officials, are also now included in the evaluation system. For example, in the current climate, the Central Committee prefers younger and more educated officials. All of these newer evaluation factors by the leadership regarding party cadres and state officials have become essential components in their decision-making. Moreover, changes in the evaluation system have institutionalized a close association between a provincial leader's political advancement and their jurisdictional economic performance, thus incentivizing them to grow their local economy (Li and Zhou 2005). In fact, it is widely believed that the powerful career concerns faced by local officials have contributed to the rapid economic growth of China over the past 30 years (Qian and Xu 1993, Maskin *et al.* 2000).

In the mid-1980s, the cadre responsibility system, the aforementioned top-down personnel control system, was introduced in China. This process links job assignments, performance appraisals, and remuneration to concrete target goals. Each target is quantifiable and comes with a numerical measure, where a cadre's performance appraisal is based on the weight allotted by each target (O'Brien and Li 1999). The quantification of the targets specified in the cadre responsibility system reinforces the connection of a politician's career advancement to the results of their evaluation. The powerful career concerns created by the center through its system of promotions and demotions provides sufficient incentive for politicians to both adhere to the goals of the central government and foster local prosperity.

Much literature on China examines the close association between local economic performance and the turnover of provincial leaders.[4] For example, Li and Zhou (2005) study the political turnover of provincial leaders from 1979 to 1995, finding that one's probability of promotion is positively correlated with economic performance and, inversely, the likelihood of their termination is negatively correlated. Chen *et al.* (2005) extend the dataset to 2002; their findings are consistent with those of Li and Zhou (2005).

However, the performance-based promotion system of political elites has also resulted in unbalanced economic development, showing how tangible economic contributions are enacted, while intangible ones are ignored. In order to impress their superiors and improve their odds of being promoted, local cadres pay more attention to easily measurable and more quantifiable projects, at the cost of less-quantifiable projects (O'Brien and Li 1999, Guo 2009). For example, Wu *et al.* (2014) study the correlation between politicians' promotion odds and their fiscal spending on infrastructure and environmental investments. Using the data of 283 city-level governments from 2000 to 2009, their results indicate that local officials have a greater incentive to invest in infrastructure projects over environmental development because spending on the former is positively correlated with their odds of promotion, whereas spending on the latter is negatively correlated.

However, unlike their democratic counterparts, political turnover in China is not formally institutionalized; it sometimes involves many extrainstitutional factors, such as personal connections and political networks, and must also deal with political competition among factions (Bo 2004b). Thus, it is not an easy task to discover the exact time point when a Chinese politician would most likely be considered for a promotion, which is exactly when they would have the greatest incentive for manipulating the budget with more visible and quantifiable projects. In any event, it is not hard to imagine that a politician's promotion concerns would likely influence their priorities regarding government spending. Building

---

[4] However, when examining the data of the 12th through the 16th Party Congresses, from 1982 to 2007, by applying a novel Bayesian method, Shih *et al.* (2012) did not find evidence of correlation between strong performance growth and higher-party rank.

upon the political uncertainty of Chinese officials' turnover, it is possible that the anticipated advancement cycle is associated with local officials' times in office on fiscal manipulation if the term in office is regulated and term limits are strictly enforced. Then Chinese officials may have the incentive to manipulate fiscal budgets according to their tenure and strategically plan a surge when there is more likelihood of having a reshuffling of general personnel. Additionally, under the politically centralized system, it is also possible that there exists a nationally coordinated budget cycle correlated with national policy. The next section will specify the pattern of these two anticipated cycles and how they are driven by politicians' fiscal incentives.

Career Concerns of Chinese Officials

The first possible anticipated cycle is correlated with a local official's tenure. According to Article 106 of the State Constitution and Article 26 of the Party Constitution, the term in office for a local official is five years, irrespective of their start date. With very few exceptions, a local official cannot stay in the same position for more than two five-year terms. Thus, if a politician expects to be evaluated during his fifth year in office, he should strategically manipulate fiscal choices at this time in order to increase the chances of being promoted. From this supposition, we should be able to observe an apparent political budget cycle associated with a local official's time in office.

The political positions at each administrative level follow the dual-party government administrative system. At each administrative level, there are two top political positions: one is the committee secretary, who represents the CCP, and the other is the governor, who represents the government and the state. Since the party dominates the state, the committee secretary, who is considered the *de facto* person in charge of the entire jurisdiction, is the one who is responsible for both shaping the direction of policy and exerting personnel control. The governor, then, is in charge of implementing party policy and the day-to-day management of the government. Both local officials have discretionary power over the use of government money; the governor has the authority to establish the annual budget, yet this process is supervised by the committee secretary.

Therefore, to study the tenure effects on public spending, both political positions should be examined.

Guo (2009) studied China's aggregate political budget cycles at the county level from 1997 to 2002 and found that local Chinese leaders strategically increase aggregate expenditures during the crucial third and fourth years of their tenures. Since a large-scale development project usually takes time, in order to ensure that the project can be implemented at the right time, meaning the moment when the upper-level party committees are about to reshuffle general personnel positions, an official needs to manipulate the budget prior to his fifth year to impress his superiors and increase his chances of being promoted. Even though, in practice, the turnover rates of county governors are more constrained by the five-year cycle of state constitutions, and they are more institutionalized — because the "candidate" still must go through the electoral process by the local people's congress at the county level — whereas the turnover of county party committee secretaries comes about by direct appointment by the CCP — the empirical results of Guo (2009) show that both political leaders at the county level have the incentive to manipulate their budgets for the sake of political advancement. In the other words, political budget cycles at the county level are driven by local officials' personal career concerns, and these are associated with their times in office.

While the empirical results show that county-level officials often plan a surge during their third and fourth years in office, the motives behind their fiscal policies may not necessarily be correlated with their personal political concerns, but rather, they may strongly correspond with the preferences of upper-level authorities. This may be especially true because, as mentioned above, since the 1994 tax-sharing reform, the political dependence of subprovincial governments on upper-level authorities has intensified (Wedeman 1999; Shen *et al.* 2012). Lower-level governments have relied more and more on the intergovernmental transfers from upper-level government bodies. In addition, most of the fiscal reforms of the 1980s focused solely on the central–provincial fiscal relationship; thus, the actual division of expenditure assignments among the various administrative governments is vague (Shen *et al.* 2012). Discretionary power over the allocation of spending at the subprovincial–government level remains debatable. For this reason, it is difficult to identify the motives and choices of political officials at the lower levels of government. Thus, instead of studying the effect of political budget cycles at the county level, Tsai (2016) examines the spending effects on the highest level of China's sub-national governments as her unit of analysis — the provinces.

According to Tsai (2016), the pattern of political budget cycles at the provincial level in China is not associated with a provincial leader's tenure, but has to do more with the timing of the national leadership transition. In the following section, the author focuses on the mechanism of such nationally coordinated cycles. Yet, before delving into this aspect, it is important to ask why the local officials' career concerns induced by the performance-based promotion system are weaker at the provincial level. Tsai (2016) attributes this to the unique political amphibian status of provincial leaders. Compared to subprovincial leaders, most provincial leaders serve as members of the Central Committee of the CCP. Thus, they are not only local leaders but also national elites. In the 16th Central Committee of the CCP, 43% of the members were provincial leaders (Bo 2004a). Moreover, when considering both the full members and the alternate members of the Central Committee between 1980 and 2006, 93% of the provincial committee secretaries and 74% of the provincial governors were part of the Central Committee (Tsai 2016). The priorities of provincial leaders are, therefore, not only to foster local prosperity but also to formulate and follow national policies.

Additionally, unlike county-level political officials, the turnover of provincial leaders is less constrained by the term-limit rules. Table 17.1 shows the frequency distribution of provincial leaders' turnover during their tenures. It includes 233 provincial committee secretaries and 278 provincial governors who left their offices between 1980 and 2015 in 31 administrative provincial units (excluding Hong Kong and Macau). Table 17.1 suggests that less than about 20% of provincial leaders remain in the same position for more than six years, and more than half of them leave before their fifth year (i.e., 69.5% of the provincial committee secretaries and 81.3% of the provincial governors). This indicates rather frequent political turnover among provincial leaders, which may largely stem from a fear of the rise of localism.

In fact, during the late 1980s, the CCP imposed several institutional mechanisms, including term limits and age limits for retirement, in order to avoid the formation of province-based factionalism. In 1999, "The Regulation of Cadre Exchange" was issued, and in it, one of the important rules emphasized and institutionalized the frequent reshuffling of provincial leaders (Li 2004). Moreover, as found in Table 17.1, officially, though a provincial leader has a five-year term, there is no clear pattern of political turnover during either the provincial leaders' fifth or tenth years in office. In other words, a politician's five-year term does not guarantee their continued appointment; rather, the party authority of the CCP can remove them from office at any time. At the same time, as mentioned, term limits tend to be strictly enforced, so we find that less than 2% of provincial leaders have held their offices more than 10 years. Overall, Table 17.1 indicates that provincial leaders' tenures are not constrained by term limits, as they can be removed from office before their terms are up, and there is only small connection between a politician's tenure and the likelihood of turnover. If a provincial leader does not expect to be promoted in their fifth year in office, they have no incentive to manipulate

Table 17.1   Frequency Distribution of Provincial Leaders' Turnover During Their Tenures (1980–2015).

	Provincial committee secretary		Provincial governor	
	Frequency	Percentage	Frequency	Percentage
1st year	5	2.15	27	9.71
2nd year	30	12.88	38	13.67
3rd year	59	25.32	80	28.78
4th year	38	16.31	44	15.83
5th year	30	12.88	37	13.31
6th year	23	9.87	24	8.63
7th year	16	6.87	10	3.60
8th year	19	8.15	7	2.52
9th year	2	0.86	4	1.44
10th year	7	3.00	5	1.80
11th year and more	4	1.72	2	0.72
Total	233	100.0	278	100.0

fiscal spending according to their time in office, so for this reason, we are unable to observe a provincial budget cycle associated with political tenure.

Nationally Coordinated Cycles

Due to the uncertainty of provincial leaders' tenures and political turnover, provincial leaders have less incentive to manipulate their fiscal budgets according to their tenures for political gain. In addition, the political amphibian status of provincial leaders may lead to fiscal policies that are consistent with the national policy that they themselves are responsible for formulating. Therefore, instead of a budget cycle coinciding with a Chinese provincial leader's time in office, Tsai (2016) finds that there exists a nationally coordinated budget cycle at the provincial level in China, consistent with the pattern of National Congress of the Communist Party (NCCP).

Since the late 1970s, the NCCP has been held regularly every five years. The NCCP involves the discussion and negotiation of practically all significant political issues in the country, and it has become the most important national occasion for determining China's future party policies. In the post-Mao reform era, fiscal and monetary cycles have been found to be responsive to the political rhythms of the plenary sessions of the NCCP, reflecting the importance of the NCCP and the normalization of political institutions in China (Tao 2006).

Tsai (2016) finds that two years prior to the NCCP, provincial leaders have had an incentive to shift public spending toward capital expenditures, such as innovation funds and capital construction, and away from current expenditures, such as agricultural subsidies. Interestingly, the opposite pattern occurs during the actual NCCP year, when provincial leaders increase current expenditures, such as, for example, social spending and government administration, while they decrease capital expenditures. The changes in taxation and total aggregate expenditure are consistent with the changes in capital expenditures. Tsai (2016) argues that because provincial leaders are part of the national elites, they want to ensure a smooth national leadership transition to show the legitimacy of the CCP, not only to the country's citizens but also internationally. We thus see that provincial leaders' fiscal behaviors are constrained by the dynamics of national leadership transition.

Because heavy government investment in infrastructure and development projects is usually sustainable but time-consuming, provincial leaders have to schedule such projects strategically in advance if they hope to have those projects implemented during the NCCP year. For this reason, according to Tsai (2016), capital expenditure reaches its peak two years prior to the NCCP. From this, we find that an increase in current expenditure reveals that the popularity of a Chinese leader still plays an important role during the transition of leadership, at least to some degree. Even though provincial leaders' political futures rely less on popular support than those of local officials in a democratic country, they are still compelled by a fear of widespread social instability. This provides indirect incentives for provincial leaders to spend money on social programs, such as education, welfare, and healthcare. Indeed, even the general secretary and the premier of the CCP, who sit atop the Chinese government hierarchy, may be removed from their positions by the Standing Committee if the destruction of public goods occur or if there is an outbreak of social unrest (Shih *et al.* 2005). To avoid these two potential scenarios that threaten their political power, the general secretary and the premier require provincial leaders to both provide essential public goods and demonstrate economic performance to the population. Since the general secretary and the premier have the ultimate power in determining a provincial leader's political future, such policies require an internalization of budget allocation considerations from the top down. Fear of demotion by the senior leaders in the CCP, which extends down to the provincial leaders, implicitly induces the provincial leaders to spend on essential social programs to keep the peace of the general public. This is why the political turnovers of provincial leaders are less bounded to term limits than subprovincial leaders and why they may be more likely to be affected by extrainstitutional factors. A provincial leader's career concern to manipulate their fiscal budget is driven by a fear of being removed from office by the general secretary and the premier of the CCP. This threat of demotion or removal from office is felt most strongly during times of leadership transition. This is why the priorities of national policies during political succession shift to public goods, and this directly corresponds to the finding that the peak of current spending occurs during the NCCP years.

Conclusion

In democracies, political budget cycles are driven by electoral cycles; they are widely perceived to be motivated by the desire of politicians to be reelected. Opportunistic democratic politicians, for example, have the incentive to manipulate fiscal budgets in order to maximize political gain. Even under a different political structure, such as that of China, similar fiscal distortion can also be found. For example, as the author has shown, the cyclical budget changes over the course of politicians' tenures are apparent at the county level. Since 1979, the Chinese government has begun to emphasize more quantifiable economic performance standards, implicitly encouraging local officials to develop their local economies. In order to maximize their chances of being promoted in their fifth years, county-level officials have the incentive to increase aggregate expenditure during their third and fourth years in office. Such powerful career concerns faced by local officials are considered as one of the main forces determining local officials' fiscal behavior and policies (Guo 2009).

However, compared to county-level officials, political turnover at the provincial level may be more constrained by the dynamics of national leadership transition rather than bound by the rules of term limits, as a nationally coordinated cycle coinciding with the NCCP can be observed at the provincial level in China. Thus, the fiscal decisions of provincial leaders are not intended to help the advancement of their personal careers but to follow national policies that they, themselves, have helped formulate. Even though there may not be a direct connection between the policy preferences of political elites in China and the wishes of the general public, Tsai (2016) found that provincial leaders shift public spending toward current expenditures to coincide with the timing of the NCCP. Her findings imply that even in the absence of downward local accountability, provincial leaders are incentivized to provide at least a bare minimum of public goods, maintaining the basic standard of living for the general public. Politicians in non-democratic countries such as China still have a vested interest in maintaining their political popularity, which has the net result of benefiting the general population in the goods and services provided to them.

As mentioned at the outset, while the impact of election cycles on policies is well established in the study of democratic countries, political turnover in China has long been considered as essentially informal, often relying on personal connections and deftly dealing with fractious politics. However, as the author has demonstrated, politicians in China also share a similar characteristic with those in Western democracies, specifically, a desire to maintain political power and remain in office. For this objective, they are willing to manipulate economic policies in order to achieve their own political goals. Just as with Western counterparts, budget cycles do exist in China. The implication is that the affairs of political elites in China may be more institutionalized than traditionally conceived, as similar fiscal distortions can also be found in both West and the East.

References

Alesina, Alberto, Gerald Cohen and Nouriel Roubini (1992), "Macroeconomic policy and elections in OECD democracies," *Economics and Politics* 4(1), 1–30.

Block, Steven (2002), "Political business cycles, democratization, and economic reform: The case of Africa," *Journal of Development Economics* 67, 205–228.

Bo, Zhiyue (2004a), "The 16th central committee of the Chinese communist party: Formal institutions and factional groups," *Journal of Contemporary China* 13(39), 223–256.

Bo, Zhiyue (2004b), "The institutionalization of elite management in China," in: Naughton, B.J. and D.L. Yang (eds.), *Holding China Together,* Cambridge: Cambridge University Press, p. 70.

Brender, Adi and Drazen Allan (2005), "Political budget cycles in new versus established democracies," *Journal of Monetary Economics*, 52(5), 1271–1295.

Chen, Ye, Hongbin Li and Li-An Zhou (2005), "Relative performance evaluation and the turnover of provincial leaders in China," *Economic Letters,* 88, 421–425.

Drazen, Allen (2001), "The political business cycle after 25 years," *NBER Macroeconomics Annual*, 2000(15), 75–138.

Drazen, Allan and Marcela Eslava (2010), "Electoral manipulation via voter-friendly spending: Theory and evidence," *Journal of Development Economics*, 92, 39–52.

Guo, Gang (2009), "China's local political budget cycles," *American Journal of Political Science*, 53(3), 621–632.

Jin, Hehui, Yingyi Qian and Barry R. Weingast (2005), "Regional decentralization and fiscal incentives: Federalism, Chinese style," *Journal of Public Economics*, 89, 1719–1742.

Jin, Jing and Heng-fu Zou (2005), "Fiscal decentralization, revenue and expenditure assignments, and growth in China," *Journal of Asian Economics*, 16, 1047–1064.

Keech, William and Kyoungsan Pak (1989), "Electoral cycles and budgetary growth in veterans' benefit programs," *American Journal of Political Science*, 33(4), 901–911.

Lawrence, V. Susan and F. Michael Martin (2013), "Understanding China's political system," *Congressional Research Service Report for Congress* (R41007; March 20), https://www.justice.gov/sites/default/files/eoir/legacy/2013/06/13/chinas%20political%20system.pdf (accessed on May 19, 2013).

Li, Cheng (2004), "Political localism versus institutional restraints: Elite recruitment in the Jiang era," in: Naughton, B.J. and D.L. Yang (eds.), *Holding China Together*, Cambridge: Cambridge University Press, p. 62.

Li, Hongbin and Li-An Zhou (2005), "Political turnover and economic performance: The incentive role of personnel control in China," *Journal of Public Economics*, 89, 1743–1762.

Lin, Justin Yifu and Zhiqiang Liu (2000), "Fiscal decentralization and economic growth in China," *Economic Development and Cultural Change*, 49(1), 1–21.

Manion, Melanie (1985), "The cadre management system, post-Mao: the appointment, promotion, transfer and removal of party and state leaders," *The China Quarterly*, 102, 203–233.

Maskin, Eric, Yingyi Qian and Chenggang Xu (2000), "Incentives, information, and organizational form," *Review of Economic Studies*, 67(2), 359–378.

McCallum, Bennett T. (1978), "The political business cycle: An empirical test," *Southern Economic Journal*, 44(3), 504–515.

National Bureau of Statistics (1980–2015), *China Statistical Yearbook*, Beijing: Chinese Statistics Press.

O'Brien, J. Kevin and Li Lianjiang (1999), "Selective policy implementation in rural China," *Comparative Politics*, 31(2), 167–186.

Persson, Petra and Ekaterina Zhuravskaya (2016), "The limits of career concerns in federalism: Evidence from China," *Journal of the European Economic Association*, 14(2), 338–374.

Qian, Yingyi and Chenggang Xu (1993), "Why China's economic reforms differ: The M-form hierarchy and entry/expansion of the non-state sector," *Economics of Transitions*, 1(2), 135–170.

Rogoff, Kenneth (1990), "Equilibrium political budget cycles," *American Economic Review*, 80(1), 21–36.

Shen, Chunli, Jing Jin and Heng-fu Zou (2012), "Fiscal decentralization in China: History, impact, challenges and next steps," *Annals of Economics and Finance*, 13(1), 1–51.

Shih, Victor, Christopher Adolph and Mingxing Liu (2012), "Getting ahead in the communist party: Explaining the advancement of central committee members in China," *American Political Science Review*, 106(1), 166–187.

Shih, Victor, Mingxing Liu and Qi Zhang (2005), "Eating budget: Determining fiscal transfers under predatory fiscal federalism," *FED Working Papers Series: FE20050009*.

Tao, Yi-Feng (2006), "The evolution of 'political business cycle' in post-Mao China," *Issues and Studies*, 42(1), 163–194.

Tsai, Pi-Han (2014), "State fiscal rules and composition changes in public spending before the election," *Public Finance Review*, 42(1), 58–91.

Tsai, Pi-Han (2016), "Fiscal incentives and political budget cycles in China," *International Tax and Public Finance*, 23(6), 1030–1073.

Vergne, Clémence (2009), "Democracy, elections and allocation of public expenditures in developing countries," *European Journal of Political Economy*, 25, 63–77.

Wedeman, Andrew (1999), "Agency and fiscal dependence in central-provincial relations in China," *Journal of Contemporary China*, 8(20), 103–122.

Wu, Jing, Yongheng Deng, Jun Huang, Randall Morck and Bernard Yeung (2014), "Incentives and outcomes: China's environmental policy," *Capitalism and Society*, 9(1), Article 2, 41.

Chapter 18

Asian Power Shift

Kumiko Haba and Steven Rosefielde

Introduction: Power Shift — Turning Point in the 21st Century

The year 2016 was a major turning point, marking the rise of the populist and decline of the globalizing world order (Rosefielde 2017; Talbott 1992).[1] The key events were the European refugee crisis, the UK Brexit referendum (Britain' exit from the European Union [EU]), and Donald Trump's US presidential electoral victory. All three spotlight populisms surge. They triggered turmoil across Europe, America, and the rest of the

[1] Friedman (2017): "The National Intelligence Council (NIC), a unit within the Office of the Director of National Intelligence, is essentially marking the potential end not just of America's status as the world's sole superpower, but also of the current foundation for much of that power: an open international economy, U.S. military alliances in Asia and Europe, and liberal rules and institutions — rules like human-rights protections and institutions like the World Trade Organization — that shape how countries behave and resolve their conflicts." Talbott (1992), "In the next century, nations as we know it will be obsolete; all states will recognize a single, global authority. National sovereignty wasn't such a great idea after all." Talbott is a well-connected and highly visible public intellectual. He served as US Deputy Assistant Secretary of State 1994–2001 under President Bill Clinton; Director of the Yale Center for the Study of Globalization. He is currently the president of the Brookings Institution in Washington, DC, and a member of the Council on Foreign Relations.

world. None of this was coincidental. Today's shocks were the predictable consequences of globalism's intensifying contradictions and decay (Rosefielde and Mills 2017). These dangers were ignored until recently because leaders across the planet implausibly thought that globalism was forever. The Roman Empire survived 500 years; the British Empire lasted for three centuries. Is the sun already setting on the American century (Kennedy 1987, 1988)?[2]

The possibility has been under discussion for nearly 50 years. Power shifts and transitions were analyzed by realists like Organski in 1968, Organski and Kugler in 1980, and Tammen *et al.* in 2000.[3] Their research led Alvin Toffler to devise his authoritative power shift paradigm in 1990, a seminal construct that illuminates today's turning point.

The key factors threatening to bring the globalist epoch to a close are the rise of Islamic terrorism; the 2008 global financial crisis; the euro crisis; resurgent nationalism, populism, and xenophobia; and Asia's "Great Ascent." They were all caused to some extent by globalism.

The 9/11 terrorist attack on the World Trade Center and the Iraq War (2001–2003) inspired Islamic terrorist guerrilla war (a type of "hybrid" war-fighting) that has staggered the West.[4] Terrorists, masquerading as ordinary citizens, began attacking soft targets in metropolitan America and Europe metropolises. These attacks have tested the limits of Western liberalism, democracy, tolerance, and secularism.

The global financial crisis triggered by Lehman Brothers' collapse not only triggered a worldwide depression euphemistically described as "the

---

[2] This article was presented at Hitotsubashi University in March 2016. The first book about power transition was about the great power's shift and was written by Paul Kennedy, first published in 1987; Soshisya, 1988.

[3] About the power transition theory after the starting of the Cold War to the end of the Cold War.

[4] The term "hybrid warfare" appeared at least as early as 2005 and was subsequently used to describe the strategy used by the Hezbollah in the 2006 Lebanon War. Modern adversaries make use of conventional/unconventional, regular/irregular, and overt/covert means and exploit all the dimensions of war to combat the Western superiority in conventional warfare. Hybrid threats exploit the "full-spectrum" of modern warfare; they are not restricted to conventional means.

Great Recession" but also ushered in a decade of secular economic stagnation that intensified the economic plight of America's middle class (Rosefielde and Mills 2015).

The "euro crisis" has three aspects: a depression that ravaged Greece, Italy, Ireland, Portugal, and Spain; a tug of war between EU members pressing for and against "more Europe"; and a polarizing battle between cosmopolitans (Strobe Talbott's Global Nation) and populists over refugees, immigrants, and Islamic terrorism.

Nationalism, populism, and xenophobia in Europe have become potent antiglobalist political forces driven by Islamic terrorism attacks against non-combatants in American and Europe and by a flood of Muslim refugees from Syria and other parts of the Islam world.[5] Eroding middle-class incomes have played a part in sparking a populist revolt that is likely to scuttle the Transatlantic Trade and Investment Partnership in the West and Trans-Pacific Partnership (TTP) in Asia.

Rapid Asian economic growth, especially in China, should have supported globalism by reducing East–West income disparities, but did not do so. Although, it brought prosperity to the region, it bolstered nationalism against the globalist tide. The attractiveness of hegemonic regional spheres of interest gradually came to outweigh the material benefits of economic globalism in the eyes of key Asian leaders like Xi Jinping. Rivalry became more attractive than mutual accommodation, ominously spurring nuclear proliferation. China seems intent on expanding its sphere of influence under the banner of its One-Belt, One-Road project.[6] Anti-Japanese, anti-Korean, and anti-Chinese feelings are running high in East Asia, and aggravating territorial disputes over the South China Sea, Senkaku (Diaoyu), Takeshima (Dokuto), and the Northern Islands.

The wheels suddenly have fallen off the globalist bandwagon. A movement that seemed unstoppable in 2015 appears to be on the ropes in 2016.

---

[5] See Chapter 5 for a thorough discuss of nationalism, populism, and xenophobia.
[6] China is also investing in South East Asia, Central Asia, Ukraine, and Africa, pressing the "Beijing Consensus" against Washington Consensus. This echoes the Cold War competition between the West's Marshall Plan and the Soviet Union's Comecon.

Power Shift or Age of Uncertainty?

Toffler's paradigm is a truncated version of the Soviet correlation of forces concept (Sergiyev 1975).[7] National (imperial) power depends on a triangle of military power, economic power, and knowledge (science and technology). Toffler claimed that economic power was the most important of these factors in the 20th century but was being displaced in the 21st century by knowledge. Military power was a tertiary force in shaping the new world order. This triangle led him to predict that world power would shift from a military-dominated to a knowledge-led, economically codriven, harmonious global ideal.

Knowledge was the key. It allowed weak nations to economically converge to and catch up with advanced countries, encouraging global integration and cooperation.[8] Knowledge was supposed to make nationalism, spheres of influence, and great power rivalries superfluous. Knowledge was supposed to destroy ethnic, racial, and religious barriers and support the cause of free global labor mobility. Knowledge was supposed to make globalism irresistible.

Toffler was right. Knowledge played a pivotal role in changing the terms of global competition, but contrary to his expectations, some nations were assisted more than others. Instead of narrowing inequalities, knowledge served as a platform for rivalry, expanding spheres of influence and war. It fueled resentments that contributed to the antiglobalist upsurge of 2016. Knowledge was not the only factor driving global relations to the turning point. Religion (Islamic fundamentalism), ideology (globalism), nationalism, imperialism, predatory competition, social struggles, politics, technology, populism, and men (world historical figures) codetermined outcomes. Toffler's triangle as should have been expected was not the whole story. There was a power shift, but no golden age, just another time of troubles.

---

[7] Marshall Nikolai Ogarkov, *Izvestiya*, May 9, 1978. The correlation of forces as the Soviet's conceived refers to the military, economic, political, social, leadership, and ideological factors codetermining national power.

[8] Millions of students from China and India studied in undergraduate and graduate schools such as Harvard and Oxford. After returning to their countries, they obtained top positions in major companies and laboratories in the developed world.

Rising Nationalism and Territorial Anxiety in East Asia

East Asia is not an exception. Like other areas in turmoil such as Israel, it made notable economic progress. Living standards in South Korea and Taiwan caught up with and surpassed the EU norm. China and the emerging nations of the Asia Pacific grew faster than their Western peers. Even Japan's growth paced the European standard. This should have promoted harmony, but it did not because Xi Jinping has chosen to harness China's economic and technological advances for hegemonic purposes. Beijing has successfully modernized and expanded its military capabilities to the point that it can dominate or conquer its neighbors, if America retreats from the Asia Pacific.

China is flexing its muscles in the East China Sea and the South China Sea.[9] The disputes are confined to a small set of maritime players but are interlocked with a larger zone extending westward to Laos, Cambodia, Myanmar, and India through the Association of Southeast Asian Nations (ASEAN), and north to the two Koreas, Japan, and Russia (East China Sea, Yellow Sea, and Sea of Japan).

The South China Sea imbroglio from a territorial perspective involves both island and maritime claims among six parties,[10] two of

---

[9] Annual Report to Congress, *Military and Security Developments Involving the People's Republic of China 2016*, Office of the Secretary of Defense, available at http://www.defense. gov/Portals/1/Documents/pubs/2016%20China%20Military%20Power%20Report.pdf.

The dispute has been affected by the fact that Japan did not designate a successor state after it renounced all claims to the Spratly Islands and other conquered islands and territories in the Treaty of San Francisco and Treaty of Peace with the Republic of China (Taiwan) signed on September 8, 1951. The Chinese government was excluded from the peace talks, but made its position clear in the Declaration on the Draft Peace Treaty with Japan by the United States and the United Kingdom on August 15, 1951. Foreign Minister Zhou Enlai asserted China's sovereignty over the archipelagos in the South China Sea, including the Spratly Islands.

[10] There are several disputes, each of which involved a different collection of countries:

1. The nine-dash-line area claimed by the Republic of China, later People's Republic of China, which covers most of the South China sea and overlaps exclusive economic zone claims of Brunei, Indonesia, Malaysia, the Philippines, Taiwan, and Vietnam. Singapore has reiterated that it is not a claimant state in the South China Sea dispute, therefore allowing it to play a neutral role in being a constructive conduit for dialogue among the claimant states.

whom do not recognize each other's legitimacy (China and Taiwan). The antagonists are the Nation of Brunei, the People's Republic of China, the Republic of China (Taiwan), Malaysia, the Republic of the Philippines, and the Socialist Republic of Vietnam.[11] America does not claim territory in the region, but, like Australia and Indonesia, participates as an out-of-area stakeholder defending the right of free navigation in international waters.

China's position is simple. It claims the entire South China Sea delineated by the nine-dashed line in Figure 18.1[12] and rejects rival counterclaims as well as alternative boundaries that can be derived from principles set forth in the United Nations Convention on the Law of the Sea (UNCLOS). It insists that it is the sole owner of the nine-dash zone

---

2. Maritime boundary along the Vietnamese coast between Brunei, Cambodia, China, Malaysia, the Philippines, Taiwan, and Vietnam.
3. Maritime boundary north of Borneo between Brunei, China, Malaysia, the Philippines, Taiwan, and Vietnam.
4. Islands in the South China Sea, including the Paracel Islands, the Pratas Islands, Scarborough Shoal, and the Spratly Islands between Brunei, China, Malaysia, the Philippines, Taiwan, and Vietnam.
5. Maritime boundary in the waters north of the Natuna Islands between Cambodia, China, Indonesia, Malaysia, Taiwan, and Vietnam.
6. Maritime boundary off the coast of Palawan and Luzon between Brunei, China, Malaysia, the Philippines, Taiwan, and Vietnam.
7. Maritime boundary, land territory, and the islands of Sabah, including Ambalat, between Indonesia, Malaysia, and the Philippines.
8. Maritime boundary and islands in the Luzon Strait between China, the Philippines, and Taiwan.
9. Maritime boundary and islands in the Pedra Branca (and Middle Rocks) between Singapore and Malaysia. This was resolved amicably between the countries through the court of arbitration and joint committees.

[11] The interests of different nations include acquiring fishing areas around the two archipelagos; the potential exploitation of crude oil and natural gas under the waters of various parts of the South China Sea, and the strategic control of important shipping lanes.

[12] The nine-dotted line was originally an "eleven-dotted-line," first indicated by the then Kuomintang government of the Republic of China in 1947, for its claims to the South China Sea. After the Communist Party of China took over mainland China and formed the People's Republic of China in 1949, the line was adopted and revised to nine as endorsed by Zhou Enlai.

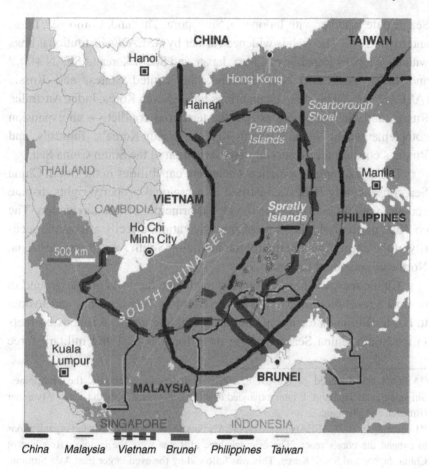

China   Malaysia   Vietnam   Brunei   Philippines   Taiwan

Figure 18.1   South China Sea Dispute.

including underwater mineral rights and has exclusive subsurface and surface naval transit authority. Beijing explicitly denies any intention to resolve the matter by force and recommends bilateral negotiation, an approach that has frozen the conflict for decades.

The territorial counterclaims of the other South China Sea nations are important but are only part of the larger geostrategic problematic. The principal southeast Asian claimants do not act independently. Brunei, Malaysia, the Philippines, and Vietnam are core members of ASEAN (and the filial Asian Economic Community 2015) and act collectively in the South China

Sea dispute together with Indonesia, Singapore, Thailand, Cambodia, Laos, and Myanmar.[13] The web is widened further by ASEAN's institutional links with the People's Republic of China, Japan, and South Korea (ASEAN + 3),[14] and India, Australia, New Zealand, the United States, and Russia (ASEAN + 8).[15] This daisy chain brings Japan, South Korea, India, Australia, Russia, and the United States into the territorial conflict — an expansion complemented by Japan's, South Korea's, North Korea's, Taiwan's, and Russia's concern for preserving free navigation in the South China Sea.

The weakening of America's deterrent capabilities in the South China Sea consequently is best construed as a regional property rights dispute and an incipient conflict over the global principle of free navigation. The conflict, particularly the issue of free navigation, directly affects the security of the entire Asia Pacific region including South Asia, Southeast Asia, Northeast Asia, and beyond.

China, recently, has been trying to change the facts on the ground to compel a resolution on its own terms (Hranjski 2016).[16] It has endeavored to bolster Beijing's territorial claims by building artificial islands on reefs in the South China Sea and using them for logistical and military force

---

[13] ASEAN was founded on August 8, 1967, by Indonesia, Malaysia, the Philippines, Singapore, and Thailand. It later expanded to include Brunei, Cambodia, Laos, Myanmar (Burma), and Vietnam.

[14] Beginning in 1997, ASEAN created "ASEAN Plus Three," adding affiliated organizations to expand the core's reach. The original three affiliates were the People's Republic of China, Japan, and South Korea. This was followed by the even larger East Asia Summit, which included ASEAN + 3 countries as well as India, Australia, New Zealand, the United States, and Russia.

[15] ASEAN operates by consensus among the original 5 and core 10 members. The core pays attention to the + 8.

[16] "Chinese warships enter South China Sea near Taiwan in show of force," *Reuters*, December 16, 2016, available at https://www.theguardian.com/world/south-china-sea: "China's air force conducted long-range drills this month above the East and South China Seas that rattled Japan and Taiwan. China said those exercises were also routine.

In December last year, the defence ministry confirmed China was building a second aircraft carrier but its launch date is unclear. The aircraft carrier programme is a state secret."

Hranjski (2016): "China has begun daily civilian flights to Sansha city on Woody Island, also known as Yongxing Dao, in the disputed Paracels that are also claimed by Vietnam and Taiwan."

projection (Watkins 2015).[17] Beijing has built at least seven such bases, equipped with access channels, helipads, radar facilities, gun and missile emplacements, piers, military facilities, and other objects of strategic importance since 2014 (Larter 2016; Perlez 2016).[18] Moreover, China has recently asserted its right to deny warships international access to the nine-dash zone claiming that the South China Sea is exclusively its property, and not an international waterway (Ku *et al.* 2016). To drive home the point, the People's Liberation Army Air Force scrambled fighter jets in response to a US Navy ship sailing near the disputed Fiery Cross Reef (Ku *et al.* 2016).

China justifies its artificial island-building as a necessary measure to deny unauthorized naval operations in its closed South China Sea, taking pains to distinguish commercial from military traffic (Ku *et al.* 2016). The legal skirmishing settles nothing, but is significant, suggesting as it does that the battle for the South China Sea is gaining momentum.[19]

Beijing's commitment to pressing the envelop is further confirmed by its response to a decision rendered in July 2016 by the UN's Arbitration Tribunal under Annex VII of the UNCLOS in favor of the Philippines's maritime claims against China. Xi Jinping brusquely rejected the UN's jurisdiction and used China's influence over Cambodia to prevent ASEAN from promulgating a consensus statement urging China to heed the ruling (Willemyns 2016).

---

[17] However, it should be noted that other nations in the dispute have also built artificial islands.

[18] "China's man-made islands in the South China Sea," available at https://southfront.org/chinas-artificial-islands-south-china-sea-review/. Larter, David (2016), "U.S. wary of Chinese moves near disputed South China Sea reef," *Navy Times*, September 7, available at https://www.navytimes.com/articles/us-wary-of-chinese-moves-near-disputed-south-china-sea-reef. Perlez (2016): Building up the reefs in the South China Sea, China pursues multiple objectives, including ensuring the safety of expanding shipping lanes, extending maritime protection to its regional waters, and developing capabilities to conduct non-conventional security operations outside the region. The PLA Navy has sufficient self-defense capabilities, but deficiency in cross-region operations and force projection is evident, thought Beijing is trying to change that.

[19] "China says Japan trying to 'confuse' South China Sea situation," *Reuters*, September 19, 2016. "China on Monday accused Japan of trying to 'confuse' the situation in the South China Sea, after its neighbor said it would step up activity in the contested waters, through joint training patrols with the United States." Available at http://www.businessinsider.com/r-china-says-japan-trying-to-confuse-south-china-sea-situation-2016-9.

The weight of the evidence thus indicates that ASEAN, ASEAN + 3, and ASEAN + 8 are going to find it difficult to offset America's waning deterrent in the Asia Pacific.[20] ASEAN members are trying to rebalance the disequilibrium within the Asia Pacific aggravated by the establishment's plight, but the effort is uphill because they are reluctant to mobilize opposition to Beijing's ambitions and because America's position is becoming precarious.

While America's establishment is intent on dithering, China continues to fortify islands in the area it claims and to patrol it with increasingly strong naval forces. *De facto*, China is gradually taking possession of the entire area and is infringing the principle of free navigation in international waters.

Japan's squabble with China over the Senkaku (Diaoyu) Islands is part of the same story. When Japan deannexed Taiwan in the San Francisco Treaty, on September 8, 1951, concluding World War II, it failed to designate its successor. Beijing declared itself to be Taiwan's sovereign, inheriting China's Kuomintang era 11-dash line claim to the Diaoyu Islands, later endorsed and revised by Zhou Enlai to a nine-dash line. This is how a minor territorial dispute dating back to Japan's annexation of the Ryukyu Kingdom in 1879 has assumed larger significance in China's eyes as an integral aspect of its expansive maritime claims in the East China Sea and the South China Sea (Haba 2013).

The problem will not be resolved by Toeffler's triangle. The conflict will either remain frozen or be determined by other forces like nationalism or rational compromise. The globalist mindset before 2016 made rational compromise seem a foregone conclusion. The events of 2016 were momentous because they invalidated this expectation. The East Asian Sea and South China Sea dispute may now end very badly.

References

Beaumont, Joan and Alfredo Canavero (eds.) (2005), *Globalization, Regionalization and the History of International Relations*, Victoria: Deakin University.

Delanty, Gerard (ed.) (2012), *Europe and Asia beyond East and West*, London: Routledge.

---

[20] The statement of course excludes China, which is a member of ASEAN + 3. India is only peripherally concerned with the Asia Pacific.

Dent, Christopher (2008), *East Asian Regionalism,* London and New York: Routledge.

Friedman, Yuri (2017), "What the world might look like in 5 years, according to US intelligence," *Atlantic,* January 11, available at http://www.defenseone.com/ideas/2017/01/what-world-might-look-5-years-according-us-intelligence/134511/?oref=d-river.

Haba, Kumiko (2012), *Asian Regional Integration in the Global Age*: *The Relation among the US–China–Japan and the Trans-Pacific Partnership (TPP),* Tokyo: Iwanami Publishers.

Haba, Kumiko (2013), "What is the 'inherent territory' in East Asia? — conflict on Senkaku (Daiaoyu) islands historical questions *Sekai (World),*" Iwanami Publisher, February.

Haba, Kumiko, Tibor Palankai and Janos Hoos (eds.) (2002), *The Enlargement of the European Union Toward Central Europe and the Role of the Japanese Economy,* Budapest, Aula.

Haggard, Stephan and Robert R. Kaufman (2008), *Development, Democracy, and Welfare States: Latin America, East Asia, and Eastern Europe,* Princeton NJ: Princeton University Press.

Hranjski, Hrvoje (2016), "Recent developments surrounding the South China Sea," *Washington Post,* December 25, available at https://www.washington-post.com/world/asia_pacific/recent-developments-surrounding-the-south-china-sea/2016/12/25/920825fe-cb10-11e6-85cd-e66532e35a44_story.html?utm_term=.899e6dd5725e.

Inoguchi, Takashi (ed.) (2007), *Citizens and the State: Attitudes in Western Europe and East and Southeast Asia,* London: Routledge.

Kennedy, Paul (trans. by Shuzei Suzuki) (1987, 1988), *The Rise and Fall of the Great Powers: Economic Change and Military Conflict from 1500 to 2000,* New York: Random House first published in 1987; Soshisya, 1988.

Ku, Julian G., M. Taylor Fravel and Malcolm Cook (2016), "Freedom of navigation operations in the South China sea aren't enough: The U.S. will need to do more if it's to stop Chinese overreach," *Foreign Policy,* May 16, available at http://foreignpolicy.com/2016/05/16/freedom-of-navigation-operations-in-the-south-china-sea-arent-enough-unclos-fonop-philippines-tribunal/.

Kupchan, Charles A. (2003), *The End of the American Era: U.S. Foreign Policy and the Geopolitics of the Twenty-First Century,* New York: Vintage.

Larter, David (2016), "U.S. wary of Chinese moves near disputed South China Sea reef," *Navy Times,* September 7, available at https://www.navytimes.com/articles/us-wary-of-chinese-moves-near-disputed-south-china-sea-reef.

Organski, A. F. K. (1968), *World Politics,* 2nd ed., New York: Knopf.

Organski, A. F. K. and Jacek Kugler (1980), *The War Ledger,* Chicago: University of Chicago Press.

Perlez, Jane (2016), "New Chinese vessels seen near disputed reef in South China Sea," *New York Times*, September 5.

Rosefielde, Steven (2017), *Trump's Populist America*, Singapore: World Scientific Publishers.

Rosefielde, Steven and Quinn Mills (2015), *Global Economic Turmoil and the Public Good*, Singapore: World Scientific.

Rosefielde, Steven and Quinn Mills (2017), *Trump-Politik: Rethinking American National Security*, London: Oxford University Press.

Sergiyev A. (1975), "Leninism on the correlation of forces as a factor of international relations," *International Affairs* (Moscow), 5, 99–107.

Tammen, Ronald, Jacek Kugler, Douglas Lemke *et al.* (2000), *Power Transitions: Strategies for the 21st Century,* New York: Chatham House.

Talbott, Strobe (1992), "America abroad: The birth of the global nation," *Time*, July 20, available at http://channelingreality.com/Documents/1992_Strobe_Talbot_Global_Nation.pdf.

Therborn, Göran and Habibul Haque Khondker (2006), *Asia and Europe in Globalization: Continents, Regions and Nations, Social Sciences in Asia*, Brill.

Toffler, Alvin (1990), *Power Shift: Knowledge, Wealth, and Violence at the Edge of the 21st Century*, New York: Bantam Books.

Watkins, Derek (2015), "What China has been building in the South China Sea," *New York Times*, October 27, available at http://www.nytimes.com/interactive/2015/07/30/world/asia/what-china-has-been-building-in-the-south-china-sea.html.

Willemyns, Alex (2016), "Cambodia blocks ASEAN statement on South China Sea," July 25, available at https://www.cambodiadaily.com/news/cambodia-blocks-asean-statement-on-south-china-sea-115834/.

Yoshinobu, Yamamoto, Kumiko Haba and Takashi Oshimura (eds.) (2012), *The East Asian Community from Standpoint of International Politics*, Kyoto: Minerva Publishers.

Conclusion

Steven Rosefielde

America's attempt to create a hegemonic global order appears to be unwinding. Globalism in it post-Soviet form inspired by Strobe Talbott's concept of the Global Nation seemed unstoppable during the 1992–2007 period when economies across the world were vibrant. The global financial crisis of 2008, Russia's military modernization, China's great power resurgence, North Korea's nuclearization, Brexit, Donald Trump's electoral victory, and the worldwide rise of populism have burst the globalist bubble.

Humpty-Dumpty globalists do not accept the possibility of a "Kuhnian revolution," concede nothing, and are committed to fighting their way forward despite recent setbacks, but their position is precarious. The Global Nation's big government-affirmative action domestic agenda offers slim prospects for economic revival and social tranquility. Globalists oppose increased defense-spending, and rival great powers such as Russia and China find the Global Nation's social message repellent. Globalism can no longer attract these rivals with its social dream and false promises of universal prosperity, nor can it intimidate them with its military power. The West's economic, social, and military problems are solvable if leaders stop overreaching, but the Global Nation refuses to make concessions.

The chapters in this volume on the European Union, Russia, and China all support the proposition that globalism is ill-conceived. The world is entering a new multipolar era where peaceful coexistence rather than hegemony should be the watchword. The wisest course for every nation in the years immediately ahead is to maximize national well-being as each sees fit, to cooperate with one another as far as possible, and avoid hegemonic confrontation. The sooner the West lowers its ambitions and attends to the well-being of all its peoples, the better are the prospects for all concerned.

Index

Printed in the United States
By Bookmasters

Printed in the United States
By Bookmasters